The New York Times
—NEW—
NATURAL FOODS
COOKBOOK

Other Avon Books by
Jean Hewitt
THE NEW YORK TIMES NATURAL FOODS COOKBOOK

The New York Times
NEW
NATURAL FOODS
COOKBOOK

Jean Hewitt

AVON
PUBLISHERS OF BARD, CAMELOT, DISCUS AND FLARE BOOKS

AVON BOOKS
A division of
The Hearst Corporation
959 Eighth Avenue
New York, New York 10019

Copyright © 1982 by Jean Hewitt
Published by arrangement with Times Books
Front cover design and illustration Copyright © 1982 by
Wendell Minor
Library of Congress Catalog Card Number: 81-52570
ISBN: 0-380-62687-X

The Times Books edition contains the following Library of
Congress Cataloging in Publication Data:

Hewitt, Jean.
  The New York Times new natural foods cookbook.

  Rev. ed. of: The New York Times natural foods
cookbook. 1972, c1971.
    Bibliography: p. 417
    Includes index.
    1. Cookery (Natural foods)   I. New York Times.
II. Title.
TX741.H48   1982   641.5'637   81-52570
                                   AACR2

First Avon Printing, June, 1983

*To Jim
who never complains about
the eclectic dinner fare*

Acknowledgments

The author would like to acknowledge the valuable contributions of Diane Hodges, Charlotte Scripture, Freddi Greenberg, and Donna Johnson in the preparation of the manuscript for this book.

CONTENTS

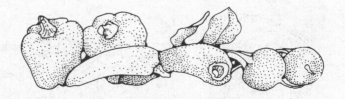

INTRODUCTION

The natural foods movement has changed dramatically in the decade since *The New York Times Natural Foods Cookbook* was originally published. Today many more people are questioning the kinds of foods they are eating. They are more concerned, and better informed, about sound nutrition practices, and they recognize the savings to be gained in cooking from scratch and finding alternatives to high-priced meats.

Government nutrition guidelines and educational efforts; nutritional labeling; the media, food companies, and supermarkets' coverage of nutrition topics have increased consumer awareness of the importance of proper eating for good health. Lighter eating, meals with less total fat, a smaller percentage of saturated or animal fat, less cholesterol, smaller amounts of red meat, lower levels of salt and sugar, and larger amounts of whole grains, fresh fruits, and vegetables have become the eating goals to strive for. Even though the evidence is not conclusive, this way of eating may lower blood cholesterol levels and be a factor in preventing atherosclerosis, high blood pressure, heart disease, and some forms of cancer.

The prudent eating regime is energy efficient, too. It takes more than twice the amount of energy that is needed for fish or chicken to produce a serving of beef. The energy input of a vegetarian dinner is less than one-third that of a beef dinner. People are learning that by mixing legumes (soybeans, dried peas, beans, and peanuts) with whole grains (wheat, rice, oats, barley, rye) or nuts and seeds in the same meal improves the quality of the protein. Also that mixing legumes, whole grains, or nuts and seeds with small amounts of poultry, fish, or low-fat dairy products provides adequate, good quality protein.

The United States Department of Agriculture Food and Nutrition Program is currently developing specifications for including low cost, low calorie, low fat, low cholesterol, but high protein tofu (bean curd) in school lunch programs. A broad segment of the population is discovering the versatility, and money-saving virtues, of the soybean and its by-products, which include tofu, textured vegetable protein, tempeh, soy flour, and soy grits. Ten years ago soybeans were only found in health food stores and co-ops, and bought by a relatively small group of believers, but today they are in hundreds of supermarkets, too.

In the early seventies health food stores were individually owned, but today the business is dominated by giant chains with emphasis on high profit vitamins, food supplements, cosmetics, and their own brands of canned and processed foods. However, the number and scope of health food sections in supermarkets is increasing, and the majority of the ingredients called for in this book can be found in supermarkets. Produce departments are carrying several varieties of sprouts, tofu, fresh ginger, Jerusalem artichokes, and Chinese vegetables. There are displays of raw nuts, dried fruits, and seed snack items; whole grain breads and flours are packaged by leading bakers and millers; plain and flavored yogurts are in every dairy case; brown rice, bulghur, kasha, and barley are on the shelves. And with salad bars everywhere and the number of natural food restaurants increasing, it is no longer difficult to eat healthy food when dining out.

My definition of a natural food as basic, fresh, unrefined, and non-highly processed, with no additives, has not changed. And the key to flavor and food value still lies in freshness. In 1980, the Federal Trade Commission proposed that a food advertised as natural may not contain synthetic or artificial ingredients and may not be more than minimally processed. Anything containing added sugar and salt and highly refined products would not qualify. Some deviations would be allowed if noted, such as "natural but contains bleached flour."

There is still a dedicated group of people convinced that organically grown produce, grains, and animals are highly desirable, but the availability of these products has not increased significantly over the past ten years. The California Organic Food Act of 1979, effective January 1981 through January 1983, has defined in detail the word "organic" as it applies to commodities, processed foods, meat, fish, and poultry to deter fraudulent labeling.

There are more vegetarians because of humanitarian, philosophical, religious, or ecological concerns than a decade ago, but less is heard about raw food and macrobiotic eating patterns. The bibliography (page 417) suggests sources for more information on these peripheral movements, but a listing does not constitute an endorsement. Anyone following a restricted diet should be examined by a physician who may suggest that a dietitian prepare a detailed food analysis and calculation of nutrients supplied.

The goal of this book is to help all individuals and families to eat better and enjoy it more; to make every mouthful taste good and contribute nutrients needed for good health. The dishes made from the recipes here can furnish a varied, well-balanced diet based on the four food groups: fruits and vegetables; dairy products; meat, fish, and other protein sources; grains and cereals. It is becoming popular to add a fifth group of fat, sugar, and alcohol, with a warning to use in moderation. The book aims to challenge the reader to know exactly what he is eating by preparing everything from scratch, eliminating additives and controlling sugar and salt intake.

Cutting down on sugar consumption from all sources is an excellent way to free calories for foods containing essential nutrients. There is virtually no difference in the way various sweeteners are transformed into glucose in the blood. Turbinado and brown sugar are almost 100 percent sucrose. Fructose syrup and powder are manufactured from cornstarch and sucrose respectively. Honey is high in glucose and fructose. However, where texture is important, as in baked goods, and tart flavors demand, the recipes in this book call for minimum amounts of sweeteners such as brown sugar, honey, and molasses.

Snacking is a way of life for most of us, and if it is considered as a fourth meal contributing to the day's nutritional requirements and not as an excuse for high-fat, highly salted or sugared foods, it can be a plus. The appetizer chapter has been expanded to include healthy and appealing snacks and sandwich ideas.

Fortunately, ethnic and foreign foods are no longer a mystery, and the popularity of Mexican and Chinese cuisines, pizzas, quiches, crêpes, and pasta is reflected among the new recipes in this book. The food processor is making many kitchen chores easier and quicker, and you will find reference to it in the recipes.

Making baby food is one operation particularly helped by the food processor, and there is a greatly expanded chapter on the subject. Infants can be started on natural foods from birth, but switching older children and adults from a diet of highly processed foods to the prudent natural pattern of eating should be done gradually to allow the body, the senses, and the mind to adjust. Next week plan to serve a vegetarian meal and a whole grain bread. Add sprouts to a salad or sandwich as a commitment to eating naturally! HAPPY COOKING!

Jean D. Hewitt
Westerly, R.I.

APPETIZERS, SNACKS, & SANDWICHES

These first-course appetizers, snacks, sandwiches, and dips are alternatives to high-fat, high-calorie, minimum-nutrition packaged products. Remember to always keep lots of raw vegetable and fruit tidbits in the refrigerator for quick nibbles.

DEEP-FRIED TOFU

1 pound tofu (bean curd),
cut into ½-inch cubes
(see page 160)
½ cup wheat germ
3 tablespoons cornstarch
Vegetable oil for deep
frying
Soy sauce or Sweet and
Sour Sauce (see below)

1. Roll the tofu cubes in the wheat germ mixed with the cornstarch. Heat the oil to 365 degrees on a deep-fat frying thermometer.

2. Fry the cubes, a few at a time, in a basket in the hot oil. Drain on paper towels and keep warm while frying the remainder.

3. Serve with soy sauce or Sweet and Sour Sauce dip.

SWEET AND SOUR SAUCE: Drain a 6-ounce can crushed pineapple packed in juice; reserve the fruit and measure ⅓ cup juice. In a small saucepan mix the juice with 2 tablespoons soy sauce, ⅓ cup cider vinegar, ½ cup sugar, and ¼ cup ketchup. Bring to a boil. Mix 2 tablespoons cornstarch with ⅓ cup water and stir into the boiling mixture. Cook, stirring, until thick. Add reserved pineapple.
Yield: Six servings.

SOY CHEESE APPETIZER

1 cup tofu (bean curd),
see page 160
¼ cup finely chopped
green pepper
1 tablespoon finely
chopped scallion
Salt to taste
2 tablespoons homemade
mayonnaise (see page
195)

Mix all the ingredients together in the container of an electric blender or food processor and serve as a spread or dip or on lettuce leaves.
Yield: Four servings.

BEAN CURD APPETIZER

1. Slice the tofu and arrange it on a small plate or dish.
2. Combine the tamari and oil and pour over the tofu.
Sprinkle with the cilantro, scallion, and pepper to taste. Chill.
Yield: Four servings.

1 cup tofu (bean curd), see page 160
1 tablespoon tamari (soy sauce)
1 teaspoon sesame oil
2 tablespoons chopped cilantro (Chinese parsley) or parsley
1 scallion, chopped
Freshly ground black pepper to taste

SPINACH DIP

1. Thaw and drain the spinach. Squeeze to remove all excess liquid.
2. Heat the oil in a medium-sized skillet and sauté the onion until tender but not browned. Stir in spinach and cook for 2 minutes.
3. Combine the yogurt, garlic, mint, salt, and pepper in a medium-sized bowl. Stir in the spinach and nuts. Mix well. Chill. Serve with vegetable dippers.
Yield: About one and one-quarter cups.

1 10-ounce package frozen chopped spinach
2 tablespoons vegetable oil
1 small onion, finely chopped
1 cup plain yogurt (see page 324)
1 small clove garlic, finely chopped
1 tablespoon finely chopped fresh mint leaves, or ½ teaspoon dried mint
¼ teaspoon salt
¼ teaspoon freshly ground black pepper
2 tablespoons finely chopped roasted walnuts or pecans
Raw vegetable dippers

HOT CHEESE PARTY DIP

½ pound Cheddar cheese, shredded
1½ cups peeled, seeded, and chopped ripe tomatoes
1 tablespoon seeded chopped hot green chili pepper, fresh or canned
Carrot sticks
Scallions
Cauliflower flowerets
Zucchini sticks
Cucumber sticks

1. Put the cheese and tomatoes in a small saucepan and heat gently until the cheese is melted. Add the chili pepper and transfer to a serving dish over a candle warmer.
2. Serve with the raw vegetable dippers.
Yield: Six servings.

NUTTY-RICE PÂTÉ

⅓ cup raw brown rice
2 tablespoons butter
2 cups sliced mushrooms
1 cup grated zucchini
½ cup grated onion
1 large clove garlic, finely chopped
1 egg
1¾ cups finely ground dry roasted peanuts, walnuts, or cashews
½ cup finely chopped parsley
¼ cup wheat germ
1 teaspoon dried leaf sage
1 teaspoon dried basil
½ teaspoon dried thyme
¼ teaspoon freshly ground black pepper
Lettuce leaves
Sour pickles

1. Cook the brown rice according to package directions (or see page 228), but eliminate the salt.
2. Melt the butter in a large skillet and sauté the mushrooms, zucchini, onion, and garlic until tender but not browned.
3. Put the sautéed vegetables in the container of an electric blender or food processor and whirl or process until smooth. Scrape into a bowl.
4. Add the cooked rice, eggs, nuts, parsley, wheat germ, sage, basil, thyme, and pepper. Transfer to an oiled 9- by 5- by 3-inch loaf pan and bake in a 375-degree oven for 30 minutes.
5. Cool, remove from pan, and chill. Serve in ¼-inch-thick slices on lettuce leaves with sour pickles.
Yield: Twelve servings.

CHOPPED CHICKEN LIVER

1. Place the egg in a small saucepan and cover it with water. Bring the water to a boil and simmer for 12 minutes. Remove the egg and cool it under cold water. Peel.
2. Cook the celery, carrot, onion, and millet in ¾ cup egg cooking water with salt to taste, until the vegetables are barely tender, adding more water if necessary.
3. Add the chicken livers and cook only until the livers are firm, about 3 minutes. Remove the livers and set them aside.
4. With a slotted spoon, lift the vegetables and millet into the container of an electric blender or food processor. Add parsley, pepper, curry powder, and enough of the cooking water to blend the mixture to a smooth paste.
5. Pass livers and peeled egg through medium blade of a food chopper or chop on a board. Mix with blended mixture, oil, wheat germ, onion juice, and chives. Pack into an oiled bowl and chill well.
6. Unmold onto a cold plate and garnish with parsley sprigs and radish roses and serve with rounds of whole wheat toast or whole wheat crackers.
Yield: Eight servings.

1 egg
1 cup water, approximately
½ celery stalk, diced
1 medium-sized carrot, diced
1 small onion, diced
1 tablespoon whole hulled millet
Salt
¾ pound chicken livers
1 tablespoon chopped parsley
¼ teaspoon freshly ground black pepper
⅛ teaspoon curry powder
2 tablespoons vegetable oil
¼ cup wheat germ
½ teaspoon onion juice
1 tablespoon chopped chives, optional
Parsley sprigs and radish roses
Whole wheat toast rounds or whole wheat crackers

EGGPLANT APPETIZER

1 medium-sized eggplant, about 1¼ pounds
Salt
¾ cup vegetable or olive oil
1 large onion, finely chopped
1 cup finely chopped celery
1 1-pound can Italian plum tomatoes, well drained
2 tablespoons tomato paste
2 anchovy fillets, drained and finely chopped, optional
2 tablespoons drained capers
3 tablespoons sliced pitted black olives
3 tablespoons wine vinegar
½ teaspoon freshly ground black pepper
¼ cup finely chopped parsley
Boston lettuce leaves

1. Peel the eggplant and cut into 1-inch cubes. Put in a colander and sprinkle with salt, tossing to coat evenly. Let stand 30 minutes. Rinse, drain, and pat dry.
2. Heat the oil in a large skillet and sauté the onion and celery until tender. Remove to a bowl with a slotted spoon. Add the eggplant to the oil remaining in the skillet and sauté until tender and golden.
3. Return the onions and celery to the skillet and add the tomatoes, tomato paste, anchovies, capers, olives, vinegar, and ¼ teaspoon salt. Cook over low heat, stirring occasionally, for 20 minutes, or until the vegetables are tender.
4. Remove from the heat and stir in the parsley. Cool, cover, and refrigerate for several hours or overnight. Serve in Boston lettuce leaf cups as a first course. Yield: Six servings.

SEVICHE

Combine all the ingredients except the scallops and lettuce in a large bowl. Mix well. Add the scallops, cover, and refrigerate for several hours. Serve on lettuce leaves as an appetizer.
Yield: Six servings.

1 cup fresh lime juice
3 tomatoes, peeled, seeded, and chopped
3 scallions, including green parts, finely chopped
½ green pepper, seeded and chopped
2 canned jalapeño peppers, finely chopped
2 cloves garlic, finely chopped
1 teaspoon salt
¼ teaspoon freshly ground black pepper
1 pound bay or sea scallops (cut sea scallops into quarters)
Lettuce leaves

MOCK HERRING APPETIZER

1. Put the onion rings and celery in a colander over boiling water and steam, covered, for 5 minutes.
2. Add the eggplant sticks and steam until they are tender but not mushy. Turn the vegetables into a bowl and cool.
3. Combine the salt, cloves, bay leaf, brown sugar, lemon juice, and yogurt. Stir into the cooled vegetables. Chill well. Serve on pumpernickel bread.
Yield: Six servings.

2 onions, cut crosswise in ½-inch-thick slices and separated into rings
2 celery stalks, cut in 1-inch pieces
1 medium-sized eggplant, peeled and cut into long strips about 1 inch thick
Vegetable salt to taste
1 teaspoon whole cloves
1 bay leaf, crumbled
1 teaspoon brown sugar
1 tablespoon lemon juice
1 cup plain yogurt (see page 324) or sour cream
Pumpernickel bread slices (see page 270)

MOCK SALMON APPETIZER

2 hard-cooked eggs
1 small onion
2 cups cooked drained
   fresh or frozen peas
3 carrots, grated
2 tablespoons vegetable
   oil
   Vegetable salt to taste
1 teaspoon paprika
¼ cup unblanched
   almonds, finely ground
   in a hand grinder or
   food processor
2 tablespoons wheat germ
2 tablespoons chopped
   parsley
6 to 8 Boston lettuce leaf
   cups

1. Grind the eggs, onion, and peas through the coarse blade of a meat grinder or in a food processor.
2. Stir in the carrots, oil, salt, paprika, almonds, wheat germ, and parsley. Mix well and chill. Serve in Boston lettuce leaf cups.

Yield: Six to eight servings.

EGG ROLLS

1 cup diced cooked
   chicken, turkey, or
   shrimp
1 cup mung or soy bean
   sprouts
⅓ cup chopped water
   chestnuts
⅓ cup chopped bamboo
   shoots
¼ cup chopped scallions
¼ cup chopped green
   pepper
⅓ cup chopped mushrooms
2 teaspoons chopped
   fresh gingerroot, or ½
   teaspoon ground ginger
1 tablespoon soy sauce
10 to 12 egg roll wrappers
1 egg, lightly beaten
   Vegetable oil for frying

1. In a medium-sized bowl combine the chicken, sprouts, water chestnuts, bamboo shoots, scallions, green pepper, mushrooms, gingerroot, and soy sauce.
2. Divide the filling evenly among the wrappers placing it down the center of each. Fold in the sides and roll like a jelly roll. Seal the edges with egg. Allow the rolls to rest for 30 minutes.
3. Heat the oil in a deep-fat fryer or kettle to 360 degrees and fry the rolls, two at a time, until golden on all sides, about 6 to 8 minutes. Drain on paper towels and serve with plum or duck sauce.

Yield: Ten to twelve egg rolls.

FALAFEL

1. Grind the chick-peas through the coarse blade of a meat grinder or in the container of a food processor.

2. Add the remaining ingredients, with the exception of the last 6 ingredients. Mix well. The mixture will be soft.

3. Preheat the oil to 365 degrees.

4. Form the mixture into 1-inch balls, coat with the flour and fry, in a basket, four or five at a time, in the hot oil. The balls rise to the surface and are light brown when cooked. This takes about 2 minutes. Drain on paper towels. Serve in whole wheat pita halves with chopped onion, tomato, and shredded lettuce.

Yield: About twenty falafel.

2 cups cooked dried chick-peas, or 1 1-pound 4-ounce can chick-peas, drained and rinsed
⅓ cup water
1 slice firm whole wheat bread, crusts removed
1 tablespoon unbleached white flour
½ teaspoon baking soda
3 cloves garlic, finely chopped
1 egg, lightly beaten
2 tablespoons chopped parsley
¾ teaspoon salt
¼ teaspoon freshly ground black pepper, optional
¼ teaspoon ground cumin
½ teaspoon ground turmeric
¼ teaspoon dried basil
¼ teaspoon dried marjoram
1 tablespoon tahini (sesame paste) or olive oil
Cayenne pepper to taste
Vegetable oil for deep frying
Flour for coating
5 whole wheat pita, halved
½ cup chopped onion
1 tomato, peeled and diced
1 cup shredded lettuce

PEANUT-CHICKEN MEATBALLS

2½ cups ground cooked chicken or turkey
½ cup grated carrot
½ cup finely chopped parsley
½ cup finely chopped scallions
¾ cup homemade mayonnaise (see page 195)
1 cup ground nuts (walnuts, peanuts, pecans, or cashews)
¼ cup butter, melted

1. In a medium-sized bowl combine the chicken, carrot, parsley, scallions, and mayonnaise. Mix well and form into 1-inch balls.
2. Roll the balls in the nuts, then on one side in the butter, and place butter side up on a baking sheet. Bake in a 400-degree oven for 15 minutes or until the meatballs are golden.
Yield: About twenty-four.

GOUGÈRE PUFFS

1 cup hot water
½ cup butter
¼ teaspoon salt
1 cup unbleached white flour or whole wheat flour
4 large eggs
⅔ cup grated Swiss or Gruyère cheese
1 teaspoon dry mustard
Few grains cayenne pepper

1. Preheat the oven to 375 degrees.
2. In a small saucepan, combine the water, butter, and salt. Heat until the butter is melted and mixture boiling. Stir in the flour all at once, stirring vigorously with a wooden spoon.
3. Continue stirring over medium heat until mixture leaves the sides of the pan clean.
4. Remove from the heat and beat in the eggs, one at a time, very well. Stir in all but three tablespoons of the cheese, the mustard, and the cayenne. Drop by teaspoons onto an oiled baking sheet, sprinkle with remaining cheese and bake for 35 to 40 minutes, or until well puffed and golden.
5. Turn off the oven heat and let puffs remain in oven for 3 minutes longer. Serve hot.
Yield: About three dozen puffs.
Note: If desired, the puffs can be filled with cheese or a clam mixture.

WHEAT GERM WAFERS

1. Preheat the oven to 350 degrees.
2. Sift the flour, baking powder, and salt into a bowl. Add ½ cup of the wheat germ. Using two knives, cut in the butter until it is well distributed.
3. Stir in water quickly but gently. Gather dough into a ball and put on a floured board. Roll to ½-inch thickness, sprinkle with the remaining wheat germ and continue to roll until the dough is wafer thin.
4. Cut with a 2-inch cutter. Put the wafers on an ungreased baking sheet. Bake for 15 minutes, or until golden.
Yield: About eighteen wafers.

½ cup unbleached white flour
2 teaspoons baking powder
½ teaspoon salt
¾ cup wheat germ
2 tablespoons firm butter
¼ cup ice water

NUTTY CRACKERS

1. Preheat oven to 375 degrees.
2. Combine whole wheat flour, wheat germ, oats, and nuts in a bowl. Mix the butter and water together and gradually add to flour mixture.
3. The dough should cling together in a ball when pressed. On a lightly floured board roll out half the dough to ⅛-inch thickness. Cut into 1½-inch circles. Put the circles on an ungreased baking sheet. Repeat with the remaining dough and scraps.
4. Bake for 8 to 10 minutes, or until lightly browned. Cool on a wire rack.
Yield: About five dozen.

¾ cup unsifted whole wheat flour
½ cup wheat germ
½ cup old-fashioned oats
½ cup ground nuts (peanuts, walnuts, or almonds)
⅓ cup butter, melted
⅓ cup water, approximately

SPICY ALMONDS

1 pound blanched whole
   almonds
3 tablespoons butter,
   melted
½ teaspoon cayenne
   pepper, or to taste
¼ cup tamari (soy sauce)

1. Toss the almonds with the butter and toast over low heat, in a heavy skillet, until golden. Add the cayenne and tamari and continue cooking, stirring often, until nuts are fairly dry.

2. Allow to cool, then store in an airtight jar in the refrigerator.

Yield: Six servings.

Note: Walnuts can be done the same way but substitute curry powder for the cayenne.

SNACK MIX

3 cups unsalted popcorn
2 cups bite-sized
   shredded wheat
2 cups puffed rice cereal
1½ cups dry roasted
   cashews or peanuts
½ cup butter
½ teaspoon paprika
¼ teaspoon curry powder
½ teaspoon garlic salt

1. Combine the popcorn, shredded wheat, puffed rice, and nuts in a jelly roll pan. Melt the butter in a small saucepan and add the paprika, curry, and garlic salt.

2. Pour the butter mixture over the popcorn mixture. Bake in a 325-degree oven for 10 minutes. Remove from oven and let stand until cool. Store in a tightly covered container.

Yield: About two quarts.

SNACKS

Banana Pops: Peel ripe bananas and cut them in half crosswise; insert an ice cream stick in the cut end. Freeze. Dip in maple syrup, honey, melted chocolate, butterscotch or melted peanut butter bits. Roll in wheat germ, chopped nuts, cookie crumbs, or granola and return to the freezer.

Frosty Grapes: Wash and drain seedless grapes or bing cherries. Arrange on a baking sheet and freeze. Place in a covered container and return to the freezer to serve partially frozen with cheese.

Eggplant Salad: Sauté 2 cups chopped onions and 1 cup chopped celery in 2 tablespoons vegetable oil. Peel two medium-sized eggplants, cut into 1-inch cubes. Add to pan with three 8-ounce cans tomato sauce, ½ teaspoon salt, ½ teaspoon dried basil, and ½ teaspoon dried oregano. Add chopped black olives if you wish and serve on lettuce, or as a stuffing for mushrooms or as a sandwich filling.

Herb Dip: Combine ⅔ cup homemade mayonnaise (see page 195), 1 cup plain yogurt (see page 324), 2 tablespoons chopped fresh parsley, 1 tablespoon snipped fresh dill weed, ¼ teaspoon salt, 1 finely chopped clove garlic, 1 tablespoon finely chopped scallion, and ⅛ teaspoon celery seed. Mix well, chill several hours, and use with raw vegetable dippers.

Avocado Dip: Combine one 8-ounce package softened cream cheese with 1 cup plain yogurt (see page 324), 1 teaspoon celery salt, 2 finely chopped scallions, 3 tablespoons lemon juice, and the cut up flesh of 2 medium-sized avocados in the container of an electric blender or food processor. Blend or process until smooth. Serve with raw vegetable dippers.

Fruity Nuts: Combine 2 cups nuts (cashews, peanuts, almonds, walnuts, pecans) of one kind or mixed, with 1 cup chopped dried apricots, 1 cup chopped dried apples, and ½ cup seedless raisins. Store in a tightly covered container in the refrigerator. Makes about four cups.

Fig Bites: Combine 1 cup dried figs and 2 tablespoons lemon juice. Pour over boiling water to cover and let stand for 10 minutes. Drain. Chop the figs in the container of an electric blender or food processor and mix with 1 cup finely chopped (in blender or food processer) walnuts. Shape the mixture into ½-inch balls and roll in unsweetened coconut. Makes about eighteen.

Apple Slush: Measure ½ cup water into the container of an electric blender or food processor. Add 6 tablespoons frozen apple juice concentrate. Whirl to blend or process and while whirring at high speed add 8 ice cubes, one at a time, through the cover opening. Serve immediately. Makes one serving.

Peanut-Coconut Balls: Combine 1 cup chunky peanut butter, ⅔ cup honey, ½ cup non-fat dry milk powder and mix well. Add 1 cup finely ground nuts (peanuts, walnuts, cashews, pecans) and enough unsweetened coconut to make a moldable mixture. Shape into tiny balls and roll in unsweetened coconut. Makes about six dozen.

Fruit Leather: Wash, pit, and cut up enough pears, peaches, plums, apricots, or cherries and whirl in the container of an electric blender or food processor to make 2 cups of purée. Add 1 tablespoon lemon juice and ¼ teaspoon ground cinnamon. Whirl or process again. Spread evenly over a lightly oiled 10- by 15-inch jelly roll pan and bake in a 175-degree oven with the door ajar for about 3 hours. Every 30 minutes check to see if leather is dry enough to peel off. If it is still wet underneath, flip and return it to the oven. Cut crosswise into 6-inch strips; cover with plastic wrap and roll up like a jelly roll. Store in an airtight container.

FLAVORED NUTS

Tropical Mix: Combine 1½ cups raw unsalted cashews, 1½ cups raw unsalted Spanish peanuts, 1 cup macadamia nuts, 1½ cups diced dried pineapple in a bowl. Beat 1 egg white, pour it over the nut mixture and toss to coat. Sprinkle with ¼ cup brown sugar and toss again. Spread in a thin layer in a jelly roll pan and bake in a 300-degree oven for 25 to 30 minutes, stirring occasionally. Spread on wax paper on a rack to cool. Transfer to a covered container and add tiny cubes of Cheddar or Gruyère cheese, if you wish. Refrigerate if the cheese is used.

Garlic Cashews: Melt ¼ cup butter in a shallow baking pan in a 350-degree oven. Stir in 1½ cups raw cashews and stir to coat with the butter. Toast in the oven for 15 to 20 minutes. Spread on wax paper on a rack to cool. Sprinkle with 2 teaspoons garlic salt.

Orange-Cinnamon Pecans: Mix 1 tablespoon unbeaten egg white and 1 teaspoon grated orange rind and pour over 1½ cups raw pecans. Toss to coat. Combine ¼ cup light brown sugar and 2 teaspoons ground cinnamon and sprinkle over the nuts. Toss well. Spread in a shallow pan and bake in a 300-degree oven for 20 to 25 minutes, stirring occasionally. Spread on wax paper on a rack to cool. Store in tightly covered containers.

Sesame and Chick-Pea Dip: Blend ¼ cup sesame seeds in the container of an electric blender until fine. Add 2 tablespoons water and 1 teaspoon vegetable oil and blend until it makes a smooth paste. Add 3 tablespoons lemon juice, 1 finely chopped clove garlic. ¼ teaspoon ground cumin, and 1 20-ounce can chick-peas, drained. Whirl and add as much of the chick-pea liquid as necessary. Stir in 2 tablespoons chopped parsley. Chill for several hours and serve with toasted pita bread triangles or raw vegetables.

Yogurt Cheese: Put 2 cups plain yogurt (see page 324) into a cheesecloth-lined sieve set over a bowl and let it stand for 30 minutes. Tie the corners of the cheesecloth together to make a bag. Tie a string around the bag and suspend from the faucet over the sink. Let drain for 8 to 12 hours. Remove the cheese to a bowl and flavor with herbs, honey, and chopped apple, nuts and dried fruits and use as a salad topping or sandwich filling. It will keep in the refrigerator about 2 weeks.

Yogurt Dip: Make the yogurt cheese as above but allow it to drip for only an hour. Turn into a bowl and add 3 sieved yolks from hard-cooked eggs, ½ teaspoon salt, ½ teaspoon freshly ground black pepper, 1 small clove garlic, finely chopped, 2 teaspoons Dijon mustard, ⅛ teaspoon liquid red pepper seasoning, 1 teaspoon Worcestershire sauce, 3 tablespoons lemon juice, 2 tablespoons vegetable oil, and 1½ tablespoons finely chopped parsley. Mix well and chill. Serve with raw vegetable dippers.

NUT BUTTERS

Put 1 cup raw cashews, blanched almonds, peanuts, pecans, or walnuts in the container of an electric blender or food processor and blend or process until very fine. While the machine is running add 1 tablespoon vegetable oil and 1 tablespoon honey and continue to blend or process until smooth and creamy. Keep refrigerated.
Yield: About one-half cup.

EGGPLANT AND NUT APPETIZER SPREAD

1. Trim off and discard the end slices of the eggplant. Cut the eggplant into ¼-inch-thick slices.
2. Heat some of the oil in a heavy skillet and cook the eggplant in it until golden brown on both sides, adding more oil as necessary. Drain browned slices on paper towels. Chop the eggplant and put it in a bowl.
3. Chop the tomatoes and add to the bowl. Add the garlic, onion, and nuts. Season with salt and pepper to taste. Chill. Sprinkle with the chopped parsley before serving with the lemon wedges and bread.
Yield: Six servings.

1 medium-sized eggplant
¾ cup olive oil, approximately
10 cherry tomatoes
1 clove garlic, finely chopped
2 tablespoons finely chopped onion
½ cup pine nuts or chopped walnuts
Salt and freshly ground black pepper
¼ cup finely chopped parsley
Lemon wedges
Whole wheat or pumpernickel bread slices (see pages 294 and 270)

RAISIN-COCONUT SPREAD

Put the raisins and coconut in the container of an electric blender or food processor. Blend or process until smooth. Mix to spreading consistency with the yogurt.
Yield: About one-half cup.

½ cup unsulphured raisins
½ cup unsweetened shredded coconut
Plain yogurt (see page 324)

SOYBEAN SPREAD

½ cup mashed cooked
  soybeans (see page 159)
  or soy flour
½ cup raw peanut butter
1 tablespoon brewer's
  yeast
3 tablespoons chopped
  scallions or chives
3 tablespoons chopped
  parsley
2 tablespoons chopped
  raw peanuts

Mix together all the ingredients until well blended.
Yield: Enough for six sandwiches.

SANDWICH RELISH

2 cups homemade
  mayonnaise (see page
  195), or soy mayonnaise
  (see page 199)
¼ cup chopped dill
  pickles
¼ cup chopped celery
1 tablespoon chopped
  sweet red pepper
1 tablespoon chopped
  parsley
¼ teaspoon dried basil
¼ teaspoon dried oregano
¼ teaspoon dried chervil
¼ cup chopped scallions
1 tablespoon tamari (soy
  sauce)
2 teaspoons ground
  turmeric
2 teaspoons lemon juice

Mix together all the ingredients, with the exception of the turmeric and lemon juice. Dissolve the turmeric in the lemon juice and add to the mixture. Chill.
Yield: About three cups.

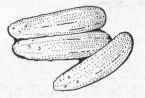

CREAMED APPLE BUTTER

1. Put the apple slices on a broiler pan, brush with the honey, and broil under a preheated broiler, set at 350 degrees, for 15 minutes, or until soft.
2. Mash the broiled apple, the cheese, and nut butter together. Add the walnut and raisins and blend until smooth.
Yield: Enough for one sandwich or salad.

½ apple, peeled and sliced
1 teaspoon honey
1½ tablespoons cream cheese
½ teaspoon raw nut butter (see page 15)
1 walnut, chopped
2 teaspoons raisins, or 2 dates, chopped

NATURAL SANDWICH SPREAD

1. In a medium-sized bowl combine the mayonnaise, yogurt, dill pickle, celery, red pepper, parsley, herbs, scallions, and soy sauce. Mix well.
2. Mix the turmeric with the lemon juice and add to mayonnaise mixture. Cover and chill.
Yield: About two and one-half cups.

1½ cups homemade mayonnaise (see page 195)
½ cup plain yogurt (see page 324)
¼ cup chopped dill pickle
¼ cup finely chopped celery
1 tablespoon finely chopped sweet red pepper
1 tablespoon chopped parsley
½ teaspoon mixed Italian herbs
¼ cup finely chopped scallions
1 tablespoon soy sauce
1 teaspoon ground turmeric
2 teaspoons lemon juice

FOUR VEGETABLE SPREADS

1. Mix together 1 cup shredded cabbage, ¼ cup chopped dried apricots, and 2 tablespoons chopped walnuts, and moisten with homemade mayonnaise (see page 195).

2. Mix together 1 cup shredded cabbage, ⅓ cup grated carrot, 1 tablespoon chopped chives, and moisten with homemade mayonnaise (see page 195).

3. Mix together 1 cup grated carrots, ¼ cup finely chopped celery, ¼ cup finely chopped apple, 2 tablespoons finely chopped green pepper, and moisten with homemade mayonnaise (see page 195).

4. Mix together 1 cup mashed home-baked navy beans or soybeans, ¼ cup finely chopped celery, 1 tablespoon chopped onion, and moisten with homemade mayonnaise (see page 195).

Yield: Each of the spreads will fill about four sandwiches.

NUT BUTTER SPREAD

2 cups raw nuts (cashews, pecans, walnuts, almonds)
1 cup sunflower seed kernels
1 cup sesame seeds
  Vegetable oil
  Honey to taste

1. Put the nuts, sunflower seed kernels, and sesame seeds in the container of an electric blender or food processor and blend or process until fine. Add enough oil to blend or process them to a paste. Sweeten with honey.

2. Store in covered jars in the refrigerator.
Yield: About two cups.

CREAM CHEESE OR COTTAGE CHEESE SPREADS

1. Mix together 3 ounces cream cheese or cottage cheese, ¼ cup chopped walnuts.

2. Mix together 3 ounces cream cheese or cottage cheese, 1 tablespoon grated onion, 1 teaspoon chopped green pepper, 1 tablespoon chopped celery, and vegetable salt to taste.

3. Mix together 3 ounces cream cheese or cottage cheese, ¼ cup sliced radishes, ¼ cup chopped, peeled, and seeded cucumber, and kelp to taste.

4. Mix together 3 ounces cream cheese or cottage cheese, ¼ cup chopped walnuts, ¼ cup chopped watercress, ¼ cup grated raw carrot, and salt to taste.

5. Mix together 3 ounces cream cheese or cottage cheese, ⅓ cup chopped dates, figs, dried apricots, or raisins, 2 teaspoons lemon juice, and ¼ cup chopped nuts.

Yield: Each of the spreads will fill three sandwiches.

MIXED CHEESE SPREAD

Put all the ingredients, with the exception of the nuts, in the container of an electric blender or food processor and blend or process until smooth. Stir in the nuts.
Yield: Enough for two sandwiches.

2½ ounces farmer cheese
2 tablespoons ricotta cheese
¼ cup diced mozzarella cheese
1 tablespoon raisins
2 tablespoons chopped walnuts

AVOCADO AND BANANA SPREAD

1 ripe avocado, peeled, pitted, and mashed
1 tablespoon lemon juice
½ ripe banana, mashed
¼ cup wheat germ
2 tablespoons coarsely chopped walnuts

Combine all the ingredients and mix lightly.
Yield: Enough for three sandwiches.

CHICKEN LIVER SPREAD

3 tablespoons butter
1 small onion, finely chopped
1 pound chicken livers
2 hard-cooked eggs, chopped
Salt and freshly ground black pepper to taste
1 tablespoon chopped parsley
¼ teaspoon dried tarragon

1. Melt the butter in a heavy skillet and sauté the onion in it until tender. Add the chicken livers and cook quickly until browned and tender. (The chicken livers will still be a little pink in the middle.) Chop finely, or grind in a meat grinder or food processor.
2. Add the remaining ingredients and mix well.
Yield: Enough for four sandwiches.

SESAME SEED SPREAD

Combine all the ingredients, with the exception of the crackers, and mix well. Chill. Serve with crackers.

Yield: Six servings.

Note: Sesame seeds can be toasted in a small dry skillet over low heat while stirring frequently.

1 cup cottage cheese
⅓ cup toasted sesame seeds
1 tablespoon chopped parsley
1 teaspoon lemon juice
Grated fresh horseradish to taste
2 tablespoons finely diced green pepper
2 tablespoons finely diced sweet red pepper
Salt to taste
Whole wheat crackers (see page 11)

SANDWICHES

Cheese 'n' Peas: Mix ⅓ cup drained cooked peas with 1½ tablespoons homemade mayonnaise (see page 195) and spread over four whole wheat English muffin halves or slices of whole wheat bread (see page 294). Top with slices of hard-cooked egg (1 egg for 4 sandwiches). Top with 8 slices of Swiss, Gruyère, Muenster, or Monterey Jack cheese. Broil until the cheese melts and starts to brown.

Beet and Apple: Grate 3 raw peeled beets and 2 peeled apples into a bowl. Stir in ¼ cup sour cream or plain yogurt (see page 324), a dash of wine vinegar, and a pinch of salt. Serve in pita halves or on whole wheat bread.

Fruit and Peanut Butter: Spread whole wheat bread with peanut butter, then a layer of ricotta. Dust lightly with ground cinnamon and top with apple or pear slices.

Bean and Cheese: Make a thick layer of warm refried beans on whole wheat bread or cornbread. Top with shredded chili-flavored cheese or shredded Monterey Jack and sprinkle with chopped chilies. Broil just to melt the cheese.

Egg and Anchovy: Combine 4 sieved hard-cooked eggs with 2 tablespoons plain yogurt (see page 324), 2 tablespoons homemade mayonnaise (see page 195), 1 teaspoon anchovy paste, and ⅛ teaspoon freshly ground black pepper.

Use to fill pita bread halves, or spread on whole wheat bread slices. Top with alfalfa sprouts.

Salmon Spread: Drain and flake one 8-ounce can salmon and remove the skin and bones. Add ¼ cup plain yogurt (see page 324), 2 tablespoons grated onion, 2 tablespoons chopped parsley, 2 teaspoons lemon juice, 1 teaspoon bottled horseradish, and 1 tablespoon homemade chili sauce or ketchup. Mix, chill, and use for sandwich filling or salad.

AVOCADO-FILLED PITA

1 large ripe avocado
1 tablespoon lemon juice
½ teaspoon garlic salt
¼ teaspoon dried oregano
½ teaspoon Worcestershire sauce
4 whole wheat pita, halved
1 tomato, peeled, seeded, and chopped
1 scallion, including green part, finely chopped
Dash of liquid red pepper seasoning
1 cup alfalfa sprouts

1. Halve the avocado and remove the pit. Peel the avocado halves and chop the flesh coarsely. Combine with the lemon juice, garlic salt, oregano, and Worcestershire.
2. Fill pita halves with the avocado mixture. Combine the tomato, scallion, and red pepper seasoning and spoon over avocado filling.
Yield: Four servings.

BANANA-CHEESE SANDWICHES

1 ripe banana
½ cup shredded Swiss or Gruyère cheese
¼ cup finely chopped walnuts
¼ teaspoon lemon juice
6 slices whole wheat raisin bread

1. Mash the banana in a small bowl. Add the cheese, nuts, and lemon juice and blend well.
2. Spread on the slices of bread and broil under a preheated broiler, about 4 inches from the heat, for about 2 minutes.
Yield: Six sandwiches.

EGG SALAD-FILLED PITA

1. Combine eggs, mayonnaise, curry, onion, salt, parsley, and cucumber in a medium-sized bowl. Mix well.
2. Fill the pita pockets with the mixture. Top with the sprouts.
Yield: Four servings.

4 hard-cooked eggs, coarsely chopped
⅓ cup homemade mayonnaise (see page 195)
1½ teaspoons curry powder
1 tablespoon grated onion
¼ teaspoon salt
2 tablespoons chopped parsley
¼ cup finely diced, peeled cucumber
4 whole wheat pita, cut in half
1 cup alfalfa sprouts

CHEESY-CLAM POCKETS

1. Combine the cheese, celery, cucumber, garlic salt, parsley, lemon juice, red pepper seasoning, and clams in a medium-sized bowl. Mix well.
2. Spoon the clam mixture into the pita halves and top with sprouts.
Yield: Six servings.

2 cups farmer or ricotta cheese
1 celery stalk, finely chopped
½ cup peeled, seeded, and finely diced cucumber
¼ teaspoon garlic salt
2 tablespoons chopped parsley
1 tablespoon lemon juice
Few drops of liquid red pepper seasoning
1 6-ounce can minced clams, drained
6 whole wheat pita, cut in half
1 4-ounce package alfalfa sprouts

SCRAMBLED EGG SANDWICHES

2 tablespoons butter
1 cup chopped
   mushrooms
1 small onion, chopped
3 eggs, lightly beaten
3 tablespoons cold water
   Salt and freshly ground
   black pepper
2 tablespoons chopped
   parsley
½ cup grated Monterey
   Jack cheese
3 whole wheat pita, cut in
   half
1 ripe tomato, peeled,
   seeded, and chopped
1 scallion, including
   green part, chopped
   Dash of liquid red
   pepper seasoning

1. Melt the butter in a small skillet and sauté the mushrooms and onion until tender but not browned.
2. Combine the eggs, water, salt and pepper to taste, and parsley. Pour over the mushroom mixture and stir over medium heat until the eggs are set but still soft. Sprinkle with the cheese, cover, remove from heat, and let stand for 1 minute.
3. Spoon the egg mixture into pita halves. Combine the tomato, scallions, and red pepper seasoning and spoon over the egg mixture.
Yield: Three servings.

TOFU-EGG SALAD

2 hard-cooked eggs,
   peeled and chopped
½ pound firm tofu,
   drained and crumbled
1 celery stalk, finely
   chopped
2 scallions, finely
   chopped
1 tablespoon finely
   chopped parsley
2 tablespoons wheat germ
¼ teaspoon turmeric
1 teaspoon Dijon mustard
¼ teaspoon celery seed
   Homemade mayonnaise
   (see page 195)

Combine all the ingredients in a bowl using just enough mayonnaise to make the mixture hold together. Use as a sandwich filling, stuffing for tomatoes, or as a salad on lettuce with alfalfa sprouts.
Yield: About two cups.

BEVERAGES

Devout followers of natural food regimes do not drink wine, liquors, flavored carbonated beverages, or artificially-flavored drinks. The beverages in this chapter fit in with the book's aim to provide good-tasting and nutritious alternates to foods with little or no food value. The recipes will provide refreshing drinks for all occasions, including breakfast quickies, and most can be made without an expensive electric juicer. The combinations of raw vegetables and fruit juices are almost limitless if one does own one of the machines.

PEACH SHAKE

1½ cups peach nectar, made
from fresh peaches
when possible
1 cup milk
1 teaspoon lemon juice
2 cups frozen homemade
eggnog, or 1 pint
vanilla ice cream

Put all the ingredients in the container of
an electric blender or food processor and
blend or process until smooth.
Yield: Four servings.

APPLE PUNCH

2 cups unsweetened
apple nectar or juice
½ cup brewer's yeast
⅛ teaspoon ground mace
1 sprig mint

Combine all the ingredients in the container of an electric blender or food processor and blend or process until smooth.
Yield: Four to six servings.

BANANA-MILK DRINK

3 tablespoons carob
powder, or 1 whole egg
1 tablespoon non-fat dry
milk powder
2 tablespoons honey
½ teaspoon smooth raw
peanut butter
½ ripe banana
4 cups skim milk

1. Put the carob powder or egg, the milk
powder, honey, peanut butter, banana,
and 1 cup of the milk in the container of
an electric blender or food processor.
2. Blend or process until smooth. Add
remaining milk and blend or process
again. Serve hot or cold.
Yield: Four servings.

LEMONADE SYRUP

1. Combine the rind and juice and let stand overnight.
2. Pour the boiling water over the sugar and stir to dissolve. Bring to a boil and boil for five minutes. Cool.
3. Combine the syrup with the lemon juice mixture.
4. To serve, dilute the lemonade syrup with equal parts of cold water. Serve over ice.
Yield: Two and one-half quarts syrup, or five quarts lemonade.

Grated rind of 6 lemons (or limes)
Juice of 12 lemons (or limes)
2 quarts boiling water
2¼ cups brown sugar
Cold water
Ice cubes

ORANGE-STRAWBERRY WAKE-UP

Put all the ingredients into the container of an electric blender or food processor and blend or process until smooth.
Yield: Four servings.

1 cup fresh orange juice
1 cup fresh strawberries
1 egg
½ cup non-fat dry milk powder
½ cup water

STRAWBERRY COOLER

1. Put the strawberries and sugar in the container of an electric blender or food processor and blend or process until smooth.
2. Add the ice cream and 1 cup of the goat's milk and blend or process again.
3. Combine the mixture with remaining goat's milk.
Yield: Eight to ten servings.

1 pint fresh strawberries
½ cup brown sugar or honey
2 cups homemade vanilla ice cream
2 quarts ice-cold goat's or cow's milk

MIDMORNING PICKUP

½ cup unsweetened prune
   juice
½ cup fresh apple juice
1 teaspoon nut butter (see
   page 15)
1 teaspoon plain yogurt
   (see page 324)
1 teaspoon sesame oil

Put all the ingredients in the container of an electric blender or food processor. Blend or process until smooth.

Yield: One serving.

WATERMELON JUICE

Force ripe watermelon, cantaloupe, or honeydew melon through a very fine conical strainer.

This juice is a particularly appealing, mild-tasting, hot weather beverage for a small infant.

PINEAPPLE-COCONUT DRINK

½ cup coconut milk
½ cup unsweetened
   pineapple juice
1 teaspoon wheat germ
1 tablespoon plain yogurt
   (see page 324)

Combine all the ingredients in the container of an electric blender or food processor. Blend or process until smooth.

Yield: One serving.

BREAKFAST IN A GLASS

1. Combine the water, milk, egg, coconut cream, wheat germ, and frozen orange juice concentrate in the container of an electric blender or food processor. Blend or process until well mixed.
2. Add the crushed ice and blend or process until smooth.
Yield: One serving.

⅓ cup water
½ cup non-fat dry milk powder
1 egg
¼ cup coconut cream
2 tablespoons wheat germ
¼ cup frozen orange juice concentrate
1 cup crushed ice

FRUITED MILK SHAKE

Put all the ingredients in the container of an electric blender or food processor. Blend or process until smooth.
Yield: Two servings.

1 cup milk
6 ice cubes, crushed
1 tablespoon honey
¾ cup diced mixed fresh fruits, such as peeled and cored apples, and pears, strawberries, blueberries, and peeled and pitted peaches and apricots

EASY BLENDER LUNCH

Put all the ingredients in the container of an electric blender or food processor. Blend or process until smooth. Pour into a bowl and eat with a spoon, or drink from a glass.
Yield: One to two servings.

1 banana
1 apple, cored
1 pear, cored
½ to ¾ cup fresh orange juice
2 tablespoons raisins

VEGETABLE COCKTAIL

1 celery stalk with leaves, chopped
½ cup fresh or frozen peas
1 small carrot, chopped
1 cup water
¼ teaspoon salt
⅛ teaspoon freshly ground black pepper
1 tablespoon chopped fresh mint
1 cup plain yogurt (see page 324)

Put the celery, peas, carrot, water, salt, pepper, and mint in the container of an electric blender or food processor. Blend or process until smooth. Add the yogurt and process just to blend.
Yield: Two servings.

HOT CAROB DRINK

1 cup granola cereal (see page 217)
1 tablespoon carob powder
1 teaspoon brewer's yeast
⅓ cup non-fat dry milk powder
1 cup hot water
2 tablespoons honey

Combine all the ingredients in the container of an electric blender or food processor. Blend or process until smooth.
Yield: Two servings.

CARROT AND DATE DRINK

1 cup water
1 carrot, diced
2 tablespoons chopped dates
2 tablespoons sesame seeds
2 tablespoons wheat germ

Put all the ingredients in the container of an electric blender or food processor. Blend or process until smooth.
Yield: Two servings.

RUSSIAN FRUIT TEA

1. Sweeten the tea with sugar or honey and add the apple.
2. Let stand several minutes then eat the apple pieces with a spoon and drink the tea.
Yield: One serving.
Note: Other fruits, such as pears, peaches, oranges, and grapes can be substituted for the apple.

1 cup, two-thirds full, hot, brewed regular or herb tea
Honey to taste
1 apple, quartered, cored, and finely diced

SESAME SEED MILK

Put the seeds and water in the container of an electric blender or food processor. Blend or process at high speed for 45 seconds. Strain through a double thickness of cheesecloth.
Yield: One serving.

½ cup sesame seeds
1½ cups water

NUT AND SEED MILK

1. Put the kernels, nuts, and 1 cup of the water in the container of an electric blender or food processor and let soak 15 minutes. Blend or process until smooth.
2. Add the remaining ingredients, including the remaining water, and blend or process until well mixed. Serve very cold.
Yield: Three servings.

¼ cup sunflower seed kernels
¾ cup cashews or blanched almonds
3 cups cold water
2 tablespoons honey
½ teaspoon soy milk powder

CARROT-MILK DRINK

½ cup carrot juice
½ cup soy milk or cow's milk
¼ cup chopped almonds
2 teaspoons wheat germ

Blend or process all ingredients in the container of an electric blender or food processor.
Yield: Two servings.

CARROT-PINEAPPLE APPETIZER

2 cups unsweetened pineapple juice
½ cup diced raw carrot
1 tablespoon lemon juice
1 tablespoon brewer's yeast
⅛ teaspoon dried basil

Put all the ingredients in the container of an electric blender or food processor. Blend or process until smooth.
Yield: Four to six servings.

COMFREY COCKTAIL

2 to 3 cups young tender comfrey leaves, washed, drained, and chopped
¼ cup celery leaves, chopped
1 small onion, chopped
2 tablespoons fresh basil
½ cup shredded escarole
1 apple, cored and chopped
3 to 4 mint leaves, chopped
Tomato juice or fresh apple cider
Salt
Honey

1. Mix together the comfrey, celery leaves, onion, basil, escarole, apple, and mint leaves in a bowl.
2. Put ½ cup of the greens mixture in the container of an electric blender or food processor with ¼ cup tomato juice. Blend briefly. Pour into a pitcher and repeat with the remaining mixture and more juice.
3. Add enough extra juice to give a drinkable consistency to the blended mixture. Season with salt and sweeten with honey to taste.
Yield: About one and one-half quarts.

WILD GREENS PUNCH DELUXE

1. Pour the boiling water over 1½ quarts of shredded mixed wild greens, orange peel, and lemon peel. Bring to a boil and simmer for 20 minutes. Strain the mixture and sweeten with honey while hot. Cool.
2. Add the orange juice concentrate and lemon juice and make up to one gallon with pineapple juice or apple juice.
3. Put 1 cup of the punch in the container of an electric blender or food processor with the remaining cup of shredded greens. Blend or process well, strain, add to punch and chill.
Yield: One gallon.

½ gallon boiling water
1½ quarts plus 1 cup shredded wild, edible greens, such as comfrey, dandelion, lamb's quarters, nettles, wild strawberry leaves, lemon geranium, watercress, rose petals, squash blossoms, chickweed, purslane, or nasturtium flowers
1 strip orange peel
1 strip lemon peel
Honey to taste
1 6-ounce can frozen orange juice concentrate
½ cup lemon juice
Unsweetened pineapple juice or fresh apple juice

GOLDEN TOMATO JUICE

1. Put tomatoes, onions, parsley, celery, and salt in a large kettle. Bring to a boil and simmer until the tomatoes are soft.
2. Press the tomatoe mixture through a food mill. Heat to boiling and pour into clean, sterilized canning jars. Process in a water bath for 15 minutes. Tighten the covers, let cool, and store in a cool dark place.
Yield: About three quarts.

½ peck (4 quarts) yellow or red plum tomatoes, washed
3 onions, chopped
1 cup chopped parsley
1 cup chopped celery
3 teaspoons salt

TOMATO-SAUERKRAUT DRINK

½ cup tomato juice
½ cup sauerkraut juice
1 teaspoon chopped
   parsley
2 teaspoons brewer's
   yeast

Blend or process all ingredients in the container of an electric blender or food processor.
Yield: One serving.

VEGETABLE COCKTAIL

1 quart peeled ripe
   tomatoes
1 large sprig parsley
1 teaspoon finely chopped
   scallion
2 tablespoons chopped
   celery leaves from the
   center of the head
1 teaspoon salt

1. Put the tomatoes in the container of an electric blender or food processor, one at a time, and blend or process until smooth after each addition.
2. Add the remaining ingredients. Blend or process until smooth. Serve very cold.
Yield: About three cups.

TAHN

1 cup plain yogurt (see
   page 324)
3 cups ice water
   Ice cubes

Combine the yogurt and water in the container of an electric blender or food processor. Blend or process for 1 minute. Pour over ice cubes.
Yield: Four servings.

DAHI

1. Put the yogurt, lime juice, and sugar to taste in the container of an electric blender or food processor. Blend or process until sugar has dissolved.
2. Pour into a gallon jug or container and fill with ice-cold spring water.
Yield: Sixteen servings.

1 quart plain yogurt (see page 324)
Juice of 12 limes
½ to 1 cup sugar or honey, approximately
Ice-cold spring water

BLUEBERRY YOGURT PICK-ME-UP

Put all the ingredients in the container of an electric blender or food processor. Blend or process until smooth.
Yield: Two servings.

2 cups plain yogurt (see page 324)
2 tablespoons honey
2 tablespoons wheat germ
2 cups fresh or frozen unsweetened blueberries
1 ripe banana, peeled

SOUPS

A homemade soup has always been superior to any dried, canned, or frozen product, and almost any of Grandmother's recipes for soups will still produce a hearty, good-tasting, and nutritious luncheon or dinner mainstay. In the recipes that follow, emphasis is on unusual recipes that are not found in standard texts but that combine honest, fresh ingredients in appetizing combinations. A good homemade broth, whether based on poultry or vegetables, is still the secret to many good-tasting soups made from scratch, and recipes for such broths are included. Vegetable cooking water contains valuable nutrients and can be the basis for vegetable broths to be used in vegetable soups, supplemented where necessary with vegetable extracts, bouillon cubes, powders, and salts. Try one of these recipes and your family or guests will urge you to make more of "those different kinds of soups," in which you control all of the ingredients.

VEGETABLE BROTH

1. Heat the oil in a large heavy kettle and sauté the carrots, celery, onions, potatoes, turnips, and parings for 15 to 20 minutes, stirring often.
2. Add the water, bay leaves, salt, pepper, and parsley. Bring to a boil, cover partially, and simmer for 2 hours. Strain through a fine strainer pushing as much of the vegetables through as possible. Cool, chill, and freeze in pints or quarts.
Yield: About two and one-half quarts.

½ cup vegetable oil
4 carrots, diced
4 celery stalks with leaves, diced
3 large onions, chopped
6 medium-sized potatoes, diced
3 turnips, diced
3 cups parings from scrubbed carrots, potatoes, turnips, parsnips if available
3 quarts water
2 bay leaves, crumbled
1 tablespoon salt
½ teaspoon freshly ground black pepper
Small bunch parsley

TURKEY BROTH

Put all the ingredients in a large heavy pot, bring to a boil, cover, and simmer for 2 hours. Strain the broth and use in soups, stews or gravies. Remove any turkey meat from the bones and add to the broth or use in casseroles.
Yield: About two quarts.

Carcass from 10- to 16-pound turkey, broken up
2 to 3 quarts water
1 large onion, quartered
2 celery stalks, quartered
1 carrot, quartered
1 tablespoon salt
8 black peppercorns, crushed in a mortar and pestle
1 bay leaf, crumbled
1 teaspoon dried thyme

HOMEMADE CHICKEN BROTH

1½ quarts boiling water
  Backs, wings, and
  necks of 2 or 3 chickens
1 onion, quartered
1 carrot, quartered
2 celery stalks with
  leaves, diced
1 teaspoon salt
4 peppercorns
2 bay leaves
2 sprigs parsley

To the boiling water in a large saucepan, add the remaining ingredients, cover, and simmer for 2 hours. Strain. Concentrate by boiling, if necessary, for a richer flavor. Yield: About one quart.

BORSCHT

2 tablespoons vegetable
  oil
3 large onions, chopped
3 beets, peeled and grated
2 beets, peeled and cubed
1 carrot, chopped
2 potatoes, peeled and
  cubed
1 medium-sized head red
  cabbage, shredded
2 quarts homemade
  vegetable broth (see
  page 37)
2 cups chopped, peeled
  fresh or canned
  tomatoes
½ teaspoon dill seeds,
  freshly ground in a
  mortar or electric
  grinder
2 bay leaves, crumbled
1 tablespoon soy flour
3 tablespoons brewer's
  yeast
1 teaspoon salt, or to taste
  Yogurt (see page 324)

1. Heat the oil in a large kettle and sauté the onions, beets, carrot, potatoes, and cabbage, for 15 minutes, stirring occasionally.
2. Add the broth, cover, and simmer until the vegetables are crisp-tender.
3. Combine the tomatoes, dill seeds, bay leaves, soy flour, brewer's yeast, and salt and add to the kettle. Cook for 10 minutes. Serve topped with yogurt.
Yield: Six to eight servings.

BEST BARLEY SOUP

1. Put the barley and broth in a heavy kettle, cover, and simmer until the barley is tender, about 1 hour. Add the remaining ingredients, with the exception of the parsley, and cook, covered, until the vegetables are barely tender.
2. Add the parsley, but do not cook any further.
Yield: Six servings.

¼ cup whole barley, washed
6 cups boiling homemade vegetable broth (see page 37)
1 cup sliced carrots
½ cup diced celery
¼ cup chopped onion
2 cups chopped peeled tomatoes
1 cup fresh peas
Salt to taste
½ cup chopped parsley

BEAN CURD SOUP

1. In a large kettle heat the broth, scallions, ginger, and soy sauce to boiling. Add the snow peas.
2. While stirring the boiling mixture with a fork or chop sticks, add the beaten eggs in a continuous stream. Add the tofu and heat through. Serve the soup garnished with mushroom slices.
Yield: Four servings.

1 quart homemade vegetable or chicken broth (see pages 37 and 38)
2 scallions, cut into 1- by ¼-inch sticks
1 tablespoon chopped fresh gingerroot
2 tablespoons soy sauce
1½ cups fresh snow peas, or 1 7-ounce package frozen snow peas
2 eggs, lightly beaten
½ pound tofu (bean curd), diced (see page 160)
1 large mushroom, thinly sliced

BLACK BEAN SOUP

3 tablespoons vegetable oil
1 onion, finely chopped
1 celery stalk with leaves, chopped
1½ cups black beans, picked over, washed, and soaked overnight
6 cups homemade vegetable or chicken broth (see pages 37 and 38)
½ teaspoon salt
Freshly ground black pepper
3 tablespoons brewer's yeast
2 tablespoons whole wheat flour
1 tablespoon celery seeds
½ cup lemon juice
Dry sherry to taste, optional
Lemon slices
1 hard-cooked egg, chopped
1 cup finely chopped onion

1. Heat the oil in a heavy kettle and sauté the onion and celery until tender. Add the drained beans and broth. Bring to a boil, cover, and simmer for 1 hour, or until the beans are tender.

2. Purée in the container of an electric blender or food processor in batches, with the salt, pepper to taste, brewer's yeast, flour, and celery seeds.

3. Return the puréed soup to the kettle and reheat, stirring, until the mixture thickens slightly. Stir in the lemon juice and sherry. If the soup is too thick, it can be thinned with more broth or water. Serve in bowls, topped with lemon slices, chopped egg, and onion.

Yield: Six to eight servings.

THICK BEAN AND GRAIN SOUP

1 cup dried soybeans, picked over and washed
1 cup whole barley, washed
¾ cup cracked wheat (bulghur)
Water

1. Put the soybeans, barley, and cracked wheat in a large bowl. Cover well with cold water and let soak overnight.

2. Put the soybeans, barley, and wheat with the soaking liquid in a large kettle. Add water to give a depth of 2 inches above the soybeans. Add salt to taste, the

garlic, onion, and bay leaf. Bring to a boil, partly cover, and simmer until the soybeans are barely tender, about 2 hours.

3. Add the split peas and lentils and continue to cook until tender, about 50 minutes. Add water as necessary.

4. Add the greens and tamari and cook until the greens are wilted.

Yield: Twelve to sixteen servings.

Salt
1 clove garlic, minced
1 onion, chopped
1 bay leaf
½ cup split peas, picked over and washed
½ cup lentils, picked over and washed
2 cups shredded kale, spinach, or escarole
Tamari (soy sauce) to taste

BULGHUR AND MUSHROOM SOUP

1. In a large Dutch oven, heat the bulghur while stirring until it browns slightly. Slowly add the broth and bring to a boil. Cover and simmer for 50 minutes, or until the bulghur is tender.

2. Meanwhile, heat the oil in a medium-sized skillet and sauté the onion until tender but not browned. Add the garlic, carrot, turnip, and mushrooms and cook, stirring, for 5 minutes longer.

3. Add the vegetables to the bulghur with the tomato, salt, pepper, thyme, and parsley. Simmer for 10 minutes, or until the vegetables are crisp-tender.

Yield: Four servings.

½ cup bulghur (cracked wheat)
1 quart homemade vegetable or chicken broth (see pages 37 and 38
3 tablespoons vegetable oil
1 large onion, finely chopped
1 clove garlic, finely chopped
1 carrot, diced
1 turnip, diced
½ pound mushrooms, sliced
1 large ripe tomato, peeled, seeded, and chopped
1 teaspoon salt
¼ teaspoon freshly ground black pepper
½ teaspoon dried thyme
2 tablespoons chopped parsley

BROCCOLI CHOWDER

¼ cup butter
1 medium-sized onion, finely chopped
1 clove garlic, finely chopped
2 medium-sized potatoes, peeled and diced
1 quart homemade vegetable or chicken broth (see pages 37 and 38)
1 teaspoon dried thyme
¾ teaspoon salt
½ teaspoon freshly ground black pepper
1 bunch broccoli, broken into tiny flowerets (save stalks for cream of broccoli soup that follows)

1. Melt the butter in a heavy kettle and sauté the onion and garlic until tender but not browned. Add the potatoes and sauté for 4 minutes longer.
2. Add the broth, thyme, salt, and pepper, bring to a boil, cover, and simmer for 15 minutes, or until the potatoes are tender.
3. Add the broccoli flowerets, cover, and cook for 7 minutes, or until the flowerets are barely tender.
Yield: Six servings.

CREAM OF BROCCOLI SOUP

¼ cup butter
1 medium-sized onion, finely chopped
1 celery stalk with leaves, chopped
1 carrot, diced
Stalks from 1 bunch broccoli, peeled and chopped
1 quart homemade vegetable or chicken broth (see pages 37 and 38)
½ teaspoon salt
¼ teaspoon freshly ground black pepper
½ teaspoon dried oregano
1 cup heavy cream or half-and-half

1. Melt the butter in a heavy kettle and sauté the onion until tender but not browned. Add the celery, carrot, and broccoli stalks and sauté for 5 minutes longer, stirring often.
2. Add the broth, salt, pepper, and oregano, bring to a boil, cover, and simmer for 25 minutes. Purée in the container of an electric blender or food processor and pour into a clean kettle.
3. Add the cream and reheat. Check the seasonings and add salt and pepper if needed.
Yield: Six servings.

CABBAGE SOUP

1. Heat the oil in a large heavy kettle and sauté the onion until tender but not browned. Add the carrot, celery, cabbage, and caraway seeds and cook, stirring, for 5 minutes.
2. Add the broth, salt, and pepper. Bring to a boil, cover, and simmer for 30 minutes. Add the spinach and cook for 5 minutes longer.
Yield: Four servings.

3 tablespoons vegetable oil
1 medium-sized onion, finely chopped
1 carrot, diced
1 celery stalk with leaves, diced
1 small head green cabbage, shredded
½ teaspoon caraway seeds
1 quart homemade vegetable or chicken broth (see pages 37 and 38)
½ teaspoon salt
¼ teaspoon freshly ground black pepper
½ pound fresh spinach, trimmed and washed, or half a 10-ounce bag, or 1 10-ounce package chopped frozen, thawed

CHEESE SOUP

1. Melt the butter in a heavy medium-sized saucepan and sauté the onion and carrot until tender but not browned.
2. Add the broth, bring to a boil, cover, and simmer for 10 minutes. Add the cream, red pepper seasoning, and pepper, and bring to a boil. Remove from the heat and stir in the cheese until it melts. Serve topped with the scallions.
Yield: Four servings.

2 tablespoons butter
1 small onion, finely chopped
1 small carrot, finely chopped
2 cups homemade vegetable or chicken broth (see pages 37 and 38)
2 cups light cream
Dash of liquid red pepper seasoning
¼ teaspoon freshly ground black pepper
2 cups grated Cheddar cheese
2 scallions, chopped

MEXICAN CHICKEN SOUP

1 2½-pound broiler-fryer, cut up
1 onion, quartered
1 carrot, quartered
2 cloves garlic, crushed
1½ quarts water
3 tablespoons vegetable oil
1 medium-sized onion, finely chopped
1 celery stalk, finely chopped
1 1-pound can whole tomatoes
2 cups cubed winter squash, such as butternut, acorn, or hubbard
¼ cup brown rice
1 10-ounce package frozen peas
1 20-ounce can chick-peas, drained
2 teaspoons ground coriander
¼ cup chopped parsley
1 teaspoon salt
1 4-ounce can jalapeño peppers, seeded and chopped

1. Put the chicken, onion, carrot, garlic, and water in a heavy kettle or Dutch oven. Bring to a boil, cover, and simmer for 45 minutes, or until the chicken is tender. Cool until the chicken can be handled. Remove and discard the skin and bones and cut the meat into bite-sized pieces. Strain the broth and reserve.

2. Meanwhile, heat the oil in a heavy kettle and sauté the onion and celery until tender but not browned. Add the tomatoes with their juice, the reserved broth, squash, and rice. Bring to a boil, cover, and simmer for 40 minutes, or until the rice is tender.

3. Add the peas, chick-peas, coriander, parsley, salt, jalapeño peppers, and chicken. Reheat.

Yield: Six servings.

CHICKEN AND CORN SOUP

1. Put the chicken, water, salt, pepper, onion, celery, and parsley in a heavy kettle or Dutch oven. Bring to a boil, cover, and simmer for 1 hour, or until the chicken is tender.

2. Remove the chicken from broth. When cool enough to handle, discard skin and bones and cut the chicken meat into bite-sized pieces. Reserve. Strain the broth and return to the kettle.

3. Bring to a boil and add the reserved chicken and corn and cook for 5 minutes. Stir in the eggs.

Yield: Four servings.

1 2½- to 3-pound broiler-fryer, cut up
1½ quarts water
1 teaspoon salt
½ teaspoon freshly ground black pepper
1 medium-sized onion, sliced
1 celery stalk with leaves, chopped
2 sprigs parsley
2 cups corn kernels cut from the cob (about 6 ears)
2 hard-cooked eggs, chopped

ORIENTAL CHICKEN AND CORN SOUP

1. Mix the chicken breast with the egg white and sherry.

2. Heat the broth, soy sauce, ginger, and pepper to boiling in a large kettle. Add the chicken and corn and stir vigorously while cooking to break up the chicken pieces. Cook for 5 minutes. Serve garnished with the scallion.

Yield: Six servings.

½ large chicken breast, skinned, boned, and cut into thin strips
1 egg white, lightly beaten
2 teaspoons dry sherry
1 quart homemade chicken broth (see page 38)
1 tablespoon tamari (soy sauce)
2 teaspoons chopped fresh gingerroot
¼ teaspoon freshly ground black pepper
1½ cups corn kernels cut from the cob (about 4 ears)
2 tablespoons chopped green scallion

CELERY CHOWDER

4 cups chopped celery, preferably the outer stalks with their leaves
2 cups boiling water
1 large potato, peeled and grated
2 tablespooons butter
1 tablespoon unbleached white flour
1 quart milk, scalded
Salt
⅛ teaspoon grated nutmeg
2 hard-cooked eggs, chopped

1. Drop the celery into the boiling water. Add the potato and let simmer until the celery is crisp-tender and the potato is cooked.

2. Meanwhile, combine the butter and flour in a saucepan. Gradually beat in the milk, bring to a boil, and stir until the mixture thickens slightly. Add salt to taste and the nutmeg and stir into the celery mixture.

3. Add the eggs, check the seasonings, and simmer, stirring continuously, until the mixture is smooth and slightly thickened. Serve immediately.

Yield: Six to eight servings.

COLD CUCUMBER SOUP

2 tablespoons butter
1 small onion, finely chopped
1 clove garlic, finely chopped
3 large cucumbers, peeled, halved lengthwise, seeded, and chopped
3 tablespoons unbleached white flour
2 cups homemade vegetable or chicken broth (see pages 37 and 38)
1 teaspoon salt
¾ cup plain yogurt (see page 324)
1 tablespoon snipped fresh dill weed
1 teaspoon grated lemon rind
⅛ teaspoon ground mace

1. Melt the butter in a heavy skillet and sauté the onion, garlic, and cucumbers for about 10 minutes, or until the onion is tender.

2. Sprinkle with the flour and stir well. Gradually stir in the broth. Add the salt and bring to a boil. Cover and simmer until the cucumber is tender. Cool. Purée the mixture, in batches, in the container of an electric blender or food processor, or push through a food mill. Stir in the yogurt, dill, lemon rind, and mace. Chill for several hours.

Yield: Four to six servings.

FRESH PEA SOUP

1. Put the peas in a saucepan with boiling water to extend ½ inch above peas. Add salt to taste, the mint, and scallion. Cover and cook until the peas are tender, about 10 minutes.

2. Put the peas and the cooking liquid in the container of an electric blender or food processor and blend or process until smooth. Add the milk and blend or process briefly.

3. The soup can be reheated and served hot, garnished with the croutons, or cooled and chilled and served cold, garnished with the chives.

Yield: Four servings.

2 pounds peas, shelled
(about 2 cups)
Boiling water
Salt
1 tablespoon chopped
fresh mint
1 scallion, finely chopped
1½ cups goat's milk or
cow's heavy cream
Whole wheat bread
croutons or chopped
chives

LENTIL SOUP

1. Heat the oil in a heavy kettle and sauté the onion until it is transparent. Add the lentils and water. Bring to a boil, cover, and simmer over low heat until the lentils are tender, about 1 hour. Watch the water level and replenish as necessary to keep the lentils covered.

2. Add the potatoes, carrot, basil, tomato juice, and salt and cook until the potato is tender. Add the spinach and cook until the spinach wilts and turns dark green, about 4 minutes after the mixture returns to the boil. Stir in the wine. Serve with grated cheese. Garnish the soup with basil sprigs.

Yield: Ten servings.

1½ tablespoons vegetable
oil
1½ cups chopped onion
2 cups dried lentils,
picked over and washed
2 quarts cold water or
homemade vegetable
broth (see page 37)
2 small potatoes,
scrubbed and diced
1 large carrot, grated
1 tablespoon chopped
fresh basil
2 cups fresh or canned
tomato juice
Salt to taste, optional
¾ cup shredded spinach
½ cup dry white wine,
optional
Grated hard goat's or
Romano cheese
Sprigs of fresh basil

LENTIL, RICE, AND TOFU SOUP

1 cup lentils, picked over
1 cup brown rice
6 cups water, homemade vegetable or chicken broth (see pages 37 and 38)
2 tablespoons vegetable oil
1 large onion, finely chopped
1 clove garlic, finely chopped
2 carrots, finely chopped
1 white turnip, finely chopped
1 green pepper, seeded and diced
½ teaspoon dried thyme
½ teaspoon freshly ground black pepper
½ teaspoon salt
1 pound tofu (see page 160), crumbled

1. Wash the lentils and put them in a large kettle or Dutch oven. Add the rice and water, bring to a boil, and cook until the rice and lentils are tender, about 50 minutes.
2. Heat the oil in a medium-sized skillet and sauté the onion until tender but not browned. Add the garlic, carrots, turnip, and green pepper and cook for 3 minutes. Add to kettle with thyme, pepper, and salt.
3. Add the tofu, bring to a simmer, and simmer for 20 minutes. Check the consistency of the soup and add more water or broth, if you wish.
Yield: Six servings.

GREEK RICE AND LEMON SOUP

2 quarts homemade chicken broth (see page 38)
½ cup brown rice
4 eggs, lightly beaten
1 tablespoon flour
2 tablespoons water
½ cup lemon juice
Salt and freshly ground black pepper

1. Put the broth and rice in a heavy saucepan, bring to a boil, cover, and simmer for 45 minutes, or until the rice is tender.
2. Mix the eggs with the flour, water, and lemon juice. Spoon 1 cup hot rice broth into the egg mixture and mix well. Return to the saucepan and cook, stirring, until mixture thickens. Do not allow to boil. Check seasonings and add salt and pepper if needed.
Yield: Eight servings.

MUSHROOM AND YOGURT SOUP

1. Melt 2 tablespoons of the butter in a large heavy skillet and sauté the leek, garlic, and carrot until tender but not browned.

2. Add the mushrooms and remaining butter and cook for 3 minutes longer.

3. Sprinkle with the flour, salt, pepper, and thyme and cook, stirring, for 1 minute.

4. Stir in the broth, bring to a boil, cover, and simmer for 30 minutes. For a creamy thick soup, purée the hot mixture in the container of a blender or food processor in batches, mix the yogurt with a little of the blended or unblended soup, return all to the skillet, and reheat but do not boil. Stir in the parsley. (I prefer the soup unblended.)

Yield: Four to six servings.

4 tablespoons butter
1 leek or medium-sized onion, finely chopped
1 clove garlic, finely chopped
1 small carrot, finely chopped
1 pound mushrooms, sliced or chopped
3 tablespoons flour
½ teaspoon salt
¼ teaspoon freshly ground black pepper
¼ teaspoon dried thyme
1 quart homemade vegetable or chicken broth (see pages 37 and 38)
1½ cups plain yogurt (see page 324), drained through two thicknesses of cheesecloth for 30 minutes
2 tablespoons chopped parsley

BLACK MUSHROOM SOUP

¼ cup dried black mushrooms (available in Italian and Oriental markets)
Warm water
1 quart homemade vegetable or chicken broth (see pages 37 and 38)
2 tablespoons vegetable oil
1 clove garlic, chopped
1 tablespoon grated fresh gingerroot
2 tablespoons tamari (soy sauce)
½ cup sliced bamboo shoots
½ cup sliced scallions

1. Put the dried mushrooms in a small bowl. Cover with warm water and let soak for 15 minutes. Drain and slice the mushrooms.
2. Put the broth in a large saucepan and heat to boiling. Meanwhile, heat the oil in a small skillet and sauté the garlic and mushrooms for 3 minutes.
3. Add the mushroom mixture to broth along with ginger, soy sauce, bamboo shoots, and scallions. Cover and simmer for 2 minutes.
Yield: Four servings.

SUNCHOKE SOUP

8 to 10 medium-sized Jerusalem artichokes (sunchokes)
2 tablespoons cider vinegar
3 tablespoons butter
1 medium-sized onion, finely chopped
1 quart homemade vegetable or chicken broth (see pages 37 and 38)
½ teaspoon salt
¼ teaspoon freshly ground black pepper
1 cup heavy cream or half-and-half

1. Peel the artichokes and slice them into a bowl of water with vinegar added to retard browning.
2. Melt the butter in a heavy kettle and sauté the onion until tender but not browned. Drain the artichokes well and add them to the pot. Cook, stirring, for 4 minutes longer.
3. Add the broth, salt, and pepper and bring to a boil. Cover and simmer for 15 minutes, or until the artichokes are tender. Purée in the container of an electric blender or food processor and pour into a clean kettle. Add the cream and reheat.
Yield: Four servings.

ROSE HIPS SOUP

1. Crush or grind the rose hips and put them in a saucepan with 1½ quarts water. Bring to a boil, cover, and simmer for 45 minutes, stirring occasionally.
2. Strain through a fine sieve. Measure the liquid and return to the saucepan. Add enough water to make liquid measure 1½ quarts. Stir in the sugar.
3. Mix the arrowroot with a small amount of water and add to rose hips liquid. Heat, stirring, until the mixture thickens.
4. Cover and chill. Serve cold with a garnish of yogurt and slivered almonds.
Yield: Six servings.
Note: Dried rose hips, also called nypon, are available at Swedish delicatessens, such as Nyborg & Nelson, 937 Second Avenue, New York, New York.

Rose hips soup may be served as a dessert, too.

2 cups (½ pound) dried rose hips (see note)
Water
½ cup brown sugar, or honey to taste
1½ tablespoons arrowroot
Plain yogurt (see page 324)
Slivered almonds

PUMPKIN SOUP

1. Heat the oil in a heavy kettle and sauté the onion until tender but not browned. Add tomatoes, pumpkin, broth, and salt and pepper to taste. Bring to a boil, cover, and simmer for 30 minutes, or until the pumpkin is tender.
2. Purée in the container of an electric blender or a food processor and return to the kettle. Stir in the cream and reheat. Check the seasonings and add salt and pepper if needed.
Yield: Four servings.

2 tablespoons vegetable oil
1 medium-sized onion, finely chopped
2 ripe tomatoes, peeled, seeded, and chopped
1 to 1½ pounds pumpkin, peeled and cubed
3 cups homemade vegetable or chicken broth (see pages 37 and 38)
Salt and freshly ground black pepper
1 cup heavy cream or half-and-half

GREEN POTATO SOUP

5 medium-sized potatoes,
peeled and diced
3 cups water
½ teaspoon salt
3 tablespoons butter
1 medium-sized onion,
finely chopped
1 clove garlic, finely
chopped
2 bunches watercress,
chopped, or 1 bunch
watercress plus 1 cup
finely chopped parsley
2 tablespoons flour
3 cups milk, scalded
½ teaspoon salt
¼ teaspoon freshly ground
black pepper
¼ teaspoon dried tarragon
¼ cup grated Gruyère or
Swiss cheese

1. In a medium-sized saucepan cook the potatoes in the water and salt until tender, about 15 minutes.
2. Meanwhile, melt the butter in a medium-sized skillet and sauté the onion and garlic until tender but not browned. Add the watercress and cook stirring until wilted.
3. Sprinkle with the flour and cook, stirring, for 1 minute. Put one third of the potatoes and potato cooking water and one third of the watercress mixture in the container of an electric blender or food processor. Blend or process until smooth and transfer to a large clean pot. Repeat with the remaining potatoes, water, and watercress mixture.
4. Stir in the milk, salt, pepper, and tarragon. Bring to a boil. Stir in the cheese but do not boil again or the cheese will string.
Yield: Eight servings.

BROWN POTATO SOUP

6 medium-sized potatoes,
peeled and diced
1 medium-sized onion,
diced
Water
2½ cups peeled, chopped
fresh or canned
tomatoes
4 tablespoons unbleached
white flour
1 tablespoon butter
Salt and freshly ground
pepper

1. Put the potatoes and onion in a saucepan and add water to cover. Bring to a boil and simmer for 15 minutes. Add the tomatoes and simmer for 5 minutes longer.
2. Meanwhile, put the flour and butter in a small, heavy skillet and heat slowly, stirring constantly, until the flour browns. (Do not allow to burn or it will be bitter.) Stir into the simmering vegetable mixture.
3. Season with salt and pepper to taste. If the mixture is too thick, add more water.
Yield: Six servings.

HOT AND SOUR VEGETABLE SOUP

1. Heat the oil in a wok or kettle and stir-fry the scallions, celery, and mushrooms briefly. Sprinkle with the ginger.

2. Add the broth, tamari, vinegar, and red pepper flakes. Bring to a boil and simmer for 10 minutes.

3. Add the water chestnuts, snow peas, and sprouts and simmer for 3 minutes. Sprinkle with the parsley.

Yield: Four to six servings.

¼ cup vegetable oil

4 to 6 scallions, including green parts, finely chopped

1 celery stalk with leaves, chopped

½ pound mushrooms, sliced

1 tablespoon chopped fresh gingerroot

1 quart homemade vegetable or chicken broth (see pages 37 and 38)

3 tablespoons tamari (soy sauce)

2 tablespoons vinegar

½ teaspoon hot red pepper flakes, or to taste

1 6-ounce can water chestnuts, drained and sliced

1½ cups fresh snow peas, or 1 7-ounce package frozen snow peas

1 cup fresh bean sprouts

1 tablespoon chopped parsley

SUNFLOWER BROTH

2 tablespoons vegetable oil
1 medium-sized onion, finely chopped, or 4 scallions, chopped
2 cups sunflower seed kernels
1 teaspoon salt
1½ quarts homemade vegetable or chicken broth (see pages 37 and 38)
1 teaspoon dried summer savory
1 cup shredded spinach or romaine lettuce, optional

1. Heat the oil in a heavy saucepan and sauté the onion until tender but not browned. Add the sunflower seed kernels, salt, and broth.
2. Bring to a boil, cover, and simmer gently for 40 minutes, or until the kernels are tender. Add the savory and spinach. Boil for 2 minutes. Alternately, the soup can be blended or processed in the container of an electric blender or food processor and the spinach omitted if a creamed texture is preferred.
Yield: Six servings.

SQUASH SOUP

3 tablespoons butter
1 medium-sized onion, finely chopped
1 celery stalk, finely chopped
1½ to 2 pounds squash, such as butternut, hubbard or acorn, peeled, seeded, and diced
1 tart apple, peeled, cored, and chopped
1 quart homemade vegetable or chicken broth (see pages 37 and 38)
1 tablespoon lemon juice
¼ teaspoon grated nutmeg
1 teaspoon salt
¼ teaspoon freshly ground black pepper
½ teaspoon dried thyme
1 cup light cream

1. Melt the butter in a heavy kettle and sauté the onion until tender but not browned. Add the celery, squash, and apple and cook, stirring, for 5 minutes.
2. Add the broth, lemon juice, nutmeg, salt, pepper, and thyme. Bring to a boil, cover, and simmer for 15 minutes, or until the squash is tender. Purée in the container of an electric blender or food processor and return to the kettle.
3. Bring to a boil and add the cream. Check seasonings and correct if necessary.
Yield: Six servings.

SORREL SOUP

1. Heat the oil in a large heavy kettle and sauté the sorrel, parsley, and potatoes for 5 minutes, stirring often.
2. Add the broth, pepper, and salt to taste, bring to a boil, cover, and simmer for 20 minutes. Purée the mixture in the container of an electric blender or food processor and pour into a clean kettle.
3. Stir in the cream and reheat.
Yield: Four servings.

3 tablespoons vegetable oil
8 ounces fresh sorrel, shredded finely
¼ cup finely chopped flat Italian parsley
2 medium-sized potatoes, peeled and diced
1 quart homemade vegetable or chicken broth (see pages 37 and 38)
¼ teaspoon freshly ground black pepper
Salt
1 cup heavy cream or half-and-half

VEGETABLE AND KASHA SOUP

1. Mix the egg with the kasha until the grains are moistened. Cook the egg-kasha mixture in a large heavy saucepan, stirring until the grains separate and dry out.
2. Add the broth, celery, turnips, carrots, salt, pepper, and thyme. Bring to a boil and simmer for 30 minutes, or until the kasha and vegetables are tender. Stir in the parsley and serve topped with dollops of yogurt.
Yield: Eight servings.

1 egg, lightly beaten
⅔ cup kasha
2 quarts homemade vegetable broth (see page 37)
1 celery stalk with leaves, finely chopped
4 medium-sized turnips, diced
4 medium-sized carrots, diced
1 teaspoon salt
¼ teaspoon freshly ground black pepper
1 teaspoon dried thyme
¼ cup finely chopped parsley
Plain yogurt (see page 324)

GREEN TOMATO SOUP

¼ cup butter
2 onions, sliced
8 green tomatoes, washed
and cut into chunks
1 cup homemade
vegetable or chicken
broth (see pages 37 and
38)
1 tablespoon arrowroot
1 cup milk
Salt
Freshly ground black
pepper, optional
Plain yogurt (see page
324)
Chopped chives or dill
weed

1. Melt the butter in a heavy skillet and sauté the onions and green tomatoes until soft but not brown. Purée in the container of an electric blender or food processor, or push through a food mill. Add the broth.
2. Blend the arrowroot with the milk and add to tomato mixture. Bring to a boil, stirring until the mixture thickens. Season with salt and pepper to taste.
3. Serve topped with yogurt and chives. Alternately, the soup may be cooled and chilled to serve cold.
Yield: Six servings.

ZUCCHINI SOUP

1 pound zucchini (3 to 4
small), washed and
sliced
1 cup homemade
vegetable or chicken
broth (see pages 37 and
38)
Salt to taste
⅛ teaspoon dried basil
⅛ teaspoon dried thyme
⅛ teaspoon dried
marjoram
2 cups milk
Whipped cottage cheese
or plain yogurt (see
page 324)

1. Put the zucchini, broth, and salt in a saucepan and bring to a boil. Cover and simmer gently until tender. Cool.
2. Add the basil, thyme, and marjoram and purée in the container of an electric blender or food processor, or push through a food mill. Return to the saucepan and stir in the milk. Heat, but do not boil. Serve topped with the cottage cheese.
Yield: Four servings.

ITALIAN-STYLE VEGETABLE SOUP

1. Heat the oil in a kettle and sauté the onion and garlic until tender but not browned. Add the broth, tomatoes, rice, and salt to taste. Bring to a boil, cover, and simmer for 20 minutes.
2. Add the zucchini and potato and cook for 20 minutes longer, or until the rice is tender. Serve with grated cheese.
Yield: Four servings.

3 tablespoons olive oil
1 medium-sized onion, chopped
1 clove garlic, finely chopped
1 quart homemade vegetable or chicken broth (see pages 37 and 38)
2 large plum tomatoes, peeled and chopped
⅓ cup raw brown rice
Salt
1 medium-sized zucchini, washed and sliced
1 medium-sized potato, peeled and cubed
Freshly grated Parmesan or Romano cheese

FRUIT SOUP

1. Combine the dried fruits and water in a large saucepan. Bring to a boil and simmer over low heat until tender, about 30 minutes.
2. Add the fresh fruits, except the berries, and cook for 5 minutes. Add the berries and cook for 5 minutes longer. Remove from the heat and add the lemon juice. Sweeten with honey. Cool and chill well.
3. Serve very cold, or hot, with a dollop of yogurt.
Yield: Eight servings.

½ pound mixed dried fruits, such as pitted prunes, apricots, raisins, pears, peaches, or apples
2½ quarts water
2 pounds mixed fresh fruits, such as cubed or sliced peaches, apricots, pears, plums, or apples, or whole strawberries, blueberries, or blackberries
¼ cup lemon juice
Honey to taste
Plain yogurt (see page 324)

ZUCCHINI AND PASTA SOUP

3 tablespoons vegetable
  oil
1 large onion, finely
  chopped
1 clove garlic, finely
  chopped
1 celery stalk with leaves,
  chopped
2 medium-sized zucchini,
  diced
1½ quarts homemade
  vegetable or chicken
  broth (see pages 37 and
  38)
1 teaspoon salt
¼ teaspoon freshly ground
  black pepper
1 1-pound can tomatoes
1 teaspoon dried basil
1 teaspoon dried oregano
½ cup orzo or pastina
2 tablespoons chopped
  parsley
  Freshly grated
  Parmesan cheese

1. Heat the oil in a large heavy kettle and sauté the onion and garlic until tender but not browned. Add the celery and zucchini and cook for 3 minutes longer.
2. Add the broth, salt, pepper, tomatoes, basil, and oregano. Bring to a boil, cover, and simmer for 10 minutes. Add the orzo and cook for 8 minutes, or until the orzo is barely tender. Add the parsley and serve with Parmesan cheese.

Yield: Six servings.

VEGETABLE-SOY SOUP

1½ cups cooked soybeans
  (see page 159), or 1 15½-
  ounce can soybeans,
  drained
¼ cup water
2 tablespoons vegetable
  oil
2 onions, chopped
1 clove garlic, chopped
2 celery stalks, diced

1. Place ¾ cup of the soybeans in the container of an electric blender or food processor with the water and blend or process until smooth.
2. Heat the oil in a kettle and sauté the onions and garlic until tender.
3. Add the celery, green pepper, and carrots and cook for 5 minutes longer, stirring occasionally.
4. Add the tomatoes, broth, thyme, pars-

ley, salt, and blended beans. Bring to a boil, cover, and simmer gently until the vegetables are crisp-tender.

5. Add the remaining whole beans and reheat.

Yield: Six servings.

1 green pepper, seeded and diced
2 carrots, scrubbed (or scraped), and diced
2 cups peeled, chopped fresh or canned tomatoes
1 quart homemade vegetable or chicken broth (see pages 37 and 38) or water
½ teaspoon dried thyme
2 tablespoons chopped parsley
1 teaspoon salt, or to taste

UNCOOKED YOGURT GAZPACHO

1. Combine the tomatoes, chilies, onion, parsley, and salt to taste. Chill in the refrigerator for at least 2 hours.

2. Stir in the yogurt. Garnish each serving with radish or cucumber slices and a sprig of watercress.

Yield: Four servings.

4 tomatoes, peeled and coarsley chopped
1 tablespoon seeded, chopped hot green chilies, fresh or canned, or to taste
1 onion, finely chopped
¼ cup chopped parsley
Salt
3 cups plain yogurt (see page 324)
Radish or cucumber slices
Watercress sprigs

GARDEN GAZPACHO

3 tomatoes, peeled and seeded
1 clove garlic
1 green pepper, seeded and quartered
1 carrot, sliced
1 onion, quartered
½ cup lemon juice
1 cucumber, peeled and cubed
2 tablespoons chopped chives
2 large sprigs parsley
¼ cup chopped fresh basil
1½ teaspoons chopped fresh chervil or summer savory
¼ cup olive oil
Salt to taste
3 cups chilled homemade vegetable or chicken broth (see pages 37 and 38)
Whole wheat bread croutons or sunflower seed kernels

Blend half of all the ingredients, with the exception of the croutons or sunflower seed kernels, in the container of an electric blender or food processor until smooth. Repeat with the other half of the ingredients. Combine the halves and chill well. Garnish with whole wheat bread croutons or sunflower seed kernels.
Yield: Four servings.

POTATO CHOWDER

3 tablespoons vegetable oil
3 tablespoons chopped onion
2 cups water
1 teaspoon salt
5 medium-sized potatoes, peeled and diced
1 cup carrots, finely diced
1 cup shredded spinach
4 cups milk, scalded

1. Heat the oil in a heavy saucepan, add the onion, and sauté until tender. Add the water, salt, potatoes, and carrots. Bring to a boil, cover, and simmer until the vegetables are tender, about 15 minutes.
2. Add the spinach and cook until it is just limp and dark green, about 3 minutes. Add the milk and bring the mixture to just below the simmer point. Do not boil. Serve immediately.
Yield: Six servings.

FISH

Fish and shellfish have an important part to play in a varied, well-balanced diet for those concerned with calories, cholesterol, and saturated-fat intake. The recipes here suggest combinations of ingredients to be used with fish, and ways of preparing it, that make it appealing and extra nourishing. Although freshness is the key to good flavor and maximum nutritive value for all ingredients, it is especially important for fish.

CLAM PIE

PASTRY

2 cups whole wheat flour
1 cup unbleached white
    flour
½ teaspoon salt
¼ cup sesame oil or
    safflower oil
    Ice water

FILLING

1½ cups clam juice
3 cups diced potatoes
1 carrot, diced
1 large onion, finely
    chopped
2 cups finely chopped
    clams
⅛ teaspoon freshly ground
    black pepper
    Kelp to taste, optional
¼ cup unbleached white
    flour
½ cup light cream

1. To prepare pastry, put the whole wheat flour, unbleached white flour, and salt in a bowl. Add the oil and work in with the fingers.

2. Add the ice water a teaspoon at a time until dough clings together. Wrap in wax paper and chill.

3. To prepare filling, put the clam juice, potatoes, carrot, and onion in a saucepan and bring to a boil. Cover and simmer until vegetables are barely tender, about 12 minutes.

4. Add clams, pepper, and kelp. Mix the flour with the cream and stir into the clam mixture. Bring to a boil, stirring until the mixture thickens cool.

5. Preheat the oven to 400 degrees.

6. Divide the pastry dough in half and roll out one half between sheets of wax paper to fit a deep, 10-inch pie plate or casserole. Pour in the cooled clam mixture. Roll out the remaining dough between sheets of wax paper and use to cover the pie. Seal edges and cut a steam hole in the center of the top crust.

7. Bake for 10 minutes, reduce the oven temperature to 350 degrees and bake until the pastry is done, about 30 minutes longer.

Yield: Six servings.

BAKED COD WITH MUSTARD SAUCE

1. Preheat the oven to 350 degrees.

2. Put the fish in a shallow, buttered baking dish. Dot with 2 tablespoons of the butter, pour the white wine over the fish, cover with wax paper, and bake for 15 minutes, or until the fish flakes easily.

3. Meanwhile, melt the remaining 2 tablespoons butter in a small saucepan and sauté the shallots until tender but not browned. Sprinkle with the flour and cook for 1 minute longer.

4. Stir in the salt and mustard and all the liquid you can drain from the cooked fish. Bring to a boil, stirring until thickened. Stir a little of the hot mixture into the yogurt. Return all to the saucepan and reheat but do not boil.

5. Pour over the fish.

Yield: Four servings.

1½ pounds cod fillets (or other firm white fish fillets), fresh or frozen, cut into serving-size portions
4 tablespoons butter
½ cup white wine, dry vermouth, or milk
2 shallots or scallions, finely chopped
2 tablespoons unbleached flour
½ teaspoon salt
1½ tablespoons Dijon mustard
1 cup plain yogurt (see page 324), drained through 2 thicknesses of cheesecloth for 30 minutes

BAKED TROUT

1. Clean the trout. Place 4 lemon wedges and the mushroom slices in the cavity. Season inside and outside of fish with salt and pepper to taste.

2. Wrap the fish in heavy-duty aluminum foil and set directly in the white-hot coals of a charcoal fire that has been allowed to burn down.

3. Cook, turning often, for 10 minutes, or until the fish flakes easily. (Trout can be cooked on a grill over hot coals but will take longer to cook.) Serve with extra lemon wedges.

Yield: Two servings.

1 trout (11 to 14 inches)
1 lemon, cut into eighths
¼ cup sliced mushrooms
Salt and freshly ground black pepper

BAKED YOGURT FISH FILLETS

1 pound firm white fish
  fillets, such as cod,
  haddock, scrod, or
  striped bass, cut into
  bite-sized pieces
1 cup plain yogurt (see
  page 324)
2 tablespoons finely
  chopped scallion,
  including the green
  parts
1 tablespoon lemon juice
1 tablespoon chopped
  parsley
1 tablespoon chopped
  chives
1 tablespoon chopped
  sweet red pepper

Put the fish fillets in a greased shallow
baking dish in one layer. Combine the
remaining ingredients and spread over
the fillets. Bake in a 350-degree oven for
25 minutes, or until the fish flakes easily.
Yield: Four servings.

BAKED FLOUNDER ROLL-UPS

½ cup cooked shredded
  kale, spinach, Swiss
  chard, or wild greens,
  well drained
1 egg, lightly beaten
¼ cup wheat germ
⅛ teaspoon grated nutmeg
  Salt to taste
2 tablespoons freshly
  grated Parmesan cheese
4 large flounder or sole
  fillets
4 thick slices tomato
  Vegetable oil

1. Preheat the oven to 350 degrees.
2. In a bowl, mix together the cooked
greens, egg, wheat germ, nutmeg, salt,
and cheese.
3. Spread over the fillets and roll up as for
a jelly roll. Secure with toothpicks and set,
seam side down, in a buttered baking
dish. Top each fillet with a slice of tomato.
Brush with oil and bake for 20 minutes, or
until the fish flakes easily.
Yield: Four servings.

QUICK FISH DINNER IN A SKILLET

1. Cook the potatoes in boiling salted water until just tender. Drain.
2. Melt the butter in a large skillet. Add the zucchini and squash. Top with the fish fillets and arrange the potatoes around the edge.
3. Sprinkle with the salt, pepper, and dill. Cover and simmer for 10 minutes, or until the fish flakes easily. Add the tomato, cover, and cook for 1 minute longer.
Yield: Four servings.

6 small new potatoes, scrubbed, with a ½-inch strip peeled around the middle
⅓ cup butter
1 medium-sized zucchini, sliced
1 small yellow squash, sliced
1 pound flounder, sole, fluke, or perch fillets, thawed if frozen
1 teaspoon salt
¼ teaspoon freshly ground black pepper
1 tablespoon snipped fresh dill weed
1 large tomato, peeled, seeded, and chopped

BAKED FISH

1. Preheat the oven to 350 degrees.
2. Combine the scallions, green pepper, carrot, tomato, salt and pepper to taste, and dill. Spread half the mixture in the bottom of an oiled baking dish.
3. Put fish on top, season with salt and pepper to taste, and sprinkle with lemon juice. Cover with remaining vegetable mixture. Pour the water over all and dot with the butter. Cover tightly and bake for 25 minutes, or until the fish flakes easily.
4. Spread the yogurt over the top of dish and return to the oven just long enough to warm the yogurt, about 4 minutes.
Yield: Two servings.

½ cup chopped scallions
1 green pepper, seeded and diced
1 carrot, finely diced
1 tomato, peeled and chopped
Salt and freshly ground black pepper
1 tablespoon snipped fresh dill weed
2 halibut or cod steaks (each ¾ inch thick)
1 teaspoon lemon juice
¼ cup water
3 tablespoons butter
1 cup plain yogurt (see page 324)

FISH IN TOMATO SAUCE

2 tablespoons olive or vegetable oil
1 onion, finely chopped
1 clove garlic, finely chopped
1½ cups peeled, chopped ripe tomatoes
1 tablespoon chopped parsley
Salt or kelp to taste
1 fresh hot chili pepper, seeded and chopped
¼ teaspoon dried oregano
1 pound boneless firm white fish, such as cod, halibut, or striped bass

1. Heat the oil in a saucepan and sauté the onion and garlic until transparent and tender but not browned.
2. Add the tomatoes, parsley, salt, chili pepper, and oregano. Bring to a boil and simmer for 20 minutes.
3. Cut the fish into 2-inch squares and add to the sauce. Cover and simmer for 8 minutes, or until the fish flakes easily.
Yield: Four servings.

COLD SALMON STEAKS WITH GREEN SAUCE

1 recipe Salmon Steaks with Scallions (see page 67), without brown rice and lemon juice
1 cup spinach leaves
1 tablespoon grated onion
¼ cup watercress leaves and stems
¼ cup parsley leaves
2 teaspoons lemon juice
1¼ cups plain yogurt (see page 324), drained through 2 thicknesses of cheesecloth for 30 minutes

1. Prepare the salmon steaks through step 4 of the recipe. Cover and refrigerate.
2. Meanwhile, put the spinach, onion, watercress, parsley, and lemon juice in the container of an electric blender or food processor. Blend until smooth adding more lemon juice if necessary.
3. Stir blended mixture into the drained yogurt. Chill. Serve the sauce with chilled salmon steaks.
Yield: Two servings.

SALMON STEAKS WITH SCALLIONS

1. Trim the scallions and wash them well. Dry and cut lengthwise into quarters and then crosswise into 2-inch lengths.
2. Heat the oil in a heavy skillet, add the scallions, and cook over medium heat until they are golden, turning with a spatula as they cook.
3. Place the salmon steaks on the scallions. Season with salt and pepper to taste, and sprinkle with basil and add vinegar. Cover and steam for 4 minutes, moving the salmon steaks twice with a spatula but not turning them.
4. Uncover and sauté the steaks for several minutes to reduce the pan juices. Lower the heat, cover, and cook for about 2 minutes longer, or until the fish flakes easily.
5. Remove the salmon and scallions to a warm platter. Add the rice to skillet and quickly stir-fry in the pan juices. Sprinkle with lemon juice and serve with the fish.
Yield: Two servings.

1 bunch scallions
2 tablespoons olive or vegetable oil
2 salmon steaks (¾ inch to 1 inch thick)
Salt and freshly ground black pepper
1 teaspoon chopped fresh basil leaves
1 tablespoon wine vinegar
1½ cups cooked brown rice (see page 228)
Lemon juice to taste

SALMON CASSEROLES

1. Drain the salmon and reserve the liquid. Flake the salmon, discarding the bones and skin, if you wish.
2. In a bowl combine the mashed potatoes, eggs, and salmon liquid. Stir in the salmon and remaining ingredients, with the exception of the cheese. Pour into four oiled 1-cup individual casseroles, au gratin, or soufflé dishes.
3. Sprinkle with the cheese and bake in a 350-degree oven for 30 minutes, or until set.
Yield: Four servings.

1 15½-ounce can salmon
2 cups mashed potatoes
3 eggs, lightly beaten
2 scallions, finely chopped
1 teaspoon grated lemon rind
3 tablespoons lemon juice
¼ teaspoon freshly ground black pepper
1 tablespoon snipped fresh dill weed
½ cup shredded Monterey Jack cheese

BAKED SHRIMP

⅓ cup vegetable oil
2 tablespoons finely chopped shallots or scallions
1 clove garlic, finely chopped
2 tablespoons chopped parsley
1 teaspoon dried savory
3 tablespoons lemon juice
1 cup dried whole wheat bread crumbs
2 tablespoons freshly grated Parmesan cheese
2 pounds cooked, shelled, and deveined shrimp
¼ cup dry white wine or clam juice

1. Preheat the oven to 350 degrees.
2. Heat the oil and sauté the shallots and the garlic until tender but not browned. Add the parsley, savory, lemon juice, crumbs, and cheese.
3. Arrange shrimp in a buttered baking dish and sprinkle the bread crumb mixture over them. Pour the wine over the shrimp and bake for 10 to 15 minutes, or until heated through.
Yield: Four to six servings.

FLOWER OF SHRIMP

1 pound shrimp
2 cups plus 3 tablespoons water
3 tablespoons vegetable oil
2 medium-sized onions, cut in eighths
½ medium-sized head cauliflower, broken into flowerets
1½ tablespoons arrowroot
¼ cup soy sauce
4 cups hot cooked brown rice (see page 228)

1. Shell and devein the shrimp, reserving the shells. Put the shells and 2 cups of water in a saucepan, bring to a boil, cover, and boil for 15 minutes. Strain the stock and discard shells.
2. Heat the oil in a skillet and sauté the onions and cauliflower for 4 minutes. Add the strained shrimp stock, cover, and simmer until the vegetables are crisp-tender, about 2 minutes.
3. Add the shrimp and cook, covered, until the shrimp turn pink, about 5 minutes. Dissolve the arrowroot in the remaining water and add to the skillet with the soy sauce. Stir until the mixture thickens. Serve over rice.
Yield: Six servings.

SHRIMP WITH AVOCADO

1. Cook the shrimp according to package directions.
2. Sauté the onion, celery, and green pepper in the oil until tender but not browned. Add the tomato sauce, oregano, basil, salt, pepper, and red pepper seasoning. Bring to a boil and simmer slowly for 15 minutes, stirring often.
3. Cut the avocados into thin slices and add to the tomato sauce with the shrimp. Heat until warmed but do not boil. Serve over brown rice, if you wish.
Yield: Four servings.

1 pound shelled and deveined frozen shrimp
1 medium-sized onion, finely chopped
1 celery stalk, finely chopped
½ green pepper, finely chopped
2 tablespoons vegetable oil
2 8-ounce cans tomato sauce
½ teaspoon dried oregano
½ teaspoon dried basil
½ teaspoon salt
¼ teaspoon freshly ground black pepper
Dash of liquid red pepper seasoning
2 medium-sized avocados, halved, pitted, and peeled

SHRIMP AND SPROUTS

1. Melt the butter in a heavy skillet. Add the shrimp and cook, stirring, until they turn pink. Add the mushrooms and cook for 2 minutes longer.
2. Stir in the clam juice and tamari and bring to a boil. Add the bean sprouts and water chestnuts and cook for 2 minutes.
3. Mix the arrowroot with the water and stir into the skillet. Cook, stirring, until the mixture thickens.
Yield: Four servings.

3 tablespoons butter
1 pound shelled and deveined shrimp
1 cup sliced mushrooms
1 cup clam juice
1 tablespoon tamari (soy sauce)
1 cup mung bean or soybean sprouts (see page 201)
½ cup sliced water chestnuts
2 teaspoons arrowroot
2 tablespoons water

SKEWERED SHRIMP WITH RICE

1½ to 2 pounds large
   shrimp (about 20)
¼ cup vegetable oil
¼ cup lime juice
2 tablespoons soy sauce
2 tablespoons butter
¼ cup chopped onion
1 cup sliced mushrooms
2 tablespoons chopped
   parsley
4 cups hot cooked brown
   rice (see page 228)
3 limes, sliced

1. Wash the shrimp. Cut the shell down the back of each and devein but leave the shell intact. Combine the oil, lime juice, and soy sauce in a bowl and add the shrimp. Marinate in the refrigerator for 30 to 60 minutes.

2. Meanwhile, melt the butter in a small skillet and sauté the onion until transparent. Add the mushrooms and cook for 3 minutes longer. Stir in the parsley and add onion mixture to the rice. Keep warm.

3. Thread the shrimp onto 4 individual skewers, alternating with the lime slices. Broil under a preheated broiler or over hot coals, about 3 minutes each side, brushing with the marinade when the skewers are turned. Serve on top of the rice mixture. Yield: Four servings.

SHRIMP WITH YOGURT

3 tablespoons butter
2 tablespoons finely
   chopped onion
1½ pounds shelled and
   deveined shrimp
⅓ cup finely chopped
   parsley
¼ teaspoon caraway seeds,
   lightly crushed
¼ clove garlic, finely
   chopped
½ cup dry white wine or
   clam juice
   Kelp to taste, optional
½ cup plain yogurt (see
   page 324)

1. Melt the butter in a skillet and sauté the onion until transparent. Add the shrimp and cook, stirring, until the shrimp turn pink.

2. Add the parsley, caraway seeds, garlic, wine, and kelp. Bring to a boil, cover, and simmer for 2 minutes. Remove from the heat and stir in the yogurt. Yield: Four servings.

SWEET AND SOUR CUCUMBER SHRIMP

1. Cut the cucumbers in half lengthwise. Peel them and remove the seeds. Slice the cucumbers thinly and sprinkle with salt. Set aside for 10 minutes.
2. Rinse the cucumbers and squeeze out any excess water. Add the shrimp to the cucumbers.
3. Soak the wakame in water to cover for 5 minutes. Cut or tear the soft portion of wakame from the core into 1-inch lengths.
4. Combine the cucumbers, shrimp, and wakame. Mix together the sugar, ½ teaspoon salt, and the vinegar. Pour over cucumber mixture and chill in refrigerator for 1 hour or longer.
Yield: Two servings.

2 cucumbers
Salt
½ cup tiny cooked, shelled, and deveined shrimp
2 or 3 1-foot-long thin strips of wakame (Japanese seaweed)
Water
1 tablespoon brown sugar
¼ cup Japanese rice vinegar

SHRIMP-AND-RICE-STUFFED PEPPERS

1. Remove a ½-inch cap from the stem end of the peppers. Seed the peppers and steam them over boiling water for 8 minutes. Put in a baking dish with ¼-inch water in the bottom.
2. Heat the oil in a medium-sized skillet and sauté the onion until tender but not browned. Add the shrimp and cook, stirring, until the shrimp turns pink and is tender.
3. Stir in the red pepper, parsley, soy sauce, pepper, tomatoes, red pepper seasoning, and cooked rice. Spoon into the peppers, cover dish tightly with aluminum foil, and bake in a 350-degree oven for 30 minutes, or until the peppers are tender and the filling is hot.
Yield: Four servings.

4 large green peppers
¼ cup vegetable oil
1 small onion, finely chopped
12 ounces fresh or frozen peeled and deveined shrimp
1 sweet red pepper, seeded and chopped
¼ cup chopped parsley
2 tablespoons soy sauce
¼ teaspoon freshly ground black pepper
2 medium-sized tomatoes, peeled, seeded, and chopped
⅛ teaspoon liquid red pepper seasoning
4 cups hot cooked brown rice (see page 228)

TUNA-CHICK RICE

¼ cup vegetable oil
1 large onion, finely
  chopped
1 clove garlic, finely
  chopped
1 28-ounce can peeled
  plum tomatoes
1 cup brown rice
1 green pepper, seeded
  and diced
1 cup water
1 tablespoon snipped
  fresh dill weed
¾ teaspoon salt
¼ teaspoon freshly ground
  black pepper
1 20-ounce can chick-
  peas, drained
1 7-ounce can tuna in
  water, drained and
  flaked
¼ cup chopped parsley
1¼ cups plain yogurt (see
  page 324), drained
  through 2 thicknesses of
  cheesecloth for 30
  minutes

1. Heat the oil in a large heavy saucepan and sauté the onion and garlic until tender but not browned. Add the tomatoes with their juice, the brown rice, green pepper, water, dill, salt, and pepper.

2. Bring to a boil, cover, and simmer for 50 minutes, or until the rice is cooked and has absorbed the liquid. Stir in the chickpeas, tuna, parsley, and yogurt and reheat. Do not boil.

Yield: Four servings.

TUNA-STUFFED POTATOES

1. Scrub the potatoes, prick, and bake in a 425-degree oven for 50 minutes, or until tender.

2. Cut a 1-inch slice off the top of each potato and scoop out the inside into a large bowl leaving a ¼-inch shell.

3. Put the potato shells on a baking sheet.

4. Add the tuna, scallion, red pepper seasoning, mayonnaise, eggs, and wheat germ to the potato flesh. Beat in the cheese, reserving 2 tablespoons. Spoon the potato mixture into the shells and sprinkle with the reserved cheese. Bake in a 375-degree oven for 20 minutes, or until thoroughly hot and browned on top.
Yield: Six servings.

6 large russet or baking potatoes
1 13-ounce can tuna, drained and flaked
¼ cup finely chopped scallion
Dash of liquid red pepper seasoning
¼ to ⅓ cup homemade mayonnaise (see page 195)
2 hard-cooked eggs, chopped
¼ cup wheat germ
1 cup shredded Cheddar cheese

POULTRY

The poultry recipes in this chapter are offered as economical, good-tasting, and nutritious alternates to the more conventional red meat roasts, pot roasts, and stews found in most cookbooks. Perhaps you have already discovered the convenience, economy, and healthful properties of raw turkey parts. If not, here are some ways to increase or begin your enjoyment.

KASHA AND CHICKEN LIVERS

1. In a small bowl, mix the egg with the kasha until the grains are moistened. In a medium-sized heavy saucepan heat the egg-kasha mixture, while stirring, until the grains separate and become dry.
2. Add the boiling water, cover, and simmer for 20 minutes. Let stand for 15 minutes.
3. Meanwhile, melt the butter in a medium-sized skillet and sauté the onion and garlic until tender but not browned. Add the chicken livers and mushrooms and cook over medium-high heat until the livers are browned on all sides but still pink in the middle.
4. Add the chicken liver mixture to the kasha. Stir in the salt, pepper, parsley, and nuts.
Yield: Four servings.

1 egg, lightly beaten
1¼ cups kasha
2 cups boiling water or homemade chicken broth (see page 38)
3 tablespoons butter
1 medium-sized onion, finely chopped
1 clove garlic, finely chopped
1 pound chicken livers, well trimmed and halved
¼ pound mushrooms, sliced
1 teaspoon salt
¼ teaspoon freshly ground black pepper
3 tablespoons chopped parsley
½ cup chopped toasted walnuts

CARAWAY CHICKEN LIVERS

1. Dredge the livers in the flour seasoned with salt and pepper.
2. Melt the butter in a heavy skillet and sauté the caraway seeds over gentle heat for 2 minutes. Turn up the heat and add the livers.
3. Sauté the livers until they are well browned on all sides but still pink in the middle. Slowly pour the wine over the livers and simmer for 2 minutes. Serve over brown rice, if desired.
Yield: Four servings.

1 pound chicken livers, rinsed and each cut into two pieces
Whole wheat flour for dredging
Salt and freshly ground black pepper
3 tablespoons butter
1 teaspoon caraway seeds, lightly bruised
⅓ cup Madeira wine or homemade chicken broth (see page 38)

LUSCIOUS CHICKEN LIVERS

1 pound chicken livers
1 tablespoon dry mustard
1 tablespoon curry
  powder
1 teaspoon ground ginger
1 teaspoon garlic powder
1 teaspoon salt
3 tablespoons olive oil
1 cup frozen peas
3 tablespoons chopped
  parsley
  Cooked brown rice (see
  page 228)

1. Put the livers in a colander and rinse with cold water. Drain. Cut each liver in half and trim well.

2. Mix together the mustard, curry, ginger, garlic powder, and salt. Heat the oil in a heavy skillet, add the dry spice mixture and stir in the oil and cook for 15 seconds.

3. Add the livers and sauté, turning frequently until browned, about 10 minutes. Add the peas, cover, and cook until they thaw, uncover and simmer for 3 minutes, or until the peas are tender. Sprinkle with parsley. Serve over brown rice.

Yield: Four servings.

CHICKEN LIVERS WITH YOGURT

2 tablespoons butter
2 medium-sized onions,
  cut into eighths
1 pound chicken livers,
  trimmed
1 teaspoon salt
⅛ teaspoon freshly ground
  black pepper
¼ teaspoon dried thyme
½ cup plain yogurt (see
  page 324)

1. Melt the butter in a heavy skillet and sauté the onions until tender. Push the onions to one side of the pan and add the livers. Brown quickly over high heat, turning frequently, a few at a time if the pan is not large enough for a single layer. Cook over medium heat until the livers are browned but still pink in the middle. Do not overcook.

2. Add the salt, pepper, and thyme.

3. Add the yogurt and reheat but do not boil.

Yield: Four servings.

CHICKEN AND VEGETABLES

1. Heat the oil in a heavy skillet. Add the onion, green peppers, salt, and pepper and cook over low heat until the onion is transparent.

2. Put the potatoes on top of the vegetables in the skillet and then lay the chicken breasts on top of the potatoes. Pour in the broth. Cover and simmer gently until chicken and potatoes are cooked, about 40 minutes.

Yield: Four servings.

3 tablespoons vegetable oil
1 large Bermuda onion, thinly sliced
3 green peppers, seeded and cut lengthwise into strips
1 teaspoon salt
¼ teaspoon freshly ground black pepper
2 large Idaho potatoes, peeled and thinly sliced
2 whole chicken breasts, halved
¼ cup homemade chicken broth (see page 38) or water

CHICKEN TANDOORI

1. Combine all ingredients, with the exception of the chicken, butter, and lime wedges and mix well. Put the chicken in a bowl and pour the yogurt mixture over all. Marinate in the refrigerator for 24 hours, turning often.

2. Preheat the oven to 375 degrees.

3. Put the chicken pieces on a rack in a shallow roasting pan and bake for 45 to 60 minutes, or until done, basting three times with the melted butter during the cooking.

4. Serve with lime wedges.

Yield: Four servings.

1 cup plain yogurt (see page 324)
3 tablespoons lime juice
1½ teaspoons grated fresh gingerroot
1½ teaspoons ground coriander
1 teaspoon ground cumin
½ teaspoon ground anise seeds
½ teaspoon cayenne pepper
1 clove garlic, finely chopped
1 2½- to 3-pound frying chicken, cut into serving pieces
⅓ cup melted butter
Lime wedges

HOT CHICKEN SALAD

4 whole chicken breasts, halved
1 cup homemade chicken broth (see page 38)
1 small whole onion, peeled
½ bay leaf
¼ cup chopped celery leaves
Salt and freshly ground black pepper to taste
2 tablespoons grated onion
½ cup diced celery
2 tablespoons chopped parsley
3 hard-cooked eggs, sliced or chopped
⅔ cup homemade mayonnaise (see page 195)
½ cup wheat germ

1. Put the chicken breasts, broth, whole onion, bay leaf, celery leaves, salt, and pepper in a skillet. Bring to a boil, cover, and simmer until tender, about 15 minutes. Cool in the broth.
2. Preheat the oven to 350 degrees.
3. Remove the chicken meat from the bones and skin; dice the meat finely. Strain and reserve the broth. Mix the diced chicken with the grated onion, celery, parsley, eggs, and salt and pepper to taste.
4. Remove the surface fat from the reserved broth and use a tablespoon or two of the broth to thin down the mayonnaise.
5. Add the thinned mayonnaise to the chicken mixture and pour into an oiled casserole. Top with the wheat germ and bake for 30 minutes, or until bubbly hot and lightly browned.
Yield: Eight servings.

HONEYED CHICKEN

2 2½- to 3-pound frying chickens, cut into serving pieces
½ cup honey, approximately
1½ cups wheat germ
1 tablespoon chopped parsley
½ teaspoon dried thyme
½ teaspoon dried basil
Salt and freshly ground black pepper to taste
Soy oil

1. Dip each piece of chicken in the honey to coat it thinly all over. Mix together the wheat germ, parsley, thyme, basil, salt, and pepper.
2. Coat honeyed chicken with the wheat germ mixture.
3. Pour soy oil to a depth of ½ to ¾ inch into a heavy skillet and heat. Add the chicken pieces in a single layer. Cook over medium to low heat until browned, turning several times.
4. Cover the skillet and cook until the chicken is done, about 10 minutes.
Yield: Six servings.

PAPRIKA CHICKEN WITH YOGURT

1. Heat the oil in a large heavy skillet and brown the chicken pieces on both sides. Remove to paper toweling and keep warm.
2. Add the onions to the skillet and cook slowly, stirring often, until golden. Add the garlic, paprika, flour, salt, and pepper and cook, stirring, for 2 minutes.
3. Add the broth to the skillet and bring the mixture to a boil. Return the chicken to the skillet, cover, and simmer for 20 minutes, or until the chicken is cooked. Add the green beans and cook until they are crisp-tender. Arrange the chicken and beans in a deep platter. Combine the yogurt and cornstarch and stir into the liquid in the skillet. Cook, stirring, until thickened but do not allow to boil. Pour over the chicken and beans.
Yield: Six servings.

½ cup vegetable oil
3 whole chicken breasts, halved
2 large onions, thinly sliced and separated into rings
1 clove garlic, finely chopped
1½ tablespoons paprika
1 tablespoon flour
1 teaspoon salt
¼ teaspoon freshly ground black pepper
1½ cups homemade chicken broth (see page 38)
½ pound green beans, cut on the bias into 1½-inch lengths
1½ cups plain yogurt (see page 324)
1 tablespoon cornstarch

SESAME BAKED CHICKEN

1. Preheat the oven to 350 degrees.
2. Beat the egg and milk together. Combine the flour, baking powder, salt, paprika, and sesame seeds in a paper bag.
3. Dip the chicken pieces in the egg mixture and then shake in the paper bag. Place the chicken pieces skin side up in a baking dish so that they do not touch each other. Pour the melted butter over and bake until done, about 1 hour.
Yield: Three to four servings.

1 egg, lightly beaten
½ cup milk
½ cup whole wheat flour
1 tablespoon baking powder
1 teaspoon salt
2 tablespoons sweet paprika
2 tablespoons sesame seeds
1 2½- to 3-pound frying chicken, cut into serving pieces
½ cup melted butter

CHICKEN SALAD

½ cup plain yogurt (see page 324)
½ cup homemade mayonnaise (see page 195)
2 tablespoons lemon juice
2 tablespoons snipped fresh dill weed
1 tablespoon chopped parsley
½ teaspoon salt
¼ teaspoon freshly ground black pepper
3 cups hot, cooked, diced potatoes
2 cups diced cooked chicken meat
1 cup cooked peas
1 cup diced cooked carrot
2 tablespoons drained capers, optional

1. Combine the yogurt, mayonnaise, lemon juice, dill, parsley, salt, pepper, and potatoes in a medium-sized bowl. Set aside until the potatoes are at room temperature.
2. Stir in the remaining ingredients. Use as a sandwich filling, salad on lettuce, or to stuff tomatoes.
Yield: Four servings.

CHICKEN AND EGG CASSEROLE

1½ slices whole wheat bread, crumbled
½ cup milk
3 cups finely diced cooked chicken
1 teaspoon grated onion
½ teaspoon salt
⅛ teaspoon freshly ground black pepper
1 tablespoon chopped parsley
2 tablespoons vegetable oil or melted butter
3 eggs, separated

1. Preheat the oven to 350 degrees.
2. Soak the bread in the milk. Add the chicken, onion, salt, pepper, parsley, and oil. Beat the egg yolks well and add.
3. Beat the egg whites until stiff but not dry and fold into chicken mixture. Pour into an oiled soufflé dish or casserole and set in a pan of boiling water. Bake until set, about 30 minutes.
Yield: Four servings.

CHICKEN CRÊPES

1. Put the chicken breast halves in a heavy kettle. Add water to barely cover, the quartered onion, celery, peppercorns, bay leaf, and ¾ teaspoon salt. Bring to a boil, cover, and simmer for 35 minutes, or until tender.

2. Let the chicken cool until it can be handled. Skin and bone the chicken and shred it. Strain the broth, return to a clean saucepan and boil to reduce to 1 cup.

3. Melt the butter in a medium-sized saucepan and sauté the onion until tender but not browned. Sprinkle with the flour and cook for 2 minutes.

4. Gradually stir in the 1 cup reduced broth and ½ cup heavy cream. Bring to a boil, stirring. Stir in the cheese, ¼ teaspoon salt, and the pepper.

5. Put the shredded chicken in a bowl and add the ricotta and egg. Mix well. Add the parsley and ¼ teaspoon salt and mix well.

6. Fill the crêpes with the chicken mixture. Spread a layer of the cheese sauce in a shallow baking dish that will accommodate the crêpes in a single layer.

7. Arrange the filled crêpes, seam side down, on top of the sauce. Spoon the remaining sauce over, sprinkle with the Parmesan, cover, and bake in a 350-degree oven for 35 minutes. Run under a preheated broiler to glaze lightly.

Yield: Four to six servings.

2 chicken breasts, halved
Water
1 small onion, quartered
1 celery stalk, diced
6 black peppercorns, crushed
1 bay leaf, crumbled
1¼ teaspoons salt
2 tablespoons butter
1 small onion, finely chopped
2 tablespoons whole wheat flour
½ cup heavy cream
½ cup grated Gruyère or Swiss cheese
⅛ teaspoon pepper
1 cup ricotta cheese
1 egg, lightly beaten
2 tablespoons chopped parsley
1 recipe whole wheat crêpes (see pages 306 and 307)
2 tablespoons freshly grated Parmesan cheese

CHICKEN STROGANOFF

3 tablespoons vegetable oil

2 large chicken breasts, skinned, boned, and cut into strips 2 by ¼ inch thick

2 tablespoons whole wheat flour

½ teaspoon salt

¼ teaspoon freshly ground black pepper

1 medium-sized onion, finely chopped

½ pound mushrooms, sliced

1½ cups homemade chicken broth (see page 38)

1¼ cups plain yogurt (see page 324), drained through 2 thicknesses of cheesecloth for 30 minutes

1. Heat the oil in a large skillet. Toss the chicken strips in the flour mixed with the salt and pepper and stir-fry in the oil over high heat until lightly browned.

2. Remove the chicken to paper towels to drain.

3. In the oil remaining in the skillet sauté the onion until tender but not browned. Add the mushrooms and cook over medium heat for 3 minutes, stirring often.

4. Stir in the broth and scrape up all browned-on bits. Return the chicken to the skillet, cover, and simmer for 5 minutes. Stir in the drained yogurt and reheat but do not boil. Serve over noodles or brown rice.

Yield: Four servings.

ORIENTAL CHICKEN PANCAKES

2 cups bean sprouts (see page 201)

1 cup julienne strips of cooked chicken or turkey

2 teaspoons chopped fresh gingerroot

1 tablespoon dry sherry, optional

½ teaspoon salt

6 eggs, lightly beaten

¼ cup vegetable oil

2 scallions, cut into 1- by

1. Mix the bean sprouts, chicken, ginger, and sherry together in a medium-sized bowl. Add the salt to the eggs and stir into the bean sprout mixture. Heat a 6-inch skillet and oil it well. Pour in the bean sprout mixture to a thickness of ¼ to ½ inch.

2. Cover the pan and cook over low heat for 8 minutes. Loosen around the edges and slide the pancake out onto a plate. Place the skillet over the pancake and invert the plate.

3. Cook the pancake for several minutes

on the second side. Slide onto a warm platter and repeat until all batter is used.

4. Meanwhile, heat 2 tablespoons of the remaining oil in a medium-sized saucepan and sauté the scallions, celery, water chestnuts, and green pepper until tender but not browned.

5. Add the broth, soy sauce, and salt and bring to a boil. Combine the cornstarch and water and stir into the vegetable mixture. Cook, stirring, until the mixture thickens.

6. When all the chicken pancakes are cooked, serve with the vegetable sauce. Yield: Four servings.

¼-inch sticks
1 celery stalk, cut into 1- by ¼-inch sticks
4 water chestnuts, sliced
1 medium-sized green pepper, seeded and diced
1½ cups homemade chicken broth (see page 38)
2 tablespoons soy sauce
½ teaspoon salt
1 tablespoon cornstarch
¼ cup water

CHICKEN WITH YOGURT

1. Heat the butter and oil in a heavy skillet and sauté the chicken pieces a few at a time, until they are golden brown. Return all the chicken to the skillet.

2. Add the cayenne, cover the skillet, and cook over moderate heat for 10 minutes, turning chicken once.

3. Add broth and wine to the chicken. Sprinkle with chives and salt to taste, cover, and cook over low heat for 20 minutes, or until the chicken is done. Remove the chicken to a warm platter.

4. Skim the surface fat from the broth. Mix the flour and yogurt together and add to the skillet. Cook until thickened but do not boil. Pour over chicken. Yield: Four servings.

1 tablespoon butter
1 tablespoon vegetable oil
1 3- to 3½-pound frying chicken, cut into serving pieces
⅛ teaspoon cayenne pepper
½ cup homemade chicken broth (see page 38) or water
½ cup dry white wine or homemade chicken broth (see page 38)
2 tablespoons chopped chives
Salt
1 tablespoon unbleached white flour
½ cup plain yogurt (see page 324)

CHICKEN WITH FRUIT

¼ cup butter
2 2½-pound frying chickens, cut into serving pieces
1 onion, sliced
¼ pound mushrooms, sliced
1¼ cups homemade chicken broth (see page 38)
3 tablespoons lemon juice
1 teaspoon salt
¼ teaspoon ground cloves
¼ teaspoon ground allspice
1 tablespoon unsulphured molasses
4 teaspoons arrowroot
2 tablespoons cold water
1 cup cubed fresh pineapple
4 green-tipped bananas, halved lengthwise and then crosswise

1. Melt the butter in a heavy skillet, add the chicken pieces and brown on all sides. Add onion and mushrooms and cook for 5 minutes longer.

2. Add the broth, juice, salt, cloves, allspice, and molasses. Cover and simmer for 30 minutes, or until the chicken is tender.

3. Blend the arrowroot with the cold water and stir into the skillet. Stir until the mixture thickens. Add the pineapple and banana pieces. Heat through but do not boil.

Yield: Eight servings.

CHICKEN GIBLET STEW

¾ pound chicken gizzards
¼ pound chicken hearts
2 cups homemade chicken broth (see page 38) or water
1 onion, chopped
1 bay leaf, crumbled
Salt and freshly ground black pepper
1 pound chicken livers, cut into bite-sized pieces
¼ cup whole wheat flour

1. Wash the gizzards and hearts very well and put them in a saucepan with the broth, onion, bay leaf, and salt and pepper to taste. Bring to a boil, cover, and simmer until tender, about 45 minutes.

2. Remove the gizzards and hearts, chop finely and reserve. Reserve the broth.

3. Coat the liver pieces with the flour seasoned with salt and pepper. (Reserve any remaining seasoned flour.) Heat the butter and 2 tablespoons of the oil in a heavy skillet.

4. Fry the livers quickly in the skillet until

browned on all sides. Remove and reserve. Add the remaining oil, the garlic, and mushrooms to the skillet and cook for 2 minutes. Add the celery and carrots and cook for 3 minutes, stirring occasionally.

5. Add the reserved broth and chopped gizzards and hearts, bring to a boil, cover, and simmer until vegetables are barely tender, about 12 minutes.

6. Add reserved liver pieces, any remaining seasoned flour, the basil, marjoram, thyme, and salt and pepper to taste.

7. Heat, stirring, until the mixture thickens slightly. Cook for 3 minutes longer. Serve over homemade noodles.

Yield: Four servings.

Note: Any combination of gizzards, hearts, wings, and necks may be used in the broth, but all skin and bone should be discarded before dicing.

1 tablespoon butter
¼ cup vegetable oil
1 clove garlic, finely chopped
¼ pound mushrooms, sliced
1 cup diced celery
1 cup diced carrots
½ teaspoon dried basil
½ teaspoon dried marjoram
½ teaspoon dried thyme
Cooked homemade whole wheat noodles (see page 314)

GIBLET SAUTÉ

1. Brown the trimmed giblets in the oil in a heavy skillet.

2. Add 1 teaspoon salt, the pepper, thyme, and wine. Cover tightly and simmer for 1 hour.

3. Meanwhile, place the trimmings and water in a saucepan, bring to a boil, cover, and simmer for 30 minutes. Drain, reserving the broth. Discard the trimmings (or give them to the dog, if you have one).

4. Put the broth in a saucepan with the rice and salt to taste. Cover and simmer for 40 minutes, or until the rice is tender.

5. Add the garlic and parsley to the cooked giblets and keep warm until the rice is cooked. Make a bed of rice on a warm platter and top with the giblet mixture.

Yield: Four servings.

1 pound chicken giblets (hearts, gizzards, livers, and necks), trimmed and cut into bite-sized pieces (reserve trimmings)
¼ cup vegetable oil
Salt
½ teaspoon freshly ground black pepper
½ teaspoon dried thyme
¼ cup dry white wine or homemade chicken broth (see page 38)
3½ cups water
1 cup raw brown rice
1 clove garlic, finely chopped
¼ cup chopped parsley

TURKEY MEAT LOAF

1 tablespoon vegetable oil
1 medium-sized onion,
   finely chopped
1 20-ounce can chick-
   peas, drained and
   puréed in a blender or
   food processor
1 pound ground raw
   turkey meat, thawed if
   frozen
1 celery stalk, finely
   chopped
1 teaspoon dried leaf sage
1 tablespoon chopped
   parsley
2 eggs, lightly beaten
1 teaspoon salt
½ teaspoon freshly ground
   black pepper

Heat the oil in a small skillet and sauté the onion until tender but not browned. In a large bowl combine the cooked onion, chick-pea purée, turkey, celery, sage, parsley, eggs, salt, and pepper. Pack into an oiled 8½- by 4½- by 2½-inch loaf pan and bake in a 350-degree oven for 50 to 60 minutes. Let stand for 10 minutes and unmold onto a serving platter.
Yield: Four servings.

TURKEY CHILI

1 large onion, finely
   chopped
1 clove garlic, finely
   chopped
2 tablespoons vegetable
   oil
1 pound ground raw
   turkey meat, thawed if
   frozen
1 28-ounce can crushed
   tomatoes in purée
1½ tablespoons chili
   powder
1 teaspoon ground cumin
1 teaspoon salt
1 20-ounce can red kidney
   beans, drained

1. Sauté the onion and garlic in the oil until tender but not browned. Add the ground turkey and cook, stirring to break up the meat, until all signs of pink have disappeared.
2. Add the tomatoes, chili, cumin, and salt. Bring to a boil and simmer for 10 minutes. Add the beans and reheat.
Yield: Four servings.

STIR-FRY TURKEY AND VEGETABLES

1. Heat the oil in a wok or a heavy skillet. Add the turkey and stir-fry until lightly browned. Add salt, pepper, basil, thyme, chervil, and savory.

2. With wok or skillet over fairly high heat, add the cauliflower, broccoli, mushrooms, alfalfa seed sprouts, mung bean sprouts, watercress, carrot, cabbage, and spinach. Season with salt and pepper and add ½ cup of the water. Cover and cook for about 3 minutes.

3. Remove from the heat. Mix the arrowroot with the tamari and the remaining water. Pour over the vegetables. Return to the heat and cook, stirring, until the mixture thickens and clears.

4. Serve with brown rice.

Yield: Four to six servings.

3 tablespoons vegetable oil
2 cups thin strips raw turkey breast
Salt and freshly ground black pepper to taste
¼ teaspoon dried basil
¼ teaspoon dried thyme
¼ teaspoon dried chervil
¼ teaspoon dried savory
1 cup sliced cauliflower flowerets
1 cup sliced broccoli flowerets
½ cup sliced mushrooms
½ cup alfalfa seed sprouts (see page 201)
1 cup mung bean sprouts (see page 201)
1 cup chopped watercress
½ cup shredded carrot
1 cup chopped or shredded cabbage
1 cup shredded spinach leaves
¾ cup water
1 teaspoon arrowroot
1 tablespoon tamari (soy sauce)
Cooked brown rice (see page 228)

SPROUTED TURKEY LOAF

1 pound ground raw
   turkey meat, thawed if
   frozen
2 eggs, lightly beaten
1 medium-sized onion,
   finely chopped
½ cup finely chopped
   scallions
¼ cup milk
½ teaspoon salt
¼ teaspoon freshly ground
   black pepper
2 tablespoons chopped
   parsley
1 tablespoon chopped
   fresh gingerroot, or ½
   teaspoon ground ginger
1 cup mung bean sprouts
   (see page 201)
1 cup sprouted wheat
   bread crumbs (see page
   293)
   Avocado sauce (see
   page 187)

1. In a large bowl combine all the ingredients except the Avocado sauce and pack into an oiled 8- by 4½- by 2½-inch loaf pan.
2. Bake in a 350-degree oven for 50 minutes. Serve with avocado sauce.
Yield: Four servings.

TURKEY SAUSAGE

1 pound raw ground
   turkey, thawed if frozen
1 teaspoon salt
1 teaspoon dried sage
¼ teaspoon freshly ground
   black pepper
¼ teaspoon hot red pepper
   flakes
1 small onion, grated
¼ cup butter, melted

1. Put the turkey meat in a bowl and sprinkle with the salt, sage, pepper, and red pepper flakes. Add the onion and melted butter and mix well.
2. Cover the bowl and refrigerate overnight.
3. Shape the mixture into 4 patties and sauté in an oiled skillet until browned. Turn and brown on the second side and cook until cooked through.
Yield: Four servings.

STUFFED TURKEY ROLL

1. To prepare the stuffing, melt the butter in a skillet and sauté the onion and celery until tender but not browned.

2. Add the carrot, mushrooms, and green pepper and cook for 3 minutes. Remove the skillet from the heat and add the crumbs, wheat germ, salt, pepper, sage, and egg. Mix well.

3. In a large bowl combine the turkey meat, crumbs, milk, egg, mustard, salt, pepper, and sage. Mix well.

4. Turn the turkey mixture onto wax paper and spread into a 12- by 8-inch rectangle. Spread the stuffing over the turkey mixture and roll up jelly-roll fashion starting with the short end and using the paper as a guide.

5. Transfer the roll to an oiled shallow baking dish and bake in a 350-degree oven for 60 minutes.

Yield: Eight servings.

STUFFING

⅓ cup butter
1 small onion, finely chopped
1 celery stalk, finely chopped
1 carrot, shredded
½ cup sliced mushrooms
½ cup finely chopped green pepper
1 cup whole wheat bread crumbs
¼ cup wheat germ
¼ teaspoon salt
¼ teaspoon freshly ground black pepper
1 teaspoon dried leaf sage
1 egg, lightly beaten

TURKEY ROLL

2 pounds ground raw turkey meat, thawed if frozen
1½ cups whole wheat crumbs
1 cup milk
2 eggs, lightly beaten
1 tablespoon Dijon mustard
1 teaspoon salt
½ teaspoon freshly ground black pepper
1 teaspoon dried leaf sage

SAVOY AND TURKEY LOAF

1 medium-sized head
   savoy cabbage, cored
2 tablespoons vegetable
   oil
1 medium-sized onion,
   finely chopped
1 celery stalk, finely
   chopped
1 6-ounce can pitted black
   olives, drained and
   chopped
1 pound ground raw
   turkey meat, thawed if
   frozen
2 tablespoons chopped
   parsley
3 tablespoons dry cream
   of rice cereal, or ½ cup
   soft whole wheat bread
   crumbs
¼ cup milk
1 egg, lightly beaten
½ teaspoon dried thyme
½ teaspoon caraway seeds

1. Plunge the head of cabbage into a large pot of boiling salted water. Cover and cook for 8 minutes, or until wilted. Drain well.
2. Heat the oil in a small skillet and sauté the onion and celery until tender but not browned. Turn into a large bowl.
3. To the onion mixture add the olives, ground turkey, parsley, rice cereal, milk, egg, thyme, and caraway seeds.
4. Line a lightly oiled 9- by 5- by 3-inch loaf pan with cabbage leaves. Spoon in half the turkey mixture. Top with more cabbage leaves, add the remaining turkey mixture and cover with remaining cabbage leaves. Bake in a 350-degree oven for 1 hour. Let stand for 10 minutes and unmold onto a serving platter.
Yield: Six servings.

TURKEY YOGURT ENCHILADAS

4 tablespoons vegetable
   oil
½ pound ground raw
   turkey meat, thawed if
   frozen
3 scallions, chopped
1 cup plain yogurt, at
   room temperature (see
   page 324)
¼ teaspoon salt
1 4-ounce can jalapeño

1. Heat 2 tablespoons of the oil in a small skillet and cook the turkey and scallions, stirring often, until all the pink has disappeared from the meat. Stir in the yogurt, salt, and 1 jalapeño pepper, seeded and chopped.
2. Divide the turkey mixture evenly among the warm tortillas, roll up and place seam side down in an oiled shallow baking dish.
3. Preheat the oven to 350 degrees.

4. Heat the remaining oil in the same skillet and sauté the onion and garlic until tender but not browned. Add the tomatoes, breaking them up with a spoon while bringing to a boil. Add the salt and remaining jalapeño peppers, seeded and chopped. Simmer for 5 minutes.

5. Spoon the sauce over the rolled tortillas and top with the shredded cheese. Bake for 20 minutes, or until the cheese has melted and the tortillas are heated through.

Yield: Six servings.

peppers
12 tortillas, warmed
 1 medium-sized onion, finely chopped
 1 clove garlic, finely chopped
 1 16-ounce can plum tomatoes, drained
 ¼ teaspoon salt
 1 cup shredded Monterey Jack cheese

TURKEY KEBABS IN PITA BREAD

1. Put the lemon juice, oil, onion, garlic, bay leaf, oregano, salt, and pepper in a large heavy plastic bag. Mix well. Add the turkey cubes, eliminate as much air as possible, and close the bag. Set in a shallow pan in the refrigerator for 4 to 24 hours. Shake once or twice.

2. Alternate turkey cubes and cherry tomatoes on skewers and broil, or grill, 4 to 6 inches from the barbecue coals or broiler heat for about 25 minutes, turning and basting with the marinade often, or until the turkey is cooked through.

3. Heat the pita bread and cut each in half. Stuff the turkey kebabs and cherry tomatoes into the bread halves. Mix the yogurt with mint and scallion and spoon on top of turkey.

Yield: Eight servings.

 2 tablespoons lemon juice
 ⅓ cup vegetable oil
 1 medium-sized onion, finely chopped
 1 clove garlic, crushed
 1 bay leaf, crumbled
 1 teaspoon dried oregano
 1 teaspoon salt
 ½ teaspoon freshly ground black pepper
 2 pounds raw turkey breast, cut into 1-inch cubes
 1 pint cherry tomatoes
 8 large whole wheat pita bread
1½ cups plain yogurt (see page 324)
 2 tablespoons chopped fresh mint, or 1 teaspoon dried mint
 1 tablespoon chopped scallion

TURKEY-RICE CASSEROLE

2 tablespoons vegetable oil
1 medium-sized onion, finely chopped
1 clove garlic, finely chopped
1 pound ground raw turkey, thawed if frozen
1 teaspoon dried oregano
1 teaspoon dried basil
½ teaspoon salt
½ teaspoon crushed red pepper flakes
1 celery stalk, finely chopped
1 16-ounce can tomatoes
1 8-ounce can tomato sauce
½ cup water
3 cups cooked brown rice (see page 228)
1 cup cottage cheese
1 egg
6 ounces mozzarella cheese, grated
¼ cup freshly grated Parmesan cheese

1. Heat the oil in a medium-sized saucepan and sauté the onion and garlic until tender but not browned. Add the turkey and cook, stirring, until all pink has disappeared.

2. Add the oregano, basil, salt, pepper flakes, celery, tomatoes, tomato sauce, and water. Bring to a boil and simmer for 25 minutes.

3. Mix together the rice, cottage cheese, and egg and spoon half the mixture over the bottom of a buttered 2½-quart baking dish. Pour over half the tomato sauce, sprinkle with half the mozzarella. Repeat with the remainder of the rice, sauce, and mozzarella. Sprinkle with Parmesan and bake in a 350-degree oven for 35 minutes. Yield: Six servings.

TURKEY 'N' EGGS

2 tablespoons vegetable oil
1 medium-sized onion, finely chopped
1 clove garlic, finely chopped

1. Heat the oil in a medium-sized skillet with an ovenproof handle and sauté the onion and garlic until tender but not browned. Add the turkey meat and cook, stirring, until the turkey loses all pinkness.

2. Preheat the oven to 400 degrees.

3. Stir in the salt, pepper, and sage. Trim the spinach, wash, shred, and cook in just the water clinging to the leaves. Squeeze out most of the liquid and add the spinach to the skillet.

4. Combine the eggs and yogurt and pour over turkey-spinach mixture. Sprinkle with the Parmesan and bake for 12 minutes, or until set. Serve in wedges.

Yield: Six servings.

½ pound ground raw turkey meat, thawed if frozen
¾ teaspoon salt
¼ teaspoon freshly ground black pepper
½ teaspoon dried leaf sage
1 pound fresh spinach, or 1 10-ounce bag
6 eggs, lightly beaten
1 cup plain yogurt (see page 324), at room temperature
¼ cup freshly grated Parmesan cheese

YOGURT TURKEY BURGERS

1. Heat the oil in a small skillet and sauté the scallion for 2 minutes. Put the turkey in a medium-sized bowl and add the cooked scallion, bread crumbs, milk, yogurt cheese, salt, pepper, sage, and parsley. Mix well and shape into 4 burgers. Cover and refrigerate for 30 minutes or longer.

2. Mix the wheat germ and sesame seeds and use to coat the burgers. Heat 2 to 3 tablespoons oil in a medium-sized skillet and pan-fry the burgers until golden on one side. Turn and fry until golden and meat is thoroughly cooked.

Yield: Four servings.

2 tablespoons vegetable oil
1 scallion, finely chopped
1 pound ground raw turkey, thawed if frozen
1 cup whole wheat bread crumbs
¼ cup milk
⅓ cup yogurt cheese (see page 14)
½ teaspoon salt
¼ teaspoon freshly ground black pepper
½ teaspoon dried leaf sage
2 tablespoons chopped parsley
⅓ cup wheat germ
1 tablespoon sesame seeds
Vegetable oil for sautéeing

MILLET AND TURKEY CASSEROLE

2 cups whole millet
1 quart boiling
homemade vegetable
broth (see page 37) or
water
1 teaspoon salt
3 tablespoons vegetable
oil
1 large onion, finely
chopped
1 clove garlic, finely
chopped
1 pound ground raw
turkey, thawed if frozen
1 teaspoon dried sage
1 teaspoon salt
¼ teaspoon freshly ground
black pepper
1 15-ounce can tomato
sauce
1 cup shredded sharp
Cheddar cheese
½ cup chopped walnuts,
pecans, peanuts, or
cashews

1. Add the millet in a steady stream to the boiling broth while stirring. Add the salt and cook until boiling and thick. Spread half the thick mush in the bottom of an oiled 2-quart casserole or baking dish.

2. Meanwhile, heat the oil in a heavy skillet and sauté the onion and garlic until tender but not browned. Add the turkey and cook, stirring, until all pink disappears. Stir in the sage, salt, pepper, and tomato sauce. Bring to a boil and simmer for 10 minutes. Spoon half over the millet in the casserole.

3. Sprinkle over half the cheese and the nuts. Top with remaining millet mush, the remainder of the tomato sauce, and the remaining cheese. Bake in a 350-degree oven for 20 minutes, or until hot and lightly browned.

Yield: Six servings.

VEGETARIAN MAIN DISHES

This is not a vegetarian cookbook, but I do recognize the many diversified groups who adhere to this regime of eating for humanitarian, philosophical, health, or religious reasons. Also, studies have suggested that many Americans, especially those in the middle-income and upper-income brackets, consume an excess of animal protein. The vegetarian main dishes offered here are meant to be occasional substitutes for animal and fish protein and to lend variety, economy, and new eating experiences to family dining.

Balancing an all-vegetable diet—with or without dairy products—based on nuts, seeds, peas, beans, whole grains, and such, requires thought, planning, and expert dietary knowledge to ensure that adequate amounts of essential amino acids and other nutrients will appear in the diet. This is particularly true for children, pregnant women, and others with special needs. A completely new regime of eating should not be undertaken lightly. Check bibliography for further reading.

FRESH CORN SOUFFLÉ

2 cups corn kernels cut
from the cob (about 4
ears)
3 scallions, finely
chopped
6 tablespoons butter
⅓ cup whole wheat flour
½ teaspoon salt
¼ teaspoon freshly ground
black pepper
½ teaspoon dry mustard
1½ cups milk
¾ cup shredded Swiss
cheese
Dash of liquid red
pepper seasoning
6 eggs, separated

1. Preheat the oven to 350 degrees.
2. In a medium-sized saucepan, sauté the corn and scallions in the butter briefly. Stir in the flour and cook for 2 minutes while stirring.
3. Add the salt, pepper, and mustard and mix well. Gradually stir in the milk and bring to a boil, stirring, until the mixture thickens. Stir in cheese and red pepper seasoning.
4. Lightly beat the egg yolks and whisk into the hot sauce. Beat the egg whites until stiff but not dry and fold into the sauce.
5. Turn into a well-buttered 2-quart soufflé dish and bake in a 350-degree oven for 50 minutes, or until puffy and browned.
Yield: Six servings.

EGGPLANT STEAKS

1 large eggplant, peeled,
and sliced lengthwise
into ¼-inch-thick slices
1 cup unbleached white
flour
4 eggs, lightly beaten
2 cups cold water
1 teaspoon salt
1 teaspoon dried thyme
2 cups whole wheat bread
crumbs
1 cup wheat germ
½ cup sesame seeds
½ cup vegetable oil,
approximately
Tomato sauce (see page
397)

1. Dredge the eggplant slices in the flour. Set aside.
2. Combine the eggs, water, salt, and thyme. Mix together the bread crumbs, wheat germ, and sesame seeds.
3. Dip the floured eggplant into the egg mixture and then into the crumb mixture.
4. Heat the oil in a heavy skillet and fry the eggplant slices until they are golden and tender. Drain on paper towels. Serve with tomato sauce.
Yield: Six servings.

EGGPLANT AND CHEESE CASSEROLE

1. Preheat the oven to 350 degrees.
2. Put the eggplant in a saucepan with water to cover, cover, and simmer until tender, about 15 minutes. Drain and mash the eggplant.
3. Meanwhile, pour the milk over the bread to cover. Let soak for 5 minutes. Squeeze the excess milk from the bread. Pull the softened bread apart and add it to the eggplant; mix.
4. Add the eggs and cheese and mix. Pour into an oiled 1½-quart casserole and bake for 1 hour, or until set and lightly browned on top.
Yield: Six servings.

1 medium-sized eggplant, peeled and cubed
Boiling water
Milk
2 slices whole wheat bread
2 eggs, beaten
1 cup grated Cheddar cheese

EGGPLANT PARMIGIANA

1. Preheat the oven to 400 degrees.
2. Peel the eggplant and slice crosswise into paper-thin slices. Blend or process the tomatoes in the container of an electric blender or food processor until smooth.
3. Butter a large casserole or baking dish and make alternate layers of eggplant, mozzarella, and tomato purée, making the top layer cheese. Bake for 45 minutes.
Yield: Six servings.
Note: One-half pound of whole-milk ricotta can be added in layers and zucchini cut into lengthwise strips can be substituted for the eggplant.

1 large eggplant
6 large tomatoes, cored and peeled
1 pound whole-milk mozzarella, thinly sliced

ZUCCHINI-CHEESE CASSEROLE

2 pounds zucchini, cut into ½-inch-thick slices
½ cup boiling water
2 eggs, lightly beaten
1 pound cottage cheese
1 cup cooked brown rice (see page 228)
1 onion, finely chopped
Salt to taste
½ teaspoon dried marjoram
1 tablespoon chopped chives
½ cup grated Parmesan cheese

1. Put the zucchini and boiling water in a saucepan, cover and boil for 5 minutes. Drain. (You can save the liquid to use for making soup.)
2. Preheat the oven to 350 degrees.
3. Combine the eggs, cottage cheese, rice, onion, salt, marjoram, and chives. Lay half the zucchini in the bottom of a buttered casserole, top with half the rice mixture, then repeat the layers.
4. Sprinkle with the Parmesan cheese and bake for 45 minutes.
Yield: Three servings.

ZUCCHINI FRITTATA

2 tablespoons vegetable oil
5 finger-length, small zucchini, cut into ¼-inch-thick slices
5 eggs, lightly beaten
1 tablespoon chopped parsley
¼ teaspoon dried thyme
3½ tablespoons grated Parmesan cheese
Salt and freshly ground black pepper

1. Heat the oil in a medium-sized omelet pan, add the zucchini, and cook until lightly browned on all sides.
2. Combine the eggs, parsley, thyme, 2 tablespoons of the cheese, and salt and pepper to taste.
3. Pour the egg mixture over the zucchini and cook, shaking the pan occasionally, over medium heat until the mixture is almost set.
4. Sprinkle with remaining cheese and run under a preheated broiler to brown lightly.
Yield: Two servings.

VEGETARIAN CUTLETS

1. Grind the beets, carrot, and onions through the finest blade of a meat grinder or in a food processor. Strain off any excess liquid (which can be used in soup).
2. Combine the vegetables with remaining ingredients and mix well. If the mixture is too wet to form into patties, add more wheat germ. Chill for 30 minutes. Shape into patties.
3. Fry the patties in a lightly oiled skillet until browned. Turn to brown the other side.
Yield: Four servings.

2 small raw beets, peeled
1 carrot, scraped
2 onions, peeled
2 eggs, well beaten
2 tablespoons vegetable oil
½ cup sunflower seed kernels, finely ground
½ teaspoon caraway seeds
½ cup wheat germ
½ teaspoon vegetable salt
Vegetable oil

PEAS AND BARLEY CASSEROLE

1. Heat the oil in a heavy saucepan and sauté the onion until tender. Add the split peas and cook for 3 minutes.
2. Meanwhile, add ½ cup broth to the grits and set aside.
3. Add the barley to the saucepan and cook for 2 minutes, stirring occasionally. Add the remaining broth, soaked grits, parsley, dill, and salt to taste. Bring to a boil and simmer, covered, until the liquid has been absorbed and the barley is tender, about 55 minutes. Add the mushrooms and cook for 5 minutes longer.
Yield: Four servings.

2 tablespoons oil
1 onion, finely chopped
½ cup yellow split peas, washed and drained
2½ cups boiling homemade vegetable broth (see page 37)
¼ cup soy grits
½ cup whole barley, washed and drained
2 tablespoons chopped parsley
3 tablespoons fresh snipped dill weed
Salt
¼ pound mushrooms, sliced

PEAS ROAST

1 pound dried split green
  peas
1 medium-sized onion
  Water
  Salt to taste
½ teaspoon dried
  marjoram
2 eggs, lightly beaten
  Tomato sauce (see page
  397)

1. Pick over and wash the split peas and put them in a saucepan with the onion and water to cover. Bring to a boil, cover, and cook gently until tender, about 30 minutes.

2. Preheat the oven to 350 degrees.

3. Drain off the excess water (and use it in soup) and purée the peas and onion in a food processor, or press through a food mill or sieve. Season with salt and marjoram.

4. Beat in the eggs and pour the mixture into an oiled 9- by 5- by 3-inch loaf pan. Bake for 30 minutes, or until the loaf is set. Let stand for 10 minutes and unmold onto a serving platter. Serve with tomato sauce.

Yield: Six servings.

LIMA BEAN LOAF

2 cups cooked fresh,
  frozen, or dried lima
  beans
1 cup whole wheat bread
  crumbs
½ cup finely chopped
  green pepper
½ cup finely chopped
  onion
½ cup chopped nuts
2 eggs, well beaten
½ cup heavy cream
  Vegetable salt to taste
  Melted butter

1. Preheat the oven to 350 degrees.

2. Mix together the lima beans, bread crumbs, green pepper, onion, nuts, eggs, cream, salt, and 2 tablespoons melted butter. Turn into a well-buttered 8½- by 4½- by 2½-inch loaf pan. Bake for 45 minutes, basting 3 times with melted butter during cooking.

Yield: Six servings.

WINTER CASSEROLE

1. Preheat the oven to 350 degrees.
2. Put the carrots, onions, celery, and green pepper in a colander over boiling water. Cover and steam until barely tender. Add the escarole and steam for 3 minutes longer.
3. Mix the steamed vegetables with the pignoli, bread crumbs, eggs, rice, sesame seeds, and salt to taste and turn into an oiled 3-quart casserole. Cover and bake for 30 minutes.
4. To make the sauce, combine all ingredients in a small saucepan and heat.
5. Just before serving, pour the sauce over casserole.
Yield: Eight servings.

4 carrots, grated
3 onions, finely chopped
4 celery stalks, diced
1 green pepper, seeded and chopped
1 cup shredded escarole
½ cup crushed pignoli (pine nuts)
1 cup whole wheat bread crumbs
3 eggs, well beaten
4 cups cooked brown rice (see page 228)
3 tablespoons toasted sesame seeds
Salt

SAUCE
½ cup butter
2 tablespoons lemon juice
3 tablespoons chopped parsley
2 tablespoons chopped fresh basil leaves

DILLED CARROT CUTLETS

1. Mash the soybeans with a potato masher until smooth. Stir in carrot, salt, cashews, and dill.
2. Shape the mixture into cutlet shapes. Dip into the egg and coat with the wheat germ.
3. Heat the oil in a skillet. Add the cutlets and fry quickly until lightly browned on both sides. Drain on paper towels.
Yield: Six servings.

2 cups cooked and drained soybeans (see page 159)
1 large carrot, grated
½ teaspoon salt
¼ cup finely chopped cashews
2 tablespoons snipped fresh dill weed
1 egg, lightly beaten
⅓ cup wheat germ
¼ cup vegetable oil

CARROT LOAF

3 cups grated raw carrots
2 cups cooked brown rice
(see page 228)
1 cup finely chopped raw
peanuts or cashews
1 cup raw peanut butter
2 cups skim milk
2 teaspoons dried sage
2 eggs, lightly beaten

1. Preheat the oven to 325 degrees.
2. Mix together the carrots, rice, and peanuts.
3. Blend together the peanut butter and milk either in an electric blender or with a rotary whisk. Add the sage and eggs.
4. Pour the milk mixture over the carrot mixture and blend well.
5. Turn into a 3-quart oiled casserole and bake for 45 minutes, or until set.
Yield: Six servings.

CHICK-PEA LOAF

3 cups cooked dried or
drained canned chick-
peas or garbanzos
1 cup chopped celery
¼ cup finely chopped
onion
1 cup whole wheat bread
crumbs
⅓ cup tomato sauce (see
page 397)
1 tablespoon soy sauce
2 tablespoons wheat germ
1 cup ground nuts
(walnuts, almonds,
pecans)
1 teaspoon dried sage
2 tablespoons vegetable
oil
2 tablespoons chopped
parsley
2 eggs, lightly beaten
Salt to taste

1. Preheat the oven to 375 degrees.
2. Mash the chick-peas and put in a large bowl. Add the remaining ingredients and mix well. Turn into a well-oiled 9- by 5- by 3-inch loaf pan and bake for 30 minutes, or until set. Let stand for 10 minutes and unmold onto a serving platter.
Yield: Six servings.

BARLEY-LENTIL KASHA

1. Combine the barley, lentils, and grits in a saucepan. Add broth until it is ½ inch above the vegetables. Cover and simmer for 30 minutes, or until the barley and lentils are tender. Add water or broth, if necessary, during cooking.
2. Meanwhile, heat the oil and sauté the onion until tender.
3. Add the onion, parsley, yeast, rosemary, and salt to taste to the barley mixture. Simmer for 10 minutes. If the mixture becomes too dry during cooking, add a little more water or broth.
Yield: Six servings.

½ cup whole barley
1 cup lentils, soaked in water to cover for 30 minutes, and drained
¼ cup soy grits
Water or boiling homemade vegetable broth (see page 37), optional
1 tablespoon vegetable oil
1 onion, finely chopped
3 tablespoons chopped parsley
3 tablespoons brewer's yeast
1 teaspoon dried rosemary
Salt

LENTIL-MILLET PATTIES WITH TOMATO SAUCE

1. Put lentils in a saucepan with water to cover, bring to a boil, and cook until tender, about 40 minutes.
2. Put the millet and 1½ cups water in a second saucepan, bring to a boil, cover, and simmer 30 minutes, or until tender and water is absorbed.
3. Drain the lentils and mix with the millet. Add the onion, salt and pepper. Form the mixture into patties. If too wet add wheat germ to bind. Dip the patties into the beaten eggs and then into the wheat germ.
4. Heat oil to a depth of ¼ inch in a heavy skillet and fry the patties until golden on both sides. Drain on paper towels. Serve with tomato sauce.
Yield: Six servings.

1 cup dried lentils, picked over and washed
Water
¾ cup whole hulled millet
1 onion, chopped
Salt and freshly ground black pepper to taste, optional
2 eggs, lightly beaten
Wheat germ
Vegetable oil for frying
Tomato sauce (see page 397)

LENTIL BURGERS

2 cups cooked and drained lentils
1 cup whole wheat bread crumbs
½ cup wheat germ
½ teaspoon salt
½ onion, grated
½ teaspoon celery seeds
Whole wheat flour for coating
3 tablespoons vegetable oil

1. Mash the lentils slightly. Add the bread crumbs, wheat germ, salt, onion, and celery seeds. Mix well.
2. Form the mixture into 8 patties. Coat with flour.
3. Heat the oil in a skillet and fry the patties on both sides until browned.
Yield: Eight servings.

BEAN AND CHEESE LOAF

1 cup whole wheat bread crumbs
1 cup milk
1 20-ounce can chick-peas, drained and ground through coarse blade of a meat grinder
¼ cup chopped parsley
½ teaspoon salt
1 large onion, finely chopped
1 celery stalk, finely chopped
3 tablespoons vegetable oil
1½ cups finely chopped walnuts
2 eggs, lightly beaten
1 tablespoon soy sauce
⅛ teaspoon cayenne
1 cup shredded Cheddar cheese

1. Soak the bread crumbs in the milk. In a large bowl combine the chick-peas, parsley, and salt.
2. Sauté the onion and celery in the oil until tender but not browned and add to chick-pea mixture. Stir in the soaked crumbs, nuts, eggs, soy sauce, cayenne, and cheese.
3. Pour into an oiled 9- by 5- by 3-inch loaf pan. Bake in a 350-degree oven for 50 minutes. Cool in the pan for 5 minutes before removing to a platter.
Yield: Six servings.

NUTTY BEAN LOAF

1. Heat the oil in a small skillet and sauté the onion until tender but not browned. Combine with the remaining ingredients except the barbecue sauce. Pack into an oiled 8½- by 4½- by 2½-inch loaf pan.

2. Bake in a 350-degree oven for 45 minutes. Serve with barbecue sauce, if you wish.

Yield: Four servings.

3 tablespoons vegetable oil
1 large onion, finely chopped
2 cups mashed, cooked pinto, pea, or kidney beans
1 cup finely chopped walnuts, pecans, or cashews
2 cups whole wheat bread crumbs
2 eggs, lightly beaten
1¼ cups light cream or milk
1 teaspoon dried sage
¾ teaspoon salt
¼ teaspoon freshly ground black pepper
¼ cup chopped parsley
⅓ cup chopped celery
Barbecue sauce (see page 392), optional

SOYBEAN SOUFFLÉ

1. Preheat the oven to 325 degrees.

2. Beat the soybean pulp together with the egg yolks and heat gently, while stirring constantly, until the mixture thickens slightly. Do not allow to boil.

3. Stir in the onion, parsley, salt, thyme, and marjoram. Beat the egg whites until stiff but not dry and fold into soybean mixture. Pour mixture into a well-buttered 1½-quart soufflé or baking dish and bake for 45 minutes, or until set.

Yield: Six servings.

3 cups warm soybean pulp or cooked soybeans forced through a food mill or colander (pulp should be fairly dry)
4 eggs, separated
1 tablespoon grated onion
2 tablespoons chopped parsley
Salt to taste
½ teaspoon dried thyme
¼ teaspoon dried marjoram

BEAN BURGERS

1 tablespoon vegetable oil
1 medium-sized onion,
  finely chopped
1 clove garlic, finely
  chopped
2 cups drained, mashed
  cooked pinto, pea, or
  kidney beans
¼ cup chopped parsley
½ cup whole wheat bread
  crumbs
2 egg yolks
2 tablespoons cream or
  milk
1 teaspoon salt
¼ teaspoon freshly ground
  black pepper
½ teaspoon dried oregano
  Wheat germ
  Butter for sautéeing
  Hot homemade
  barbecue sauce (see
  page 392)

1. Heat the oil in a small skillet and sauté the onion and garlic until tender but not browned. Combine with the beans, parsley, crumbs, egg yolks, cream, salt, pepper, and oregano and mix well.
2. Shape into 4 burgers and coat with wheat germ. Chill for 1 hour or longer.
3. Melt the butter in a large heavy skillet and sauté burgers until lightly browned. Serve with barbecue sauce.
Yield: Four servings.

VEGETARIAN SAUSAGES

2 cups cooked soybeans
  (see page 159)
1 cup cooked dried lima
  beans
1 cup cooked dried navy
  beans
2 teaspoons vegetable salt

1. Preheat the oven to 500 degrees.
2. Press the soybeans, lima beans, and navy beans through a colander or purée in a food processor. Add the salt, paprika, butter, sage, thyme, marjoram, and savory. Add enough wheat germ to make a moldable mixture.

3. Shape the bean mixture into sausage shapes. Combine the egg and milk. Dip the sausages first into the egg and milk mixture and then into the cornmeal. Put the sausages in a large, well oiled, shallow roasting pan. Bake until the sausages are browned on all sides, turning during the cooking.

Yield: Four servings.

⅛ teaspoon paprika
1 tablespoon butter, melted
½ teaspoon powdered sage
½ teaspoon dried thyme
¼ teaspoon dried marjoram
¼ teaspoon dried summer savory
Wheat germ
1 egg, lightly beaten
⅔ cup milk
1 cup cornmeal
Vegetable oil

PRESSURE-COOKED SOYBEANS

1. Pick over and wash the soybeans. Mix the beans with the onion and water and refrigerate overnight. Put the beans, onion, soaking liquid, salt, molasses, oil, cinnamon, and cloves in a pressure cooker. The cooker should not be more than half full.

2. Close the cover tightly, place pressure regulator on vent pipe, set for 15 pounds if there is a choice, and cook, according to manufacturer's directions, for 30 minutes.

3. Allow the pressure to reduce of its own accord. Remove pressure regulator and cover. Add the remaining ingredients and mix, while stirring over low heat.

Yield: Six servings.

Note: The soaked beans may be cooked in a regular covered saucepan for several hours. Add extra water as needed.

1 cup dried soybeans
1 large onion, grated
3¼ cups water
1 teaspoon salt
3 tablespoons unsulphured molasses
1 tablespoon vegetable oil
¼ teaspoon ground cinnamon
¼ teaspoon ground cloves
¼ cup chopped dates
¼ cup chopped apple
2 tablespoons unsweetened shredded coconut
1 tablespoon lime juice or lemon juice

SOYBEAN AND NUT LOAF

4 cups cooked and drained soybeans (see page 159)
½ cup ground pecans
½ cup ground almonds
⅓ cup sesame seeds
⅓ cup flax seeds, soaked in warm water for 30 minutes and drained, optional
2 tablespoons vegetable oil
1 cup chopped celery
1 cup chopped onions
1 teaspoon paprika
1 teaspoon dried oregano
1 teaspoon ground cumin

1. Preheat the oven to 350 degrees.
2. Grind the beans through a meat grinder and mix with the pecans, almonds, sesame seeds, and flax seeds.
3. Heat the oil and sauté the celery and onions until tender. Add to the bean mixture with the remaining ingredients. Pack into a 9- by 5- by 3-inch loaf pan and bake for 1 hour. (Alternately, the loaf mixture may be formed into patties and fried in a little oil in a skillet.)
Yield: Eight servings.

SOYBEAN AND VEGETABLE CASSEROLE

3 tablespoons vegetable oil
1 cup chopped celery
1 cup chopped onion
2½ cups peeled, chopped fresh tomatoes or canned tomatoes
2 cloves garlic, finely chopped
½ teaspoon salt
½ cup wheat germ
½ cup homemade vegetable broth (see page 37)
3 tablespoons brewer's yeast
3 cups cooked soybeans (see page 159)

1. Preheat the oven to 350 degrees.
2. Heat the oil in a skillet and sauté the celery and onions until tender. Mix the onion mixture with the remaining ingredients and turn into an oiled 3-quart casserole. Bake for 30 minutes.
Yield: Six servings.

BAKED SOYBEANS I

1. Preheat the oven to 300 degrees.
2. Combine the beans with the onion and oil. Put in a bean crock or casserole with a narrow top opening.
3. In a measuring cup, combine the molasses, salt, mustard, and enough hot water to fill the cup. Pour over the beans. Add enough reserved soybean cooking liquid to cover the beans.
4. Cover the crock and bake for 6 to 8 hours. Add more water as necessary to maintain the level until the last hour, then uncover and do not add any more water.
Yield: Four to six servings.

2 cups cooked dried soybeans, with cooking liquid reserved (see page 159)
1 large onion, chopped
¼ cup vegetable oil
2 tablespoons unsulphured molasses
4 teaspoons salt, or to taste
½ teaspoon dry mustard
Hot water

BAKED SOYBEANS II

1. Put the beans in a large freezer container, or several smaller ones, and cover the beans with cold water. There should be plenty of room for the beans to expand.
2. Let soak for 5 hours and then put in the freezer for at least 24 hours. (This reduces length of cooking time required.)
3. Put the frozen beans and liquid in a large kettle. Bring to a boil and simmer gently until tender, adding more water if necessary. The beans will take 2½ hours to 3½ hours to cook.
4. Meanwhile, heat the oil and sauté the onion and green pepper until tender. Transfer to a 3-quart casserole. Add the tomato paste, kelp, honey, salt, and molasses.
5. Preheat the oven to 325 degrees.
6. Add the beans and cooking liquid to the casserole. Mix well and add more water if the beans are not covered. Bake, uncovered, for about 1½ hours, or until browned.
Yield: Eight servings.

1 pound yellow soybeans, picked over and washed
Cold water
¼ cup vegetable oil
1 small onion, chopped
1 green pepper, seeded and diced
¾ cup tomato paste
½ teaspoon kelp, optional
2 tablespoons honey
1½ teaspoons salt
2 tablespoons unsulphured molasses

SOY BURGERS

1 15½-ounce can soybeans, drained and rinsed, or 2 cups cooked and drained soybeans (see page 159)
1 small onion, finely grated or chopped
2 eggs, lightly beaten
1 cup wheat germ
1 tablespoon vegetable broth seasoning
1 tablespoon tamari (soy sauce)
1 tomato, peeled and puréed in the container of an electric blender or food processor

1. Preheat the oven to 350 degrees.
2. Mash the soybeans with a potato masher.
3. Combine all the ingredients in a large bowl.
4. Using a small ice cream scoop, measure out portions of the mixture onto a lightly oiled baking sheet. Flatten each scoop slightly.
5. Bake for 25 minutes, turn and bake for 15 minutes longer.
Yield: Four servings.

SOY-RICE BURGERS

1 15½-ounce can soybeans, drained and rinsed, (2 cups) or dried soybeans, soaked, cooked, and drained (2 cups) (see page 159)
1 cup cooked brown rice (see page 228)
2 tablespoons chopped onion
2 eggs, lightly beaten
½ teaspoon salt
½ teaspoon celery salt
1 cup whole wheat bread crumbs
¼ teaspoon paprika
2 tablespoons chopped parsley
½ cup wheat germ
8 slices whole wheat bread

1. Grind the soybeans, using the coarse blade of the meat grinder. Mix the soybeans with the other ingredients, with the exception of the wheat germ and bread slices.
2. Form into 4 burgers. Coat with the wheat germ.
3. Broil over a charcoal fire, or under the broiler, until lightly browned. Alternately, the burgers may be baked on a baking sheet in a 350-degree oven for 35 minutes.
4. Serve between whole wheat bread slices.
Yield: Four servings.

MILLET-STUFFED PEPPERS

1. Put the millet, water, and salt in a saucepan. Bring to a boil and simmer, covered, until tender, about 30 minutes. Drain.
2. Steam the pepper halves over boiling water for 5 minutes.
3. Preheat the oven to 350 degrees.
4. Heat the oil in a large heavy skillet and sauté the onions and garlic until tender. Add the mushrooms and cook for 2 minutes longer.
5. Stir in the parsley, oregano, basil, and tamari.
6. Add the cooked millet, eggs, and cottage cheese. Cook, stirring gently, for a minute or two. Fill the pepper halves with the millet mixture.
7. Set in a baking dish with ½ inch of hot water in the bottom. Top each pepper half with a tomato slice and some cheese.
8. Bake for 25 to 30 minutes.
Yield: Four servings.

1 cup whole hulled millet
3 cups water
Salt to taste
4 medium-sized green peppers, halved lengthwise and seeded
⅓ cup vegetable oil
1½ cups chopped onion
1 clove garlic, chopped
½ cup sliced mushrooms
3 tablespoons chopped parsley
1 teaspoon dried oregano
½ teaspoon dried basil
1 teaspoon tamari (soy sauce)
2 eggs, lightly beaten
½ cup cottage cheese
8 slices tomato
Grated Cheddar cheese

MILLET CASSEROLE

1. Put the millet, water, and salt to taste in a saucepan. Bring to a boil, cover, and simmer until tender, about 30 minutes.
2. Preheat the oven to 350 degrees.
3. Add the remaining ingredients to the cooked millet and turn into an oiled 9- by 5- by 3-inch loaf pan or casserole. Bake for 1 hour, or until set.
Yield: Six servings.
Note: One-half cup grated Cheddar cheese can be added if desired.

1 cup whole hulled millet
4 cups water
Salt
2 onions, finely chopped
1 clove garlic, finely chopped
2 cups tomato purée
2 cups wheat germ
2 tablespoons vegetable oil
2 tablespoons chopped fresh basil
2 tablespoons chopped parsley
½ teaspoon celery seeds

MILLET STEW

1 tablespoon vegetable oil
½ cup chopped onion
1 cup peeled butternut
    squash cubes (about ½-
    inch cubes)
1 cup whole hulled millet
4½ cups water
1 tablespoon tamari (soy
    sauce)

1. Heat the oil in a saucepan and sauté the onion in it.
2. Add the squash, millet, water, and tamari. Bring to a boil, cover, and boil for 45 minutes. Stir to mix and let stand for 10 minutes before serving.
Yield: Four servings.

MILLET 'N' VEGETABLES

1 cup chopped carrots
½ cup chopped onion
1 cup diced peeled potato
½ cup chopped parsnip or
    white turnip
1 cup shredded cabbage
¼ cup chopped parsley
½ cup whole hulled millet
1 teaspoon salt
2½ cups water or
    homemade vegetable
    broth (see page 37),
    approximately
1 tablespoon vegetable oil

1. Put all the vegetables in a heavy porcelanized iron casserole. Add the parsley, millet, salt, and 2½ cups water. Bring to a boil, cover, and cook gently for 45 minutes.
2. If mixture seems too thick, add a little water and cook for 15 minutes longer. Drizzle the oil over surface before serving.
Yield: Four servings.

MILLET SOUFFLÉ

3 eggs, separated
1¾ cup cooked millet (see
    page 221)
½ teaspoon salt
⅓ cup plus ¼ cup grated
    Cheddar cheese
⅔ cup milk

1. Preheat the oven to 350 degrees.
2. Beat the egg yolks lightly. Mix with the millet, salt, ⅓ cup cheese, and the milk.
3. Beat the egg whites until stiff but not dry and fold into the millet mixture. Pour into a 1½-quart soufflé dish. Sprinkle the remaining cheese on top. Set the soufflé dish in a pan of hot water and bake for about 20 minutes, or until set.
Yield: Four servings.

NOODLE CASSEROLE

1. Preheat the oven to 300 degrees.
2. Mix together all ingredients except the noodles. Drain the noodles and rinse with cold water. Add to the cheese mixture and toss.
3. Turn into a buttered 2½-quart casserole or baking dish and bake for 45 to 60 minutes.
Yield: Six servings.

1 cup ricotta cheese or large curd cottage cheese
1 cup plain yogurt (see page 324)
¼ cup butter, melted
Salt and freshly ground black pepper to taste, optional
1 egg, lightly beaten
⅛ teaspoon grated nutmeg
⅓ cup freshly grated Parmesan cheese
8 ounces whole wheat noodles, cooked al dente (see page 314)

CORNMEAL, KALE, AND BEANS

1. Put the beans in a bowl, cover with water and let soak overnight. Next morning, drain, cover with fresh water and add the onion, garlic, celery, parsley, salt to taste, and tamari. Bring to a boil and simmer, covered, until tender, about 30 minutes.
2. Break the kale into pieces and cook in the boiling water until tender.
3. Remove the onion, garlic, parsley, and celery from beans and discard.
4. Drain the kale, adding the liquid to the bean mixture. Stir the cornmeal and salt to taste into the boiling bean mixture, beating vigorously to prevent lumping. Cover and simmer slowly for 30 minutes, or until the cornmeal is done.
5. Add the kale and oil and check the seasonings. Serve hot. Or, slice when cold and fry in oil.
Yield: Twelve servings.

1 pound dried red kidney beans, picked over and washed
Water
1 large unpeeled onion, halved
2 cloves garlic, crushed
3 celery stalks, quartered
4 sprigs parsley, tied together
Salt
1 tablespoon tamari (soy sauce)
2 pounds kale, stems and tough veins removed
2 quarts boiling water
1½ cups stoneground cornmeal
1 cup olive or vegetable oil

BROWN RICE AND CHEESE CASSEROLE

2 eggs, lightly beaten
½ cup heavy cream
⅓ cup water
1½ cups cooked brown rice
(see page 228)
1¼ cups grated Cheddar
cheese
Salt
¼ cup chopped green
pepper
2 tablespoons grated
onion

1. Preheat the oven to 350 degrees.
2. Beat the eggs together with the cream and water. Stir into the rice. Add cheese, salt to taste, green pepper, and onion. Mix well.
3. Turn into an oiled 2-quart casserole and bake for 45 minutes, or until set.
Yield: Two servings.

VEGETARIAN RICE CASSEROLE

¼ cup vegetable oil
1 onion, finely chopped
1 large carrot, diced
1 cup shredded Chinese
cabbage
1 cup snow peas
1 cup shredded spinach
leaves
1 cup shredded romaine
lettuce or escarole
1½ cups bean sprouts (see
page 201)
2 tablespoons sesame
seeds
½ cup finely chopped
walnuts
Salt
Tamari (soy sauce) to
taste
4 cups cooked brown rice
(see page 228)
2 eggs, lightly beaten

1. Heat the oil in a large heavy skillet and sauté the onion and carrot until the onion is tender. Add Chinese cabbage, snow peas, spinach, and romaine lettuce. Cover the pan and cook, without added liquid, until wilted.
2. Add the bean sprouts, sesame seeds, walnuts, salt to taste, and tamari. Cover and steam for 3 minutes. Mix in the rice and reheat.
3. Make a well in the center of the vegetable mixture and add the eggs. Cook, stirring, until the eggs are cooked. Check the seasonings. Transfer to a casserole and keep warm for serving.
Yield: Six to eight servings.

ORIENTAL-STYLE BROWN RICE

1. Heat the oil in a wok or a heavy iron skillet. Add the scallions and cook quickly for 1 minute. Add the garlic and celery and cook for 1 minute.

2. Add the water chestnuts, bean sprouts, and parsley. Cook, stirring, for 1 minute. Stir in the oregano, basil, and sunflower seed kernels.

3. Combine the ginger, honey, soy sauce, and lemon juice and stir into the vegetable mixture. Add salt to taste. Stir in the cooked rice and reheat.

Yield: Four servings.

3 tablespoons vegetable oil
2 bunches scallions, chopped
1 clove garlic, finely chopped
4 celery stalks, diced
1 5-ounce can water chestnuts, sliced
2 cups bean sprouts (see page 201)
3 tablespoons chopped parsley
1 teaspoon dried oregano
½ teaspoon dried basil
¾ cup sunflower seed kernels
2 tablespoons grated fresh gingerroot
¾ cup honey
½ cup soy sauce
1 tablespoon lemon juice
Salt
4 cups cooked brown rice (see page 228)

BUCKWHEAT AND PEANUT CASSEROLE

1. Preheat the oven to 350 degrees.

2. Make a layer of half the potatoes in a buttered 1½-quart casserole. Add the buckwheat, onions, green pepper, and salt. Top with remaining potatoes.

3. Finely chop the peanuts in an electric blender or food processor. Add the water and blend until the mixture is smooth. Pour over the potatoes in the casserole. Cover and bake for 1 hour, or until buckwheat is cooked.

Yield: Six servings.

4 cups peeled sliced potatoes
½ cup whole buckwheat (kasha)
2 medium-sized onions, finely chopped
½ green pepper, seeded and chopped
1 teaspoon salt
½ cup shelled raw peanuts
3 cups water

BUCKWHEAT GROATS-VEGETABLE BAKE

2 cups cooked buckwheat
groats (kasha)
2 cups cooked brown rice
(see page 228)
3 cups steamed diced
vegetables, such as
celery, carrot, turnip,
parsnip, green pepper,
and potatoes
2 cups shredded Cheddar
cheese
Salt to taste

1. Preheat the oven to 325 degrees.
2. Combine the groats, rice, vegetables, and 1 cup of the cheese in a bowl. Add salt to taste and mix well.
3. Turn into an oiled 3-quart casserole or ovenproof bowl. Sprinkle the remaining cheese over the top and bake for 40 minutes.
Yield: Six servings.

WILD RICE AND BUCKWHEAT LOAF

½ cup whole buckwheat
groats (kasha)
½ cup raw brown rice
½ cup raw wild rice
1 quart water or
homemade vegetable
broth (see page 37),
approximately
2 tablespoons vegetable
oil
2 medium-sized onions,
finely chopped
1 cup chopped celery
1½ teaspoons salt
¼ cup chopped parsley
2 teaspoons ground
cumin

1. Put the buckwheat, rice, and wild rice in a kettle. Add 1 quart water. Bring to a boil, cover, and simmer until tender, about 40 minutes. Add more water as necessary during cooking.
2. Preheat the oven to 350 degrees.
3. Heat the oil in a skillet and sauté the onion and celery until tender. Add to the cooked grains with the remaining ingredients. Turn into an oiled 3-quart casserole and bake for 1 hour.
Yield: Six servings.

BUCKWHEAT-STUFFED CABBAGE ROLLS

1. Sauté the onion in the oil until tender. Add groats and cook, stirring, until coated with oil.
2. Add salt, pepper, and 1 quart water and bring to a boil. Cover and simmer for 20 minutes, or until the water has been absorbed. Stir in the dill.
3. Meanwhile, core the cabbage and steam over boiling water until the leaves are soft.
4. Preheat the oven to 350 degrees.
5. Separate the cabbage leaves and place 2 to 3 heaping tablespoons of the groats mixture on each big leaf. Roll up, tucking in the sides as you go. Use two smaller leaves together for making other rolls.
6. Put the rolls seam side down in an oiled baking dish or casserole. Pour the warm water over the rolls until the liquid reaches three quarters of the way up the layers of rolls. Cover and bake for 2 hours, or until cabbage is tender.
Yield: Ten servings.

1 medium-sized onion, finely chopped
¼ cup vegetable oil
2 cups buckwheat groats (kasha)
Salt and freshly ground black pepper to taste
1 quart water
2 tablespoons snipped fresh dill weed
1 3-pound head cabbage
Warm water or tomato sauce (see page 397)

WHEAT LOAF

1. Preheat the oven to 350 degrees.
2. Mix together the nuts, wheat germ, and cheese. Add the remaining ingredients and mix well. Turn into an oiled 8½- by 4½- by 2½-inch loaf pan. Bake for 45 minutes. Serve like meatloaf.
Yield: Four to six servings.

1 cup finely ground walnuts or pecans
1 cup wheat germ
1 cup grated mild Cheddar cheese
¾ cup tomato juice (see page 33)
3 eggs, well beaten
1 large onion, finely chopped
1 teaspoon dried thyme
¼ teaspoon dried marjoram
Salt to taste

WHEAT AND NUT LOAF

¼ cup vegetable oil
1 onion, finely chopped
4 eggs, lightly beaten
3 cups cooked brown rice
  (see page 228)
1 quart milk
3 cups stoneground whole
  wheat raisin bread
  crumbs
1 teaspoon salt
2 tablespoons dried sage
2 cups finely chopped
  walnuts
  Tomato sauce (see page
  397)

1. Preheat the oven to 350 degrees.
2. Heat the oil and sauté the onion until tender. Mix the eggs and rice together. Pour 2 cups of the milk over the raisin bread crumbs and let stand for 5 minutes.
3. In a large bowl, combine the onion mixture, rice mixture, crumb mixture, salt, sage, walnuts, and remaining milk. Pack into an oiled 9- by 5- by 3-inch loaf pan or 2-quart casserole.
4. Place the pan or casserole in a pan of hot water and bake for 1 hour. Serve hot with tomato sauce.
Yield: Eight servings.

CHEESE AND NUT LOAF

3 tablespoons vegetable
  oil
1 onion, chopped
1½ cups chopped celery
1 cup chopped cashews
1 cup chopped walnuts
2 cups cooked brown rice
  (see page 228)
2 cups (1 pound) cottage
  cheese
2 tablespoons chopped
  chives
¼ cup toasted sesame
  seeds
¼ cup chopped parsley
½ teaspoon dried thyme
  Salt to taste
3 eggs, lightly beaten
¼ cup wheat germ

1. Preheat the oven to 375 degrees.
2. Heat the oil in a skillet and sauté the onion until tender. Add the celery and cook for 5 minutes longer.
3. Combine the cashews, walnuts, rice, cottage cheese, chives, sesame seeds, parsley, thyme, salt, and eggs in a large bowl. Stir in the cooked onion mixture.
4. Oil a 9- by 5- by 3-inch loaf pan and dust generously with wheat germ. Turn the cheese-rice-nut mixture into the pan and sprinkle the remaining wheat germ over the surface. Bake for 1 hour. Unmold to serve.
Yield: Eight to ten servings.

NUT LOAF

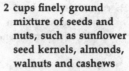

1. Preheat the oven to 350 degrees.
2. Mix all ingredients together in a large bowl until well blended. Turn into an oiled 9- by 5- by 3-inch loaf pan and bake for 40 minutes. Serve like meatloaf.

Yield: Six servings.

Note: The cold nut loaf can be spread on crackers with cream cheese.

2 cups finely ground mixture of seeds and nuts, such as sunflower seed kernels, almonds, walnuts and cashews
1 medium-sized onion, finely chopped
3 cloves garlic, finely chopped
3 celery stalks, finely chopped
2 eggs, lightly beaten
¾ cup wheat germ
3 tablespoons brewer's yeast
1 cup cooked brown rice (see page 228) or raw rolled oats
1 tablespoon tamari (soy sauce)
½ teaspoon chopped fresh rosemary, or ⅛ teaspoon dried rosemary
½ teaspoon chopped fresh sage, or ¼ teaspoon dried sage
1 teaspoon caraway seeds
Salt to taste

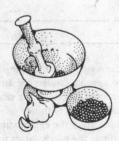

SUNFLOWER SEED LOAF

1½ cups sunflower seed
    kernels, ground in an
    electric blender or hand
    grinder
¾ cup sesame seeds,
    ground in an electric
    blender or Moulinex
    grinder
½ cup chopped walnuts or
    pecans
1 cup cooked dried lentils
½ cup grated raw beets or
    carrots
3 tablespoons chopped
    onion
2 eggs, lightly beaten
1 tablespoon apple cider
    vinegar
2 teaspoons lemon juice
½ cup diced celery
½ cup chopped parsley
    Salt to taste
    Chopped fresh sage or
    crumbled dry sage to
    taste

1. Preheat the oven to 325 degrees.
2. Combine all the ingredients in a large
bowl. Mix well. Turn into an oiled 2-quart
casserole or baking dish and bake for 40
minutes.
Yield: Six servings.

CHINESE PANCAKES

8 eggs, lightly beaten
1 cup mung bean sprouts
    (see page 201)
½ cup diced water
    chestnuts
½ cup sliced (¼-inch
    thick) snow peas
2 tablespoons soy sauce
3 tablespoons vegetable
    oil

1. To the eggs in a medium-sized bowl
add the sprouts, water chestnuts, snow
peas, and soy sauce. Heat a small 5- to 6-
inch skillet. Brush with oil.
2. Pour ½ cup of the egg mixture into the
skillet, tilting the pan to cover the surface.
Cover and cook over low heat for about 5
minutes, or until eggs are set. Slide onto a
warm platter and keep warm while cooking the remaining pancakes.
3. Stack the pancakes and serve in wedges
or whole pancakes with plum sauce.
Yield: Four servings.

EGG FOO YONG

1. Heat the oil in a skillet and sauté the celery and onion until crisp-tender. Add the mushrooms, water chestnuts, and bean sprouts and cook for 2 minutes longer.

2. Stir in the eggs and salt and soy sauce to taste. Drop by tablespoons into a hot, well-oiled skillet and brown lightly on both sides. Serve with brown rice.

Yield: Four servings.

2 tablespoons vegetable oil
1 cup diced celery
½ cup chopped onion
½ cup sliced mushrooms
½ cup sliced water chestnuts
2 cups bean sprouts (see page 201)
5 eggs, lightly beaten
Salt
Soy sauce
4 cups cooked brown rice (see page 228)

TOFU LASAGNE

1. Spread a layer of tomato sauce in the bottom of a 13- by 9- by 2-inch baking dish. Make a layer of noodles.

2. Sauté the mushrooms in the oil in a medium-sized skillet. Add the spinach and cook until wilted. Drain. Stir in the eggs and pour over noodles.

3. Add half the tofu and half the mozzarella. Repeat the layers again, starting with the tomato sauce, until all the ingredients are used.

4. Sprinkle with the Parmesan cheese and bake in a 350-degree oven for 40 minutes. Let stand for 15 minutes before serving.

Yield: Six servings.

1 quart tomato sauce (see page 397)
12 ounces whole wheat lasagne noodles (made from recipe, page 314), cooked al dente, drained
½ pound mushrooms, sliced
3 tablespoons vegetable oil
1 pound fresh spinach, or 1 10-ounce bag, trimmed and shredded
2 eggs, lightly beaten
1 pound tofu, crumbled (see page 160)
12 ounces mozzarella cheese, shredded
¼ cup freshly grated Parmesan cheese

TOFU-STUFFED TOMATOES

4 large ripe tomatoes
1 pound firm tofu,
   crumbled (see page 160)
½ cup chopped celery
½ cup scallions
2 tablespoons Dijon
   mustard
½ cup homemade
   mayonnaise (see page
   195)
1 teaspoon lemon juice
1 tablespoon grated onion
¼ teaspoon freshly ground
   black pepper
2 teaspoons soy sauce
1 tablespoon finely
   chopped parsley

1. Cut a ¼-inch slice from the blossom end of the tomatoes. Scoop out the pulp leaving a ¼-inch shell. (Reserve the pulp for soup, stew, or gravy.) Turn the tomatoes upside down to drain.

2. Mix the remaining ingredients together in a bowl. Spoon into the tomato shells and serve on lettuce leaves or place in a shallow baking dish and add water to just cover the bottom of the dish. Sprinkle the tops with grated Parmesan cheese and bake in a 350-degree oven for 25 minutes, or until heated through.

Yield: Four servings.

TOFU BURGERS

1 pound tofu, drained
   and crumbled (see page
   160)
½ cup finely grated carrot
¼ cup chopped scallions
6 tablespoons wheat germ
1 tablespoon chopped
   parsley
1 4-ounce package alfalfa
   sprouts
1 tablespoon soy sauce
¼ cup whole wheat bread
   crumbs
   Homemade mayonnaise
   (see page 195)
   Vegetable oil

Put all ingredients (reserving 4 tablespoons wheat germ) in a bowl and mix well, using only just enough mayonnaise to make the mixture hold together for shaping. Shape into 4 to 6 burger patties, coat with the reserved wheat germ, and pan-fry in a small amount of oil until browned and hot.

Yield: Four servings.

TOFU CHILI

1. Heat oil in a heavy saucepan and sauté the garlic, green pepper, and onion until tender but not browned.

2. Sprinkle with chili powder, cumin, and pepper flakes. Cook, stirring, for 1 minute.

3. Add the oregano, tomatoes, salt, and tofu. Bring to a boil and simmer for 5 minutes. Add the beans. Let stand for several hours or refrigerate overnight, before reheating to serve.

Yield: Four to six servings.

- 2 tablespoons vegetable oil
- 1 clove garlic, finely chopped
- 2 small green peppers, seeded and chopped
- 1 large onion, finely chopped
- 4 teaspoons chili powder, or to taste
- 1 teaspoon ground cumin
- ¼ teaspoon hot red pepper flakes, optional
- 1 teaspoon dried oregano
- 1 28-ounce can crushed tomatoes in purée
- ½ teaspoon salt, optional
- ½ pound tofu (see page 160), drained and crumbled, mixed with a little gravy browning, if you wish
- 1 20-ounce can cannellini beans, drained
- 1 20-ounce can kidney beans, drained

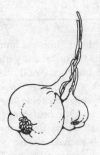

STIR-FRIED TOFU AND BROCCOLI

3 tablespoons vegetable
oil, approximately
1 bunch scallions,
chopped
1 clove garlic, finely
chopped
1 pound firm or pressed
tofu, cut into ½-inch
cubes (see page 160)
2 slices fresh gingerroot,
finely chopped
2 cups tiny broccoli
flowerets
¼ pound mushrooms,
sliced
1 cup homemade
vegetable broth (see
page 37)
2 tablespoons cornstarch
¼ cup soy sauce
½ cup water

1. Heat the oil in a wok or skillet and stir-fry the scallions and garlic for 1 minute. Remove with a slotted spoon to paper toweling and keep warm.
2. Add the tofu to the wok and stir-fry until lightly browned. Remove and add to the scallions. Add more oil if necessary and stir-fry the ginger and broccoli for 3 minutes. Add the mushrooms and stir-fy for 2 minutes longer. Stir in the broth and bring to a boil.
3. Return the reserved scallions, garlic, and tofu to the wok. Combine the cornstarch, soy sauce, and water in a small bowl. Mix well. Stir the mixture into the wok and cook, stirring, until the mixture thickens and vegetables are coated.
Yield: Four servings.

BROCCOLI AND RICE BAKE

2 tablespoons vegetable
oil
1 large onion, finely
chopped
1 clove garlic, finely
chopped
½ pound mushrooms,
sliced
3 cups hot cooked brown
rice (see page 228)
1½ cups grated sharp
Cheddar cheese

1. Heat the oil in a medium-sized skillet and sauté the onion and garlic until tender but not browned. Add the mushrooms and cook, stirring, for 5 minutes longer.
2. Meanwhile, combine the rice, ¾ cup cheese, 2 lightly beaten eggs, and ¼ teaspoon salt. Press firmly into two 9-inch pie plates to make shells.
3. Beat the remaining eggs lightly. Stir in the remaining salt, pepper, and yogurt. Cut the broccoli into small flowerets and the stalks into julienne strips. Cook the

stalks in boiling salted water for 5 minutes. Add the flowerets and cook for 4 minutes longer, or until crisp-tender. Add to skillet with the mushrooms.

4. Pour egg-yogurt mixture over the broccoli and mix well. Pour into the two rice-lined pie plates. Bake in a 375-degree oven for 20 minutes. Sprinkle with the remaining cheese and bake for 10 minutes longer, or until set. Cool for 5 minutes before cutting into wedges.
Yield: Six servings.

6 eggs
¾ teaspoon salt
¼ teaspoon freshly ground black pepper
1 cup plain yogurt (see page 324)
1 bunch broccoli

CURRIED BROCCOLI AND BEAN CURD

1. Heat the oil in a wok or heavy skillet and stir-fry the onions until tender but not browned. Add the mushrooms and broccoli and stir-fry for 3 minutes.

2. Sprinkle with the curry powder and ginger. Gradually stir in the broth and bring to a boil. Cover and cook for 2 to 3 minutes, or until the vegetables are crisp-tender.

3. Mix the soy sauce and cornstarch with the water. Add to the wok and cook, stirring, until the mixture thickens. Add the tofu and reheat. Add tomatoes and toss.
Yield: Six servings.

3 tablespoons vegetable oil
2 medium-sized onions, sliced and rings separated
¼ pound mushrooms, sliced
3 cups small broccoli flowerets
1 to 2 teaspoons curry powder
1 tablespoon chopped fresh gingerroot
1 cup homemade vegetable broth (see page 37)
1 tablespoon soy sauce
1 tablespoon cornstarch
¼ cup water
1 pound firm tofu, diced (see page 160)
12 cherry tomatoes, halved

NUTTY MUSHROOMS

5 tablespoons butter
1 clove garlic, finely chopped
1 medium-sized onion, finely chopped
1½ pounds mushrooms, sliced
3 tablespoons whole wheat flour
2 tablespoons tomato paste
1 8-ounce can tomato sauce
2 tablespoons soy sauce
1 cup plain yogurt (see page 324)
¼ teaspoon salt
¼ teaspoon freshly ground black pepper
1 cup toasted, unsalted walnuts, cashews, pecans, or peanuts

1. Melt the butter in a large skillet and sauté the garlic and onion until tender but not browned. Add the mushrooms and cook until wilted.
2. Add the flour, tomato paste, tomato sauce, and soy sauce to the skillet. Bring to a boil, stirring until the mixture thickens.
3. Stir in the yogurt, salt, pepper, and nuts and reheat but do not boil. Serve over brown rice, if you wish.
Yield: Four servings.

SPINACH QUICHE

1 9-inch unbaked whole wheat pastry shell (see page 344)
2 tablespoons butter
1 large onion, finely chopped
1 small green pepper, seeded and chopped
1 pound fresh spinach, or 1 10-ounce bag, well trimmed
¾ cup chopped pecans, walnuts, or peanuts

1. Bake the pastry shell in a preheated 400-degree oven for 10 minutes. Remove from the oven. Reduce the oven temperature to 350 degrees.
2. Meanwhile, melt the butter in a large skillet and sauté the onion until tender but not browned. Add the green pepper and spinach and cook until the spinach is wilted. Squeeze the spinach mixture and pour off excess liquid into a bowl.
3. Sprinkle nuts and cheese in the bottom of the partially baked pie shell. Spread the spinach mixture over the cheese.

4. Add the half-and-half and eggs to the bowl with the reserved spinach liquid. Add salt, pepper, and nutmeg and pour into the pie shell. Bake for 35 minutes, or until puffy and set. Let stand for 5 minutes before cutting.
Yield: Six servings.

1¼ cups grated Swiss or Gruyère cheese
1¼ cups half-and-half
4 eggs, lightly beaten
¾ teaspoon salt
¼ teaspoon freshly ground black pepper
⅛ teaspoon grated nutmeg

VEGETABLES WITH YOGURT-CHEESE SAUCE

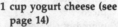

1. In a food processor or bowl, process or beat the yogurt cheese with the yolks, salt, and jalapeño peppers until smooth.
2. Slowly beat in the oil and then the yogurt. Stir in the scallions, chives, and parsley. Peel and slice the potatoes into a bowl. Add the green beans and pour the sauce over all. Mix the chopped egg whites with the parsley and use as a garnish around the edge of bowl.
Yield: Four to six servings.

1 cup yogurt cheese (see page 14)
4 hard-cooked eggs, yolks and whites separated
½ teaspoon salt
1 to 2 canned jalapeño peppers, seeded and chopped
¼ cup vegetable oil
1 cup plain yogurt (see page 324)
½ cup chopped scallions
1 tablespoon chopped chives, or 1 teaspoon freeze-dried chives
2 tablespoons finely chopped parsley
2 pounds new red-skinned potatoes, scrubbed and cooked in boiling salted water, drained
½ pound green beans, cut on the diagonal and cooked in boiling water until barely tender, drained

VEGETABLE CURRY WITH TOFU

1 tart apple, peeled,
  cored, and diced
2 celery stalks, diced
1 large onion, finely
  chopped
3 tablespoons vegetable
  oil
1 small green pepper,
  seeded and diced
1 large potato, peeled and
  diced
¼ pound mushrooms,
  sliced
2 tablespoons whole
  wheat flour
2 tablespoons curry
  powder
4 cups homemade
  vegetable broth (see
  page 37)
1 20-ounce can chick-
  peas, drained
½ pound firm tofu (see
  page 160), drained and
  cubed or crumbled
2 tablespoons chopped
  Italian parsley
4 cups hot cooked brown
  rice (see page 228)

1. Sauté the apple, celery, and onion in the oil in a heavy skillet until tender but not browned. Add the green pepper, potato, and mushrooms and sauté for 5 minutes longer, stirring occasionally.

2. Sprinkle over the flour and curry powder and cook, stirring, for 3 minutes. Stir in the broth, bring to a boil, add the chick-peas and tofu, cover, and simmer for 30 minutes. Stir in the parsley and serve over rice.

Yield: Four servings.

VEGETABLE LOAF

1 20-ounce can chick-
  peas, drained and
  ground in an electric
  blender, food processor
  or meat grinder

1. Mix the chick-peas and rice together in a large bowl. Trim and cook the fresh spinach in just the water clinging to the leaves. Drain well and squeeze dry. (Squeeze any extra liquid from the thawed

frozen spinach and add to rice mixture.)

2. Heat the oil in a medium-sized skillet and sauté the onion until tender but not browned. Add the carrot and garlic and cook, stirring, for about 3 minutes. Add to the rice.

3. Combine the eggs, soy sauce, walnuts, and pepper in a small bowl. Add to the rice and mix well. Stir in the cheese and parsley and turn into an oiled 9- by 5- by 3-inch pan. Bake in a 350-degree oven for 35 minutes, or almost set. Cool in the pan for 10 minutes before serving.

Yield: Six servings.

1 cup cooked brown rice (see page 228)

1 pound fresh spinach, or 1 10-ounce bag, or 1 10-ounce package frozen chopped spinach, thawed

3 tablespoons vegetable oil

1 medium-sized onion, finely chopped

1 large carrot, grated

1 clove garlic, finely chopped

3 eggs, lightly beaten

2 tablespoons soy sauce

½ cup finely chopped walnuts

½ teaspoon freshly ground black pepper

½ cup shredded Monterey Jack cheese

2 tablespoons finely chopped parsley

RATATOUILLE WITH EGGS

Divide the ratatouille among six lightly oiled individual au gratin dishes or casseroles. Make a depression in each and break an egg into the hole. Bake in a 350-degree oven for 20 minutes, or until the eggs are set and the ratatouille is hot.

Yield: Six servings.

1 recipe ratatouille (see page 147)

6 eggs

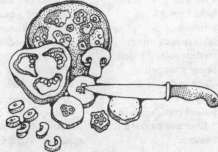

CRUSTLESS VEGETABLE QUICHE

3 tablespoons butter
1 large onion, finely
   chopped
1 celery stalk, finely
   chopped
1 carrot, finely chopped
1 white turnip, finely
   chopped
1 cup cut green beans
1 cup cauliflower
   flowerets
¼ cup homemade
   vegetable broth (see
   page 37)
6 eggs, lightly beaten
1 cup half-and-half
1 cup ricotta cheese
1 tablespoon whole wheat
   flour
¼ cup freshly grated
   Parmesan cheese
¾ cup teaspoon salt
¼ teaspoon freshly ground
   black pepper
2 tablespoons chopped
   parsley

1. Melt the butter in a medium-sized heavy skillet and sauté the onion until tender but not browned. Add the celery, carrot, and turnip and cook for 3 minutes longer.
2. Add the green beans, cauliflower, and broth. Bring to a boil, cover, and cook for 3 minutes, or until the vegetables are crisp-tender.
3. Combine the eggs, half-and-half, ricotta, flour, Parmesan, salt, pepper, and parsley. Add the vegetables to the egg mixture and pour into an oiled 1½-quart casserole or baking dish. Bake in a 350-degree oven for 40 minutes, or until set. Let stand for 5 minutes before cutting.
Yield: Four servings.

YOGURT QUICHE

1 partially baked 9-inch
   whole wheat pastry pie
   shell (see page 344),
   baked for 8 to 10
   minutes
2 tablespoons butter
1 medium-sized onion,
   finely chopped
1 clove garlic, finely
   chopped
1 pound fresh spinach, or
   1 10-ounce bag, well
   trimmed

1. Prepare pie shell. Preheat the oven to 400 degrees.
2. Melt the butter in a small skillet and sauté the onion and garlic until tender but not browned. Meanwhile, put the trimmed and washed spinach in a pan, cover, and simmer with just the water clinging to the leaves until wilted, about 5 minutes. Drain and squeeze dry.
3. Add the cooked onion to the spinach and spread in the bottom of the partially baked pie shell. Combine the eggs, yogurt, yogurt cheese, dill, parsley, salt,

and pepper in a bowl. Pour over the spinach.

4. Sprinkle with the Parmesan and bake for 10 minutes, reduce oven temperature to 350 degrees and bake for 40 minutes longer, or until almost set. Let stand for 5 to 10 minutes before cutting.

Yield: Four to six servings.

4 eggs, lightly beaten
1¼ cups plain yogurt (see page 324) drained through 2 thicknesses of cheesecloth for 30 minutes
1 cup yogurt cheese (see page 14)
1 tablespoon snipped fresh dill weed
1 tablespoon chopped parsley
¾ teaspoon salt
¼ teaspoon freshly ground black pepper
¼ cup freshly grated Parmesan cheese

MACARONI AND YOGURT CASSEROLE

1. Heat the oil in a large heavy skillet, and sauté the onion and garlic until tender but not browned.

2. Meanwhile, trim and shred the spinach and cook, in a covered saucepan, with just the water clinging to the leaves until wilted. Squeeze out the excess liquid and add the spinach to skillet.

3. Stir the cinnamon, nutmeg, and elbow macaroni into the skillet. Melt the butter in a small saucepan and stir in the flour. Cook, stirring, for 1 minute. Gradually blend in the milk and bring to a boil, stirring until thick. Add the salt, pepper, and yogurt.

4. Blend or beat the yogurt cheese until smooth and add to the sauce. Stir into the spinach-macaroni mixture. Reheat and serve with cheese passed separately or turn into a buttered casserole, sprinkle with the Parmesan, and bake in a 375-degree oven for 25 minutes.

Yield: Four servings.

¼ cup vegetable oil
1 medium-sized onion, finely chopped
1 clove garlic, finely chopped
1 pound fresh spinach, or 1 10-ounce package
¼ teaspoon ground cinnamon
⅛ teaspoon grated nutmeg
8 ounces whole wheat elbow macaroni, drained
2 tablespoons butter
2 tablespoons whole wheat flour
1½ cups milk
¾ teaspoon salt
¼ teaspoon freshly grated black pepper
1 cup plain yogurt (see page 324), at room temperature
1 cup yogurt cheese (see page 14)
½ cup freshly grated Parmesan cheese

LENTIL AND VEGETABLE STEW

1 cup lentils, picked over and washed

1 quart homemade vegetable broth (see page 37) or water

1 medium-sized onion, chopped

2 cloves garlic, finely chopped

4 carrots

1 leek, sliced

2 white turnips, diced

2 medium-sized potatoes, peeled and diced

1 celery stalk, chopped

1 teaspoon crushed dried rosemary

1 2-pound 3-ounce can Italian plum tomatoes

3 tablespoons tomato paste

1 teaspoon salt

½ teaspoon freshly ground black pepper

12 small white onions

2 tablespoons vegetable oil

1 tablespoon lemon juice or vinegar

3 tablespoons chopped parsley

1. Put the lentils, broth, onion, garlic, 2 diced carrots, leek, turnip, potato, celery, and rosemary in a large heavy kettle. Bring to a boil, cover, and simmer for 50 minutes, or until the lentils are tender.

2. Add the tomatoes with their juice, the tomato paste, salt, and pepper and simmer gently for 10 minutes, while breaking up the tomatoes.

3. Meanwhile, brown the onions in the oil. Add the remaining 2 carrots cut into 2-inch pieces and cook for 5 minutes longer. Add the onions and carrots to the lentil mixture and cook for 15 minutes longer. Yield: Four servings.

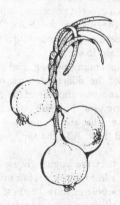

VEGETABLE-TOFU CASSEROLE

1. Put the eggplant in a colander, sprinkle generously with salt, and let stand for 30 minutes. Rinse well and pat dry with paper towels. Cut into cubes.

2. Heat ¼ cup of the oil in a large heavy skillet and sauté the eggplant until lightly browned. Drain on paper towels and transfer to an oiled 3-quart baking dish.

3. In the oil remaining in the skillet, sauté the zucchini until lightly browned and transfer to a bowl. Add the potatoes to the skillet and sauté until lightly browned and transfer to a second bowl.

4. Add the remaining tablespoon of oil to the skillet and sauté the onion and garlic until tender but not browned. Add the tomatoes, broth, ½ teaspoon salt, ¼ teaspoon pepper, tomato paste, parsley, and cinnamon. Bring to a boil and simmer for 10 minutes. Pour half the tomato sauce over the eggplant.

5. Add the green pepper to the zucchini and arrange over the tomato sauce. Sprinkle the tofu (or spread the ricotta) over the sauce. Add the potatoes in a layer.

6. Melt the butter in a small saucepan and blend in the flour. Cook, stirring, for 2 minutes. Gradually stir in the milk. Bring to a boil, stirring, and cook for 3 minutes. Add ¼ teaspoon salt, ⅛ teaspoon pepper, nutmeg, egg, and half the cheese.

7. Pour the white sauce over potato slices and sprinkle with the remaining cheese. Bake in a 350-degree oven for 1 hour. Let stand for 10 minutes before serving.

Yield: Six servings.

Note: This recipe lends itself to doubling and the use of other vegetables.

1 small eggplant, cut into ¼-inch-thick slices
Salt
¼ cup plus 1 tablespoon vegetable oil
3 small zucchini, cut into ½-inch-thick slices
3 medium-sized potatoes, pared and cut into ½-inch-thick slices
1 clove garlic, finely chopped
1 large onion, finely chopped
1 16-ounce can tomatoes
½ cup homemade vegetable broth (see page 37) or water
⅜ teaspoon freshly ground black pepper
2 tablespoons tomato paste
2 tablespoons chopped parsley
¼ teaspoon ground cinnamon
1 green pepper, seeded and cut into strips
1 cup diced tofu (about ½ pound, see page 160) or 1 cup ricotta cheese
3 tablespoons butter
¼ cup whole wheat flour
2 cups milk
¼ teaspoon salt
Pinch nutmeg
1 egg, lightly beaten
¼ cup freshly grated Parmesan cheese

ZUCCHINI AND FETA SOUFFLÉ

2 cups coarsely shredded
  zucchini
1 teaspoon salt
¼ cup butter
¼ cup chopped scallions
¼ cup whole wheat flour
1 cup milk
⅓ cup crumbled feta
  cheese
¼ teaspoon freshly ground
  black pepper
4 eggs, separated
1 egg white
2 tablespoons freshly
  grated Parmesan cheese

1. Preheat the oven to 375 degrees.
2. Put the zucchini in a colander and sprinkle with the salt and let stand for 30 minutes. Rinse well, drain, and put in a double thickness of cheesecloth to squeeze out as much liquid as possible. Reserve.
3. Melt the butter in a large saucepan and sauté the scallions briefly. Stir in the flour and cook, stirring, for 2 minutes. Gradually stir in the milk. Bring to a boil, stirring, and cook for 2 minutes.
4. Stir in the zucchini, feta, and pepper. Blend some of the hot mixture into the egg yolks and return to the pan. Beat the five egg whites until stiff but not dry and fold into the zucchini mixture until no streaks of white remain. Turn into an oiled 2-quart soufflé dish. Bake for 40 minutes, or until well puffed and golden.
Yield: Four servings.

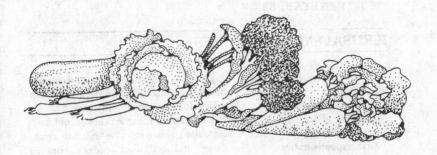

VEGETABLES

National food consumption surveys conducted in recent years have indicated that Americans are eating increasing amounts of fresh fruits and vegetables. This shows that nutrition education has been a strong, positive force. Fresh vegetables that are not overcooked—served alone or in combinations—can add variety, flavor, texture, color, and essential nutrients to the diet. Bought-in-season fresh vegetables are usually cheaper than their frozen, boil-in-the-bag, and canned counterparts and infinitely preferable at all seasons. Undercooking, rather than overcooking, and utilization of all cooking liquids in soups, stews, beverages or gravies are probably the two most important rules to bear in mind for successful vegetable cookery. The recipes in this chapter rely on such natural supplements as seeds, nuts, and herbs to enhance flavor and food value too. Dried peas and beans, for which various recipes are included, are splendid sources of essential nutrients, especially protein. Combining a whole grain, such as brown rice, with beans or peas provides protein value beyond the protein value of either eaten alone.

JERUSALEM ARTICHOKES

1½ pounds Jerusalem
   artichokes
 1 tablespoon lemon juice
   Boiling water
   Salt
 3 tablespoons butter
⅛ teaspoon grated nutmeg

1. Peel the artichokes and place immediately in a bowl of cold water with lemon juice added to prevent browning.

2. Drain and put the artichokes and boiling salted water to cover in a saucepan. Cover and boil until tender, about 20 minutes.

3. Drain the artichokes and mash together with butter, salt to taste, and nutmeg.

Yield: Four servings.

Note: Cooked Jerusalem artichokes can also be served in a cheese sauce. Raw, chopped, peeled Jerusalem artichokes can be used in salads or as dippers when cut into sticks, and are delicious pickled.

GREEN BEANS AND TOMATO

 ¼ cup vegetable oil
 2 large onions, thinly
   sliced
1½ pounds green beans, cut
   into 2-inch lengths
 1 sweet red pepper,
   seeded and cut into
   strips
 1 teaspoon salt
 1 teaspoon dried oregano
 ½ teaspoon dried thyme
 ¼ teaspoon freshly ground
   black pepper
 1 clove garlic, crushed
 ½ cup soft whole wheat
   bread crumbs
 2 tablespoons chopped
   parsley
 3 tomatoes, sliced
 1 2-ounce can anchovy
   fillets, chopped

1. Heat 3 tablespoons of the oil in a large heavy skillet and sauté the onions until tender but not browned. Add the beans, red pepper, salt, oregano, thyme, and pepper and stir-fry until the beans are crisp-tender. Turn into an ovenproof baking dish.

2. Add remaining tablespoon of oil to the skillet, and cook the garlic until brown. Discard the garlic. Add the crumbs and parsley to the skillet and toss.

3. Arrange the tomato slices over beans, sprinkle with the anchovies, and then the crumbs. Broil under a preheated broiler until the crumbs are brown.

Yield: Eight servings.

GREEN BEANS WITH SUNFLOWER SEED KERNELS

1. Mix the butter with marjoram, basil, chervil, parsley, chives, savory, and thyme.
2. Wash beans and remove the ends. Put the onion and garlic in boiling salted water (the water should only just cover the bottom of the pan) in a large skillet. Add the beans, cover, and cook until crisp-tender.
3. Pour off the excess liquid. Add the herb butter and sunflower seed kernels and swirl around to melt the butter. Add salt and pepper to taste and toss over medium heat for 1 minute.
Yield: Four to six servings.

¼ cup butter, softened
½ teaspoon dried marjoram
½ teaspoon dried basil
½ teaspoon dried chervil
1 teaspoon chopped parsley
1 teaspoon chopped chives
⅛ teaspoon dried savory
⅛ teaspoon dried thyme
1 pound green beans
1 small onion, chopped
1 clove garlic, finely chopped
Boiling salted water
¼ cup sunflower seed kernels
Salt and freshly ground black pepper

SPANISH GREEN BEANS

1. Preheat the oven to 275 degrees.
2. Melt the butter and stir in the flour. Gradually blend in the tomato juice. Bring to a boil, stirring, and cook until thickened.
3. Combine the beans, cheese, onion, green pepper, and salt to taste and mix well. Pour into an oiled baking dish. Pour the tomato mixture over all.
4. Sprinkle with crumbs and bake for 25 minutes.
Yield: Eight servings.

2 tablespoons butter
1 tablespoon whole wheat flour
1½ cups tomato juice (see page 33)
1 quart whole cooked green beans, drained
1 cup grated Swiss or Cheddar cheese
1 onion, finely chopped
1 green pepper, seeded and finely chopped
Salt
1 cup buttered whole wheat bread crumbs

ASPARAGUS CASSEROLE

1 tablespoon butter
1 tablespoon unbleached
white flour
1 cup milk
4 hard-cooked eggs,
sliced
1½ cups cooked asparagus,
cut on the diagonal into
1-inch pieces
Salt and freshly ground
black pepper to taste,
optional
½ cup buttered whole
wheat bread crumbs

1. Preheat the oven to 350 degrees.
2. Melt the butter, blend in the flour, and gradually stir in the milk. Bring to a boil, stirring until mixture thickens.
3. Fold in the eggs, asparagus, salt, and pepper. Pour into a 1-quart buttered baking dish, sprinkle with the crumbs and bake for 15 minutes.
Yield: Four side servings or two main-dish servings.

PURÉE OF BROCCOLI

1 bunch broccoli (about 2
pounds), stems peeled
and julienned, and
flowerets made
uniformly small
¼ cup heavy cream
3 tablespoons butter
3 tablespoons whole
wheat flour
1 cup plain yogurt (see
page 324)
½ teaspoon salt
¼ teaspoon freshly ground
black pepper
⅛ teaspoon grated nutmeg

1. Cook the stalks in boiling salted water until they are almost tender. Add the flowerets and cook until they are tender.
2. Purée the broccoli in batches in the container of an electric blender or in a food processor, using as much of the cream as needed. Transfer the purée to saucepan.
3. Melt the butter in a small skillet and sprinkle in the flour. Cook, stirring, until the mixture is nut-colored. Do not allow to burn. Stir into the broccoli purée.
4. Stir in the yogurt, salt, pepper, and nutmeg. Reheat but do not boil.
Yield: Eight servings.
Note: You can substitute 2 pounds of green beans or peas for the broccoli.

CITRUS BEETS

1. Cook the beets in boiling salted water to cover until tender, about 40 minutes, depending on size. Drain and reserve ¼ cup of the cooking liquid. Slice the beets.
2. In a medium-sized saucepan combine the reserved cooking liquid, sugar, orange juice concentrate, lemon juice, orange rind, and cornstarch. Bring to a boil stirring until thickened and clear. Add the beets to the sauce.
3. Melt the butter in a small skillet and toast the nuts until golden.
4. Top the beets with slices of orange and sprinkle with the toasted nuts.
Yield: Eight servings.

2 bunches beets, tops removed to be used in salads
¼ cup light brown sugar
¼ cup frozen orange juice concentrate
2 tablespoons lemon juice
1 tablespoon grated orange rind
1 tablespoon cornstarch
2 tablespoons butter
½ cup chopped walnuts, pecans, or cashews
1 orange, thinly sliced

SWEET AND SOUR CABBAGE

Put all the ingredients in a kettle or saucepan, bring to a boil, and simmer gently for 10 minutes, or until wilted, stirring occasionally.
Yield: Six servings.

4 cups shredded red or green cabbage
3 onions, grated
Juice of 2 lemons
4 tart apples, cored and diced
¼ cup apple cider
3 tablespoons honey
3 tablespoons vegetable oil
1 tablespoon caraway seeds
½ cup raisins
⅛ teaspoon ground allspice

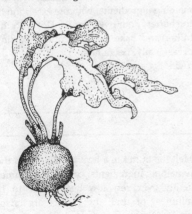

TOASTED CARROTS

8 large carrots, scrubbed
and quartered
lengthwise
¼ cup boiling water,
approximately
⅛ teaspoon salt
1 tablespoon brown sugar
1 tablespoon butter
1 cup wheat germ

1. Put the carrots in a saucepan and add the water. Cover tightly and simmer gently until tender, about 15 minutes. Add more water if necessary to prevent scorching.
2. Preheat the oven to 350 degrees.
3. Sprinkle the carrots with the salt and sugar and shake the pan to coat carrots.
4. Roll the carrot sticks in the wheat germ. Put on a buttered baking sheet and bake for 15 minutes, or until toasted.
Yield: Eight servings.

CARROT CASSEROLE

6 to 8 large carrots,
scrubbed and cut into
¼-inch-thick slices
¼ cup boiling salted water
2 tablespoons lemon
juice, or to taste
½ teaspoon grated lemon
rind
½ cup honey
½ teaspoon ground
cinnamon
⅛ teaspoon ground cloves
¼ cup raisins
2 tablespoons butter

1. Put the carrots and water in a saucepan. Cover tightly and simmer gently until almost tender, about 10 minutes.
2. Preheat the oven to 300 degrees.
3. Drain the carrots, reserving the cooking liquid. Arrange the carrots in a buttered baking dish.
4. Combine the reserved liquid with remaining ingredients, with the exception of the butter. Pour over carrots. Dot with the butter and bake for 30 minutes, basting occasionally. Serve hot.
Yield: Six servings.

BASIL CARROTS

2 tablespoons butter
6 medium-sized carrots,
thinly sliced diagonally
¼ teaspoon salt
1 tablespoon chopped
fresh basil, or ½
teaspoon dried basil

Melt the butter in a heavy skillet. Add the remaining ingredients, cover, and simmer gently over very low heat for 10 to 12 minutes, or until the carrots are crisp-tender. No water is needed.
Yield: Six servings.

FRUITED CARROTS

1. Melt the butter in a skillet. Stir in the orange juice and sugar. Cook for 2 minutes, stirring constantly, over low heat.
2. Add the carrots. Arrange the orange slices over the carrots. Sprinkle with the cinnamon and nutmeg. Cook, stirring, over fairly high heat until the juice has almost evaporated. The carrots will be crisp-tender.
Yield: Six servings.

3 tablespoons butter
1 cup fresh orange juice (2 oranges)
2 tablespoons brown sugar
8 carrots, scrubbed and scraped, left whole
2 oranges, peeled and sliced
⅛ teaspoon ground cinnamon
⅛ teaspoon grated nutmeg

CAULIFLOWER CURRY

1. Heat the oil in a skillet or casserole. Add the mustard seeds and when they pop add the garlic and onions and cook until wilted.
2. Add the remaining ingredients, with the exception of the cauliflower, and heat to just below the boiling point. Add the cauliflower and cook over very low heat for 10 minutes. Do not allow to boil.
Yield: Six servings.

2 tablespoons vegetable oil
¼ teaspoon mustard seeds
1 clove garlic, finely chopped
2 onions, finely chopped
1 tomato, peeled and diced
1 cup plain yogurt (see page 324)
¾ cup water
¾ teaspoon grated fresh gingerroot
½ teaspoon ground cumin
¼ teaspoon ground turmeric
½ teaspoon ground coriander
1 head cauliflower, broken into tiny flowerets and steamed for 8 minutes or until crisp-tender

MINTED CAULIFLOWER

1 medium-sized head
cauliflower, broken into
flowerets and steamed
until crisp-tender
½ cup chopped fresh mint
leaves
1 clove garlic, finely
chopped
½ cup olive or vegetable
oil
⅓ cup wine vinegar
Salt and freshly ground
black pepper

1. Put the hot, cooked cauliflower pieces on a platter or in a serving bowl. Sprinkle with the mint and garlic and toss with the oil.
2. Refrigerate for 1 hour. Toss with the vinegar and salt and pepper to taste. Drain and use as an appetizer or as a vegetable or salad with lamb.
Yield: Six servings.
Note: The cauliflower can be combined with other cooked vegetables, or hard-cooked egg slices can be added to make it a luncheon main course.

CAULIFLOWER, ONIONS, AND SESAME SEEDS

2 large Spanish onions,
finely sliced
¼ cup vegetable oil
1½ tablespoons brown
sugar
1 medium-sized head
cauliflower, broken into
flowerets
Salt
½ cup tomato juice (see
page 33)
2 tablespoons toasted
sesame seeds

1. Sauté the onions in the oil in a skillet until tender and lightly browned. Add the sugar and cook for 2 minutes longer.
2. Add the cauliflower, salt to taste, and tomato juice. Cover and cook over medium heat until the cauliflower is crisp-tender.
3. Sprinkle with seeds just before serving.
Yield: Six servings.

CELERY AND CABBAGE

1. Put the butter, water, celery, and cabbage in a saucepan. Heat to boiling, cover, and cook for 10 minutes, stirring at least three times.
2. Add the vinegar and salt and pepper to taste. Cover and cook until the cabbage is barely tender, about 5 minutes. Stir in the yogurt and caraway seeds. Reheat but do not boil.
Yield: Six servings.

3 tablespoons butter
3 tablespoons water
1½ cups diagonally sliced celery
1 small head cabbage, shredded
1 tablespoon cider vinegar
Salt and freshly ground black pepper, optional
1 cup plain yogurt (see page 324)
1 tablespoon caraway seeds

CHICK-PEAS

1. Pick over and wash the chick-peas and put in a bowl. Pour in enough water to cover the peas. Let stand overnight.
2. Next day, drain the peas and put them in a kettle with 5 cups of water. Bring to a boil, cover, and simmer for 2 hours, or until tender.
3. Add remaining ingredients and simmer until tender, about 30 minutes.
Yield: Six servings.

2 cups dried chick-peas
Cold water
4 vegetable broth cubes or 4 packages powder
¼ cup cider vinegar
¼ cup vegetable oil
2 cloves garlic, very finely minced
Salt and freshly ground black pepper to taste

CHICK-PEA CASSEROLE

2 tablespoons vegetable
oil
2 medium-sized onions,
finely chopped
4 cups cooked dried
chick-peas (see page 143)
or drained canned
chick-peas
2 large tomatoes, peeled
and chopped
1 6-ounce can tomato
paste
1 cup water
1 teaspoon ground
coriander
1 teaspoon ground cumin
seed
¼ teaspoon ground
turmeric
2 tablespoons chopped
parsley

1. Heat the oil in a saucepan and sauté the onions until wilted. Add the chick-peas, tomatoes, tomato paste, water, coriander, cumin, and turmeric and simmer for 30 minutes.
2. Sprinkle with parsley.
Yield: Six servings.

EGGPLANT GOULASH

1 large eggplant, peeled
and cut into ½-inch
cubes
¼ cup wheat germ
⅓ cup vegetable oil,
approximately
2 large onions, sliced
1 green pepper, seeded
and diced
1 tablespoon paprika
½ teaspoon salt
¼ teaspoon freshly ground
black pepper
1 28-ounce can peeled
Italian plum tomatoes
1 teaspoon dried oregano

1. Coat the eggplant pieces with wheat germ. Heat the oil in a large heavy skillet and brown the eggplant cubes. Transfer to a heavy Dutch oven or casserole.
2. Add the onions to the skillet and cook slowly until golden. Add the green pepper and cook for 5 minutes longer. Sprinkle with the paprika, salt, and pepper and cook for 1 minute. Add the tomatoes and their juice, and the oregano. Bring to a boil, cover, and simmer until the eggplant is tender. Serve over brown rice.
Yield: Four servings.

EGGPLANT AND SQUASH

1. Put the squash and eggplant in a saucepan. Cover with boiling salted water and simmer for 3 minutes. Drain the vegetables. (The liquid can be used in soups, stews, or gravies.)

2. Combine the squash and eggplant with the tomatoes.

3. Heat the oil in a skillet and sauté the onion until tender. Add the garlic, bay leaf, parsley, salt and pepper to taste, and the squash mixture. Simmer gently, uncovered, until the vegetables are crisp-tender.

4. Pour mixture into a shallow ovenproof serving dish, sprinkle with the cheese and brown under a preheated broiler.

Yield: Four servings.

1 medium-sized zucchini or summer squash, washed and thickly sliced
1 medium-sized eggplant, peeled and cubed
Boiling salted water
4 tomatoes, peeled and diced
3 tablespoons vegetable oil
1 small onion, finely chopped
1 clove garlic, finely chopped
1 bay leaf
1 tablespoon chopped parsley
Salt and freshly ground black pepper
¼ cup freshly grated Parmesan cheese

EGGPLANT CROQUETTES

1. Put the cubed eggplant in a saucepan and cover with boiling salted water. Cover and simmer for 15 minutes, or until eggplant is tender. (The liquid can be used in soups or stews.)

2. Drain the eggplant and chop very finely. Mix with the eggs, nutmeg, bread, cheese, salt, and parsley until well blended.

3. Shape the mixture into cutlets, cylinders, or patties. Dredge in flour. Heat the oil in a large heavy skillet and fry the croquettes until they are browned on all sides.

Yield: Six to eight servings.

2 large eggplants, peeled and cubed
Boiling salted water
2 eggs, lightly beaten
⅛ teaspoon grated nutmeg
2 slices whole wheat bread, soaked in water and squeezed dry
2 tablespoons grated Swiss or Parmesan cheese
Salt to taste
2 tablespoons chopped parsley
Unbleached white flour
1 cup soy or other vegetable oil

EGGPLANT CASSEROLE

3 tablespoons butter
1 onion, finely chopped
3 celery stalks, chopped
½ cup diced green pepper
¼ cup canned tomatoes, or
  1 small tomato, peeled,
  seeded, and diced
½ cup water
½ teaspoon dried basil
1 medium-sized or ½
  large eggplant, peeled
  and cubed
2 tablespoons chopped
  parsley
  Salt and freshly ground
  black pepper
½ teaspoon dried oregano
2 slices whole wheat
  bread
  Water
2 eggs, lightly beaten

1. Preheat the oven to 325 degrees.
2. Melt the butter in a heavy skillet and sauté the onion and celery until tender. Add the green pepper, tomatoes, water, basil, cubed eggplant, parsley, salt and pepper to taste, and oregano. Bring to a boil and simmer until tender.
3. Meanwhile, soak the bread in water. Squeeze out any excess water and mix the bread with the eggs and add to the eggplant mixture. Pour into a buttered casserole or baking dish and bake, covered, for 30 minutes. Uncover and bake for 15 minutes longer.
Yield: Four to six servings.

EGGPLANT HUSH PUPPIES

2 large eggplants, peeled
  and cubed
½ cup yellow cornmeal
1 cup whole wheat flour
1½ teaspoons baking
  powder
1½ teaspoons salt
2 tablespoons grated or
  finely chopped onion
  Oil for deep frying

1. Put the eggplant cubes into a colander and steam, covered, over boiling water until tender, about 25 minutes.
2. Meanwhile, combine the cornmeal, flour, baking powder, and salt in a bowl. Push the eggplant through the colander into the bowl in small amounts, mixing in enough eggplant to make a medium-stiff dough.
3. Stir in the onion. Set the mixture aside for 15 to 30 minutes.
4. Drop the mixture by teaspoons into deep oil heated to 365 degrees and fry until golden. Drain on paper towels.
Yield: Six servings.

BAKED EGGPLANT

1. Preheat the oven to 350 degrees.
2. In a well-oiled casserole or baking dish, place alternate layers of onions, eggplant, and tomatoes until all are used.
3. Combine the oil, salt, paprika, cayenne, and marjoram and pour over the vegetables. The oil should come about ¾ way up the vegetables.
4. Cover and bake for 40 minutes. Increase the oven temperature to 400 degrees. Combine the cheese and cream and pour over the top of the vegetables. Bake, uncovered, until the top is browned, about 10 minutes.
Yield: Six to eight servings.

2 large onions, sliced
1 medium-sized eggplant, sliced into ¼-inch-thick slices
6 tomatoes, sliced
1 cup olive or vegetable oil, approximately
Salt to taste
1 teaspoon sweet paprika
⅛ teaspoon cayenne pepper
¼ teaspoon dried marjoram
¼ cup grated Parmesan cheese
¼ cup heavy cream

RATATOUILLE

1. Sprinkle the eggplant slices with salt and set aside.
2. Heat the oil in a skillet and sauté the garlic and onion until tender but not browned. Toss the zucchini with 1 tablespoon of the flour and add to the skillet.
3. Rinse the eggplant slices, quarter each slice, pat dry, and dust with the remaining flour. Add to the skillet. Add the green pepper and tomatoes and cook, uncovered, until all the vegetables are tender and any excess liquid has evaporated. Serve warm or cold, garnished with olives.
Yield: Six servings.

1 medium-sized eggplant, peeled and sliced into ¼-inch-thick slices
Salt
⅓ cup olive or vegetable oil
3 cloves garlic, finely chopped
1 medium-sized onion, finely chopped
3 zucchini, washed and sliced
2 tablespoons flour
2 green peppers, seeded and diced
4 tomatoes, peeled and chopped
⅓ cup sliced pitted black olives

STUFFED CORNHUSKS

6 ears of corn with husks
1 egg, lightly beaten
3 tablespoons brown
  sugar or honey
1 teaspoon salt
3 ounces soft cream
  cheese
¼ cup melted butter
1 teaspoon baking
  powder
¼ cup yellow cornmeal
2 cups water

1. Remove the husks from the corn and set aside. Scrape the kernels from the cobs and reserve the cobs.
2. Put the kernels in the container of an electric blender or food processor and blend or process very briefly at low speed. Do not liquefy. Scrape from the blender into a bowl and add the egg, sugar, salt, cream cheese, butter, baking powder, and cornmeal. The mixture should be on the heavy side.
3. Divide the mixture into 12 and place each portion on a double husk, roll to enclose, and then wrap in aluminum foil.
4. Place a layer of corncobs in the bottom of a large pot and add the water. Place the packages on top of cobs, cover, and steam for 45 minutes, or until done.
Yield: Six servings.

SPRING GREENS PURÉE

1 pound young lamb's
  quarters, violet leaves,
  mustard greens,
  dandelion greens, or
  other wild or cultivated
  spring greens,
  combined or used
  separately
1 tablespoon butter
1 tablespoon vegetable oil
1 clove garlic, crushed
  Water if necessary
  Salt to taste
  Freshly ground black
  pepper to taste, optional
1 tablespoon heavy cream
1 hard-cooked egg,
  chopped

1. Wash and drain the greens but do not dry thoroughly. Put in a large saucepan with the butter, oil, and garlic. Cook for 2 minutes, stirring constantly.
2. Remove the garlic and cook the greens for 5 to 7 minutes longer, or until tender. Do not overcook. Add a tablespoon or two of water, if necessary, to prevent scorching.
3. Transfer the greens to the container of an electric blender or food processor. Add salt, pepper, and cream and blend or process until smooth. Reheat.
4. Serve garnished with the egg.
Yield: Six servings.

BEET GREENS

1. Put the greens, with only the water clinging to the leaves, in a large kettle, add salt to taste, cover tightly, and cook until wilted.
2. Meanwhile, heat the oil and sauté the onion until golden. Sprinkle with the flour and stir to mix.
3. Add the onion-flour mixture to the cooked greens and heat, stirring, until the mixture thickens slightly.
Yield: About four servings.

2 quarts beet greens, well washed and shaken dry
Salt
2 tablespoons vegetable oil
1 small onion, finely chopped
1 tablespoon flour

SWEET AND SOUR DANDELION GREENS

1. Put the dandelion greens in a large kettle and cover with water. Bring to a boil, turn off the heat, and let stand for 10 minutes. Drain well.
2. Combine the egg, sugar, vinegar, butter, and ¼ cup water in a saucepan. Heat slowly, while stirring, until slightly thickened.
3. Remove from the heat, add the greens, and stir to coat evenly.
4. Serve garnished with chopped egg.
Yield: Six servings.

6 to 8 quarts tender young dandelion leaves, well washed (a dishpan full)
Cold water
1 egg, lightly beaten
¼ cup brown sugar
½ cup cider vinegar
2 tablespoons butter
2 hard-cooked eggs, chopped

COMFREY GREENS

1. Put the greens and water in a saucepan, bring to a boil, cover, and cook until tender, about 10 minutes.
2. Drain very well. Add the salt and butter and toss well.
Yield: Four servings.

2 quarts tender young comfrey leaves, washed well and coarsely shredded
⅓ cup boiling salted water
Salt to taste
2 tablespoons butter

RADISH AND SPINACH GREENS

Tops from about 18
radishes (2 bunches),
trimmed, washed, and
shredded
1 cup shredded spinach
leaves
1 tablespoon vegetable oil
½ cup plain yogurt (see
page 324)
Salt to taste

1. Combine the radish and spinach greens.
2. Heat the oil in a heavy skillet, add the greens, and cook quickly, tossing with a pancake turner, until wilted. Reduce the heat and simmer, covered, for 5 minutes. Arrange on a hot platter.
3. Add the yogurt to the skillet. Do not heat, but stir around in the hot pan until warm. Season with the salt and pour over the greens.
Yield: Three to four servings.

BROWN RICE AND SPINACH CASSEROLE

2 quarts washed spinach
leaves
2 tablespoons butter
2 tablespoons unbleached
white flour
2 cups milk
½ cup vinegar
½ cup freshly grated
Parmesan or Swiss
cheese
Salt to taste
¼ teaspoon grated nutmeg
6 cups cooked brown rice
(see page 228)
½ cup buttered whole
wheat bread crumbs

1. Preheat the oven to 325 degrees.
2. Put the spinach in a large kettle with just the water clinging to the leaves. Cover and cook until wilted. Drain well, squeeze out the excess water, and chop.
3. Melt the butter, stir in the flour, and gradually blend in the milk. Stir in the vinegar. The mixture will curdle but as it heats, and is stirred, it will smooth out. Heat, stirring, until the mixture thickens. Stir in the cheese, salt, and nutmeg.
4. Mix the spinach and rice into the sauce and pour into a buttered 2-quart casserole. Sprinkle the top with the bread crumbs and bake for 20 minutes.
Yield: Eight to ten servings.
Note: The dish may be prepared early in the day, stored in the refrigerator, and heated for 45 to 60 minutes before serving.

SWISS CHARD

1. Remove the stalks from the chard and cut into 1½-inch lengths. Heat 3 tablespoons oil in a heavy skillet and sauté the onion and 1 clove garlic until tender but not browned. Add the stalks and cook for 5 minutes, stirring often.

2. Add the water, lemon juice, and salt and pepper to taste. Cover and simmer for 10 minutes, or until tender.

3. Put the chard leaves in a large pot with boiling salted water and cook for 3 minutes. Drain. In a second skillet heat the remaining oil and sauté the remaining garlic clove. Add the greens and salt and pepper to taste to the skillet and cook for 5 minutes, or until the greens are tender. Serve the stalks and leaves sprinkled with sesame seeds and with lemon wedges.

Yield: Six servings.

1 bundle Swiss chard
(about 2 to 2½ pounds)
⅓ cup vegetable oil
1 small onion, finely
chopped
2 cloves garlic, finely
chopped
¼ cup water, or
homemade vegetable or
chicken broth (see
pages 37 and 38)
2 tablespoons lemon juice
Salt and freshly ground
black pepper
2 tablespoons toasted
sesame seeds
Lemon wedges

GREEN VEGETABLE SAUCE

1. Put the water and scallions in the container of an electric blender or food processor and blend or process until smooth. While blending or processing slowly, gradually add the lettuce, spinach, beet tops, avocado, parsley, mint, and basil.

2. Season mixture with kelp and lime juice to taste.

Yield: About five cups.

Note: The mixture can be eaten as a cold soup or heated and served as a soup or as a sauce over whole wheat noodles or brown rice.

2½ cups water
⅓ cup chopped scallions
1 cup shredded romaine
lettuce or escarole
1 cup shredded spinach
¼ cup shredded beet tops
½ pitted avocado, peeled
2 tablespoons chopped
parsley
2 teaspoons chopped
fresh mint leaves
2 teaspoons chopped
fresh basil, optional
Kelp
Lime juice

LEEKS

2 large leeks, washed
  well and sliced
½ cup boiling water
1 tablespoon raisins
  Salt
1 tablespoon flour
2 teaspoons butter,
  softened

1. Put the leeks, water, and raisins in a saucepan. Cover and simmer until tender, about 15 minutes.
2. Season with salt to taste. Mix the flour and butter together and gradually whisk into the leek mixture. Heat, stirring, until the mixture thickens.
Yield: Four servings.

LEEK AND VEGETABLE STEW

6 large leeks, washed
  well and sliced into ½-
  inch slices, including
  some of the green part
2 large potatoes, peeled
  and thinly sliced
4 carrots, scrubbed and
  thinly sliced
¼ head cabbage, shredded
1½ cups water
¼ teaspoon kelp
  Vegetable salt or salt to
  taste
3 tablespoons butter

1. In a large heavy casserole, layer the leeks, then the potatoes, then the carrots, and finally the cabbage. Pour the water over all.
2. Season with the kelp and salt. Dot with the butter. Cover tightly and cook very slowly until all vegetables are tender, about 40 minutes.
Yield: Eight servings.

GLAZED PARSNIPS

1 pound (6 medium-sized)
  parsnips
3 tablespoons butter
¼ cup brown sugar
¼ teaspoon salt
¼ cup cider vinegar
3 tablespoons frozen
  orange juice concentrate
¼ cup wheat germ

1. Pare the parsnips and cut into sticks of even thickness. Cook in boiling salted water until barely tender, about 10 minutes.
2. In a medium-sized skillet melt the butter and add the sugar, salt, vinegar, and orange juice concentrate. Bring to a boil. Add the parsnips and cook over high heat, spooning the liquid over the parsnips to glaze. Sprinkle with wheat germ.
Yield: Four servings.

CURRIED LENTILS

1. Heat the oil in a heavy 3- to 4-quart saucepan until hot. Add the onion and sauté until lightly browned.
2. Add the garlic, ginger, bay leaves, and cloves and cook for 1 minute. Add the tomatoes and continue cooking.
3. Mix the curry powder and turmeric with ¼ cup of the water. Add curry powder mixture to the pan and cook, stirring, for 3 minutes, adding a tablespoon of water if necessary to prevent sticking.
4. Add the lentils and salt and cook for 2 minutes. Add the remaining water, bring to a boil, cover, and simmer for 1 hour, or until lentils are tender and the liquid is absorbed. More water may be added during the cooking if necessary.
Yield: Eight servings.

¼ cup vegetable oil
1 onion, quartered and thinly sliced
1 clove garlic, chopped
2 tablespoons finely chopped fresh gingerroot
2 bay leaves, chopped
8 whole cloves
2 tomatoes, quartered
2 to 4 tablespoons Madras-style curry powder
1 teaspoon ground turmeric
6¼ cups water, approximately
1½ pounds dried lentils, preferably those with a reddish cast, cleaned and drained
2½ teaspoons salt

LENTILS

1. Pick over the lentils; wash and drain. Put in a kettle with the water, onion, carrot, celery, and garlic.
2. Bring to a boil, cover, and simmer until the lentils are tender, about 1 hour. Season with salt to taste.
Yield: Two quarts lentils.

2 cups (1 pound) dried lentils
1½ quarts water
1 small onion, sliced
1 carrot, quartered
2 celery stalks with leaves, quartered
1 clove garlic, crushed
Salt

SWEET AND SOUR LENTILS

2 cups homemade vegetable or chicken broth (see pages 37 and 38)
1 bay leaf, crushed
Salt to taste
1 cup picked-over and washed dried lentils, yellow or green split peas, or black-eyed peas
1 clove garlic, finely chopped
⅛ teaspoon ground cloves
⅛ teaspoon grated nutmeg
3 tablespoons vegetable oil
3 tablespoons apple cider
3 tablespoons cider vinegar
3 tablespoons brown sugar, molasses, or honey

1. Bring the broth to a boil in a kettle and add the bay leaf, salt, and lentils. Cover and simmer gently for 30 minutes.
2. Add the remaining ingredients. Stir to mix well and cook for 5 minutes, or until the lentils are tender.
Yield: Four servings.

PEAS AND ONIONS

4 cups shelled fresh peas
3 small white onions, thinly sliced
1 sprig parsley
2 stalks fresh basil
¼ cup butter
¼ teaspoon salt
6 small cauliflower flowerets
½ cup water
3 Boston lettuce leaves

1. Put the peas, onions, parsley, basil, butter, salt, cauliflower, and water in a saucepan. Cover with the lettuce leaves and a tight-fitting pan cover.
2. Bring to a boil and cook over medium heat until the peas are tender, about 12 minutes.
Yield: Six servings.

ITALIAN PEPPER CASSEROLE

1. Heat the oil in a heavy skillet and sauté the onion until tender.
2. Add the remaining ingredients, cover, and simmer over low heat until ingredients are very soft and a sauce has formed.
Yield: Four servings.

¼ cup vegetable oil
1 large onion, sliced
6 Italian sweet green peppers, seeded and quartered
3 medium-sized tomatoes, skinned and sliced
1 teaspoon salt

POKEWEED AU GRATIN

1. Cut off the lower, tough parts of the stalks, stripping off all but the uppermost leaves. Wash well and put in a saucepan with boiling water to half-cover the stalks. Cover and cook until tender, about 15 minutes. Drain well. Arrange stalks in a buttered shallow baking dish.
2. Melt the butter in a small saucepan and sauté the onion until tender. Stir in the flour and cook for 1 minute.
3. Gradually blend in the milk; bring to a boil, stirring. Add salt to taste and the mace and cook over hot water for 15 minutes, stirring often.
4. Preheat the oven to 400 degrees.
5. Remove sauce from the heat and stir in the cheese. Pour over the pokeweed. Cover loosely with aluminum foil and bake for 15 minutes. Sprinkle with bread crumbs before serving.
Yield: Four servings.

36 young pokeweed stalks
   Boiling water
1 tablespoon butter
2 teaspoons chopped onion
1 tablespoon flour
1½ cups milk, scalded
   Salt
⅛ teaspoon ground mace
1 cup grated Cheddar cheese
½ cup toasted whole wheat bread crumbs

PARSNIP PIE

CRUST

¾ cup rolled oats
¼ cup chestnut or soy flour
¼ cup whole wheat flour
Salt to taste
Water

FILLING

5 large parsnips, peeled, sliced and steamed until tender
1 tablespoon sesame butter or tahini (sesame paste)
Salt to taste

1. Preheat the oven to 350 degrees.
2. For the crust, mix together the oats, chestnut flour, whole wheat flour, and salt. Stir in enough water to make a moist but not sticky dough.
3. Pat the mixture into an oiled 9-inch pie plate to form a pie shell. Bake for 10 minutes.
4. Meanwhile, for the filling, mash the parsnips and stir in the sesame butter and salt.
5. Fill crust and bake for 30 minutes. Serve with poultry.
Yield: Six servings.

POTATOES WITH YOGURT

2 tablespoons vegetable oil
1 pound small red-skinned new potatoes, boiled until tender and peeled
¼ teaspoon ground cloves
½ teaspoon ground cinnamon
½ teaspoon ground cardamom
2 bay leaves, crumbled
¼ cup water
½ teaspoon grated fresh gingerroot
¾ cup plain yogurt (see page 324)
Salt

1. Heat the oil in a skillet and add the potatoes. Cook quickly until lightly browned. Remove the potatoes and drain them on paper towels; keep warm.
2. Add the cloves, cinnamon, cardamom, bay leaves, and water to skillet and bring to a boil. Stir in the ginger and yogurt.
3. Reheat but do not boil. Add potatoes and season with salt to taste.
Yield: Six servings.

DILLED POTATOES

1. Melt the butter in a large heavy saucepan and sauté the onion until tender but not browned. Add the potatoes, broth, salt, and pepper. Bring to a boil, cover, and simmer for 10 minutes, or until the potatoes are tender.
2. Stir in the vinegar and cook for 2 minutes. Remove from the heat, stir in the yogurt and dill.
Yield: Six servings.

2 tablespoons butter
1 medium-sized onion, finely chopped
2 pounds red-skinned small potatoes, scrubbed and thinly sliced
¾ cup homemade vegetable broth (see page 37)
1 teaspoon salt
½ teaspoon freshly ground black pepper
2 tablespoons vinegar
½ cup plain yogurt (see page 324), at room temperature
1 tablespoon snipped fresh dill weed

NEW POTATOES

1. Put the potatoes in the boiling water in a saucepan so that they are covered. Add the salt and garlic. Cover and simmer for 10 to 15 minutes, or until the potatoes are barely tender. Discard the garlic.
2. Drain the potatoes and toss with the butter, lemon juice, paprika, and dill. Serve hot or cold.
Yield: Six servings.

2 pounds tiny new potatoes, scrubbed or scraped to remove skins
Boiling water
1 teaspoon salt
1 clove garlic, halved and crushed
¼ cup butter, melted
2 tablespoons lemon juice
½ teaspoon paprika
1 tablespoon snipped fresh dill weed

BAKED YAMS

2 large yams, peeled and
cut into cubes
2 carrots, sliced
½ cup pitted prunes
1 cup water
1 apple, cored and cubed
Honey to taste

1. Put the yams, carrots, prunes, and water in a saucepan. Bring to a boil, cover, and simmer for 25 minutes, or until tender.

2. Add apple and honey and cook for 25 minutes longer.

3. Preheat the oven to 300 degrees.

4. Turn the mixture into an oven-proof serving dish and bake, uncovered, for 15 to 20 minutes.

Yield: Four servings.

SWEET POTATOES AND APPLES

6 medium-sized sweet
potatoes
Boiling salted water
2 tablespoons molasses
½ cup butter
4 medium-sized red
apples, cored and cut
into ½-inch-thick slices
¼ cup orange juice
1 tablespoon grated
orange rind
½ teaspoon salt

1. Scrub the sweet potatoes, cover with the boiling salted water, cover, and simmer for 30 minutes, or until the potatoes are tender.

2. Meanwhile, heat 1 tablespoon molasses with ¼ cup of the butter in a skillet. Add the apple slices and turn to coat with the mixture. Simmer very gently until barely tender, about 10 minutes, turning twice during the cooking.

3. Drain the potatoes, peel and mash or purée them. Add the remaining butter, remaining molasses, the orange juice, orange rind, and salt. Beat until light and fluffy.

4. Mound the mixture on top of the apple rings and serve immediately.

Yield: About ten servings.

COOKING DRIED SOYBEANS

1. Pick over the beans, wash well, and put in a bowl with cold water to cover. If beans are to be cooked in a pressure cooker, add the oil. The beans expand up to three times their bulk on soaking, so make sure that the bowl is large enough and the water level is 2 to 3 inches above the beans. Soak overnight in the refrigerator.

2 cups (1 pound) dried green or yellow soybeans
Cold water
¼ cup oil if beans are to be cooked in a pressure cooker
Salt to taste, optional

Method I

2. To cook the beans in a kettle, put in a heavy kettle with soaking liquid and extra water if necessary to almost cover. Add salt if desired, bring to a boil and simmer over low heat for 3 to 4 hours, or until tender.

Method II

3. Alternately, to cook the beans in the oven, preheat the oven to 325 degrees. Put the beans, soaking liquid, and enough extra water to barely cover beans in a heavy casserole. Cover tightly and bake for 2 hours, or until the beans are barely tender. Remove cover and bake for at least 30 minutes longer, or until tender.

Method III

4. To cook the beans in a pressure cooker, put the beans, oil, cooking liquid, and salt, if desired, in the cooker, adding enough water to cover the beans. Do not fill pressure cooker more than half full. Close the cover tightly. Place pressure regulator on vent pipe (set for 15 pounds, if there is a choice of pressures) and cook according to manufacturer's instructions for 30 minutes. If pressure regulator ceases to rock, the vent pipe may have become clogged; cool cooker rapidly. At the end of the 30 minutes cooking at 15 pounds pressure, allow pan to cool of its own accord. Do not remove pressure regulator until pressure is completely reduced.
Yield: Eight to ten cups cooked beans.

Note:
To make a pulp or purée of soybeans, force the cooked beans through a coarse sieve, food grinder, electric blender, or food processor. Other seasonings such as brewer's yeast, diced onion, chopped celery, and bay leaves may be added during the last hour of cooking in methods I and II.

TOFU, SOYBEAN CURD, OR CHEESE

1 pound soybeans
Non-stick vegetable
spray
3 teaspoons epsom salts
(pharmaceutical grade)
Cheesecloth
1 quart plastic container
with holes punched all
over

1. Rinse the beans and put in a large bowl with water to cover to a depth of 3 inches. Soak overnight at room temperature. Drain beans and rinse again.

2. Spray a large kettle with non-stick vegetable spray. Pour in 2 cups water and set over low heat, preferably using a Flametamer. In an electric blender whirl each cup of beans with 1½ cups water. Add to the kettle.

3. Partially cover the kettle and bring to a boil. Reduce heat and simmer for 20 minutes.

4. Line a colander with 4 thicknesses of cheesecloth. Set over a big bowl or kettle. Pour the bean mixture into the colander. Clean the kettle and spray again. Transfer the strained soy milk to the clean sprayed kettle. Run 12 more cups of water through bean solids in the colander and add the drained liquid to the soy milk.

5. Twist and press solids to extract as much liquid as possible. The solids are okara and can be used in baked goods.

6. Mix the epsom salts with 2 cups cold water. Reheat the soy milk to boiling. Off the heat stir in ¾ cup of the epsom salts mixture, stirring vigorously. Let stand for 5 minutes. If the mixture has not curdled add another ¼ cup epsom salts mixture. Let stand for 5 minutes and check again. The liquid or whey around the curdled part should be yellow and clear.

7. Line the holey plastic container with 4 thicknesses of cheesecloth, place in a large pan in the sink. Ladle the whey and then the curds into the container. Fold the cheesecloth over top curd and weight the top with cans. Press for 20 minutes, or until whey stops dripping. Remove soybean curd from container and store covered with water in the refrigerator.

Change the water every other day and it will keep for a week. The whey can be used in soups, stews, gravies, and baked goods.

Yield: About one and one-half pounds.

SOYBEAN PISTOU

1. In an electric blender, food processor or a mortar and pestle, mash together the garlic, basil, and tomato paste. While blending on low speed or beating with an electric mixer, add the oil drop by drop until the mixture begins to thicken. Then add the oil more quickly.
2. Beat in the cheese and the few tablespoons of soybean cooking liquid. Pour the mixture over the beans and serve warm or cold.

Yield: Four servings.

Note: Cut string beans, sliced zucchini, or sliced carrots (cooked until barely tender) may be mixed with the soybeans.

4 cloves garlic
1 tablespoon dried basil
4 tablespoons tomato paste
½ cup olive or vegetable oil
½ cup grated Parmesan cheese
2 cups cooked soybeans with a little cooking liquid (see page 159)

BAKED HONEYED TURNIP

1. Preheat the oven to 325 degrees.
2. Put the turnip in a buttered 2-quart casserole. Mix the broth with the honey and pour over.
3. Cover and bake for 1 hour, or until tender.

Yield: Four servings.

1 medium-sized yellow turnip, peeled and cubed
½ cup homemade vegetable or chicken broth (see pages 37 and 38)
2 tablespoons dark honey, or to taste

WILTED SPINACH

1 pound fresh spinach, or
  1 10-ounce bag,
  trimmed
1 head Boston lettuce
2 tablespoons butter
1 medium-sized onion,
  finely chopped
½ teaspoon salt
¼ teaspoon freshly ground
  black pepper
⅓ cup wine vinegar
1 tablespoon brown sugar
1 tablespoon chopped
  fresh mint
2 hard-cooked eggs,
  chopped

1. Wash and dry the spinach and lettuce and tear into bite-sized pieces.
2. Melt the butter in a large heavy skillet and sauté the onion until tender but not browned. Add the salt, pepper, vinegar, sugar, and mint and bring to a boil.
3. Add the spinach and lettuce and toss with dressing until just wilted. Turn into a serving dish and top with the egg.
Yield: Six servings.

SPINACH-NUT RING

2 tablespoons vegetable
  oil
1 small onion, finely
  chopped
½ cup diced celery
½ green pepper, seeded
  and diced
2 cups cooked well-
  drained spinach,
  chopped
1 cup finely chopped nuts
1 teaspoon lemon juice
2 eggs, lightly beaten
¼ teaspoon grated nutmeg
1 cup soft whole wheat
  bread crumbs
  Salt to taste
3 tablespoons wheat germ

1. Preheat the oven to 375 degrees.
2. Heat the oil and sauté the onion until tender. Add the celery and green pepper and cook for 2 minutes longer. Mix in the spinach.
3. Stir in the remaining ingredients, with the exception of the wheat germ.
4. Oil a 1-quart ring mold and sprinkle with the wheat germ to give it an even coating.
5. Pour in the spinach mixture. Set the mold in a pan of hot water and bake for 40 minutes, or until set.
Yield: Six servings.

SQUASH BLOSSOMS

1. Allow the blossoms to remain in the towel while preparing the batter so that the excess water drains from them.
2. Beat together the eggs, salt, flour, and baking powder. The batter should be a fairly thick coating consistency. Add the parsley, garlic, and cheese.
3. Add oil to depth of ½ inch in a heavy saucepan. Heat the oil to 360 degrees on a deep-fat thermometer. Dip the blossoms in the batter and fry, one at a time, in the oil until golden. Drain on paper towels.
Yield: Four to six servings.

24 squash blossoms, picked in the early morning, washed, drained and placed in a towel
3 eggs
½ teaspoon salt
½ cup unbleached white flour
½ teaspoon baking powder
1 tablespoon chopped parsley
½ clove garlic, finely chopped
1 tablespoon freshly grated Parmesan cheese
Vegetable oil

YELLOW SQUASH

1. Put the squash, onion, garlic, oil, salt, honey, celery, parsley, and oregano in a skillet. Bring to a boil, reduce the heat, cover, and cook slowly until the squash is barely tender, about 15 minutes.
2. Sprinkle the flour over all and cook, stirring, until the liquid in skillet thickens. Stir in the sunflower seed kernels.
Yield: Four servings.

3 large yellow summer squash, sliced
1 onion, finely grated
1 clove garlic, finely chopped
2 tablespoons vegetable oil
½ teaspoon salt
1 tablespoon honey
⅓ cup diced celery
2 tablespoons chopped parsley
½ teaspoon dried oregano
1 tablespoon whole wheat flour
¼ cup sunflower seed kernels

SQUASH PUFF

3 cups mashed, cooked acorn or butternut squash
2 tablespoons molasses
3 tablespoons whole wheat flour
1¼ teaspoons salt
¼ teaspoon grated nutmeg
¼ teaspoon ground ginger
3 eggs, separated
¼ cup finely chopped pecans or walnuts

1. Preheat the oven to 350 degrees.
2. In a large bowl, blend together the squash, molasses, flour, salt, nutmeg, ginger, and egg yolks. Beat the egg whites until stiff but not dry. Fold into the squash mixture.
3. Turn into an oiled 1½-quart baking dish. Sprinkle the nuts around outside edge and bake for 1 hour, or until golden and crusty.
Yield: Six servings.

SQUASH, POTATO, AND YOGURT PURÉE

6 medium-sized potatoes, scrubbed
1 medium-sized butternut squash, peeled, seeded, and cubed
2 tablespoons butter
¾ cup plain yogurt (see page 324), drained through 2 thicknesses of cheesecloth for 30 minutes
½ teaspoon salt
¼ teaspoon freshly ground black pepper
1 tablespoon chopped chives, or 1 teaspoon freeze-dried chives

1. Cook the potatoes in lightly salted boiling water to cover for 25 minutes, or until tender. Drain, peel, and put in a bowl.
2. Meanwhile, cook the squash in lightly salted boiling water to cover for 20 minutes, or until tender. Drain and add to bowl with the potatoes. Add the butter, drained yogurt, salt, pepper, and chives and mash with a potato masher. Beat well with a fork and serve at once or turn into a casserole and keep warm.
Yield: Four to six servings.

SPAGHETTI SQUASH

1. Halve the squash and scoop out the seeds and fibers. Put cut side down in a shallow baking dish and add ½-inch of water. Bake in a 350-degree oven until the squash is tender, about 40 minutes.
2. Scrape out the squash into a warm serving bowl. (It resembles threads of spaghetti.) Dot with the butter, sprinkle with the salt and pepper, and toss to mix.
Yield: Four servings.

1 medium-sized spaghetti squash
¼ cup butter
½ teaspoon salt
¼ teaspoon freshly ground black pepper

VEGETABLES AND RICE

1. Put the carrots, onion, celery, squash, and green pepper in a saucepan with the tomato and water. Cover tightly, bring to a boil, and simmer gently over low heat until carrots are tender, about 15 minutes. Stir in the almonds.
2. Add rice and stir to mix. Reheat over very low heat while stirring. Season with salt and pepper, if desired.
Yield: Eight servings.

2 carrots, finely diced
1 onion, sliced
2 celery stalks, diced
1 zucchini or yellow squash, washed and diced
½ green pepper, seeded and diced
1 tomato, peeled, seeded, and chopped
¼ cup boiling salted water
¼ cup halved raw unblanched almonds
4 cups cooked brown rice (see page 228), chilled several hours so that the grains separate
Salt and freshly ground black pepper to taste, optional

VEGETABLE-RICE MELANGE

¼ cup vegetable oil
2 medium-sized onions,
   chopped
4 cloves garlic, finely
   chopped
½ bunch broccoli
   flowerets, chopped
1 large carrot, chopped
½ pound mushrooms,
   sliced if large
8 cups cooked brown rice
   (see page 228)
½ cup mung bean sprouts
   (see page 201)
½ cup alfalfa sprouts (see
   page 201)
   Tamari (soy sauce) to
   taste

1. Heat the oil in a large skillet and sauté the onions, garlic, broccoli, and carrot until crisp-tender. Add the mushrooms and cook for 3 minutes longer.
2. Add rice, toss, and reheat. Sprinkle with the sprouts and tamari and heat for 5 minutes longer.
Yield: Eight to twelve servings.

FRIED GREEN TOMATOES

8 large firm green
   tomatoes
   Unbleached white flour
   or cornmeal
¼ cup butter
¼ cup brown sugar
   Salt and freshly ground
   black pepper
1 cup heavy cream

1. Cut off and discard a thin slice from top and bottom of each tomato. Cut each tomato into 3 thick slices. Dip each slice in flour or cornmeal.
2. Melt the butter in a heavy skillet. Add the tomato slices and sprinkle half the sugar over the slices. Fry until browned on the bottom. Turn slices, sprinkle with remaining sugar, and brown on the second side.
3. Turn the slices and reduce the heat. Season with salt and pepper to taste. Add the cream and heat until hot but do not allow to boil. The tomato slices should remain firm.
Yield: Six to eight servings.

BAKED TOMATOES

1. Preheat the oven to 375 degrees.
2. Combine the corn kernels, tomatoes, shallots, egg yolks, and salt and pepper.
3. Beat the egg whites until stiff but not dry and fold into the vegetable mixture. Pour into a buttered 1½-quart baking dish, casserole, or soufflé dish.
4. Sprinkle with the crumbs and bake until set, about 40 minutes.
Yield: Six servings.

3 cups corn kernels cut from the cob (about 8 ears)
3 tomatoes, peeled and diced
4 shallots, finely chopped
2 eggs, separated
Salt and freshly ground black pepper to taste, optional
3 tablespoons buttered whole wheat bread crumbs

BAKED ZUCCHINI

1. Preheat the oven to 350 degrees.
2. Combine the wheat germ, bread crumbs, and salt. Dip the zucchini slices into the beaten eggs and then into the seasoned crumbs. Arrange the slices on a buttered jelly roll pan.
3. Place a small dot of butter on each slice and sprinkle with cheese. Bake for 40 minutes, or until tender.
Yield: Six servings.

½ cup wheat germ
1 cup dry bread crumbs
Salt to taste
3 medium-sized zucchini, washed and cut slightly on the diagonal into ½-inch-thick slices
2 eggs, lightly beaten
¼ cup butter
3 tablespoons grated Parmesan or Cheddar cheese

SALADS

Salads depend more on the freshness and quality of the raw ingredients than on any fanciful recipes. Growing your own vegetables, fruits, and herbs is the ultimate, if not always practical, insurance of an adequate source of supply. City green markets and roadside stands are excellent sources, and supermarkets are improving their selection and the quality of produce offered. The recipes here offer unusual ingredient combinations and ways of preparation for salads, regardless of the source of the fresh fruits and vegetables. When the cook's imagination takes over to utilize available supplies, the choice of a suitable and flavorful dressing can make the difference between the delectable and the mundane. In this chapter, particular emphasis is placed on providing recipes for a variety of salad dressings made from natural ingredients that will enhance even the simplest duo of salad greens.

APPLE-LEMON SALAD

1. Using a very sharp knife, slice lemons very thin. Remove seeds and make a layer of lemon slices in a serving bowl.
2. Cut the apples twice the thickness of the lemon slices. Sprinkle a little brown sugar over the lemon layer, top with apple slices, sprinkle with sugar, and continue making layers until all the fruit is used. Do not use too much sugar.
3. Pour about ½ cup white wine over all and chill for 4 hours. If the wine is absorbed by the apples, add a little more during the chilling.
Yield: Twelve servings.
Note: This is good served as a relish with pork or ham.

4 lemons, washed
6 to 8 red-skinned apples, cored but unpeeled
Brown sugar
½ cup dry white wine or apple juice

APPLE-BANANA SALAD

1. Core the apples but do not peel them. Cut them into bite-sized pieces and put in a salad bowl. Slice bananas and add to apples.
2. Sprinkle with the nuts and toss with the mayonnaise. Serve in lettuce cups.
Yield: Twelve servings.

6 pounds sweet apples, some red and some yellow
3 to 4 bananas
1 cup toasted peanuts
Homemade mayonnaise (see page 195) or salad dressing, preferably homemade
12 Boston lettuce cups

CARROT SALAD

Combine all ingredients and chill well.
Yield: Two servings.

1 large carrot, finely grated
1 tablespoon finely chopped onion
¼ cup currants
Salt to taste
2 tablespoons lemon juice

GREEN BEAN SALAD

1 pound fresh young
green beans
Boiling salted water
5 tablespoons vegetable
oil
2 large Spanish onions,
finely chopped
4 hard-cooked eggs
2 celery stalks, chopped
½ green pepper, chopped
¼ cup chopped walnuts
2 tablespoons wine
vinegar
Salt and freshly ground
black pepper to taste,
optional

1. Cut the beans on the diagonal into 1-inch pieces and cook in the boiling salted water until barely tender. Do not overcook.

2. Heat 3 tablespoons of the oil in a skillet and sauté the onions until tender and lightly golden.

3. In a large wooden salad bowl, chop the beans and add the onions. Grate the eggs over the beans and onions. Add the celery, green pepper, and nuts.

4. Add the remaining oil, the vinegar, and salt and pepper and toss.

Yield: Six servings.

PICKLED BEET SALAD

4 bunches beets, leaves
removed for use in
green salads
Boiling water
1 quart apple cider
vinegar
1 cup honey
½ cup maple syrup or
honey
8 red onions, thinly sliced
1 teaspoon salt
3 teaspoons kelp,
optional
3 teaspoons chopped
fresh tarragon
1 quart safflower oil,
approximately
½ cup brewer's yeast,
optional

1. Wash the beets and put them in a large pot with boiling water to cover. Cook until tender, about 35 minutes. Skin the beets and slice or dice.

2. Meanwhile, heat remaining ingredients, with the exception of the oil and yeast, to the boil point. Cool. Gradually beat in enough oil to cover the beets. Add the yeast and pour over the beets. Refrigerate for several hours.

Yield: About twelve servings.

FRUITED CABBAGE SALAD

Combine all the ingredients in a bowl. Toss to mix and chill well. There will be enough juice from the pineapple and apples to serve the salad without further dressing or add a little mayonnaise.
Yield: Eight servings.

1 small head red cabbage, finely shredded
½ large pineapple, peeled, cored, and finely shredded
2 apples, cored and grated
1 celery root (celeriac), peeled and grated or finely shredded
1 cup coarsely chopped pecans
Homemade mayonnaise (see page 195), optional

COLESLAW WITH YOGURT

1. In a salad bowl combine the cabbage, carrot, peppers, onion, and zucchini.
2. In a small bowl mix together the drained yogurt, mayonnaise, and celery seeds. Pour the dressing over the vegetables and toss to mix. Chill.
Yield: Six servings.

½ head cabbage, shredded
2 carrots, shredded
1 small green pepper, seeded and diced
1 small red sweet pepper, seeded and diced
2 tablespoons chopped red onion
1 small zucchini, shredded
¾ cup yogurt (see page 324), drained in a bag of 2 thicknesses of cheesecloth for 30 minutes
½ cup homemade mayonnaise (see page 195)
½ teaspoon celery seeds

SLAW WITH VINEGAR DRESSING

2 cups shredded cabbage
1 apple, cored and grated
½ cup grated carrot
½ cup pecans, chopped
½ cup sunflower seed
  kernels
1 cup heavy cream
2 tablespoons honey
2 tablespoons apple cider
  vinegar
Salt to taste

1. Combine the cabbage, apple, carrot, pecans, and sunflower seed kernels in a salad bowl.
2. Combine the remaining ingredients and mix well. Pour over the cabbage and chill well.
Yield: Four servings.

COLESLAW

2 cups finely shredded
  cabbage
½ green pepper, diced
½ carrot, shredded
½ cucumber, peeled,
  seeded, and chopped
1 sweet onion, finely
  sliced
3 tablespoons brown
  sugar
2 tablespoons red wine
  vinegar
1 tablespoon cold water
1 tablespoon white
  vinegar
2 tablespoons vegetable
  oil
1 teaspoon salt
1 clove garlic, finely
  chopped

1. Combine the cabbage, pepper, carrot, cucumber, and onion in a ceramic or glass bowl.
2. Mix together the remaining ingredients and pour over the vegetables. Allow to marinate in the refrigerator for a few hours or overnight.
Yield: Six servings.

GRATED SALAD

1. In a large salad bowl, combine the cabbage, carrots, broccoli stalks, and sesame seeds.
2. Use the tomato, avocado, cucumber, green pepper, and celery to garnish the salad in an attractive pattern.
3. Toss with the dressing at the table.
Yield: Eight servings.

3 cups grated cabbage
2 cups grated carrots
½ cup finely chopped peeled broccoli stalks
⅓ cup sesame seeds, ground or left whole
1 tomato, diced
½ avocado, peeled, pitted, and cubed, then dipped in lemon juice to prevent darkening
½ cup chopped cucumber
¼ cup chopped green pepper
¼ cup chopped celery Salad dressing, preferably homemade

DANDELION SALAD

1. Rub a salad bowl with the garlic clove. Discard the garlic. Add the dandelion greens, parsley, scallions, onion, and watercress to the salad bowl.
2. Beat together the lemon juice and sesame paste. Add the tarragon, savory, and salt and pour over the greens mixture. Toss with a wooden spoon and fork.
Yield: Four servings.

½ clove garlic
1 quart young tender dandelion leaves, picked before flower blossoms, washed, dried, and torn up
2 tablespoons chopped parsley
1 tablespoon chopped scallions
2 tablespoons finely chopped onion
1 cup watercress sprigs
1 tablespoon lemon juice
2 tablespoons sesame paste (tahini)
⅛ teaspoon dried tarragon
⅛ teaspoon dried summer savory Salt to taste

SHREDDED CABBAGE SALAD

3 cups shredded green
  cabbage
½ cup chopped parsley
¼ cup chopped scallions,
  including green parts
¼ cup honey
1 teaspoon vegetable salt
¼ cup cider vinegar
2 tablespoons safflower
  oil or sesame oil
  Sliced radishes or black
  olives

1. Combine the cabbage, parsley, and scallions and chill well.
2. Combine the honey, salt, vinegar, and oil. Shake well and chill. Pour the dressing over the vegetables and toss lightly.
Yield: Six servings.

CHEF'S SALAD BOWL

1½ quarts washed, drained,
  and crisped
  Buttercrunch, Bibb, or
  Boston lettuce
1 cup chopped celery
1 cup sliced radishes
1 large Bermuda onion,
  chopped
2 tomatoes, cut into
  wedges
1 green pepper, cut into
  thin strips
½ cucumber, skin scored
  and thinly sliced
1 cup diced Cheddar
  cheese
1 cup julienne strips
  cooked turkey or
  chicken breast
2 hard-cooked eggs,
  sliced
  Salad dressing,
  preferably homemade

1. In a large salad bowl, combine the lettuce, celery, radishes, onion, tomatoes, green pepper, and cucumber. Toss to mix.
2. Arrange the cheese, turkey, and eggs attractively on top of the vegetables. Toss with the dressing, at the table, just before serving.
Yield: Four servings.

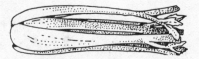

CHICK-PEA PLATTER

1. Combine the chick-peas, scallions, and parsley. Blend together the oil, lemon juice, salt, mustard, and pepper and pour over the vegetables. Toss lightly. Chill for at least 1 hour, tossing twice during chilling.

2. Serve on a bed of crisp salad greens. Yield: About ten servings.

Note: Add 1 13-ounce can tuna, flaked, to make a main dish salad for four.

2 20-ounce cans chick-peas, drained, or 1 cup dried chick-peas, soaked, cooked, and drained
⅓ cup chopped scallions
2 tablespoons chopped parsley
¼ cup vegetable oil
2 tablespoons lemon juice
½ teaspoon salt
⅛ teaspoon dry mustard
Freshly ground black pepper to taste
Salad greens

DILLED CUKE SALAD

Put the cucumbers in a salad bowl and add the remaining ingredients, with the exception of the lettuce. Mix well. Chill for 2 hours and serve in Boston lettuce cups. Yield: Six servings.

2 large cucumbers, peeled and chopped
1 small onion, finely chopped
¾ cup plain yogurt (see page 324)
1 teaspoon prepared mustard
1 tablespoon vinegar
½ teaspoon salt
⅛ teaspoon freshly ground black pepper
½ teaspoon celery seed
1 tablespoon snipped fresh dill weed
6 Boston lettuce cups

EGGPLANT SALAD

1 medium-sized eggplant
1 small onion, chopped
2 celery stalks with
  leaves, chopped
2 hard-cooked eggs,
  chopped
¼ cup vegetable oil
¼ cup lemon juice
  Kelp to taste
  Vegetable salt to taste
  Romaine lettuce
  Tomato wedges and
  cucumber slices
2 tablespoons chopped
  parsley

1. Preheat the oven to 400 degrees.
2. Put eggplant directly on the oven shelf and bake for 30 minutes, or until tender and soft to the touch.
3. When cool enough to handle, peel and chop the eggplant and put into a bowl. Add the onion, celery, and eggs. Mix well.
4. Add the oil, lemon juice, kelp, and vegetable salt. Mix well and chill.
5. Scoop eggplant mixture onto a bed of romaine lettuce and garnish with tomato wedges and cucumber slices. Sprinkle with the parsley.
Yield: Four servings.

FRUIT AND VEGETABLE SALAD

1 carrot, coarsely grated
1 apple, washed and
  grated whole
2 celery stalks, grated
6 radishes, grated
1 cup shredded red
  cabbage
¼ cup chopped parsley
1 cup finely chopped
  raisins, dried apricots,
  and dates, mixed
¼ cup unblanched toasted
  almonds, roughly
  chopped
1 cup vegetable oil
½ cup lemon juice
½ cup coconut water
  (drained from a fresh
  coconut)
1½ teaspoons salt
2 tablespoons honey
  Wheat germ

1. In a salad bowl, combine the carrot, apple, celery, radishes, cabbage, parsley, dried fruits, and almonds. Toss to mix.
2. Put the remaining ingredients, with the exception of the wheat germ, in a jar and shake to mix well. Pour over salad ingredients and toss. Sprinkle with the wheat germ.
Yield: Four servings.

TROPICAL FRUIT SALAD

1. Combine all the ingredients, with the exception of the ice cream, in a large salad bowl. Chill for at least 3 hours.
2. Add scoops of the ice cream just before serving.
Yield: Twelve to sixteen servings.
Note: Other fresh fruits can be added or substituted, and the salad can be served with cottage cheese sprinkled with wheat germ instead of the ice cream, if you prefer.

1 large cantaloupe, cubed or made into melon balls
8 bananas, sliced
½ pound cherries, halved and pitted
1 pint strawberries, halved
4 fresh peaches, pitted and sliced
1 fresh pineapple, peeled, cored, and cubed
2 cups seedless grapes
1 8-ounce can papaya juice or nectar
1 quart bottled or canned guava juice
1 quart homemade strawberry ice cream (see page 331)

MELON SALAD

1. Combine the melon, cheese, raisins, and sunflower seed kernels.
2. Arrange the watercress on 2 salad plates. Pile the melon mixture on top of the watercress. Sprinkle with juice or dressing.
Yield: Two servings.

1 large cantaloupe, cubed or made into melon balls
1 cup grated or cubed Swiss cheese
¼ cup raisins
3 tablespoons sunflower seed kernels
2 cups watercress sprigs Lemon juice or homemade Honey Yogurt Dressing (see page 198)

FULL MEAL SALAD

1 clove garlic, crushed
½ cup diced celery
½ cup sliced onion
¼ cup chopped scallion
2 apples, scrubbed and finely chopped including core
1½ cups chopped raw broccoli flowerets
4 radishes, sliced
2 hard-cooked eggs, chopped or sliced
½ cup diced green pepper
6 cold cooked new potatoes, skins left on, diced
½ cup tangerine or orange sections
1 cup mixed raw nuts
2 cups diced hard cheeses (2 or 3 kinds)
1 head romaine lettuce, core chopped and leaves shredded
½ cup diced raw yellow turnip
The hard core of one large cabbage, chopped
1 cup raisins
1½ cups whole wheat or rye bread toast cubes
2 tablespoons butter
1½ to 2 cups homemade mayonnaise (see page 195)

1. Rub a salad bowl with the clove of garlic. Discard the garlic.
2. Combine all the ingredients, with the exception of the toast cubes, butter, and mayonnaise, in the bowl and mix well.
3. Sauté the toast cubes in the butter.
4. Add enough mayonnaise to moisten the salad and toss well. Sprinkle with the sautéed toast cubes.
Yield: Six servings.

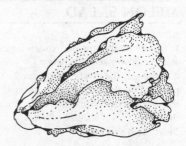

RAW BEET SALAD

1. Grate the beets finely into a salad bowl. Add the cabbage and carrots.
2. Beat together the lemon juice, honey, oil, and salt. Pour over the beet mixture, toss, and chill well.
Yield: Eight to ten servings.

1 bunch small young beets (tops removed for a tossed salad bowl), peeled
2 cups shredded red cabbage
1 cup shredded carrots
¼ cup lemon juice
¼ cup honey
¼ cup vegetable oil
Salt or vegetable salt to taste

MARINATED BROCCOLI SALAD

1. Put the broccoli in a large skillet and add boiling water to cover the bottom of the pan to a depth of ½ inch. Cover and simmer until the broccoli is crisp-tender, about 8 minutes. Drain.
2. Meanwhile, beat together the remaining ingredients.
3. Pour the dressing over the hot broccoli. Chill well before serving.
Yield: Six to eight servings.

1 bunch broccoli, broken into small flowerets (discard stems or use in grated salad—see page 173)
Boiling salted water
½ cup vegetable oil
½ cup lemon juice
Salt and freshly ground black pepper to taste
1 clove garlic, finely chopped

SAUERKRAUT SALAD

Combine all ingredients and chill well before serving.
Yield: Six servings.

2 cups fresh sauerkraut, drained
2 medium-sized apples, cored and finely diced
1 onion, halved and then cut into thin slices
3 tablespoons vegetable oil
1 tablespoon grated horseradish, or to taste
½ cup chopped nuts

MUSHROOM SALAD

⅓ cup vegetable oil
2 tablespoons vinegar
½ teaspoon salt
¼ teaspoon dried tarragon
¼ pound mushrooms, sliced
1 red onion, thinly sliced
1 to 1½ quarts salad greens, such as escarole, chicory, romaine lettuce, Boston lettuce, and leaf lettuce, crisped
1 tomato, cut into wedges

1. In a glass or ceramic bowl, combine the oil, vinegar, salt, and tarragon. Beat with a rotary beater until well blended.
2. Add the mushrooms and onion. Chill well.
3. Place the crisped salad greens in a salad bowl. Add mushroom–onion mixture and toss. Garnish with tomato wedges and serve immediately.
Yield: Six servings.

SWEET POTATO SALAD

2 cups grated raw sweet potato (for those who cannot tolerate raw sweet potato, steam or boil potatoes in their skins until barely tender, peel, cool, and grate)
2 cups finely chopped green peppers
1 cup finely ground peanuts, pecans, cashews, or almonds
2 tablespoons homemade mayonnaise (see page 195), approximately
Salad greens
½ cup diced peeled cucumber

1. Combine the sweet potato, green peppers, and nuts in a bowl. Stir in the mayonnaise to barely moisten, or to taste.
2. Spoon onto a bed of salad greens and garnish with the cucumber.
Yield: Eight servings.

POTATO SALAD WITH YOGURT DRESSING

1. Cook the potatoes in boiling water for about 20 minutes, or until barely tender. Peel and slice into a bowl.
2. Add the scallions and French dressing, toss to coat, and let marinate for 30 minutes, or longer.
3. Add the celery, dill, parsley, egg, salt, and pepper. Mix together the yogurt and the mayonnaise and stir into potato mixture. Chill well.
Yield: Six servings.

3 pounds small new, red-skinned potatoes, well scrubbed
1 bunch scallions, including green parts, finely chopped
½ cup French dressing (see page 190)
2 celery stalks, diced
2 tablespoons snipped fresh dill weed
2 tablespoons chopped parsley
2 hard-cooked eggs, peeled and chopped
½ teaspoon salt
¼ teaspoon freshly ground black pepper
1 cup plain yogurt (see page 324), drained through 2 thicknesses of cheesecloth for 30 minutes
½ cup homemade mayonnaise (see page 195)

FRESH ORANGE AND ONION SALAD

1. Peel and section the oranges and grapefruit. Cut each section into two or three pieces and put in a salad bowl. Add all the juices from the oranges and grapefruit and the onion.
2. Add about two turns of the pepper mill and salt to taste. Pour the oil over all, toss, and chill.
3. Sprinkle with the nuts and serve on salad greens, with warm whole wheat bread.
Yield: Three servings.

2 navel oranges
1 grapefruit, optional
1 red onion, thinly sliced and separated into rings
Freshly ground black pepper
Salt
⅓ to ½ cup olive oil
2 tablespoons chopped walnuts
Salad greens
Warm whole wheat bread (see page 294)

PEAS AND CARROT SALAD

1½ cups fresh peas
12 baby carrots, or 4 regular-sized carrots, scraped and sliced
Water
6 celery stalks with leaves, diced
1 bunch tiny radishes, sliced
1 green pepper, seeded and chopped
4 to 6 scallions, including some of the green, sliced
4 ears of corn, steamed 4 minutes, and kernels scraped off
4 cooked new potatoes, diced
2 cooked beets, diced
1 cup cooked green beans
Homemade French dressing (see page 190)
Salt
Buttercrunch or Boston lettuce leaves
2 hard-cooked eggs, sliced
3 tomatoes, cut into wedges

1. Put the peas and sliced carrots in a saucepan. Add enough water to barely cover the bottom of the saucepan, cover, and simmer for 8 minutes.

2. Drain the vegetables (save the water for soup) and put the vegetables in a bowl. Cool and chill. Add the celery, radishes, green pepper, scallions, corn, potatoes, beets, and green beans.

3. Toss with dressing, adding salt while tossing. Turn mixture into a salad bowl lined with lettuce leaves. Garnish with egg slices and tomato wedges.

Yield: Eight servings.

BROWN RICE SALAD

1. Put the hot rice in a large bowl and pour the French dressing over it. Toss to mix and let stand for 30 minutes.
2. Add the onion, celery, sweet pepper, and olives. In a small bowl mix together the mayonnaise, yogurt, and mustard. Add to the rice mixture and toss. Chill for several hours.
Yield: Four servings.
Note: Adding 2 cups shredded cooked chicken or turkey and 2 hard-cooked eggs, peeled and chopped, will turn the salad into a main dish.

4 cups hot cooked brown rice (see page 228)
⅓ cup French dressing (see page 190)
½ cup finely chopped red onion
2 celery stalks, finely chopped
1 medium-sized sweet red pepper, seeded and diced
½ cup chopped pitted ripe olives
¼ cup homemade mayonnaise (see page 195)
¾ cup plain yogurt (see page 324), drained through 2 thicknesses of cheesecloth for 30 minutes
1 tablespoon Dijon mustard

ZUCCHINI SALAD

1. Wash the zucchini and dice very fine. Put in a salad bowl with the scallions, dill, parsley, and oregano.
2. Combine the yogurt, lemon juice, and honey and pour over the zucchini. Toss to mix well. Refrigerate for 30 minutes or longer before serving.
Yield: Four to six servings.

3 small young zucchini (about 1 pound)
3 scallions, finely chopped
2 tablespoons snipped fresh dill weed
1 tablespoon chopped parsley
¼ teaspoon dried oregano
1 cup plain yogurt (see page 324)
1 tablespoon lemon juice
1 teaspoon honey

PEACHY SPROUT SALAD

8 unsulphured dried
peach halves
Water
Lettuce leaves (Boston,
romaine, or leaf)
1½ cups alfalfa sprouts (see
page 201)
1 cup blanched almonds,
flaked or finely grated
in a Moulinex grinder
Honey to taste
(optional)

1. Put the peaches in a jar. Pour enough water into the jar to cover the peaches. Cover the jar and refrigerate for 1 to 2 days. Drain the peaches.
2. Arrange the drained peaches on a bed of lettuce leaves. Top with the sprouts. Sprinkle with the nuts or make a nut cream dressing by beating the nuts with honey and a little water until mixture is thick and smooth. Spoon the nut cream over the sprouts.
Yield: Six to eight servings.

MAIN DISH SHRIMP SALAD

2 cups shredded romaine
lettuce
2 cups shredded spinach
leaves
1 tablespoon vegetable oil
1 hard-cooked egg,
chopped
1 dozen cooked, shelled,
and deveined shrimp
4 thin carrot sticks
4 ripe olives
1 tomato, cut into wedges
1 tablespoon chopped
fresh basil
1 tablespoon snipped
fresh dill weed
Lemon juice to taste
Salt and freshly ground
black pepper

1. Combine the romaine and spinach in a salad bowl. Add the oil and toss until all the leaves glisten.
2. Add egg, shrimp, carrot sticks, olives, tomato, basil, and dill. Toss. Add the lemon juice and season with salt and pepper to taste.
Yield: Two servings.

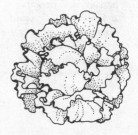

TOSSED SPROUT SALAD

1. Combine the lettuce, alfalfa seeds, mung beans, chick-peas, lentils, dandelion leaves, and mint in a salad bowl. Toss.
2. Sprinkle with the sesame seeds and toss with the oil, lemon juice, and salt.
Yield: Six servings.

1 quart buckwheat or curly leaf lettuce, torn apart
2 cups sprouted alfalfa seeds (see page 201)
2 tablespoons sprouted mung beans (see page 201)
2 tablespoons sprouted chick-peas (see page 201)
2 tablespoons sprouted lentils (see page 201)
¼ to ⅓ cup finely chopped dandelion or sorrel leaves
3 tablespoons chopped fresh mint leaves
3 tablespoons sesame seeds
Oil and lemon juice to taste
Salt to taste

BLUEBERRY-RICE SALAD

1. In a serving bowl, combine the rice, berries, coconut, nuts, and honey.
2. Put the dry milk powder, salt, and 1 tablespoon honey in the container of an electric blender or food processor. While blending or processing at high speed, add the oil slowly until mixture becomes thick.
3. Stir in the lemon juice. Fold the dressing into the rice mixture and sprinkle with wheat germ.
Yield: Four servings.

2 cups cooked cold brown rice (see page 228)
2 cups fresh blueberries
½ cup unsweetened shredded coconut
½ cup chopped pecans or almonds
¼ cup honey, or to taste
½ cup non-fat dry milk powder
⅛ teaspoon salt
⅔ cup vegetable oil
2 tablespoons lemon juice
Wheat germ

MARINATED SOYBEAN SALAD

3 cups hot cooked
drained soybeans (see
page 201)
¾ cup vegetable oil
⅓ cup vinegar
Salt and freshly ground
black pepper
1 clove garlic, finely
chopped
½ cup chopped scallions
½ cup chopped green
pepper
⅓ cup chopped celery
2 tablespoons chopped
parsley
2 tablespoons snipped
fresh dill weed

1. Put the hot beans in a bowl. Combine the oil, vinegar, salt and pepper to taste, and garlic and pour over the hot beans. Cover and marinate in the refrigerator for several hours.
2. Stir in remaining ingredients and chill again.
Yield: Four servings.

SPRINGTIME SALAD

2 cups leaf lettuce, torn
apart
2 cups dandelion greens,
torn apart
1 cup shredded comfrey
leaves
1 cup shredded plantain
leaves
1 bunch radishes, thinly
sliced

HONEY
DRESSING
1 teaspoon salt
¼ teaspoon dry mustard
¼ teaspoon freshly ground
black pepper
2 tablespoons honey
⅓ cup apple cider vinegar
1 cup vegetable oil

1. Combine all the salad greens and the radishes in a salad bowl and toss to mix.
2. Put all the dressing ingredients, with the exception of the oil, in the container of an electric blender or food processor and blend or process on low speed. Turn the speed to high and very gradually blend in the oil. Pour the dressing over the greens and toss. Serve at once.
Yield: Twelve servings.

TABOOLEY

1. In a large ceramic or glass crock, make a layer of the bulghur. Add the olive oil and lemon juice.
2. Layer the vegetables in the order listed, scallions first and cucumbers last. Sprinkle the vegetable salt over the top.
3. Cover the crock loosely and store in the refrigerator until ready to serve, at least 24 hours, and up to 2 weeks.
4. To serve, toss the salad so that all ingredients are well mixed. Check the seasonings. The salad may be served on a bed of lettuce, or Lebanese style, wrapped by the fingers in single leaves of lettuce and eaten out-of-hand.
Yield: Six to eight servings.

1 cup medium-fine bulghur (cracked wheat)
½ cup olive or vegetable oil
Juice of 4 lemons (about ¾ cup)
1 bunch scallions, including green part, finely chopped
2 large bunches parsley, chopped
4 large tomatoes, very finely chopped
1 small bunch celery, very finely chopped
2 small cucumbers, very finely chopped
Vegetable salt to taste
Romaine lettuce leaves

AVOCADO SAUCE

1. Mash the avocado in a bowl until smooth.
2. Stir in the remaining ingredients. Cover surface with clear plastic wrap and chill. This is good on cold fish or salads.
Yield: About two cups.

2 large avocados, halved, pitted, and peeled
½ teaspoon grated lime rind
3 tablespoons lime juice
2 tablespoons olive oil
2 scallions, finely chopped
2 tablespoons chopped parsley
Dash of liquid red pepper seasoning
¼ teaspoon salt

AVOCADO DRESSING

1 ripe avocado, peeled, pitted, and mashed or puréed
1 cup plain yogurt (see page 324)
1 tablespoon tamari (soy sauce)
⅛ teaspoon dried oregano

Combine all ingredients and mix well.
Yield: About two and one-half cups.
Note: This dressing is good served over tossed green salads, garnished with sprouts.

AVOCADO-TOFU DRESSING

3 cloves garlic
⅓ cup vegetable oil
½ bunch parsley, chopped
2 slices fresh gingerroot
1 ripe avocado, peeled and pitted
1 cup fresh tofu, soybean curd, or cheese (see page 160)
Tofu liquid or water
1 teaspoon tamari (soy sauce)
½ cup raw nut butter or sprouted sunflower seed kernels
1 peeled lemon, pulp and juice
1 teaspoon kelp, optional

Put the garlic, oil, parsley, and ginger in the container of an electric blender or food processor. Blend or process until smooth. Add the remaining ingredients and blend or process until thick and smooth, using enough tofu liquid to blend easily. The dressing should be the consistency of thin mayonnaise.
Yield: About three and one-third cups.

DILLED YOGURT DRESSING

Combine all ingredients and chill for several hours. Beat well before using.
Yield: About two cups.

1 cup plain yogurt (see page 324)
2 tablespoons lemon juice
¼ cup chopped scallions
2 tablespoons snipped fresh dill weed
½ teaspoon salt
¼ teaspoon white pepper
1 clove garlic, crushed

CAESAR SALAD DRESSING

1. Put the lemon juice, water, vinegar, salt, pepper, garlic, anchovy paste, honey, and cheese in the container of an electric blender or food processor. Blend or process until smooth.
2. While blending on medium speed, add the oil gradually until the mixture thickens. Chill well.
Yield: About one and one-half cups.

¼ cup lemon juice
¼ cup water
¼ cup cider vinegar
¼ to ½ teaspoon vegetable salt
¼ teaspoon freshly ground black pepper
1 clove garlic, finely chopped
1 tablespoon anchovy paste
1 teaspoon honey
3 tablespoons grated Romano cheese
¾ cup vegetable oil

CHEESE AND TOMATO DRESSING

1 cup goat's or cow's milk cottage cheese
¼ cup homemade mayonnaise (see page 195)
1 tomato, peeled and mashed
1 teaspoon lemon juice
2 or 3 tablespoons tamari (soy sauce)
½ teaspoon dried oregano
½ teaspoon dried thyme
1 teaspoon vegetable salt
1 clove garlic, very finely chopped

1. By hand, in an electric blender or in a food processor, blend or process the cottage cheese and mayonnaise together until smooth.
2. Mix the tomato, lemon juice, tamari, oregano, thyme, salt, and garlic together until well blended. Combine the two mixtures.
Yield: About two cups.

FRENCH DRESSING

¼ teaspoon dry mustard
⅛ teaspoon freshly ground black pepper
¾ teaspoon salt
¼ teaspoon paprika
¾ cup olive or peanut oil
¼ cup wine vinegar

Shake all ingredients together in a bottle.
Yield: About one and one-quarter cups.
Note: This dressing is particularly good on raw spinach salad.

FRUIT AND OIL DRESSING

1 tablespoon vegetable oil
3 tablespoons orange juice or pineapple juice
1½ tablespoons papaya juice

Shake ingredients together in a jar and use on salads.
Yield: About one-quarter cup.

FRUIT SALAD DRESSING

1. Beat the egg whites until stiff but not dry. Set aside.
2. Beat the egg yolks with the lemon juice and honey in the top of a double boiler. Cook, stirring, until the mixture thickens. Cool. Fold in the egg whites.
Yield: About two cups.

3 eggs, separated
¾ cup lemon juice
¾ cup honey

HOMEMADE TAHINI

Put the lime juice, oil, kelp, and water in the container of an electric blender or food processor and blend or process at medium speed, while adding the ground sesame seeds. Continue blending or processing until the mixture is like thick heavy cream.
Yield: About three-quarters cup.
Note: Use on sprout salad or any other salad.

1½ tablespoons lime juice
1 teaspoon vegetable oil
1 teaspoon kelp
6 tablespoons water
½ cup sesame seeds, finely ground in a Moulinex grinder

RUSSIAN DRESSING

1. Put the cottage cheese and vinegar in the container of an electric blender or food processor. Add ¼ cup tomato juice and blend or process until very smooth, adding more tomato juice if necessary.
2. Stir the egg into the dressing just before using.
Yield: About one cup.

1 cup cottage cheese
1 tablespoon vinegar or lemon juice
¼ cup tomato juice (see page 33), approximately
1 hard-cooked egg, chopped

HONEY-CREAM DRESSING FOR FRUITS

2 eggs
½ cup honey
½ cup lemon juice
¼ cup orange juice
⅛ teaspoon salt
½ cup heavy cream,
    whipped
2 teaspoons grated orange
    rind
Unsweetened flaked or
    shredded coconut

1. Beat the eggs in a small saucepan and stir in the honey, lemon juice, orange juice, and salt.
2. Cook, stirring, over low heat until the mixture coats the back of the spoon. Cool thoroughly.
3. Fold in the cream and orange rind. Serve over fresh fruit salad and sprinkle with coconut.
Yield: About two and one-half cups.

PEANUT DRESSING

2 tablespoons raw peanut
    butter
¼ cup water
2 tablespoons lemon juice

Mix the ingredients together with a fork and serve over sliced banana and apple salad.
Yield: About one-half cup.

BASIC TOFU DRESSING

Water
1 cup tofu, soybean curd,
    or cheese (see page 160)
1 clove garlic
2 tablespoons tamari (soy
    sauce)
Juice and pulp of half a
    lemon
¼ teaspoon kelp
1 teaspoon lecithin
¼ teaspoon dried oregano
¼ teaspoon dried
    marjoram

Adding only the minimum water that is necessary, put all ingredients in the container of an electric blender or food processor and blend or process until thick and creamy.
Yield: About one and one-half cups.
Note: Variations are possible by adding 2 large mushrooms, or 1 small tomato, or 2 tablespoons chopped scallion.

SOY SALAD DRESSING

Mix the tahini and tamari together with enough water to make the correct consistency for a salad dressing.
Yield: About one-third cup.

3 tablespoons tahini (sesame paste)
3 tablespoons tamari (soy sauce)
Water

SALAD DRESSING

Combine all ingredients in the container of an electric blender or food processor and blend or process until thick and smooth.
Yield: About two cups.

2 teaspoons vegetable salt or coarse kosher salt
1½ teaspoons coarsely ground black pepper
2 cloves garlic, cut into pieces
½ teaspoon dry mustard
1 teaspoon prepared mustard
1 teaspoon dried tarragon
1 teaspoon lemon juice
3 to 5 tablespoons wine vinegar
2 tablespoons olive oil
10 tablespoons soy oil
1 egg yolk

GREEN DRESSING

Put all the ingredients in the container of an electric blender or food processor and blend or process until smooth. Store in a tightly covered jar in the refrigerator.
Yield: About three-quarters cup.

¼ cup safflower oil
2 tablespoons cider vinegar
¼ cup chopped watercress
1 egg
⅛ teaspoon salt
1 sprig fresh dill
1 sprig fresh thyme, or ⅛ teaspoon dried thyme
½ teaspoon brown sugar

HERB DRESSING

¼ cup apple cider vinegar
2 tablespoons water
2 teaspoons vegetable
broth flavoring
1 teaspoon salad herbs, or
your own choice of
several herbs
1 teaspoon salt
⅔ cup vegetable oil

Put all ingredients, with the exception of the oil, in a jar and shake well. Add the oil and shake again. Chill for several hours before using.
Yield: About one cup.

SESAME DRESSING

½ cup ground sesame
seeds
1 cup water,
approximately
1 teaspoon kelp
Juice of ½ lemon
½ clove garlic

Put the seeds and 1 cup water in the container of an electric blender or food processor and blend or process until smooth. Add the remaining ingredients and blend until smooth, adding more water if necessary to give dressing the correct consistency.
Yield: About one cup.
Note: Add ½ cup chopped onions, ½ cup chopped celery, and ½ cup mixed alfalfa, mung bean, and lentil sprouts. Blend until smooth for a mock-tuna sandwich spread.

PERFECT DRESSING

1 ripe avocado, peeled,
pitted, and mashed
1 large grapefruit, peeled
and sectioned
1 large tomato, peeled
and diced

Put the ingredients in the container of an electric blender or food processor and blend or process until smooth.
Yield: About three cups.

THOUSAND ISLAND DRESSING

Combine all the ingredients until well mixed.
Yield: About two and one-half cups.

- 1 cup homemade mayonnaise (see page 195)
- 1 tablespoon chopped chives
- ½ green pepper, seeded and chopped
- 2 hard-cooked eggs, chopped
- 2 tablespoons chili sauce (see page 393)
- 1 tablespoon lemon juice
- 1½ teaspoons brown sugar
- ½ teaspoon celery salt
- ¼ teaspoon salt
- ½ teaspoon paprika
- ½ sweet red pepper, seeded and finely diced

HOMEMADE MAYONNAISE

1. Put the egg, mustard, salt, vinegar, and ½ cup of the oil in the container of an electric blender or food processor. Blend or process until smooth.
2. Continue blending or processing while adding the remaining oil very slowly in a steady stream into the center of the egg mixture. Use a small rubber spatula to scrape the mayonnaise into a jar. Store, covered, in the refrigerator.
Yield: About two cups.
Note: If the mayonnaise curdles, blend or process 1 egg in the container of a clean electric blender or food processor and gradually pour the curdled mayonnaise back in while blending or processing at high speed.

- 1 egg
- 1 teaspoon prepared mustard
- ½ teaspoon salt
- 3 tablespoons apple cider, vinegar, or lemon juice
- 1 cup sunflower or safflower oil

CASHEW MAYONNAISE

½ cup raw cashews
1 teaspoon kelp or dulse, optional
½ teaspoon paprika
1 clove garlic, crushed
1 cup water
1 cup vegetable oil
⅓ cup lemon juice
¼ teaspoon dried chervil
¼ teaspoon dried summer savory

1. Put the cashews, kelp, paprika, garlic, and water in the container of an electric blender or food processor. Blend or process until smooth.
2. While still blending, gradually add the oil until the mixture is thick. Mix in the lemon juice, chervil, and savory.
Yield: About two and one-half cups.
Note: This dressing is good with vegetable and fruit salads.

TOFU MAYONNAISE

3 tablespoons lemon juice
2 tablespoons wine vinegar
1 clove garlic, crushed
1 tablespoon Dijon mustard
¼ cup cashew mayonnaise (see page 196)
1 tablespoon tamari (soy sauce)
1½ cups drained and crumbled tofu (bean curd, see page 160)
2 tablespoons vegetable oil
2 tablespoons plain yogurt (see page 324)
½ teaspoon salt
¼ teaspoon freshly ground black pepper

Combine all the ingredients in the container of an electric blender or food processor and blend or process until smooth.
Yield: About two cups.

THICK MAYONNAISE

1. Put all the ingredients, with the exception of the oil and vinegar, in the container of an electric blender or food processor and blend or process until smooth.

2. While still blending or processing, add the oil, 1 tablespoon at a time, until the mixture thickens. When ½ cup of the oil has been used, add the vinegar. Add the remaining oil very slowly.

Yield: About two and one-half cups.

1 slice onion
2 egg yolks
½ teaspoon dry mustard
¼ teaspoon paprika
⅛ teaspoon dried thyme
⅛ teaspoon dried chervil
⅛ teaspoon dried summer savory
⅛ teaspoon dried marjoram
¼ teaspoon vegetable salt
1 teaspoon salt
1½ cups vegetable oil
3 tablespoons cider vinegar

TOMATO JUICE DRESSING

Put all the ingredients in a screw-top jar and shake well. Chill and shake again before using.

Yield: About two cups.

1 cup homemade tomato juice (see page 33)
¼ cup vegetable oil
3 tablespoons wine vinegar
2 tablespoons lemon juice
2 cloves garlic, crushed
1 teaspoon anchovy paste, optional
½ teaspoon dry mustard
1 teaspoon Italian herbs
2 tablespoons chopped parsley
½ teaspoon salt
¼ teaspoon freshly ground black pepper

TOFU SALAD DRESSING

½ cup vegetable oil
3 tablespoons lemon juice
½ pound tofu, drained
    and crumbled (see page
    160)
2 tablespoons snipped
    fresh dill weed
¼ cup chopped parsley
2 tablespoons finely
    chopped scallions
1 teaspoon Dijon mustard
½ teaspoon salt
¼ teaspoon freshly ground
    black pepper

Put all the ingredients in the container of an electric blender or food processor and blend or process until smooth. This dressing can also be used as a dip for raw vegetables.

Yield: About two cups.

HONEY YOGURT DRESSING

⅓ cup plain yogurt (see
    page 324)
1 tablespoon lemon juice
1 tablespoon honey
1 tablespoon sesame
    seeds, toasted
    Blue cheese to taste,
    optional

Mix all the ingredients together. Pour over the salad and toss.

Yield: About one-third cup.

SOY MAYONNAISE

1. Put the soy flour, water, salt, paprika, cayenne, and onion in the container of an electric blender or food processor. Blend or process until smooth.
2. With blender on high speed, add the oil, drop by drop to begin with, until the mixture starts to thicken. As it thickens, add the oil a little faster.
3. Add the lemon juice and chill well.
Yield: About two cups.

½ cup soy flour
1 cup water
½ teaspoon salt
½ teaspoon paprika
⅛ teaspoon cayenne
   pepper
1 teaspoon grated onion
1 cup vegetable oil
¼ cup lemon juice

EGGLESS MAYONNAISE

Put all the ingredients in the container of an electric blender or food processor and blend or process until smooth.
Yield: About three cups.

1 cup evaporated milk
1 teaspoon salt
¼ cup lemon juice
1 cup vegetable oil

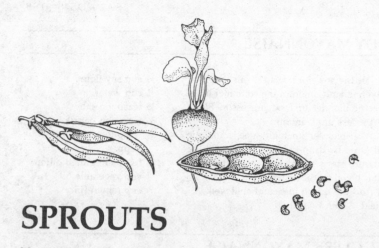

SPROUTS

Most people associate bean sprouts with Chinese restaurants, dark, damp cellars, and cans of bleached, less-than-crisp canned sprouts on supermarket shelves. Growing your own sprouts from a wide variety of seeds and grains can be an adventure in horticulture and gastronomy, even for the city apartment dweller. And now most supermarkets sell at least two kinds of fresh sprouts in their produce departments. Researchers working at such reputable institutions as Yale, the University of Pennsylvania, the University of Minnesota, and McGill University have demonstrated that the nutritional value of seeds increases dramatically during the first two to three days of sprouting. The vitamin C content of soybeans increases more than 500 percent by the third day. There are significant increases in many of the B vitamins and in vitamin E in many sprouted seeds, while the protein level remains generally high. Starch content is reduced as it is converted to sugar. However, no two varieties of seeds follow the same nutritional content pattern during sprouting.

Sprouts are tasty, economical, low in calories, and provide good amounts of vitamin C and protein:

One cup radish, mung, or alfalfa sprouts has 16 calories.

One cup soy, pea, or lentil sprouts has 65 calories.

Sprouts can be palatable snacks, or added to soups, salads, vegetable dishes, sandwich fillings, omelets, breads, and beverages. They are also good as garnishes, so they are well worth the small investment it takes to produce them. In choosing seeds to sprout, buy only those which have not been chemically treated and are sold specifically for sprouting or eating. These seeds are available in health food stores, some garden supply houses, and by mail order from growers and suppliers (see source list, page 422). Among the most popular seeds and grains for sprouting are alfalfa, mung bean, lentils, chick-peas, watercress, sunflower, wheat, and flax. They are relatively inexpensive when one considers that ¼ cup swells to 1½ cups after soaking and explodes into one quart of edible sprouts, costing about one cent a serving. Avoid tomato seeds and potato sprouts because they are poisonous. Sophisticated equipment sold in health food stores and by mail order is not necessary for successful sprouting. Below are three simple methods utilizing equipment found in most homes. One variety can be sprouted in one receptacle, or two, such as alfalfa and lentils, can be sprouted together.

Five important factors to check:

1. Temperature (75 to 85 degrees is ideal)
2. Amount of moisture
3. Circulation of air
4. Rinsing (often—at least three times a day)
5. Number of seeds in each container (fewer is better)

General Methods for Sprouting Seeds and Grains

For all methods, first pick over the seeds carefully, retaining only clean whole seeds for sprouting. Wash ¼ cup of the seeds well, put in a non-transparent bowl or jar and cover with lukewarm water. Let stand overnight. Drain, retaining the soaking liquid for a beverage or use in a soup or stew. Rinse the seeds thoroughly, pouring off all excess water.

Method I

Put 2 to 3 tablespoons of the soaked seeds in a non-transparent quart jar. Cover top of jar with cheesecloth or nylon mesh and secure tightly. Turn the jar on its side, so that the seeds form a thin layer, and put the jar in a dark place where it is warm and humid. At least three times every day rinse the sprouts by pouring lukewarm water into the jar, swirling it around, and pouring out the excess water. Seeds should be kept moist but not wet. Depending on the variety of seeds, sprouts will develop in three to five days. They should be removed before rootlets appear, but when the first young leaves appear the jar may be placed in direct sunlight for development of green chlorophyll. Rinse and drain the sprouts when they have reached the optimum length (see below) and store in covered containers in the refrigerator. The sprouts will keep for three to five days. Use the whole sprouted seed.

Method II

The soaked seeds, 2 to 3 tablespoons at a time, can be spread on several layers of dampened paper towels, flannel, or muslin fitted into a colander or over a perforated plastic tray. Enclose the colander or tray in an opaque plastic bag for darkness and humidity but do not forget to rinse the seeds thoroughly three times a day as in Method I. One end of the bag must be left open for ventilation, and the opaque bag can be replaced by a clear bag when the first leaves appear. Follow the general directions in Method I for harvesting and storing.

Method III

The seeds can be placed in a new, porous, clay flowerpot, which has been well soaked in water, with a cloth screen over the bottom hole and entirely covered with muslin. In general, sprouts are best harvested when they reach the length of the seed or grain. The harvesting schedule for some popular seed and grain sprouts is as follows:

Seeds	Best when
alfalfa sprouts	about 1 inch long
chick-peas	½ to ¾ inch long
flax	about ¾ inch long
lentil seeds	no longer than 1 inch
mung bean sprouts	1½ to 2½ inches long
sesame and sunflower	as soon as sprouts are visible
soybeans	½ inch long

Whenever possible, sprouted seeds should be used without cooking for full retention of all nutrients. If some of the larger sprouts seem to be tough, they may be blanched in steam or boiling water for a moment or two before being added to a dish. To use in breads and other baked goods, it is a good idea to grind the sprouts in a food grinder. In this form they can be added to a cooked cereal without their presence being obvious, though many people prefer the texture and appearance that sprouts give to pancakes, salads, and sandwiches. According to the publication *Natural Life Styles*, it is possible to travel with bean sprouts wrapped between thick damp towels, or in a jar, as long as the sprouts are kept moist. *Natural Life Styles* subscribers suggest taking seeds along on camping trips this way. Following are a number of recipes calling for various kinds of sprouts.

General Uses for Sprouts

- Add ½ to 1 cup sprouts, ground if you prefer, to any of the yeast breads in the bread chapter for a new taste and texture treat.
- Add 1 cup sprouts to your favorite bread or rice stuffing for poultry, fish, peppers, tomatoes, and other vegetables.

- Add sprouts to vegetables, poultry, fish, or egg salad.
- Include in all sandwiches instead of lettuce.
- Sprinkle on the top of tacos and include in the fillings for tortillas and crêpes.
- Add to pasta sauces.
- Add to baked beans.
- Add to cottage cheese for salads or to ricotta fillings.
- Toast in a slow oven for a snack.
- Stir into soups and stews just before serving.
- Mix with cheese and use as a topping for casseroles.
- Chop and add to pancake and waffle batters.
- Add to scrambled eggs and omelets.
- Add to raw vegetables and dip platters.
- Stir into fresh fruit compotes.

STIR-FRIED BEAN SPROUTS WITH RAISINS

2 tablespoons vegetable
  oil
1 clove garlic, crushed
½ pound (about 3½ cups)
  mung or soybean
  sprouts (see page 201)
1 tablespoon soy sauce
½ cup raisins
¼ cup chopped walnuts

1. In a wok or skillet, heat the oil gently with the garlic. Remove the garlic and discard. Add the sprouts and stir-fry briefly without browning, just long enough to warm the sprouts through.
2. Add the soy sauce, raisins, and nuts. Serve immediately.
Yield: Four servings.

PICKLED SPROUT SALAD

2 cups red wine vinegar
1 cup water
¼ cup olive or vegetable
  oil
¼ cup brown sugar
2 tablespoons mixed
  pickling spice
1 tablespoon salt
1 pound carrots, cut into
  julienne strips
½ pound button or
  medium-sized
  mushrooms, sliced
2 large green peppers,
  seeded and cut into
  strips
½ pound (about 3½ cups)
  soybean sprouts (see
  page 201)
½ pound (about 3½ cups)
  mung bean sprouts (see
  page 201)
4 ounces (2 cups) alfalfa
  sprouts (see page 201)

1. In an enamel or stainless steel pan combine the vinegar, water, oil, sugar, spices, and salt. Bring to a boil and simmer for 5 minutes. Cool.
2. Steam the carrot pieces for 2 minutes, cool in ice water, and drain.
3. Arrange layers of carrots, mushrooms, green pepper, and sprouts in a widemouth glass jar or bowl. Strain the cooled marinade over. Cover and refrigerate overnight. Serve on lettuce.
Yield: Twelve servings.
Note: Drain off the marinade and this is a great salad to take to a picnic.

YOGURT SPROUT SALAD

1. For the dressing, mix the yogurt, salt, mustard, orange rind, orange juice concentrate, honey, and wheat germ until smooth.

2. Put the lettuce in a salad bowl and arrange the orange slices, sprouts, cheese, avocado, and raisins in a pattern on top. Sprinkle with the seeds. Toss with the dressing at the table.

Yield: Eight to ten servings.

1 cup plain yogurt (see page 324)
1 teaspoon salt
1 teaspoon dry mustard
1 teaspoon grated orange rind
1 tablespoon undiluted frozen orange juice concentrate
2 tablespoons honey
2 tablespoons wheat germ
6 cups torn romaine, Bibb, or Boston lettuce
2 large navel oranges, peeled and cut into slices
1 pound (6 to 7 cups) mung or soybean sprouts (see page 201)
4 ounces (2 cups) alfalfa sprouts (see page 201)
½ pound Muenster, Monterey Jack, or mild Cheddar cheese, cut into tiny cubes
1 avocado, peeled, pitted, and cubed, tossed with 2 tablespoons lemon juice
½ cup golden raisins
¼ cup sunflower seeds, or 1 tablespoon sesame seeds

BEAN SPROUT LUNCH

1½ quarts shredded salad
   greens, including
   escarole, spinach,
   romaine lettuce, and
   Boston lettuce
½ bunch watercress
½ cup diced celery
½ cucumber, skin scored
   and thinly sliced
2 hard-cooked eggs,
   sliced
½ cup julienne strips
   Swiss or Cheddar
   cheese
1 cup julienne strips
   cooked chicken breast
1 cup alfalfa, flax, or
   sunflower sprouts (see
   page 201)
½ cup homemade
   mayonnaise (see page
   195)
¼ cup homemade French
   dressing (see page 190)

1. Put the salad greens in the bottom of a large shallow bowl. Sprinkle the watercress and celery over the greens.
2. Divide the surface area of the salad into fifths and arrange cucumber slices in one section, then the eggs, cheese, chicken, and sprouts in the other sections.
3. Combine the mayonnaise and dressing. Toss the salad with the mixture at the table just before serving.
Yield: Six servings.

BEAN SPROUT OMELET

4 eggs, lightly beaten
2 tablespoons water
   Salt and freshly ground
   black pepper to taste
1½ tablespoons butter
1 cup alfalfa, lentil, soy,
   or mung bean sprouts
   (see page 201)
1 tablespoon chopped
   parsley

1. Combine the eggs, water, salt, and pepper.
2. Melt the butter in a heavy omelet pan. Pour in the egg mixture and immediately stir with a fork until the mixture begins to set on the bottom.
3. Continue cooking, without stirring, until the bottom is golden. Sprinkle with sprouts and parsley. Fold over and tip onto a warm plate.
Yield: One serving.

CHICKEN CHOW MEIN

1. Heat the oil in a wok or skillet and stir-fry or sauté the onions until golden. Add the mushrooms and celery and cook briefly.
2. Stir in the broth and soy sauce and bring to a boil.
3. Mix the arrowroot with a little water until smooth and whisk into the onion mixture. Add the chicken and sprouts. Reheat, but do not boil. Serve over rice.
Yield: Four servings.

2 tablespoons vegetable oil
3 medium-sized onions, chopped
1 cup sliced mushrooms
3 cups chopped celery or Chinese cabbage
2 cups homemade chicken broth (see page 38)
2 teaspoons soy sauce, or to taste
2 teaspoons arrowroot
Water
2 cups slivered cooked chicken
1 cup mung bean sprouts (see page 201)
4 cups cooked brown rice (see page 228)

CUCUMBER AND OLIVE SALAD

1. Combine the cucumber, olives, and cheese.
2. Toss the watercress and sprouts together and arrange on four salad plates. Top with the cheese mixture and serve dressing separately or spooned over.
Yield: Four servings.

1 large cucumber, peeled and diced
12 stuffed olives
⅓ cup diced Swiss cheese
1 bunch watercress
1 cup alfalfa, flax, or lentil sprouts (see page 201)
Homemade French dressing (see page 190)

MUSHROOM AND SPROUT SALAD

2 cups alfalfa, lentil, or
   radish seed sprouts (see
   page 201)
2 cups sliced mushrooms
3 cups small or torn-up
   spinach leaves
¼ cup chopped scallions
   Homemade French
   dressing (see page 190)
1 to 2 tablespoons
   prepared mustard

1. Combine the sprouts, mushrooms, spinach, and scallions in a salad bowl.
2. Mix the dressing with the mustard and toss with spinach mixture just before serving.
Yield: Four servings.

LUCERNE SALAD

1 cucumber, skin scored
   and thinly sliced
4 tomatoes, thinly sliced
   Homemade French
   dressing (see page 190)
   Salad greens
1 cup alfalfa sprouts (see
   page 201)

1. Put the cucumber slices and tomato slices alternately in a shallow dish. Pour the dressing over and allow to marinate in the refrigerator for an hour or so.
2. Garnish the outside edges of the dish with salad greens and sprinkle the sprouts over the top of the cucumbers and tomato slices.
Yield: Six servings.

SWEET AND SOUR BEAN SPROUTS

1. Put the sprouts in a saucepan with the water, 1 tablespoon sugar, and ½ teaspoon salt. Stir and cook for 1 minute.
2. Drain well and cool.
3. Combine the remaining ingredients and pour over the sprouts. Marinate in the refrigerator overnight. The sprouts will keep in the refrigerator for a week or so.
Yield: Twelve servings.

1 pound (6 to 7 cups) mung bean sprouts (see page 201)
2 cups water
3 tablespoons brown sugar
¾ teaspoon salt
⅓ cup wine vinegar
¼ cup olive or vegetable oil
¼ teaspoon freshly ground black pepper, optional

BEAN SPROUT SALAD

1. Combine the celery, nuts, sprouts, and seeds. Spoon into lettuce cups.
2. Dress to taste with honey and lemon juice mixed together.
Yield: Two servings.

2 celery stalks, finely chopped
½ cup chopped walnuts
1½ cups mung bean or soybean sprouts (see page 201)
½ teaspoon caraway seeds
2 Boston lettuce cups
Honey and lemon juice to taste

SAUTÉED BEAN SPROUTS

3 tablespoons vegetable oil
1 scallion, finely chopped
1 quart mung bean, soybean, chick-pea, or sprouted wheat berries (see page 201)
1 slice fresh gingerroot, finely chopped
1 tablespoon soy sauce
⅓ cup sliced water chestnuts

1. Heat the oil in a wok or heavy skillet. Add scallion and cook, stirring, for 30 seconds. Add the sprouted wheat berries and cook, stirring, for 1 minute.
2. Add the ginger, soy sauce, and water chestnuts. Mix well. Cover and cook for 4 minutes. Serve hot.
Yield: Four to six servings.

SPROUT SLAW

2 cups grated carrots
2 cups sprouted alfalfa, lentil, millet, and fenugreek seeds mixed in any proportion (see page 201)
1 cup diced celery
½ cup chopped nuts
2 tablespoons chopped parsley
2 tablespoons grated onion
¼ cup raisins
1 cup homemade mayonnaise (see page 195), approximately
1 hard-cooked egg, cut into wedges

1. Combine the carrots, sprouts, celery, nuts, parsley, onion, and raisins in a salad bowl.
2. Add enough mayonnaise to moisten and toss to mix.
3. Garnish with the egg wedges.
Yield: Six servings.

SPROUTED WHEAT BALLS

1. Put the sprouted wheat berries, almonds, and onion through the fine blade of a meat grinder or process in a food processor. Turn into a bowl.
2. Add the crumbs, salt, 3 tablespoons oil, and enough milk to make a mixture that holds together.
3. Form into 1-inch balls. Heat enough oil to cover the bottom of a heavy skillet to a depth of ⅛ inch. Fry the balls in the oil until golden. Drain on paper towels.
Yield: Four servings.

2 cups sprouted wheat berries (see page 201)
1 cup unblanched almonds
1 large onion, peeled
2 cups whole wheat bread crumbs
1 teaspoon salt
3 tablespoons vegetable oil
1 cup milk, approximately
Vegetable oil for frying

BROILED SPROUTED WHEAT PATTIES

1. Put all the ingredients, with the exception of the bread crumbs, in the container of an electric blender or food processor and blend or process until smooth. Turn into a bowl.
2. Stir in enough crumbs to make a mixture that is stiff enough to be molded into patties.
3. Form into 6 patties and put on an oiled baking sheet. Broil under a preheated broiler until browned; turn and brown on the other side.
Yield: Six servings.

2 cups sprouted wheat berries (see page 201)
1 cup nuts
1 onion, quartered
1 cup milk
1 tablespoon soy flour
1 teaspoon salt
3 tablespoons brewer's yeast
1 sprig parsley
1 egg
2 cups whole wheat bread crumbs, approximately

SPROUT AND HAZELNUT SALAD

2 cups sprouted alfalfa
seeds with green leaves
(see page 201)
Herb dressing (see page
194)
Salad greens
⅓ cup finely chopped
hazelnuts

Toss the sprouts with dressing. Arrange on a bed of salad greens and sprinkle with the nuts. Serve at once.
Yield: Four servings.

SPROUTED TABOOLEY SALAD

2 cups sprouted wheat
berries (¼ inch) (see
page 201)
1 cucumber, peeled and
diced
1 green pepper, seeded
and diced
1 tomato, diced
1 scallion, chopped
¼ cup celery with leaves,
diced
2 tablespoons chopped
parsley
Vegetable salt to taste
½ cup vegetable oil
½ cup lemon juice

1. Combine all the ingredients in a large ceramic or glass bowl or crock. Toss to mix.
2. Cover and refrigerate at least overnight before serving. The mixture will keep several days in the refrigerator.
Yield: Six to eight servings.

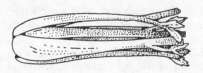

RED CABBAGE AND SPROUTS

1. Heat the oil in a wok or heavy skillet. Add the cabbage and sauté for 3 minutes. Add the sprouts and sauté for 2 minutes longer.
2. Add the remaining ingredients and reheat, tossing lightly. Serve hot.
Yield: Six servings.

3 tablespoons safflower oil
4 cups shredded red cabbage
2 cups mung bean sprouts (see page 201)
1 tablespoon caraway seeds
  Salt and freshly ground black pepper to taste
1 tablespoon soy sauce
1 tablespoon vinegar

SPROUTED CHICK-PEA SALAD

Combine all ingredients and toss to mix.
Yield: Four to six servings.

2 cups sprouted chick-peas (see page 201)
1 clove garlic, finely chopped
¼ cup chopped scallions
1 tomato, diced
¼ cup chopped parsley
2 tablespoons wine vinegar
½ cup olive or vegetable oil
  Salt and freshly ground black pepper to taste

GRAINS & CEREALS

Much has been written on the disadvantages of packaged, processed foods containing a minimum of essential nutrients and quantities of non-nutritive additives. More recently, the advisability of spraying vitamins and minerals over essentially non-nutritious cereals has also been questioned. The recipes in this chapter may persuade the reader to try alternates. Cook brown rice and fix a couple of the combination dishes calling for it. Compare the nutritive values with other kinds of rice. Compared with enriched white rice it has more niacin and protein but less thiamine and iron. But brown rice has more riboflavin, calcium, phosphorus, potassium, and vitamin E. Savor the texture and flavor of a homemade cereal, fruit and honey mixture and calculate the cost per serving compared with store-bought packages. Explore the culinary possibilities of little-known cereals such as millet, which has a delicate flavor, and contains a complete protein and little starch; bulghur, the cracked wheat staple of Mediterranean lands; and kasha or buckwheat groats. Cooking cereals and whole grains takes a little extra time so make sure to get a bonus by fixing extra and using it later in combination dishes included in this chapter and among the vegetarian main dishes.

NUT-APPLE BREAKFAST

1. In a hand grinder or food processor, grind the sunflower seed kernels, sesame seeds, almonds, hazelnuts, and pumpkin seeds. Stir in the wheat germ and date sugar.
2. Grind the apples until fine in the container of an electric blender or food processor. Add with raisins to nut mixture. Mix well. Serve in cereal bowls with milk. This mixture can be stored in a tightly closed plastic bag or covered container in the refrigerator.
Yield: Four servings.

2 tablespoons sunflower seed kernels
2 tablespoons sesame seeds
2 tablespoons unblanched almonds
2 tablespoons hazelnuts
2 tablespoons pumpkin seeds
2 tablespoons wheat germ
2 tablespoons date sugar or brown sugar
½ cup dried apples
½ cup raisins
Milk

BREAKFAST NUTRIMENT

Combine all the ingredients, with the exception of the milk. Moisten with milk and serve.
Yield: Four to six servings.

2 cups pecans, chopped
1 tablespoon wheat germ
1 unpeeled apple, cored and finely diced
1 banana, sliced
1 unpeeled pear, cored and diced
1 cup raisins
1 teaspoon brown sugar
Reconstituted non-fat dry milk powder

SIMPLE BREAKFAST

Combine all the ingredients, with the exception of the milk, and mix well. Serve in a cereal bowl with milk.
Yield: One serving.

¼ cup wheat germ
¼ cup sunflower seed kernels, coarsely ground
¼ cup sesame seeds
2 tablespoons rice polishings, optional
2 tablespoons chopped walnuts
Milk

HONEY-OATS CEREAL

½ pound rolled oats
2 cups wheat germ
1 cup almonds
1 cup cashews
1 cup sunflower seed
  kernels
1 cup honey
⅔ cup water
1 teaspoon pure vanilla
  extract
⅔ cup vegetable oil

1. Preheat the oven to 350 degrees.
2. Combine the oats, wheat germ, almonds, cashews, and sunflower seed kernels.
3. Combine the remaining ingredients in a separate bowl. Pour over the dry ingredients and mix well. Spread out on a baking sheet and bake for 15 minutes.
4. Turn mixture over and bake for 15 minutes longer. Serve with milk. Store, when cool, in a covered container in the refrigerator.
Yield: Eight servings.

HEAVENLY MUNCH

2 pounds rolled oats
½ teaspoon salt
1¼ cups soy oil
⅓ cup honey
¾ cup non-fat dry milk
  powder
1 cup soy flour
1¾ cups wheat germ
1 pound finely chopped
  dates
1½ cups unsweetened
  coconut
1¾ cups sesame seeds
1½ cups chopped dried
  bananas, optional
1 cup sunflower seed
  kernels
1½ cups raisins
1½ cups nuts
1 cup pumpkin seeds
1 cup squash seeds

1. Preheat the oven to 300 degrees.
2. Put the rolled oats in a large bowl and add the salt, oil, and honey. Mix well.
3. Combine all the remaining ingredients in another large bowl, and mix well. Stir in the oats mixture and mix well again.
4. Spread out enough of the mixture to cover a large baking sheet and bake for 15 minutes. Transfer to a bowl to cool. Repeat with the remaining oats mixture. Serve as a dry snack or in cereal bowls with milk. Store in a tightly covered container in the refrigerator.
Yield: About thirty-six servings.

COCONUT CEREAL

1. Put the almonds and coconut in a lightly oiled heavy skillet and cook over low heat, stirring frequently, until lightly toasted. Drain on paper towels.

2. Bring the water to a boil in a medium-sized saucepan. Stir in the oats, bring to a boil, cover, and simmer for 1 minute.

3. Stir in the raisins, apples, and cinnamon and serve topped with the coconut and nuts.

Yield: Two servings.

¼ cup sliced almonds
¼ cup unsweetened coconut
1½ cups water
⅔ cup quick-cooking oats
⅓ cup raisins
⅓ cup dried apple slices
¼ teaspoon ground cinnamon

GRANOLA FOR THE EIGHTIES

1. In a large bowl mix together the oats, soy flour, wheat germ, cornmeal, sesame seeds, dry milk, sugar, pulverized sunflower seeds, oil, and water. Mix very well.

2. Spread in shallow baking pans so that the layers are not thicker than 1 inch. Bake in a 300-degree oven until golden, about 35 minutes. Stir several times. Cool.

3. Mix the raisins, apples, apricots, and pineapple and store in a tightly capped container.

Yield: About two quarts.

2 cups quick-cooking oats
½ cup soy flour
½ cup wheat germ
½ cup cornmeal
½ cup sesame seeds
½ cup non-fat dry milk powder
½ cup brown sugar
½ cup sunflower seeds (pulverized in a blender)
½ cup vegetable oil
½ cup water
1 cup raisins
1 cup dried apple slices
½ cup snipped dried apricots
½ cup diced dried pineapple

BARLEY SALAD

1 cup quick-cooking
  barley
1 teaspoon salt
3 cups boiling water
2 cups slivered cooked
  chicken
2 celery stalks, sliced
½ cup sliced water
  chestnuts
1 small avocado, peeled
  and diced
1 tablespoon lemon juice
½ cup chopped red onion
2 tablespoons chopped
  parsley
1 cup plain yogurt (see
  page 324)
2 tablespoons soy sauce
¼ teaspoon freshly ground
  black pepper

1. Stir the barley into the salt and water mixture. Cover and simmer for 12 minutes, or until the barley is tender, stirring once or twice. Drain and cool.
2. Add the chicken, celery, water chestnuts, avocado tossed with lemon juice, the onion, parsley, yogurt, soy sauce, and pepper to the cooled barley. Chill and serve in lettuce leaf cups, if you wish.
Yield: Eight servings.

BUCKWHEAT POLENTA

3 cups skim milk
1 tablespoon honey
½ cup buckwheat groats
  Wheat germ
  Butter
  Honey, maple syrup, or
  fruit syrup

1. The night before you want to serve this dish, put the milk, honey, and groats in a heavy saucepan. Bring to a boil and cook, stirring, for 25 minutes, or until the buckwheat is tender. Pour into a 9- by 9- by 2-inch oiled pan and refrigerate.
2. The next morning, cut the mixture into 2-inch squares, coat with wheat germ, and fry in butter until lightly browned and heated through. Serve with more honey, butter, and syrup.
Yield: Four servings.

APPLE-OATS

Mix all ingredients together.
Yield: About four servings.

2 cups quick-cooking oats
¾ cup raisins
3 apples, peeled, cored,
   and cubed
3 cups applesauce
2 cups milk
   Honey or maple syrup
   to taste

LENTIL-CORN BURGERS

1. Mash the lentils roughly in a large bowl. Add the corn germ and oats. Heat the oil in a small skillet and sauté the onion and garlic until tender but not browned. Add to the lentils.
2. Stir in the carrot, salt, pepper, thyme, lemon juice, and egg. Mix well and let stand for 10 minutes. Form into burgers. Let stand for 30 minutes. Coat with bread crumbs and fry in ⅛-inch oil in a large heavy skillet until browned on both sides. Yield: Four servings.

1 cup lentils, cooked in
   boiling salted water
   until tender, about 40
   minutes, and drained
½ cup corn germ
¼ cup quick-cooking oats
2 tablespoons vegetable
   oil
1 small onion, finely
   chopped
1 small clove garlic, finely
   chopped
1 carrot, grated
½ teaspoon salt
¼ teaspoon freshly ground
   black pepper
½ teaspoon dried thyme
1 tablespoon lemon juice
1 egg, lightly beaten
   Vegetable oil for frying
2 tablespoons whole
   wheat bread crumbs,
   approximately

KASHA

1 cup kasha (buckwheat
groats)
1 egg, lightly beaten
½ teaspoon salt
½ cup finely chopped
onion
2½ cups boiling water
3 tablespoons butter,
optional
3 tablespoons chopped
parsley

1. Mix the kasha with the egg and heat the mixture in a dry skillet over medium to low heat, stirring occasionally, until all the grains become separate. Do not let the mixture scorch.

2. Add the remaining ingredients. Bring to a boil, cover tightly, and simmer for 25 minutes, or until grain is tender and has absorbed all the liquid. Fluff with a fork before serving.

Yield: Six to eight servings.

Note: For use as a breakfast cereal, omit the onion and parsley and serve with honey and cream or fruit.

PISTACHIO-RAISIN BRUNCH LOAF

2 cups boiling water
1 teaspoon salt
1 tablespoon safflower oil
6 ounces (about 1 cup)
stoneground yellow
cornmeal
¼ cup butter
¼ cup raisins
¼ cup non-dyed shelled
pistachios or other nuts
2 eggs, lightly beaten
Wheat germ
Butter
Maple syrup or honey

1. Bring the water to a rolling boil in a saucepan. Add the salt and oil and gradually pour in the cornmeal, while stirring constantly. Cook, stirring, until mixture is thickened and smooth.

2. Add the raisins and pistachios. Cook for 15 minutes, stirring occasionally, adding a little extra water if the mixture seems dry.

3. Pour into a greased baking dish to make a ½-inch-thick layer. Cool and cut into squares. Dip the squares into the eggs and then into the wheat germ.

4. Heat enough butter to cover the bottom of a heavy skillet and brown the squares in the butter. Turn and brown other side, adding more butter as necessary. Serve with maple syrup or honey.

Yield: Four servings.

PUFFED BROWN RICE

1. Spread the rice out and let it dry at room temperature for 3 days, turning occasionally. It should be hard.
2. Heat the oil to 350 degrees in a deep-fat fryer.
3. Put ¼ cup of the rice at a time in a stainless steel basket or sieve and lower it into the hot oil. Fry for about 20 seconds, or until lightly golden. Drain on paper towels. Serve as a cereal or snack.
Yield: About two quarts.

4 cups cooked brown rice, cooked so that grains are separate and dry (see page 228)
1 quart soy or sesame oil

MILLET CEREAL

1. Combine the millet, water, and salt in a saucepan. Bring to a boil, cover, and simmer for 30 minutes, or until the millet is cooked.
2. Plain, made with water or milk, the cereal can be eaten for breakfast with honey and cream. Made with broth, the cereal can be the basis for many savory dishes, such as the one below, to take the place of starchy vegetables.
Yield: About four servings.

½ cup whole hulled millet
1½ cups water, milk, or vegetable or chicken broth (see pages 37 and 38)
Salt to taste

MILLET WITH CHEESE

Put the millet, water, butter, and half the cheese in a saucepan. Heat, stirring, until the cheese has melted. Serve sprinkled with the remaining cheese.
Yield: Four servings.

1 recipe millet cereal, prepared as in Millet Cereal with broth (see above)
2 tablespoons water
2 tablespoons butter
1 cup grated Cheddar cheese

MILLET PILAF I

½ pound whole millet
5 tablespoons vegetable oil
1 quart water, or homemade vegetable or chicken broth (see pages 37 and 38)
1 large onion, finely chopped
1 carrot, diced
1 white turnip, diced
1 celery stalk, diced
¼ pound mushrooms, sliced
½ teaspoon salt
¼ teaspoon freshly ground black pepper
½ cup chopped walnuts
½ cup shredded Monterey Jack or mild Cheddar cheese

1. Wash and drain the millet. Toast the millet in a dry skillet over low heat to remove excess moisture.
2. Add 2 tablespoons oil to the millet and sauté for 5 minutes, stirring frequently. Add the water, bring to a boil, cover, and simmer for 40 minutes, or until the millet is tender.
3. Meanwhile, heat the remaining oil in a second skillet. Sauté the onion until tender but not browned. Add carrot, turnip, celery, and mushrooms and sauté, stirring, until the vegetables are crisp-tender.
4. Drain the millet of any excess moisture. Stir in the vegetables, salt, pepper, nuts, and cheese. Stir until the cheese melts.
Yield: Four servings.

MILLET PILAF II

1 cup whole hulled millet
2 tablespoons vegetable oil
2 onions, chopped
1 carrot, quartered
1 teaspoon salt
¼ teaspoon freshly ground black pepper
1 quart homemade vegetable or chicken broth (see pages 37 and 38), approximately
1 cup sliced mushrooms
1 cup plain yogurt (see page 324)

1. Preheat the oven to 350 degrees.
2. Put the millet in a dry, heavy pot and brown slowly over low heat. Remove the millet. Add the oil to the casserole and sauté the onions until lightly browned.
3. Return the millet to the pot and add the carrot, salt, and pepper. Pour 1 quart of broth over all and bake, tightly covered, for 1½ hours, or until the millet is tender. It may be necessary to add more broth during cooking. When the millet is fully cooked it is like rice with each grain separate.
4. Stir in the mushrooms and yogurt and serve with fowl or game. Millet pilaf can be served as a main dish.
Yield: Six servings.

MILLET BREAKFAST CEREAL

1. Put the millet, water, and salt in a saucepan. Bring to a boil, cover, and simmer for 45 minutes, or until the millet is soft.
2. Add the apples and raisins and cook for 15 minutes longer. Serve with honey and skim milk.
Yield: Four to six servings.

1 cup whole hulled millet
1 quart water or milk
1 teaspoon salt
1 cup chopped, unpeeled, cored apples
1 cup raisins
Honey and cream

CORNMEAL MUSH

1. Pour the boiling water into a saucepan. Mix together the cornmeal and cold water and gradually stir into the boiling water.
2. Add the salt and cook, stirring, for about 20 minutes. Serve with honey and milk. Or, cornmeal mush can be served in place of potatoes at dinner.
Yield: Four servings.

1 cup boiling water
1 cup stoneground yellow cornmeal
1 cup cold water
1 teaspoon salt
Honey and milk

CORNMEAL MUSH AND SOY GRITS

1. Mix the cornmeal, salt, and dry milk together.
2. Put the grits in a small bowl and cover with boiling water. Let stand for 5 minutes. Drain and add to the cornmeal mixture.
3. Stir in the cold milk. Stir the cornmeal mixture gradually into the simmering scalded milk in a saucepan. Heat, stirring, for 5 minutes, or until thick and smooth. Pour into an oiled 13- by 9- by 2-inch pan. Cool and cut into squares or rounds.
4. Dip the squares or rounds into the potato starch. Heat enough butter to cover the bottom of a heavy skillet and fry the cornmeal pieces in the butter until browned on both sides.
Yield: Four to six servings.

1 cup yellow cornmeal
1 teaspoon salt
½ cup non-fat dry milk powder
½ cup soy grits
Boiling water
1 cup cold milk
2 cups scalded milk
Potato starch or potato flour
Butter

CORN TORTILLAS

2 cups Masa Harina
(specially treated
cornmeal from Quaker)
1¼ cups water,
approximately
⅛ teaspoon salt

1. In a large bowl combine the Masa Harina, water, and salt and work with the hands until it holds together. Add more water if necessary.

2. Divide the dough into 12 balls and roll each one between sheets of wax paper to 6-inch rounds. Trim.

3. Heat a 6- or 7-inch skillet. Add a tortilla and cook for 30 seconds. Turn and cook for 1 minute. Continue to flip and cook until flecks of brown appear on both sides. Keep warm while cooking the rest of tortillas.

Yield: Twelve tortillas.

BULGHUR PILAF

1 cup bulghur (cracked
wheat), rinsed in cool
water and drained
2 cups water,
approximately
3 tablespoons butter
1 onion, finely chopped
2 cups homemade
vegetable or chicken
broth (see pages 37 and
38)
¼ teaspoon dried sage
Salt to taste
¼ teaspoon dried summer
savory
2 tablespoons chopped
parsley

1. Put the bulghur and 2 cups water in a saucepan. Bring to a boil, cover tightly, and simmer for 40 minutes, or until tender, adding more water during cooking if necessary.

2. Preheat the oven to 200 degrees.

3. Spread the bulghur out on baking sheets and dry in the oven.

4. Bulghur can be left whole for a chewy product or cracked by passing through a coffee mill. Store in a closed container in the refrigerator.

5. Melt the butter in a heavy casserole and add 1 cup of the dried bulghur and the onion. Sauté for 5 minutes.

6. Add the broth, salt, savory, and parsley. Cover tightly and simmer over low heat until the liquid is absorbed, about 25 minutes.

Yield: Four servings.

FOUR-GRAIN HOMEMADE CEREAL

1. Combine the rye, oats, wheat germ, bran, and cornmeal and mix well. Store in covered jars in refrigerator and use as needed. The mixture yields 3½ pounds.

2. To cook, heat the water to boiling. Add salt to taste and 1 cup of the mixed cereal while beating vigorously. Bring to a boil and then set in a warm place (in a thermos bottle or in a yogurt maker) until the next morning. Reheat. Add the rice polishings and serve with raisins and milk.
Yield: Two servings.

1 pound whole rye, ground in seed grinder to medium fine
1 pound whole oats, ground in seed grinder to medium fine
1 pound wheat germ
½ pound whole bran, ground in seed grinder if coarse
1 pound yellow cornmeal, optional

TO COOK
2½ cups water
Salt
1 cup mixed cereal
2 tablespoons rice polishings, optional
Raisins and milk or nut milk

CRACKED WHEAT CEREAL

1. Spread the wheat grains on a pan and place under a broiler set at 400 degrees. Toast until the grain smells toasted. Do not allow to burn.

2. Grind the toasted grains in a coffee mill or Moulinex grinder and discard any floury residue.

3. Put 1 cup cracked toasted wheat in a saucepan with the water and salt. Heat, stirring, until the mixture boils. Reduce the heat and cook slowly, stirring occasionally, until tender, about 40 minutes. Alternately, the mixture can be cooked in the top of a double boiler over boiling water for 1 hour.

4. Serve with cream or honey.
Yield: Four servings.

1 cup whole wheat grains
4 cups water or milk
½ teaspoon salt
Cream or honey

BREAKFAST RICE

1 cup raw brown rice
4 cups milk
1 cup raisins
   Maple syrup

1. Grind the rice in an electric blender or food processor until the kernels are half their original size. Combine rice in a saucepan with the milk and raisins.
2. Bring to a boil, cover, and simmer until the rice is cooked, about 10 to 15 minutes. Serve with maple syrup.
Yield: Four servings.

BARLEY PILAF

¼ cup oil, approximately
1 pound mushrooms, sliced
2 onions, sliced
1¾ cups whole hulled barley
1 quart boiling homemade vegetable or chicken broth (see pages 37 and 38) approximately
3 tablespoons brewer's yeast
   Salt
2 tablespoons snipped fresh dill weed

1. Preheat the oven to 350 degrees.
2. Heat ¼ cup oil in a heavy skillet and sauté the mushrooms for 5 minutes. Remove the mushrooms and set aside. Add the onions to the skillet and sauté until golden. Remove and set aside.
3. Add the barley to the skillet and cook, stirring, until all the grains are coated with oil, adding more oil if necessary.
4. Return the mushrooms and onions to the skillet. Add 1 quart broth, the yeast, salt to taste, and dill. Mix and turn into an oiled casserole. Cover and bake for 30 minutes, adding more broth if the pilaf becomes too dry.
Yield: Six servings.

VEGETABLE COUSCOUS

1. Spread the couscous on a baking sheet, sprinkle with the water, and mix lightly with the fingers to moisten all grains.

2. Place grains in a muslin-lined colander over a pan of boiling water, or in a special couscous pot. Cover and steam for 20 minutes. Stir the grains and steam for 20 minutes longer. Stir in the butter.

3. Meanwhile, put the carrots, celery, green pepper, beans, cabbage, broccoli, and peas in a heavy saucepan. Add salt to taste and pour the broth over all. Cover and cook the vegetables until barely crisp-tender, about 10 minutes. Add the mushrooms and chick-peas and cook for 5 minutes longer.

4. To serve, arrange the couscous in a large deep dish (a paella pan is ideal) and pile it into a conical shape. Arrange the drained vegetables neatly around and pour some of the vegetable broth over the couscous.

Yield: Six servings.

2 cups couscous
½ cup water
¼ cup butter
1 cup cubed carrots
1 cup diced celery
1 green pepper, seeded and cubed
1 cup 1-inch pieces green beans
1½ cups shredded red cabbage
1 cup tiny broccoli flowerets
1 cup fresh peas
Salt
3 cups boiling homemade vegetable broth (see page 37)
1 cup button mushrooms
2 cups cooked dried chick-peas or drained canned chick-peas

RICE 'N' WHEAT BERRIES

Put all the ingredients in a heavy kettle. Bring to a boil, cover, and simmer gently for 1 hour. Do not remove the cover during cooking.

Yield: Four to six servings.

1½ cups raw brown rice, rinsed and drained
½ cup whole wheat berries, rinsed and drained
½ cup pine nuts
6 cups water
1 teaspoon salt

BROWN RICE
(METHOD I—BOILING)

1 cup raw brown rice,
  rinsed and drained
2 to 3 cups water
  Salt to taste

Put the rice, water, and salt in a saucepan, bring to a boil, cover tightly, and cook over low heat for 45 minutes, or until the rice is tender and has absorbed the liquid. Do not stir during cooking. (The larger amount of water will give a softer rice grain.)

Yield: About four cups cooked rice.

BROWN RICE
(METHOD II—PRESSURE COOKING)

1 cup raw brown rice,
  rinsed and drained
2 cups water
½ teaspoon salt

1. Put the rice, water, and salt in a pressure cooker. Cover tightly. Put the pressure regulator in place. Heat the pan until the regulator jiggles evenly, or reaches 15 pounds of pressure.

2. Reduce the heat to maintain the regulator just jiggling gently and cook for 20 minutes. Allow the pan to cool by itself, about 20 minutes.

3. Remove the regulator when the pressure has been reduced, open the pan, and serve the rice.

Yield: About four cups cooked rice.

Note: Cooking for a shorter time, say 15 minutes, will give a firmer grain.

BROWN RICE
(METHOD III—BAKING)

1 cup raw brown rice,
  rinsed and drained
2 to 3 cups water
  Salt to taste
2 tablespoons butter

1. Preheat the oven to 350 degrees.

2. Put all the ingredients in a flameproof casserole and bring to a boil on top of the stove. Cover and bake for 50 minutes.

Yield: About four cups cooked rice.

GREEN RICE

1. Preheat the oven to 325 degrees.
2. Beat the egg lightly and gradually beat in the milk. Stir in remaining ingredients, with the exception of the oil, and mix well.
3. Spread the oil over the inside of a casserole. Turn the rice mixture into the casserole and bake for 30 minutes, or until set.
Yield: Four servings.

1 egg
1 cup milk
½ cup finely chopped parsley
1 small onion, finely chopped
2 cups cooked brown rice (see page 228)
½ cup grated Cheddar cheese
Vegetable salt to taste
2 teaspoons olive oil

GLORY RICE

1. Preheat the oven to 350 degrees.
2. Combine all the ingredients, with the exception of the almonds and sunflower seed kernels. Turn into an oiled casserole. Top with the almonds. Bake for 35 minutes, or until set.
3. Garnish with sunflower seed kernels before serving.
Yield: Four servings.

2 cups cooked brown rice (see page 228)
2 cups grated Cheddar cheese
½ teaspoon salt
2 cups milk
3 eggs, lightly beaten
3 tablespoons chopped parsley
¼ cup melted butter
1 onion, finely chopped
Blanched slivered almonds
Sunflower seed kernels

FRUIT AND RICE

3¾ cups homemade
vegetable or chicken
broth (see pages 37 and
38)
2 cups raw brown rice,
rinsed and drained
1 medium-sized onion,
chopped
3 carrots, sliced
1 cup whole dried
apricots
1 teaspoon salt
¼ teaspoon saffron,
optional
½ cup whole unblanched
almonds

1. Heat the broth to boiling in a large saucepan. Add the rice, onion, carrots, apricots, salt, and saffron.
2. Bring to a boil, cover, and simmer gently for 45 minutes, or until the rice is tender. Serve garnished with the almonds.
Yield: Four to six servings.
Note: This can be served with curries, fowl, and fish, or as a luncheon main dish.

CHILI BROWN RICE

2¾ cups water
1 small onion, finely
chopped
2 tablespoons butter
2 tablespoons seeded and
chopped canned green
chilies
1 teaspoon chili powder
¼ teaspoon ground cumin
1 teaspoon salt
1 cup raw brown rice
1 16-ounce can tomatoes
½ cup plain yogurt (see
page 324)
½ cup shredded Monterey
Jack or mild Cheddar
cheese
Pitted black olives,
optional

1. Put the water, onion, butter, chilies, chili powder, cumin, and salt in a large heavy saucepan. Bring to a boil and add the rice. Cover and simmer for 45 minutes, or until the rice has absorbed the liquid.
2. Break up the tomatoes and add to the rice with their juice. Turn the mixture into a 1½-quart casserole or baking dish. Spread the yogurt over the top, sprinkle with the cheese, and bake in a 400-degree oven for 15 minutes, or until heated through and cheese has melted. Garnish with olives, if you wish.
Yield: Six servings.

BROWN RICE WITH CHICKEN

1. Heat 3 tablespoons oil in a saucepan and add the rice. Cook rice, stirring, until all the grains are coated with oil.
2. Add the broth, cover, and simmer gently until the rice is almost tender, about 40 minutes.
3. Meanwhile, heat the remaining oil and sauté the celery and onions until tender. Add to the rice with the wine and almonds and cook for 5 minutes longer.
Yield: Four servings.

4 tablespoons vegetable oil
1 cup raw brown rice, rinsed and drained
3 cups boiling homemade chicken broth (see page 38)
2 celery stalks, chopped
2 onions, chopped
1 cup diced cooked chicken
1 tablespoon dry white wine, optional
1 tablespoon finely ground unblanched almonds

SPICY CHEESE 'N' RICE BALLS

Combine all the ingredients, with the exception of the bread crumbs. Chill. Form into 1-inch balls. Roll the balls in the bread crumbs and fry, a few at a time, in deep oil heated to 375 degrees on a deep-fat thermometer, for about 3 minutes, or until golden. Drain on paper towels.
Yield: About two and one-half dozen.

2 cups hot cooked brown rice (see page 228)
¾ cup grated sharp Cheddar cheese
1 egg, lightly beaten
½ teaspoon salt
⅛ teaspoon freshly ground black pepper
2 tablespoons grated onion
1½ tablespoons spicy creole or Dijon mustard
1 4-ounce can jalapeño peppers, seeded and chopped
1 cup fine dry whole wheat bread crumbs
Vegetable oil for deep frying

CARROT AND RICE BAKE

6 large carrots, sliced
2 cups cooked brown rice
(see page 228)
¼ pound mushrooms,
sliced
⅓ cup finely chopped
walnuts
1 medium-sized onion,
finely chopped
1½ cups frozen tofu,
thawed, drained, and
mashed (see page 160)
¾ cup soy whey or milk
1 egg, lightly beaten
⅓ cup freshly grated
Parmesan cheese
⅛ teaspoon freshly ground
black pepper

1. Cook the carrots in water to cover until barely tender. Drain. Mix together the rice, mushrooms, and nuts.
2. In four individual buttered baking dishes spread a layer of rice, top with the onion and then the carrots.
3. Combine the tofu, whey, egg, cheese (with the exception of 2 tablespoons), and pepper in the container of an electric blender or food processor. Blend or process until smooth. Pour over the carrots and sprinkle with the remaining cheese.
4. Bake in a 350-degree oven for 30 minutes, or until hot and bubbly.
Yield: Four servings.

BROWN RICE LOAF WITH AVOCADO SAUCE

1 cup raw brown rice,
cooked (see page 228)
3 carrots, finely grated
3 eggs, lightly beaten
3 scallions, finely
chopped
1 cup raw cashews, finely
chopped
½ teaspoon dried oregano
or mixed Italian herbs
½ teaspoon salt
¼ teaspoon freshly ground
black pepper
½ cup shredded Monterey
Jack or mild Cheddar
cheese
Avocado sauce (see
page 187)

1. In a large bowl mix the cooked rice, carrots, eggs, scallions, nuts, oregano, salt, pepper, and cheese.
2. Pack into an oiled 8½- by 4½- by 2½-inch loaf pan. Cover with aluminum foil and bake in a 350-degree oven for 45 minutes. Remove the foil and cook for 10 minutes longer. Serve with avocado sauce. Good cold, too.
Yield: Six servings.

PILAF PRIMAVERA

1. Remove and reserve asparagus tips and broccoli flowerets. Finely chop and reserve stems.

2. Heat the oil in a large heavy kettle and sauté the onion and garlic until tender but not browned. Add the zucchini and vegetable stems and cook for 3 minutes longer.

3. Add the rice, tomatoes with their juice, tomato paste, broth, salt, and pepper. Bring to a boil, cover, and simmer for 45 minutes, or until the rice is tender. Add more water if necessary. Steam the asparagus tips and broccoli flowerets for 5 minutes in a separate pan.

4. Stir the sugar snap peas into the rice and garnish with the reserved asparagus tips and broccoli flowerets. Serve with freshly grated Parmesan cheese.

Yield: Four servings.

12 asparagus spears
1 small bunch broccoli
¼ cup vegetable oil
1 large onion, finely chopped
1 clove garlic, finely chopped
1 medium-sized zucchini, cubed
1 cup raw brown rice
1 16-ounce can tomatoes
2 tablespoons tomato paste
2 cups homemade vegetable or chicken broth (see pages 37 and 38)
1 teaspoon salt
¼ teaspoon freshly ground black pepper
2 cups sugar snap peas or snow peas, cut into thirds on the bias
Freshly grated Parmesan cheese

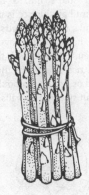

ONION AND MUSHROOM PILAF

¼ cup vegetable oil
2 large onions, sliced and
    separated into rings
1¼ cups brown rice
½ pound mushrooms,
    sliced
3 cups homemade
    vegetable or chicken
    broth (see pages 37 and
    38)
1 teaspoon salt
½ teaspoon freshly ground
    black pepper
1 tablespoon snipped
    fresh dill weed
¼ cup chopped parsley

1. Heat the oil in a large heavy kettle or Dutch oven and sauté the onion rings over medium-low heat until golden, stirring often.
2. Add the rice and mushrooms and cook, stirring, for 3 minutes longer. Add the broth, salt, pepper, and dill, bring to a boil, and simmer for 45 minutes, or until the rice is tender. Stir in the parsley.
Yield: Six servings.

ORIENTAL RICE BALLS

½ cup raw brown rice,
    cooked (see page 228)
1½ cups sesame seeds,
    approximately
⅛ teaspoon salt

1. Cook the rice and while it is still warm, press 1 to 2 tablespoons at a time into a quarter cup measure. Remove to your wet hands and shape into a ball or oval. Continue until all the rice is used.
2. Meanwhile, toast the seeds until golden in a large heavy skillet over low heat, stirring often. Sprinkle with the salt.
3. Roll the rice shapes in the seeds. Eat out of hand or serve with poultry and fish.
Yield: About twelve rice balls.

BROWN RICE AND PUMPKIN SEED STUFFING

1. Slice 1 onion and dice 1 celery stalk and put in a saucepan. Add the giblets, water, bay leaf, and salt to taste. Bring to a boil, cover, and simmer for 45 minutes.

2. Remove the giblets. Discard the skin and bones and dice the meat. Reserve.

3. Boil the broth rapidly until only 2 cups remain. Reserve.

4. Chop remaining onion. Heat the oil in a saucepan, add the chopped onion, and sauté.

5. Add the rice to the saucepan and cook for 3 minutes. Add the reserved broth, bring to a boil, cover, and simmer until the rice has absorbed all the liquid, about 45 minutes.

6. Finely chop the remaining celery and add with the pumpkin seeds, parsley, sage, marjoram, and the reserved meat. Season with salt to taste. Use to stuff a five-pound roasting chicken or turkey.

Yield: About one and one-half quarts.

2 onions
3 celery stalks with leaves
   Giblets from chicken or
   turkey
3 cups water
1 bay leaf
   Salt
2 tablespoons vegetable
   oil
1 cup raw brown rice
¼ cup pumpkin seeds
¼ cup chopped parsley
½ teaspoon dried sage
¼ teaspoon dried
   marjoram

WHEAT AND SOY CEREAL MIX

1. In the container of a food processor or an electric blender grind the wheat and grits into a coarse powder in small batches.

2. Mix the ground mixture with the date sugar and store in a tightly covered container.

3. To make hot cereal add 1 cup of the mix to 2 cups boiling water with salt added, if you wish, and cook for about 8 minutes. Length of cooking depends on how finely ground the mixture is.

Yield: About five cups mix.

4 cups wheat berries
4 cups soy grits
2 cups date sugar or
   finely chopped dates

BARLEY PILAF

⅔ cup regular barley
4 cups homemade vegetable or chicken broth (see pages 37 and 38)
3 tablespoons butter
¼ pound mushrooms, sliced
3 scallions, chopped
1 clove garlic, finely chopped
¼ teaspoon dried thyme
½ teaspoon salt
¼ teaspoon freshly ground black pepper
2 tablespoons chopped parsley

1. Spread the barley in a shallow baking pan and roast in a 350-degree oven for 20 minutes, or until golden.
2. Combine the toasted barley and broth in a large heavy kettle. Bring to a boil, cover, and simmer for 1 hour, or until the barley is tender. Drain and use the drained liquid in soup or stew.
3. Melt the butter in a large skillet and sauté the mushrooms, scallions, and garlic until tender but not browned.
4. Add the barley, thyme, salt, and pepper and reheat. Stir in the parsley.
Yield: Four servings.

WHOLE WHEAT STUFFING

3 tablespoons butter
1 small onion, finely chopped
1 celery stalk with leaves, chopped
¾ cup regular uncooked whole wheat hot cereal
1⅓ cups homemade vegetable or chicken broth (see pages 37 and 38)
½ teaspoon salt
¼ teaspoon freshly ground black pepper
¼ teaspoon dried thyme
2 tablespoons chopped parsley

1. Melt the butter in a medium-sized skillet and sauté the onion until tender but not browned. Add the celery and cook for 1 minute.
2. Add the cereal, broth, salt, pepper, thyme, and parsley. Cook, stirring, for about 5 minutes, or until the liquid has been absorbed and the cereal is tender.
Yield: Four servings.

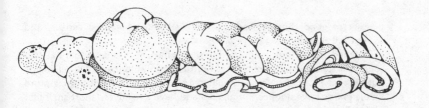

BREADS

This chapter is a collection of recipes for breads with different textures, flavors, and nutritive contributions to add variety and pleasure to family meals, snacks, and lunch boxes. Try offering a child a slice of hot buttered bread straight from the oven as an after-school snack. He could get to like the bread better than store-bought cookies.

There are quick breads, leavened with baking powder and baking soda, yeast breads, and, for the really adventurous, a few unleavened loaves. Most of the recipes call for whole grains, that is, the entire kernel ground into flour so that nothing is lost. Stoneground grains are favored where possible because the slow-moving stones generate less heat and cause less damage than high-speed mills. Slow-moving stones leave more flavor in the flour, too.

In their ability to absorb moisture, whole wheat flours vary tremendously, depending on the strain of wheat, the area where it is grown, and the climatic conditions of storage and usage. Therefore, especially in yeast mixtures, it is difficult to give exact amounts of liquid or flour needed. Experience in dealing with doughs will tell you how the dough should feel.

Wheat flour is the only grain with any appreciable amount of gluten. Gluten is the protein that forms the structure of the bread; it is developed by kneading. The quantity of gluten in unbleached white flour is greater than in whole wheat flour, and, for that reason, many recipes call for a combination of the two. Now that bread flour is available in most supermarkets it can replace unbleached white flour in yeast breads for improved results.

Other grains, such as corn, buckwheat, rye, and oatmeal, are mixed with the wheat flours in the recipes. Hard wheats contain most gluten, with Deaf Smith County, Texas, wheat having up to 20 percent gluten. A good bread flour should have at least 12 percent. If stoneground whole wheat flour is sifted for a recipe, retain the bran siftings left in the sieve that contain all manner of good things to add to coarser breads, breakfast cereals, and cooked hot puddings.

Enriched white flour is not used in the recipes. This is flour that has had roughly sixteen elements removed in processing and four synthetic elements put back in. This flour is usually sold in a bleached form. Fresh stoneground whole grains have not been fumigated and have a relatively short shelf-life. They should be bought in small quantities and stored in tightly closed containers in the refrigerator. Most of the mixed-grain breads in this chapter are fortified with a variety of natural, nutritious additions, such as soy flour, soy grits, raw wheat germ, and brewer's yeast.

Yeast is the favored raising agent and is available as baker's compressed yeast, bulk dry active yeast, and packaged dry active yeast. The latter contains BHA as a preservative. (One tablespoon dry active yeast equals one 1½-ounce cake of compressed yeast.)

Some natural foods purists eschew baking powder and baking soda completely as unnecessary synthetic chemicals, but for most people their use makes a wide selection of nourishing quick breads more palatable. Some groups consider Rumford brand (a phosphate-based powder) less obnoxious than regular double-acting or tartrate-type baking powders.

Whole grain breads tend to be heavier in texture, and you have to work harder, by kneading, to develop the gluten to get a good-textured loaf. Whole grain breads should not be allowed to over-rise, especially after shaping, and just prior to baking, or they will collapse later due to a lack of structure.

There's as much art as science in bread making because you're dealing with living things, such as yeast, that need warmth and moisture—and tender loving care.

BROWN RICE AND WHOLE WHEAT MUFFINS

1. Preheat the oven to 425 degrees.
2. In a bowl, combine the flour, baking powder, salt, and brown sugar, if used, and mix well.
3. Add the rice, butter, eggs, milk and molasses, if used. Spoon the mixture into oiled and floured muffin tins. Bake for 15 to 20 minutes, or until done. ·
Yield: One dozen medium-sized muffins.
Note: The rice gives a crunchy texture to the muffins.

1¼ cups whole wheat flour
2 teaspoons baking powder
¼ teaspoon salt
2 tablespoons brown sugar or molasses
1 cup cold (not chilled) cooked brown rice (see page 228)
¼ cup butter, melted
2 eggs, lightly beaten
⅔ cup milk

THREE-GRAIN MUFFINS

1. Preheat the oven to 350 degrees.
2. In a bowl, combine the cornmeal, sugar, soy flour, whole wheat flour, salt, and baking soda.
3. Mix the egg and yogurt together lightly and stir into the dry ingredients. Stir in the butter.
4. Fill the muffin tins two-thirds full and bake for 25 minutes, or until done.
Yield: One dozen medium-sized muffins.

⅓ cup stoneground cornmeal
⅓ cup sugar
⅓ cup soy flour
1 cup whole wheat flour
½ teaspoon salt
1 teaspoon baking soda
1 large egg, lightly beaten
1 cup plain yogurt (see page 324)
⅓ cup butter, melted

WHOLE WHEAT MUFFINS

1. Preheat the oven to 375 degrees.
2. Sift the flour, sugar, salt, and baking powder into a bowl.
3. Combine the eggs, milk, and melted butter and stir into the dry ingredients until they are just moistened.
4. Fill oiled muffin tins two-thirds full and bake for 20 minutes, or until done.
Yield: Eighteen medium-sized muffins.

3 cups whole wheat flour
⅓ cup brown sugar
¾ teaspoon salt
4½ teaspoons baking powder
2 eggs, beaten
1⅓ cups milk
⅓ cup butter, melted

CORN MUFFINS

1½ cups cornmeal
½ cup whole wheat flour
2 teaspoons aluminum-
  free baking powder
  (Rumford)
¼ teaspoon salt
½ cup honey
½ cup molasses
1 egg, lightly beaten
1¼ cups cow's or goat's
  milk
¼ cup butter, melted

1. Preheat the oven to 400 degrees.
2. Combine the cornmeal, whole wheat flour, baking powder, and salt in a bowl.
3. Add the honey, molasses, egg, milk, and butter. Stir just enough to moisten the ingredients (the batter should be lumpy). Fill well-oiled two-inch muffin tins two-thirds full. Bake for 20 to 25 minutes.
Yield: Twelve muffins.

BUCKWHEAT-CORN MUFFINS

1 cup buckwheat flour
½ cup cornmeal
2½ teaspoons baking
  powder
¼ teaspoon salt
1 to 2 tablespoons brown
  sugar
2 eggs
1¼ cups milk
¼ cup butter, melted

1. Preheat the oven to 400 degrees.
2. Mix together the buckwheat flour, cornmeal, baking powder, salt, and sugar.
3. Combine the eggs, milk, and butter and stir into the dry ingredients until just moistened (the batter will be thin).
4. Fill the oiled muffin tins two-thirds full and bake for 15 to 20 minutes, or until done.
Yield: One dozen medium-sized muffins.

BLUEBERRY MUFFINS

4 cups whole wheat flour
¾ teaspoon salt
⅓ cup brown sugar
1 tablespoon baking
  powder
1 tablespoon brewer's
  yeast
1 cup milk,
  approximately
¼ cup soy or vegetable oil
2 eggs, lightly beaten
1 cup blueberries

1. Preheat the oven to 400 degrees.
2. In a mixing bowl, combine the flour, salt, sugar, baking powder, and yeast. Stir in enough milk to make a stiff dough.
3. Stir in the oil, eggs, and blueberries. Spoon into oiled 2-inch muffin tins so that they are two-thirds full. Bake for 30 minutes, or until done.
Yield: About three dozen two-inch muffins.

SPICY APPLE-CARROT MUFFINS

1. Preheat the oven to 400 degrees.
2. In a large bowl, combine the dry milk, baking powder, salt, allspice, nutmeg, cinnamon, and flour.
3. Combine the honey, oil, and eggs and stir into the dry ingredients. Fold in the apple and carrot. Spoon into oiled muffin tins until they are two-thirds full.
4. Bake for 15 to 20 minutes or until done.
Yield: About two dozen medium-sized muffins.

½ cup non-fat dry milk powder
3 teaspoons baking powder
½ teaspoon salt
½ teaspoon ground allspice
½ teaspoon grated nutmeg
1 teaspoon ground cinnamon
2½ cups stoneground whole wheat flour
1 cup honey
1 cup safflower or other oil
4 eggs
1 teaspoon pure vanilla extract
1 cup grated unpeeled apple
1 cup grated carrot

YOGURT MUFFINS

1. Preheat the oven to 375 degrees.
2. Combine the eggs and yogurt. Beat in the oil and molasses. Sift together the whole wheat flour, soy flour, and salt.
3. Add the egg mixture to the dry ingredients and stir until just moistened. Stir in the raisins and nuts.
4. Fill oiled muffin tins two-thirds full. Bake for 20 minutes, or until done.
Yield: One dozen medium-sized muffins.
Note: These muffins have no raising agent and will be compact in texture.

2 eggs, lightly beaten
1 cup plain yogurt (see page 324)
2 tablespoons vegetable oil
¼ cup molasses
1½ cups whole wheat flour
2 tablespoons soy flour
1 teaspoon salt
¼ cup raisins
¼ cup chopped nuts

PEANUT BUTTER-APRICOT MUFFINS

Boiling water
½ cup unsulphured dried apricots
½ cup stoneground whole wheat flour
¼ cup unbleached white flour
1 tablespoon wheat germ
¼ teaspoon salt
½ teaspoon baking soda
3 tablespoons natural peanut butter
1 tablespoon butter
2 tablespoons molasses
1 egg
½ cup buttermilk
1 tablespoon sugar
⅛ teaspoon ground cinnamon

1. Preheat the oven to 400 degrees.
2. Pour boiling water over the apricots. Let stand for 3 minutes. Drain the apricots and dice finely using scissors.
3. In a bowl, mix together the whole wheat flour, unbleached flour, wheat germ, salt, and baking soda.
4. With two knives, cut in the peanut butter and the butter until well distributed. (Add diced apricots.)
5. Combine the molasses, egg, and buttermilk and add all at once to the peanut butter mixture. Stir only until the dry ingredients are moistened.
6. Spoon the batter into 8 oiled 2½-inch muffin tins. Combine the sugar and cinnamon and sprinkle over the muffins. Bake for 15 minutes, or until done.
Yield: Eight muffins.

OAT-WHEAT GERM MIX FOR BREADS

1½ cups quick rolled oats
½ cup wheat germ
1 cup unbleached white flour
1 cup whole wheat flour
½ cup non-fat dry milk powder
4 teaspoons baking powder
½ teaspoon salt
1 cup butter, softened

1. Mix the oats, wheat germ, white flour, whole wheat flour, dry milk, baking powder, and salt together in a bowl.
2. Cut in the butter to form a coarse meal.
3. Store covered in the refrigerator and use as directed in the following recipes.
Yield: Five and one-half cups.

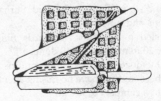

OAT–WHEAT GERM MUFFINS

1. Preheat the oven to 400 degrees.
2. Beat the egg, sugar, and water together.
3. Stir into mix only until dry ingredients are moistened. Add raisins.
4. Fill six oiled muffin tins two-thirds full.
5. Bake the muffins for 15 to 20 minutes. Cool on a wire rack.
Yield: Six muffins.

1 egg
3 tablespoons brown sugar
¼ cup water
1 cup oat–wheat germ mix (see page 242)
⅓ cup raisins

OAT–WHEAT GERM PANCAKES

1. Beat the egg yolk with the water until blended. Stir into the mix until just moistened.
2. Beat the egg white until stiff. Fold into the pancake mixture.
3. Drop by tablespoons onto a lightly oiled, moderately hot griddle.
4. Bake until browned on both sides and serve hot with syrup.
Yield: Four servings or eight to ten three-inch cakes.

1 egg, separated
½ cup warm water
¾ cup oat–wheat germ mix (see page 242)
Syrup, honey, or preferred topping (see page 312)

OAT–WHEAT GERM WAFFLES

1. Follow the directions for oat–wheat germ pancakes (see above).
2. Bake on a lightly oiled preheated waffle iron, following manufacturer's directions. Serve hot with syrup.
Yield: Four servings or two nine-inch square waffles.

2 eggs, separated
1 cup warm water
1½ cups oat–wheat germ mix (see page 242)
Syrup

BRAN MUFFINS

1 cup whole bran cereal
2 cups whole wheat flour
¼ cup non-fat dry milk powder
3 tablespoons baking powder
¼ teaspoon salt
1 cup milk
⅓ cup honey
¼ cup vegetable oil
½ cup raisins

1. Preheat the oven to 400 degrees.
2. Combine the bran, flour, dry milk, baking powder, and salt in a large bowl. Mix together the milk, honey, and oil and stir into the dry ingredients until just moistened.
3. Stir in the raisins and spoon into well oiled 2½-inch muffin tins until two-thirds full. Bake for 12 minutes, or until browned. Cool on a rack.
Yield: Eighteen muffins.

MAKE–AHEAD REFRIGERATOR BRAN MUFFINS

2½ cups unbleached white flour
1 cup whole bran cereal
1 cup raisin bran
½ cup wheat germ
2 teaspoons baking soda
½ teaspoon salt
½ cup sugar
2 eggs
¾ cup vegetable oil
¼ cup molasses
2 cups buttermilk

1. Mix together the flour, cereals, wheat germ, baking soda, salt, and sugar and set aside.
2. Beat the eggs, oil, and molasses together. Add with the buttermilk to dry ingredients, mixing only until the ingredients are moistened.
3. Store covered in refrigerator until ready to use.
4. When ready to bake, preheat the oven to 375 degrees.
5. Stir the batter and spoon into oiled muffin tins, filling two-thirds full.
6. Bake for 20 minutes, or until well browned. Cool on a wire rack.
Yield: About two dozen two-and-three-quarter-inch muffins.
Note: Recipe can be doubled, if you wish. Batter keeps for about two weeks.

BANANA-OATMEAL MUFFINS

1. Preheat the oven to 375 degrees.
2. Combine the oats, flour, salt, and sugar in a bowl.
3. Lightly beat the egg yolks and stir in the hot milk. Beat until very light and thick. Beat in the oil, vanilla, and mashed banana. Sprinkle the dry ingredients over the yolk mixture and fold in gently.
4. Beat the egg whites until stiff but not dry and fold into the batter. Spoon into oiled muffin tins until they are two-thirds full.
5. Bake for 30 minutes, or until golden and done. Cool on a rack.
Yield: About twenty medium-sized muffins.

1 cup quick-cooking oats
1 cup unbleached white flour
1 teaspoon salt
2 tablespoons brown sugar
2 eggs, separated, at room temperature
½ cup milk, scalded
⅓ cup vegetable oil
1 teaspoon pure vanilla extract
1 small banana, mashed

SQUASH-NUT MUFFINS

1. Preheat the oven to 400 degrees.
2. Mix together the flour, baking powder, salt, spices, sugar, and nuts.
3. Add the egg, oil, squash, and milk and mix only until dry ingredients are moistened.
4. Spoon batter into oiled muffin tins, filling two-thirds full.
5. Bake for about 25 minutes. Cool on a wire rack.
Yield: Twelve two-and-three-quarter-inch muffins.

1½ cups whole wheat flour
2 teaspoons baking powder
½ teaspoon salt
1 teaspoon ground cinnamon
¼ teaspoon ground cloves
¼ teaspoon grated nutmeg
⅓ cup brown sugar
¾ cup chopped nuts
1 egg, lightly beaten
⅓ cup vegetable oil
¾ cup cooked mashed winter squash or thawed frozen squash
¾ cup undiluted evaporated milk

SPICY FRESH PEACH-OATMEAL MUFFINS

1 medium-sized ripe
  peach
1 cup whole wheat flour
½ cup quick rolled oats
⅓ cup brown sugar
1¼ teaspoons baking
  powder
½ teaspoon baking soda
¼ teaspoon salt
½ teaspoon ground
  cinnamon
¼ teaspoon grated nutmeg
1 egg
½ cup milk
2 tablespoons vegetable oil

1. Preheat the oven to 400 degrees.
2. Peel the peach and cut into ½-inch dice (there will be about ½ cup).
3. Mix together the flour, oats, sugar, baking powder, baking soda, salt, and spices. Combine the peach, egg, milk, and oil and add to the dry ingredients. Mix only until the dry ingredients are moistened.
4. Spoon into oiled muffin tins, filling about two-thirds full.
5. Bake for about 15 minutes. Cool on a wire rack.
Yield: One dozen two-and-three-quarter-inch muffins.

WHOLE WHEAT POPOVERS

3 eggs
1½ cups milk
1 cup sifted stoneground
  whole wheat flour
½ teaspoon salt
3 tablespoons butter,
  melted
6 to 8 teaspoons vegetable
  oil

1. Preheat the oven to 475 degrees.
2. Put the eggs, milk, sifted flour, and salt in the container of an electric blender and blend for half a minute or, if using an electric mixer, beat at high speed for 1 minute.
3. Stir in the melted butter.
4. Pour 1 teaspoon oil in the bottom of eight iron popover forms or six large muffin tins. Heat for 2 minutes in the oven.
5. Fill the forms or tins three-quarters full and bake for 15 minutes. Lower the oven temperature to 350 degrees and bake for 25 minutes longer. For drier popovers, prick each one, turn oven off, and let them stand in the hot oven for 5 minutes. Serve hot.
Yield: Six to eight popovers.
Note: Rye popovers can be made by substituting ½ cup rye flour and ½ cup unbleached white flour for the whole wheat flour.

CARROT-PINEAPPLE BREAD

1. Preheat the oven to 325 degrees.
2. Mix together the flour, baking soda, salt, and cinnamon and set aside.
3. With a spoon beat together the eggs, sugars, oil, and vanilla. Stir in the pineapple. Stir in the dry ingredients.
4. Fold in the carrots and nuts and turn into an oiled and lightly floured 9- by 5- by 3-inch loaf pan.
5. Bake for 50 to 60 minutes, or until a toothpick inserted in the center comes out clean. Let stand in the pan on a wire rack for 5 minutes, then turn out on the rack to cool.
Yield: One loaf.

1½ cups whole wheat flour
½ teaspoon baking soda
½ teaspoon salt
1 teaspoon ground cinnamon
2 eggs
½ cup brown sugar
½ cup granulated sugar
½ cup vegetable oil
1 teaspoon pure vanilla extract
¾ cup finely chopped fresh pineapple, well drained
1 cup grated peeled carrots (1 large)
½ cup chopped walnuts or pecans

RICE MUFFINS

1. Preheat the oven to 375 degrees.
2. Combine the rice flour, baking powder, sugar, and salt in a bowl. Mix together the water, milk, vanilla, oil and eggs.
3. Stir the liquids into the dry ingredients and mix just to moisten. Spoon into paper-lined muffin tins and fill two-thirds full. Bake for 25 minutes. Cool on a wire rack.
Yield: About one dozen muffins.
Note: Before spooning the batter into muffin tins, you can stir in ½ cup blueberries, nuts, raisins, corn kernels, or cranberries.

2 cups rice flour
1½ tablespoons baking powder
¼ cup brown sugar
¼ teaspoon salt
½ cup water
⅔ cup water
⅔ cup skim milk
1 teaspoon pure vanilla extract
¼ cup vegetable oil
2 eggs, lightly beaten

BARLEY FLOUR DROP BISCUITS

1 cup barley flour
¼ teaspoon salt
2 teaspoons baking
  powder
2 tablespoons butter
⅓ to ½ cup buttermilk
1 egg

1. Preheat the oven to 425 degrees.
2. Sift the barley flour, salt, and baking powder into a bowl.
3. With a pastry blender or two knives, cut the butter into the dry ingredients.
4. With a fork, beat ⅓ cup buttermilk and the egg together and stir into the flour mixture just to moisten. If necessary, add a little more milk. The dough should be soft but firm enough to hold its shape when dropped from a spoon onto an oiled baking sheet.
5. Bake for 12 to 15 minutes, or until done.
Yield: Ten to twelve small biscuits.

MEXICAN SKILLET CORNBREAD

1 cup yellow cornmeal
½ teaspoon salt
1 tablespoon baking
  powder
⅓ cup melted butter
2 eggs, lightly beaten
1 cup plain yogurt (see
  page 324)
1 cup cream-style canned
  corn
1 medium-sized onion,
  finely chopped
1 cup grated sharp
  Cheddar cheese
1 4-ounce can chopped
  jalapeño peppers

1. Preheat the oven to 350 degrees.
2. Combine the cornmeal, salt, and baking powder in a medium-sized bowl. Oil a 12-inch cast-iron or heavy porcelainized iron skillet and heat in the oven.
3. Combine the eggs, yogurt, and corn in a small bowl. Stir into the cornmeal mixture. Stir in the onion, cheese, and peppers.
4. Pour into the hot skillet and bake for 30 minutes, or until done and lightly browned. Serve in wedges with butter and eat with a fork.
Yield: Eight servings.
Note: This is great under or with chili.

ALL-CORN CORNBREAD

1. Preheat the oven to 400 degrees.
2. Mix together the cornmeal, baking soda, and salt.
3. Add the egg, butter, and buttermilk and mix only until the dry ingredients are moistened. Turn into a well-oiled deep 9-inch pie plate.
4. Bake on the top rack of the oven for 30 to 35 minutes, or until well browned.
5. Cut in wedges and serve hot with butter.
Yield: Six servings.

1¾ cups cornmeal
1 teaspoon baking soda
½ teaspoon salt
1 egg, lightly beaten
2 tablespoons butter, melted
1½ cups buttermilk

CORN BREAD

1. Preheat the oven to 425 degrees.
2. In a bowl, combine the cornmeal, flour, dry milk, baking powder, and salt.
3. Add the remaining ingredients and stir just enough to moisten. Turn into an oiled 8-inch square baking pan. Bake for 20 to 25 minutes, or until done. Serve hot.
Yield: Six servings.

1¾ cups stoneground yellow cornmeal
¼ cup stoneground whole wheat flour
¼ cup non-fat dry milk powder
3 teaspoons baking powder
¾ teaspoon salt
1 egg, lightly beaten
1 tablespoon honey or dark brown sugar
2 tablespoons vegetable oil
1½ cups milk

BAKED BROWN BREAD

½ cup *each* cornmeal, rye, and whole wheat flours
¼ cup wheat germ
1 teaspoon baking soda
¾ teaspoon salt
½ cup raisins
1 egg
2 tablespoons vegetable oil
1 cup buttermilk
½ cup molasses

1. Preheat the oven to 350 degrees.
2. Mix together the flours, wheat germ, baking soda, salt, and raisins.
3. Stir in the egg, oil, buttermilk, and molasses only until the dry ingredients are moistened.
4. Turn into an oiled and lightly floured 8- by 4- by 2-inch loaf pan.
5. Bake for 45 minutes, or until a toothpick inserted in the center comes out clean. Let stand in the pan on a wire rack for a few minutes, then turn out on the rack. To serve, cut with a serrated knife. This makes a moist loaf similar to steamed brown bread and is good with baked beans.
Yield: One loaf.

SPOON BREAD

3 cups milk
1 cup stoneground yellow cornmeal
¾ teaspoon salt
1 teaspoon baking powder
1 tablespoon sugar
2 tablespoons vegetable oil
3 eggs, separated
Butter

1. Preheat the oven to 350 degrees.
2. Heat 2 cups of the milk in a saucepan. When the milk begins to simmer, add the cornmeal and continue to cook, stirring, until mixture is thick.
3. Remove from the heat and add the salt, baking powder, sugar, oil, and the remaining milk. Beat the egg yolks lightly and add to the cornmeal mixture.
4. Beat the egg whites until stiff but not dry and fold into the cornmeal mixture. Turn into a buttered 2-quart soufflé dish and bake for 1 hour, or until well puffed and brown on top.
5. Serve by the spoonful directly from the dish and top with butter.
Yield: Six to eight servings.

HONEY-DATE LOAF

1. Preheat the oven to 350 degrees.
2. Cream the butter and gradually beat in the honey. Beat in the egg, lemon rind, and lemon juice.
3. Combine the flour, salt, baking soda, and baking powder and add alternately with the buttermilk to the batter. Fold in the dates and walnuts.
4. Turn the mixture into an oiled 9- by 5- by 3-inch loaf pan.
5. Bake for 50 to 60 minutes or until done.
Yield: One loaf.

2 tablespoons butter
½ cup honey
1 egg
1 teaspoon grated lemon rind
2 teaspoons lemon juice
1½ cups unbleached white flour
¼ teaspoon salt
⅛ teaspoon baking soda
1 teaspoon baking powder
½ cup buttermilk
1 cup chopped dates
½ cup chopped walnuts

FRUITY AND NUTTY TEA LOAF

1. Preheat the oven to 350 degrees.
2. Sprinkle the blueberries with 2 tablespoons flour.
3. Sift together the remaining flour, sugar, baking powder, and salt. Stir in the oatmeal.
4. Blend together the eggs, butter, and bananas. Add to the dry ingredients, stirring until combined. Add the pecans, raisins, and blueberries gradually and stir only enough to distribute them evenly through the batter.
5. Pour the batter into an oiled and floured 8½- by 4½- by 2½-inch loaf pan. Bake for 1 hour. Allow the loaf to cool in the pan for 15 minutes. Remove from the pan gently and cool completely. Wrap cooled loaf in aluminum foil and store overnight before slicing.
Yield: One loaf.

½ cup fresh blueberries
1½ cups unbleached white flour or whole wheat flour
⅔ cup brown sugar
2½ teaspoons baking powder
½ teaspoon salt
½ cup old-fashioned oatmeal
2 eggs, lightly beaten
⅓ cup butter, softened
1 cup mashed ripe bananas
½ cup chopped pecans
¼ cup raisins

BANANA RICE BREAD

2 cups rice flour
½ teaspoon salt
2 tablespoons baking powder
½ teaspoon baking soda
⅓ cup honey
½ cup vegetable oil
3 eggs, separated
1 cup buttermilk
1 cup mashed bananas (2 to 3)

1. Preheat the oven to 325 degrees.
2. Sift the rice flour, salt, baking powder, and baking soda together. Beat together the honey, oil, and egg yolks and stir the flour mixture alternately with the buttermilk into the oil mixture.
3. Stir in the banana. Beat the egg whites until stiff but not dry and fold into the batter. Pour into an oiled 9- by 5- by 3-inch loaf pan and bake for 50 minutes. Cool on a wire rack.
Yield: One loaf.

NUT BUTTER LOAF

2 cups unbleached white flour
4 teaspoons baking powder
½ teaspoon salt
1 tablespoon wheat germ
¼ cup brown sugar or ⅛ cup honey
⅔ cup natural non-homogenized nut butter (cashew, peanut, or almond)
1¼ cups milk or plain yogurt (see page 324)
Honey butter (see page 312)

1. Preheat the oven to 350 degrees.
2. Sift together the flour, baking powder, and salt. Add the wheat germ and sugar, if used.
3. Combine the honey, if used, with the nut butter and the milk until thoroughly blended. Add to the dry ingredients and mix well. Turn the soft mixture into an oiled 8½- by 4½- by 2½-inch loaf pan. Bake for 50 minutes, or until done. Remove from the pan and cool.
4. Wrap in a moisture-proof wrapper and store for 1 day before slicing. Serve with honey butter.
Yield: One loaf.

BUTTERMILK ROLLS

1. Crumble the compressed yeast and put it, or the dry yeast, in a bowl. Add the honey and, while stirring, pour in the buttermilk. Continue to stir until the yeast is dissolved.

2. Stir in the melted butter.

3. Mix in 2 cups of the flour, the baking soda, and salt. Beat well. Cover and set in a warm place until the mixture rises about 2 inches up the bowl, about 25 minutes.

4. Stir down and add enough of the remaining flour to make a soft dough. Beat well. Cover and let rise in a warm place until nearly doubled in bulk, about 30 minutes. Punch down.

5. Divide the dough into 24 pieces and form each piece into a ball. Put 1 inch apart in oiled cake pans or on baking sheets.

6. Cover and let rise until doubled in bulk, about 10 minutes.

7. Preheat the oven to 400 degrees.

8. Bake for 20 minutes, or until the rolls are golden brown.

Yield: Two dozen rolls.

2 cakes compressed yeast, or 2 tablespoons dry active yeast
¼ cup honey
1½ cups buttermilk, heated to lukewarm
½ cup butter, melted
5 cups unbleached white flour or bread flour, approximately
1 teaspoon baking soda
¾ teaspoon salt

PUMPKIN-ALMOND BREAD

1½ cups whole wheat flour
½ teaspoon baking powder
1 teaspoon baking soda
½ teaspoon salt
½ teaspoon ground ginger
½ cup vegetable oil
⅔ cup brown sugar
⅓ cup granulated sugar
1 cup pumpkin purée
1 egg
1 tablespoon grated orange rind
½ cup toasted chopped or slivered almonds

1. Preheat the oven to 350 degrees.
2. Mix together the flour, baking powder, baking soda, salt, and ginger.
3. Beat the oil, sugars, pumpkin, egg, and orange rind until blended.
4. Stir in the dry ingredients until well mixed. Add the almonds.
5. Turn into an oiled and lightly floured 8- by 4- by 2-inch loaf pan.
6. Bake for 1 hour, or until a toothpick inserted in the center comes out clean. Remove from the pan and cool on a wire rack.
Yield: One loaf.

PRUNE-NUT BREAD

1½ cups (10 ounces) soft pitted prunes
¾ cup boiling water
¾ cup whole wheat flour
1 cup unbleached white flour
½ cup brown sugar
1 teaspoon baking soda
½ teaspoon salt
1 teaspoon ground cinnamon
1 egg
2 tablespoons vegetable oil
2 tablespoons undiluted evaporated milk
½ cup to 1 cup chopped walnuts, pecans, or other nuts

1. Preheat the oven to 350 degrees.
2. Snip the prunes in small pieces with a scissors. Cover with boiling water and set aside.
3. Mix together the whole wheat flour, white flour, brown sugar, baking soda, salt, and cinnamon.
4. Beat the egg with the oil and milk and add to the dry ingredients with the nuts and prunes (do not drain). Mix well and turn into a greased 8- by 4- by 2-inch loaf pan lined with wax paper.
5. Bake for 45 minutes, or until a toothpick inserted in the center comes out clean. Turn out of pan, peel off paper, and cool on a wire rack.
Yield: One loaf.

ORANGE-WHEAT GERM SODA BREAD

1. Preheat the oven to 350 degrees.
2. Mix the wheat germ, flour, baking powder, baking soda, salt, raisins, and orange rind.
3. Add the oil, buttermilk, and orange juice.
4. Turn into an oiled 1½-quart casserole.
5. Bake for 50 minutes, or until a toothpick inserted in the center comes out clean. Turn out on a wire rack to cool.
Yield: One loaf.

2 cups wheat germ
2 cups unbleached white flour
3 teaspoons baking powder
½ teaspoon baking soda
½ teaspoon salt
1 cup raisins
1 tablespoon grated orange rind
¼ cup vegetable oil
1 cup buttermilk
½ cup orange juice

CORN AND WHEAT BREAD

1. Combine ½ cup cornmeal, the oil, molasses, salt, and the boiling water in a mixing bowl. Let stand until lukewarm. Mix well.
2. Sprinkle the yeast over the warm water and stir to dissolve.
3. Add the yeast mixture, egg, and 1½ cups whole wheat flour to the cornmeal mixture. Beat well. Work in enough of the remaining flour to make a smooth dough that can be kneaded.
4. Knead until smooth. Place dough in an oiled 9- by 5- by 3- inch loaf pan. Cover and let rise in a warm place until the dough reaches top of pan, about 3 hours.
5. Preheat the oven to 375 degrees.
6. Combine the remaining cornmeal and salt and sprinkle over loaf. Bake for 35 minutes, or until well browned and done. Turn onto a wire rack to cool.
Yield: One loaf.

½ cup plus 1 tablespoon stoneground yellow cornmeal
3 tablespoons safflower oil
¼ cup molasses
1 teaspoon salt
¾ cup boiling water
1 tablespoon dry active yeast, or 1 cake compressed yeast
¼ cup warm water
1 egg, lightly beaten
2½ cups whole wheat flour, approximately
¼ teaspoon salt

QUICK FAT-FREE RAISIN BREAD

2 cups whole wheat flour
1 cup raisins
2 tablespoons brown sugar
1 teaspoon baking soda
¾ teaspoon salt
½ cup molasses
1 cup buttermilk
2 tablespoons hot water

1. Preheat the oven to 350 degrees.
2. Mix together the flour, raisins, sugar, baking soda, and salt.
3. Add the molasses, buttermilk, and hot water. Mix well, then turn into an oiled 8- by 4- by 2-inch loaf pan.
4. Bake for 45 minutes, or until a toothpick inserted in the center comes out clean. Turn out of the pan onto a wire rack to cool.
Yield: One loaf.

BRAN ENGLISH MUFFINS

2 cups whole wheat flour
1 package dry active yeast
¾ teaspoon salt
1 tablespoon brown sugar
1 cup milk
½ cup water
3 tablespoons vegetable oil
1 cup unprocessed bran
2 cups unbleached white flour, approximately

1. Mix 1 cup whole wheat flour, the yeast, salt, and brown sugar in large bowl.
2. Heat the milk, water, and oil until very warm. Stir into the first mixture. Then beat with an electric mixer at medium speed for 2 minutes.
3. Stir in the remaining whole wheat flour, the bran, and enough white flour to make a firm dough. Turn out onto a floured surface and knead for 10 minutes, or until elastic. Put in an oiled bowl, turning to oil top. Cover with a sheet of plastic wrap, allowing the wrap to touch dough. Let rise in warm place for 1 hour, or until doubled.
4. Turn the dough out and punch down. Pat or roll to ¾-inch thickness. Cut with a floured 3-inch cutter. Put on a baking sheet or board and let rise for 25 to 30 minutes, or until light.
5. Lift the rounds with a pancake turner and put on a hot, lightly oiled griddle.
6. Bake for 10 to 12 minutes on each side or until lightly browned. Cool on a rack and when ready to serve, split, butter, and toast.
Yield: Sixteen to eighteen muffins.

WALNUT-VEGETABLE BREAD

1. Preheat the oven to 350 degrees.
2. Mix together the flour, sugar, baking powder, baking soda, and salt.
3. Beat the eggs with milk and oil and add with carrot, celery, and nuts to the dry ingredients. Mix well, then turn into an oiled 9- by 5- by 3-inch loaf pan.
4. Bake for 50 minutes, or until a toothpick inserted in the center comes out clean.
5. Let stand in the pan on a wire rack for 10 minutes, then turn out and cool completely.
Yield: One loaf.

2 cups whole wheat flour
½ cup brown sugar
1½ teaspoons baking powder
½ teaspoon baking soda
½ teaspoon salt
2 eggs
½ cup milk
⅓ cup vegetable oil
1 cup grated carrot (1 large)
½ cup finely diced celery
¾ cup chopped walnuts

ZUCCHINI-NUT BREAD

1. Preheat the oven to 350 degrees.
2. Mix together the flour, baking powder, baking soda, salt, spices, and nuts.
3. Beat the egg with the oil and buttermilk. Stir in the zucchini.
4. Add the liquids to the dry ingredients and mix well.
5. Turn into an oiled 8- by 4- by 2-inch loaf pan.
6. Bake for 45 minutes, or until a toothpick inserted in the center comes out clean. Let stand in the pan on a wire rack for 10 minutes. Then turn out of the pan onto a wire rack and cool completely.
Yield: One loaf.

1½ cups whole wheat flour
1 teaspoon baking powder
½ teaspoon baking soda
¼ teaspoon salt
½ teaspoon ground cinnamon
½ teaspoon grated nutmeg
¼ teaspoon ground allspice
½ cup chopped nuts
1 egg
¼ cup vegetable oil
½ cup buttermilk
¾ cup grated zucchini (1 small)

WATCH HILL ZUCCHINI BREAD

2 cups sifted unbleached
    flour
2 teaspoons baking soda
1 teaspoon salt
¼ teaspoon baking
    powder
3 teaspoons ground
    cinnamon
3 eggs
1 cup vegetable oil
1½ cups brown sugar
2 medium-sized zucchini,
    grated (2 cups)
2 teaspoons pure vanilla
    extract
1 cup raisins
1 cup chopped walnuts

1. Preheat the oven to 350 degrees.
2. Sift together the flour, baking soda, salt, baking powder, and cinnamon.
3. Combine the eggs, oil, sugar, zucchini, and vanilla in a large bowl. Mix well. Stir in the flour mixture.
4. Stir in the raisins and nuts and pour into an oiled 13- by 9- by 2-inch pan.
5. Bake for 40 minutes, or until done. Cool on a wire rack.
Yield: Twelve squares.

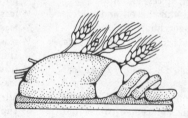

PERFECT PECAN ROLLS

1. Pour the soy milk into a bowl and add the yeast, honey, and ⅓ cup oil. Stir until the yeast dissolves.
2. Add the orange rind, salt, raisins, whole wheat flour, soy flour, and enough unbleached flour to make a dough that is sticky but can be kneaded.
3. Turn out onto a floured board and knead until smooth and elastic. Place the dough in an oiled bowl, turn to oil top, cover, and let rise in a warm place until doubled in size.
4. Punch down. Divide into two pieces. Roll each piece into a rectangle about 12 by 6 inches. Brush with the remaining oil. Sprinkle with sugar and coriander. Sprinkle each rectangle with ½ cup of the pecans.
5. Roll each rectangle like a jelly roll and cut into about 15 slices. Butter generously three 9-inch layer pans or 30 large muffin tins. Sprinkle with the brown sugar and the remaining pecans.
6. Place the rolls, cut side down, ½-inch apart in pans, or in muffin tins. Cover and let rise until doubled in bulk.
7. Preheat the oven to 375 degrees.
8. Bake for 25 to 35 minutes, or until the rolls are done. Immediately turn upside down onto a serving dish. Serve warm.
Yield: About thirty rolls.

2 cups soy or cow's milk, heated to lukewarm
1 tablespoon dry active yeast
½ cup honey
⅓ cup plus 3 tablespoons vegetable oil
2 teaspoons grated orange rind
1 teaspoon salt
1 cup unsulphured raisins
3 cups whole wheat flour
¼ cup soy flour
3 cups unbleached white flour or bread flour, approximately
½ cup date or brown sugar
1 teaspoon ground coriander
1½ cups chopped pecans
½ cup butter, melted
½ cup brown sugar

WHOLE WHEAT COFFEECAKE DOUGH

BASIC DOUGH

2 tablespoons dry active
yeast
½ cup lukewarm water
½ cup plus 1 teaspoon
brown sugar
2 eggs, lightly beaten
¾ teaspoon salt
½ cup butter, melted
1 teaspoon grated lemon
rind
½ cup evaporated milk
½ cup hot water
3½ to 4 cups sifted whole
wheat flour

FOR COFFEECAKE TWIST

1 recipe basic dough as
above
⅔ cup plus 1 tablespoon
butter, softened
½ cup brown sugar
1½ teaspoons ground
cinnamon
2 tablespoons brown
sugar
¼ cup honey
Slivered almonds

1. In a small bowl, mix together the yeast, warm water, and 1 teaspoon sugar.
2. In a large bowl, combine the eggs, remaining sugar, salt, butter, lemon rind, milk, and hot water and mix well. Stir in the yeast mixture.
3. Add enough flour to make a soft dough. Beat well. Cover and let rise for 15 minutes. Turn onto a floured board and knead until dough is smooth and satiny, about 10 minutes.
4. Put in a buttered bowl, turn to butter top, cover, and let rise until more than doubled in bulk, about 1 hour.
5. Punch down dough; now the dough is ready to shape and flavor according to your whim.
Yield: Enough dough for two coffeecakes.
1. Cover the punched-down dough with a towel and let rest for 5 minutes.
2. Divide the dough in half and roll out each half into a rectangle 9 by 12 inches. Brush each half with ⅓ cup butter. Combine the brown sugar and cinnamon and sprinkle half over the first rectangle.
3. Roll like a jelly roll and put on a buttered baking sheet in the form of a crescent ring with ends pinched together, or twisted into a knot. Repeat with second half of the dough.
4. Cover and let rise until doubled in bulk, about 1 hour.
5. Preheat the oven to 350 degrees.
6. Bake for 20 to 30 minutes. Watch carefully because the coffeecakes burn easily.

7. Meanwhile, put the remaining butter, the sugar, and honey in a small saucepan and bring to a boil, stirring.

8. Brush the hot glaze over the hot coffeecakes and sprinkle with almonds. Cool on a rack.

Yield: Two coffeecakes.

BRAN, BANANA, CURRANT, AND NUT BREAD

1. Preheat the oven to 350 degrees.

2. Mix the white flour, whole wheat flour, bran, baking soda, and salt in a bowl. Stir in the nuts and currants.

3. With a spoon, beat the oil, sugar, bananas, and egg together. Add the dry ingredients and mix well. Turn into an oiled 9- by 5- by 3-inch loaf pan.

4. Bake for 60 minutes, or until a toothpick inserted in the center comes out clean. Let stand in the pan on a wire rack for 10 minutes. Then turn out onto the rack and cool completely.

Yield: One loaf.

1 cup unbleached white
   flour
½ cup whole wheat flour
½ cup unprocessed bran
1 teaspoon baking soda
½ teaspoon salt
½ cup chopped nuts
¼ cup currants
½ cup vegetable oil
1 cup brown sugar
1 cup mashed bananas
   (2 large)
1 egg

HONEY-WHOLE WHEAT ROLLS

2 tablespoons dry active yeast
½ cup lukewarm water
1 tablespoon brown sugar
⅓ cup sweet butter
⅓ cup honey
1 tablespoon salt
1 cup boiling water
1⅔ cups cold water
3 cups whole wheat flour
2 cups old-fashioned oatmeal
4 cups unbleached white flour or bread flour, approximately
1 teaspoon ground cardamom

1. In a cup, combine the yeast, lukewarm water, and sugar. Set in a warm place until mixture starts to bubble.

2. Put the butter, honey, and salt in a large bowl. Pour the boiling water over and stir to melt the butter. Pour in the cold water and stir in the yeast mixture which has started to bubble.

3. Stir in the whole wheat flour, oatmeal, and enough of the white flour to make a fairly stiff dough. Work in the cardamom.

4. Turn dough onto a lightly floured board and knead until it is smooth and satiny and all traces of stickiness are gone.

5. Put the dough in a clean buttered bowl and turn to butter the top of the dough. Cover and set in a warm place until doubled in bulk, about 1½ hours.

6. Punch dough down and turn onto a floured board. Pull off pieces of dough the size of a large plum. Roll each piece into a rope ¼ inch in diameter. Knot the rope and place on an oiled baking sheet 2 inches apart. Repeat until all the dough is used.

7. Cover and set in a warm place to rise until doubled in bulk, about 30 minutes.

8. Preheat the oven to 375 degrees.

9. Bake the rolls for 30 minutes, or until golden and done. Cool on racks.

Yield: Three dozen rolls.

CURRANT BUNS

1. Cool the apple juice to lukewarm and stir in the yeast.

2. In a large bowl, mix together the honey and oil. Stir in the yeast mixture and add the oatmeal. Mix thoroughly.

3. Beat in the eggs and let the mixture rest for 10 minutes.

4. Slowly add the whole wheat flour, stirring vigorously. Then, work in enough of the unbleached flour to make a dough that leaves the sides of the bowl clean.

5. Knead in the salt and the currants and continue to knead either in the bowl or on a floured board until the dough becomes smooth and elastic, about 10 minutes.

6. Put the dough in a clean oiled bowl, turn to oil top, cover with a damp towel, and let rise in a warm place until the dough doubles in bulk, about 1 hour.

7. Punch dough down and let rise to double its size again, about 30 minutes.

8. Divide the dough into 12 balls and put them on two oiled large heavy baking sheets. With a sharp knife, slash a superficial X on the top of each ball. Cover and let rise in a warm place until doubled in bulk.

9. Preheat the oven to 350 degrees. Place a pan of water on the bottom of the oven.

10. Bake for 40 minutes, or until buns sound hollow when tapped on the bottom. Remove to a rack and brush with milk. Cool under a damp cloth.

Yield: One dozen buns.

½ cup apple juice, heated to just below simmering point
1 cake compressed yeast, or 1 tablespoon dry active yeast
¼ cup honey
¼ cup vegetable oil
1 cup old-fashioned oatmeal
2 eggs
4 cups whole wheat flour
2 cups unbleached white flour or bread flour, approximately
½ teaspoon salt
1 cup currants
Milk

QUICK WHOLE WHEAT SANDWICH ROLLS

3 cups whole wheat flour,
approximately
1 package dry active yeast
1 tablespoon brown sugar
1 teaspoon salt
Undiluted evaporated
milk
¾ cup very hot tap water
1 egg
¼ cup vegetable oil
Toasted sesame seeds,
optional

1. Mix together 1 cup flour, the yeast, brown sugar, and salt.

2. Add ¼ cup evaporated milk and the water. Beat with an electric mixer at medium speed for 2 minutes. Add 1 cup more flour, the egg, and oil and beat at high speed for 2 minutes. Stir in enough flour to make a firm dough.

3. Cover with a sheet of plastic wrap, allowing the wrap to touch dough. Let rise in warm place for 15 minutes.

4. Turn out onto a floured surface and punch down. Divide in 10 equal portions. With your hand, flatten and pull each portion to form a 4-inch circle.

5. Arrange 5 circles on each of two oiled baking sheets. Cover and let rise for 15 minutes. Brush with evaporated milk and, if you wish, sprinkle with sesame seeds.

6. Preheat the oven to 375 degrees.

7. Bake for about 15 minutes. Remove to wire racks to cool. When ready to serve, split with serrated knife and fill as desired.

Yield: Ten sandwich rolls.

BAGELS

1. Sift the flour and salt into a bowl. Soften the yeast in ⅓ of the potato water and stir into the flour.

2. Add the honey and oil to the remaining potato water and stir into the flour mixture. Add the eggs and beat to form a dough.

3. Turn onto a lightly floured board and knead for 10 minutes. The dough should be quite firm. Add more flour if necessary.

4. Return the dough to a clean buttered bowl, cover, and let rise at room temperature until doubled in bulk, about 1½ to 2 hours.

5. Preheat the oven to 450 degrees.

6. Knead the dough again until smooth and elastic.

7. Pinch off pieces of dough and roll into ropes 6 inches long and ¾ inch wide.

8. Bring the ends of the dough together and pinch to form doughnut shapes.

9. Drop the sugar into a pot with the boiling water. Drop the bagels into the water one at a time and, when they come to the surface, turn them over. Boil for 1 minute longer.

10. Put the bagels on an oiled baking sheet and bake for 10 to 15 minutes, or until golden brown and crisp.

Yield: About thirty bagels.

Note: Potato water is made by boiling peeled diced potatoes in excess water until they are tender. Drain and use the liquid.

8 cups whole wheat flour
1 tablespoon salt
2 cakes compressed yeast
2 cups lukewarm potato water (see note)
⅓ cup honey
¼ cup vegetable oil
4 eggs, lightly beaten
2 tablespoons brown sugar
2 quarts boiling water

CARAWAY PUFFS

1 tablespoon dry active
  yeast
1⅓ cups whole wheat flour
2 teaspoons caraway
  seeds
1 cup cream-style cottage
  cheese
¼ cup water
2 tablespoons honey
1 tablespoon butter
1 teaspoon salt
1 egg
2 teaspoons chopped
  onion
1 cup unbleached white
  flour or bread flour

1. In the large bowl of an electric mixer, combine the yeast, whole wheat flour, and caraway seeds. Combine the cottage cheese, water, honey, butter, salt, egg, and onion in the container of an electric blender. Blend until smooth.

2. Add the blended ingredients to the dry ingredients and beat at low speed for ½ minute. Beat for 3 minutes longer at high speed. Stir in the unbleached white flour.

3. Put the dough in a clean buttered bowl, cover, and let rise until doubled in bulk, about 1½ hours.

4. Divide the dough among 12 well-buttered large muffin tins. The tins should be about half full. Cover and let rise until doubled in bulk.

5. Preheat the oven to 400 degrees.

6. Bake for 2 to 15 minutes. Serve hot.

Yield: One dozen large muffins.

Note: The muffins can be frozen and reheated.

YEAST-RAISED CORN BREAD

2 cakes compressed yeast,
  or 2 tablespoons dry
  active yeast
1 cup milk, heated to
  lukewarm
2 eggs, lightly beaten
1 tablespoon vegetable oil
2 tablespoons honey
1 cup stoneground yellow
  cornmeal
1 cup whole wheat flour
¼ teaspoon salt
3 tablespoons brewer's
  yeast

1. Soften the compressed or dry active yeast in the milk. Blend in the remaining ingredients. Turn into a buttered 8-inch-square pan. Cover and set in a warm place to rise until almost doubled, about 30 minutes.

2. Preheat the oven to 350 degrees.

3. Bake for 30 minutes, or until the bread is done.

Yield: Six servings.

SUGARLESS DOUGHNUTS

1. Scald the milk and sour cream. Add the butter and honey and let stand until lukewarm.
2. Crumble and stir in the yeast until dissolved. Add the egg yolks and salt.
3. Beat in the cinnamon, lemon rind, whole wheat flour, and unbleached white flour. The dough will be soft. It can be put in the refrigerator and punched down when necessary, or left at room temperature until light.
4. Roll the dough to a ½-inch thickness. Cut with a doughnut cutter and set on a board, covered, for 5 minutes.
5. Fry, a few at a time, until golden, in oil heated to 375 degrees. Drain on paper towels and serve warm.
Yield: About eighteen doughnuts.

½ cup milk
½ cup sour cream
2 tablespoons butter
2 teaspoons honey
1 cake compressed yeast
3 egg yolks
½ teaspoon salt
1 teaspoon ground cinnamon
Grated rind of one lemon
2 cups whole wheat flour
½ cup unbleached white flour or bread flour
Vegetable oil for deep frying

BREADSTICKS

1. Dissolve the yeast in the warm water.
2. Combine the salt, sugar, and 3 cups flour in a bowl. Stir in the yeast mixture and enough of the remaining flour to make a fairly stiff dough.
3. Preheat the oven to 425 degrees.
4. Turn the dough onto a lightly floured board and knead until smooth and satiny. Divide dough into 48 pieces and roll each one into a rope ½ inch in diameter and 9 inches long. Place on oiled baking sheets.
5. Brush with the beaten egg and sprinkle generously with coarse salt. Bake for 12 to 15 minutes, or until browned.
Yield: Four dozen breadsticks.

1 tablespoon dry active yeast
1½ cups lukewarm water
1 teaspoon salt
1 tablespoon brown sugar
4 cups whole wheat flour, approximately
1 egg, beaten
Coarse salt

YEAST-RAISED WHOLE WHEAT DOUGHNUTS

2 tablespoons dry active
yeast
1½ cups lukewarm water
2 teaspoons brown sugar
¼ cup honey
¼ cup vegetable oil
3 eggs, well beaten
¾ teaspoon salt
⅓ cup non-fat dry milk
powder
4½ cups sifted whole wheat
flour, approximately
Vegetable oil for deep
frying
Sugar

1. Sprinkle the yeast over ½ cup water and stir in the sugar. Set aside for 10 minutes, or until the yeast is bubbling actively.

2. Stir in the remaining water, the honey, oil, eggs, salt, and dry milk. Mix well. Stir in enough of the sifted flour to make a soft dough. Let stand for 10 minutes.

3. Turn out onto a floured board and knead until the dough is smooth and elastic, about 10 minutes. Put in a clean oiled bowl, cover, and let rise until doubled in bulk, about 40 minutes.

4. Roll out the dough to a ½-inch thickness and cut with a doughnut cutter. Place the rings well apart on a lightly floured baking sheet.

5. Cover and let rise in a warm place until almost doubled in bulk.

6. Meanwhile, heat the oil to 375 degrees. Fry the doughnuts, a few at a time, until golden, turning once. Drain on paper towels, and sugar-coat if desired.

Yield: About three dozen doughnuts.

PUMPKIN BATTER BUNS

1. Mix together ½ cup flour, the yeast, spices, salt, and baking soda in bowl.

2. Heat the milk, water, brown sugar, and oil until very warm. Stir into the dry mixture and beat with an electric mixer at medium speed for 2 minutes.

3. Stir in the pumpkin, egg, and wheat germ and beat at medium speed for 1 minute. Add the nuts and raisins and stir in enough more flour to make a thick batter.

4. Cover the bowl and let rise in a warm place for 45 minutes, or until light and bubbly.

5. Stir the batter down and fill muffin tins three-fourths full. Let rise in a warm place for 45 minutes, or until light.

6. Preheat the oven to 375 degrees.

7. Bake buns for 20 minutes, or until done. Let stand in pans for 5 minutes, then turn out on a rack to cool.

Yield: One dozen two-and-three-quarter-inch buns.

1¾ to 2 cups unbleached white flour
1 package active dry yeast
1 teaspoon ground cinnamon
½ teaspoon grated nutmeg
¼ teaspoon ground cloves
¼ teaspoon ground ginger
½ teaspoon salt
¼ teaspoon baking soda
¼ cup milk
¼ cup water
½ cup brown sugar
2 tablespoons vegetable oil
½ cup pumpkin purée
1 egg
¼ cup wheat germ
¼ cup chopped pecans or walnuts
¼ cup raisins

DILLED BATTER BREAD

¾ cup evaporated milk
¾ cup boiling water
2 teaspoons caraway
seeds
1 tablespoon grated onion
1 tablespoon snipped
fresh dill weed
2 tablespoons brown
sugar
2 teaspoons salt
¼ cup butter
2 tablespoons dry active
yeast
½ cup lukewarm water
2 eggs, beaten
4 to 4½ cups sifted whole
wheat flour
Melted butter

1. In a large bowl, combine the milk, boiling water, caraway seeds, onion, dill, sugar, salt, and butter. Stir to melt the butter. Cool to lukewarm.

2. Dissolve the yeast in the warm water. Add to the milk mixture along with the eggs and beat well.

3. Beat in enough of the flour to give a soft, sticky dough.

4. Beat vigorously for 3 minutes. Cover and let the dough rise in a warm place until doubled in bulk. Stir down and beat for 1 minute.

5. Turn into an oiled 2-quart round casserole. Let rise for 10 to 15 minutes.

6. Preheat the oven to 375 degrees.

7. Bake for 40 minutes, or until the loaf sounds hollow when tapped on the bottom. Brush with melted butter for a soft crust.

Yield: One loaf.

OLD-FASHIONED PUMPERNICKEL

¾ cup stoneground
cornmeal
1½ cups cold water
1½ cups boiling water
1½ teaspoons salt
2 tablespoons
unsulphured molasses
2 tablespoons safflower
oil
2 tablespoons dry active
yeast or 2 cakes
compressed yeast
¼ cup cup lukewarm
water
2 cups mashed potatoes

1. Mix the cornmeal with the cold water in a saucepan. Stir in the boiling water and cook, stirring, until thick.

2. Add the salt, molasses, and oil and set aside until lukewarm.

3. Dissolve the yeast in the lukewarm water.

4. Add the dissolved yeast, mashed potatoes, and wheat germ to the cooled cornmeal mixture. Let stand for 5 minutes.

5. Add the rye flour and enough of the whole wheat flour to make a fairly stiff dough. Knead in the bowl or on a lightly floured board until smooth and satiny.

6. Place in an oiled bowl and turn the dough to oil the top. Cover and let rise until doubled in bulk, about 1½ hours. Divide the dough into two equal portions.

7. Roll each piece of dough into a rectangle twice as big as a 9- by 5- by 3-inch pan. Fold the ends of each into the center, press sides to seal, and fold over to fit into a well-oiled 9- by 5- by 3-inch pan. Cover loaves and let rise until doubled in bulk, about 1 hour.

8. Preheat the oven to 375 degrees.

9. Brush loaves with egg white and sprinkle each with 2 tablespoons of sesame seeds. Bake for 1½ hours, or until loaves sound hollow when tapped on the bottom. Cool on wire racks.

Yield: Two loaves.

1 cup wheat germ
3¼ cups rye flour
4¼ cups whole wheat flour, approximately
1 egg white, lightly beaten
4 tablespoons sesame seeds

BROWN RICE SPOON BREAD

1. Preheat the oven to 350 degrees.

2. Mix the cornmeal, wheat germ, whole wheat flour, and salt with the cold water.

3. Stir into the boiling water in a saucepan and cook, stirring, for 2 to 3 minutes. Add the rice and oil and mix well.

4. Beat the egg yolks with the milk. Then beat the whites until stiff.

5. Stir the yolks and milk into the hot mixture, then fold in the whites. Turn into an oiled 1½-quart casserole.

6. Set the casserole in a shallow pan of hot water and bake for 1 hour and 20 minutes, or until set. Serve hot with butter.

Yield: Six servings.

¼ cup cornmeal
1 tablespoon wheat germ
1 tablespoon whole wheat flour
½ teaspoon salt
½ cup cold water
½ cup boiling water
1 cup cooked brown rice (⅓ cup raw)
1 tablespoon vegetable oil
2 eggs, separated
1 cup milk

BLUEBERRY BREAD

¼ cup stoneground yellow cornmeal
1 cup boiling water
1 tablespoon vegetable oil
¼ cup molasses
1 egg, well beaten
1 tablespoon dry active yeast
¼ cup lukewarm water
3 cups unbleached white flour or bread flour, approximately
2 cups blueberries

1. Stir the cornmeal into the boiling water and stir until the mixture thickens. Remove from the heat and stir in the oil, molasses, and egg. Cool.

2. Dissolve the yeast in the warm water. When the cornmeal mixture is lukewarm, stir in the dissolved yeast.

3. Beat in enough flour to make a stiff dough. Turn the mixture onto a floured board. Knead until the mixture is smooth and elastic, about 10 minutes.

4. Put the dough in a cleaned buttered bowl and turn to butter the top.

5. Cover the bowl and let the dough rise in a warm place until doubled in bulk, about 1 hour.

6. Punch the dough down and roll into a 10-inch square. Sprinkle the blueberries over the square and press in gently.

7. Roll up the dough like a jelly roll, tuck under the ends and put, seam side down, in a well greased 9- by 5- by 3-inch loaf pan. Cover and let rise until doubled in bulk, about 45 minutes.

8. Preheat the oven to 375 degrees.

9. Bake the loaf for 45 to 50 minutes, or until it sounds hollow when tapped on the bottom. Cool on a rack. Do not slice until thoroughly cool.

Yield: One loaf.

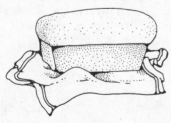

BASIC REFRIGERATOR BREAD

1. In a large bowl, combine 6 cups flour with the dry yeast, sugar, salt, dry milk, and wheat germ. Stir well.

2. In a second bowl, combine the butter and the hot water. Stir to melt the butter and then add to the flour mixture. Mix well.

3. Add more flour, 1 cup at a time, stirring well after each addition until the dough is soft but leaves the sides of the bowl clean.

4. Turn onto a well-floured board and knead until very smooth and elastic, about 10 minutes. Cover with plastic wrap and a towel and let rest for 20 minutes. Punch down the center of the dough and reshape into a ball.

5. Divide the dough into 4 portions. Roll each into a rectangle double the size of an 8½- by 4½- by 2½-inch loaf pan. Roll up tightly like a jelly roll, tuck under the ends and place in 4 well-buttered 8½- by 4½- by 2½-inch loaf pans. Brush the surface of the loaves with melted butter.

6. Cover the loaves loosely with plastic wrap and refrigerate for 2 to 24 hours at a moderately cold setting.

7. Preheat the oven to 400 degrees.

8. Remove the loaves from refrigerator and let stand for 10 minutes.

9. Just before baking, carefully puncture any surface bubbles. Bake for 35 to 40 minutes on a rack set low in the oven. Remove from the pans, brush the crust with butter, and cool on wire racks.

Yield: Four loaves

Note: This is a firm-textured bread which can be sliced very thinly, using an electric knife, for low-calorie sandwiches.

8 to 10 cups unbleached white flour or bread flour, approximately
4 tablespoons dry active yeast
¼ cup brown sugar
1 tablespoon salt
1 cup non-fat dry milk powder
½ cup wheat germ
½ cup butter
1 quart hot tap water
Melted butter

CRUSTY WHITE BREAD

5 cups unbleached white flour or bread flour
1 teaspoon salt
1 tablespoon dry active yeast
1 cup lukewarm water
¼ cup clarified melted butter (milky solids discarded) or olive oil
⅔ cup plus 1 tablespoon milk
1 egg, lightly beaten

1. Combine the flour and salt.
2. Dissolve the yeast in the warm water, add the butter, and ⅔ cup milk and mix very well.
3. Combine the yeast mixture with the flour mixture and mix well. This takes the place of kneading so mixing should be done vigorously and well. Put in an oiled bowl.
4. Cover and let rise in a warm place until the dough is doubled in bulk and is very light, about 1½ hours.
5. Punch down, turn onto a board, and pat or roll to a ½-inch thickness. Cut dough in half and roll each half like a jelly roll with tapered ends. Place, seam side down, on an oiled baking sheet.
6. Cover and let rise in a warm place until half-risen.
7. When half-risen, slash the tops of the loaves diagonally with a sharp knife. Combine the remaining milk with the egg and brush over the loaves. Set in a warm place to rise until very light, another hour or so.
8. Preheat the oven to 400 degrees.
9. Put a pan of hot water on the bottom of the oven. Bake the loaves in the middle of the oven for about 15 minutes. Reduce the oven temperature to 350 degrees and bake for 15 minutes longer or until well browned.
Yield: Two loaves.

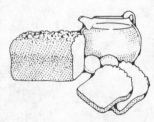

BREAD-PERFECT EVERY TIME

1. Put the salt, 3 tablespoons oil, and the honey in a bowl. Pour the milk over all and cool to lukewarm.

2. Dissolve the yeast in the lukewarm water and add to the cooled milk mixture.

3. Stir in enough flour to make a stiff dough. Turn onto a floured board and knead for 10 minutes, or until the dough is smooth and elastic. It will lose its stickiness as it is kneaded.

4. Put dough in a clean oiled bowl and brush top lightly with oil. Cover and set in a warm place to rise until doubled in bulk, about 2 hours. (When the dough is pressed lightly with a finger, an impression will remain.)

5. Punch the dough down, fold and turn so that the smooth side is on top. Let rise again until almost doubled in bulk, about 30 minutes.

6. Divide into 2 pieces and let rest, covered with a cloth or bowl upside down, on the board for 10 minutes.

7. Roll or pat each piece of dough until it is twice the size of an 8½- by 4½- by 2½-inch loaf pan. Fold in the sides and then the edges. Roll tightly into a loaf shape and set, seam side down, in the pans.

8. Cover the pans and let the dough rise until doubled in bulk, about 1 hour.

9. Preheat the oven to 400 degrees.

10. Bake the bread for 35 to 45 minutes, or until it sounds hollow when tapped on the bottom. Cool on a rack. Brush with melted butter if a soft crust is desired.

Yield: Two loaves.

2 teaspoons salt
Vegetable oil

2 tablespoons honey

2 cups skim milk or reconstituted non-fat dry milk powder, scalded

1 tablespoon dry active yeast or 1 cake compressed yeast

3 tablespoons lukewarm water

6 cups sifted whole wheat pastry flour, unbleached white flour; or bread flour, approximately
Melted butter, optional

HEALTH LOAF

2 tablespoons dry active yeast
1 tablespoon honey
3 cups lukewarm water
¼ cup safflower oil
1 egg, lightly beaten
¼ cup honey or molasses
1½ teaspoons salt
8 to 9 cups unsifted stoneground whole wheat flour
½ cup non-fat dry milk powder
½ cup low-fat soy flour
¼ cup brewer's yeast
3 tablespoons wheat germ
1 cup sunflower seed kernels

1. Put the dry active yeast, 1 tablespoon honey, and ½ cup lukewarm water in the large mixing bowl of an electric mixer. Let stand for 10 minutes.

2. Stir the yeast mixture and add to it the oil, egg, honey, salt, and remaining warm water.

3. Mix in 4 cups whole wheat flour. Mix at moderate speed for 7 to 10 minutes, or until the mixture becomes very elastic.

4. Add the dry milk, soy flour, brewer's yeast, and wheat germ. Mix well. Work in enough of the remaining whole wheat flour to make a dough that can be kneaded. It will be slightly sticky at first.

5. Turn onto a floured board and knead for 5 to 8 minutes, or until smooth and elastic.

6. Put dough in a well-oiled very large bowl and turn to oil top of dough. Cover with a damp towel and let rise in a warm place until doubled in bulk, about 1 hour.

7. Sprinkle in the sunflower kernels over the dough, punch the dough down, and mix in the seeds as well as possible. Shape the dough into 3 balls, cover, and let rest for 10 minutes.

8. Shape into 3 loaves and place in well-oiled 9- by 5- by 3-inch pans. Cover and let rise until barely doubled in bulk, about 30 minutes. Do not let bread rise too high or it will fall.

9. Put the loaf pans in a cold oven. Turn the oven temperature to 400 degrees. After 15 minutes reduce the oven temperature to 375 degrees and bake for 25 to 35 minutes longer, or until the loaves sound hollow when tapped on the bottom.

Yield: Three loaves.

QUICK BRAN BREAD

1. Combine 1 cup flour, the sugar, salt, and yeast in a large bowl. Stir in the bran.
2. Combine the milk, water, honey, and butter in a saucepan and heat until warm, 120 to 130 degrees. Pour into the dry ingredients and beat at medium speed with an electric mixer, for 2 minutes, scraping the bowl occasionally.
3. Add the eggs, wheat germ, and enough of the remaining flour to make a thick batter.
4. Beat at high speed for 2 minutes. Stir in enough of the remaining flour to make a soft dough. Turn out onto a lightly floured board and knead until the dough is smooth and elastic, about 10 minutes.
5. Put the dough in a buttered bowl and turn to grease top. Cover and let rise in a warm place until doubled in bulk, about 45 minutes.
6. Punch the dough down. Turn onto the board. Divide the dough in half. Shape each half into a loaf and put in an oiled 8½- by 4½- by 2½-inch loaf pan. Cover and let rise in a warm place until doubled in bulk, about 60 minutes.
7. Preheat the oven to 375 degrees.
8. Bake in the lower half of the oven for 30 to 35 minutes, or until the loaves sound hollow when tapped on the bottom. Cool on wire racks.
Yield: Two loaves.

4½ to 5½ cups unbleached white flour or bread flour
2 tablespoons brown sugar
2 teaspoons salt
2 tablespoons dry active yeast
2 cups whole bran
1 cup milk
½ cup water
2 tablespoons honey
⅓ cup butter
2 eggs, lightly beaten
¼ cup wheat germ

BUTTERMILK WHOLE GRAIN BREAD

6 cups whole wheat flour
1 tablespoon brown sugar
3 teaspoons salt
½ teaspoon baking soda
2 packages active dry yeast
2½ cups buttermilk
2½ cups water
⅔ cup vegetable oil or butter
2 cups *each* cracked wheat and rye flour, approximately

1. Put 4 cups whole wheat flour, the brown sugar, salt, baking soda, and yeast in very large bowl. Mix well.

2. Heat the buttermilk, water, and oil until very warm. Add to the dry ingredients and beat at medium speed of an electric mixer for 2 minutes. Add 2 cups whole wheat flour and beat at high speed for 2 minutes. Add enough cracked wheat and rye flour to make a firm dough.

3. Turn out onto a floured surface and knead for 10 minutes, or until elastic. Put in an oiled bowl and turn to oil the top. Cover with plastic wrap, allowing the wrap to touch the dough. Let rise in a warm place for 1 hour, or until doubled.

4. Punch the dough down and turn out on a floured surface. Cover with the same sheet of plastic wrap and let rest for 15 minutes.

5. Shape into four loaves and put in oiled 8- by 4- by 2-inch loaf pans. Let rise for 30 minutes or until doubled.

6. Preheat the oven to 375 degrees.

7. Bake the breads for about 35 minutes. Turn out on racks to cool.

Yield: Four loaves.

OATMEAL-DILL BREAD

2 cups whole wheat flour
2 tablespoons dry active yeast
¼ cup chopped onion
½ cup hot water
2 cups cream-style cottage cheese
Butter

1. Put the whole wheat flour and yeast in the large bowl of an electric mixer.

2. Combine the onion, water, cottage cheese, 3 tablespoons butter, the salt, sugar and eggs in the container of an electric blender or food processor. Blend or process until smooth. Add to the dry ingredients and beat for 2 minutes.

3. Stir in the oats, dill seeds, and un-bleached flour. Turn into a clean buttered bowl, cover, and let rise in a warm place until doubled in bulk, about 1 hour.

4. Stir down and turn into a well-buttered 1½-quart casserole. Let rise, uncovered, until almost doubled in bulk, about 45 minutes.

5. Preheat the oven to 350 degrees.

6. Bake for 35 minutes, or until the loaf sounds hollow when tapped on the bottom. Brush top with butter for a soft crust. Cool on a wire rack.

Yield: One loaf.

2 teaspoons salt
¼ cup brown sugar
2 eggs
1 cup quick-cooking or regular rolled oats
2 tablespoons dill seeds
1½ cups unbleached white flour or bread flour

GINGER-OATMEAL-MOLASSES BREAD

1. Mix 1 cup white flour, the whole wheat flour, oats, yeast, salt, brown sugar, and ginger in a large bowl.

2. Heat the milk, molasses, and oil until very warm. Stir into the dry ingredients. Then beat with an electric mixer at medium speed for 2 minutes.

3. Gradually stir in enough white flour to make a firm dough. Turn out on a floured surface and knead for 5 minutes, or until smooth and elastic. Put in an oiled bowl, turning to oil top.

4. Cover with a sheet of plastic wrap, allowing the wrap to touch dough. Let rise in warm place for 1 hour, or until doubled.

5. Turn out, punch the dough down, and let rest, covered with the same sheet of plastic, for 15 minutes. Then shape in a loaf and put in an oiled 9- by 5- by 3-inch loaf pan.

6. Let rise for 30 minutes, or until light.

7. Preheat the oven to 350 degrees.

8. Bake the bread for 35 minutes, or until well browned and done.

Yield: One loaf.

2½ to 3 cups unbleached white flour
½ cup whole wheat flour
½ cup quick rolled oats
1 package dry active yeast
¾ teaspoon salt
1 tablespoon brown sugar
1 teaspoon ground ginger
1 cup milk
¼ cup molasses
2 tablespoons vegetable oil

DELICIOUS OATMEAL BREAD

1½ cups boiling water
1 cup rolled oats
¾ cup molasses
3 tablespoons butter, softened
2 teaspoons salt
1 tablespoon dry active yeast
2 cups lukewarm water
8 cups unbleached white flour or bread flour, approximately
Butter

1. Pour the boiling water over the oats and let stand for 30 minutes.
2. Add the molasses, softened butter, and salt. Dissolve the yeast in the warm water and add to the oat mixture.
3. Beat, and work in, enough flour to make a medium-soft dough. Turn onto a floured board and knead until smooth, about 10 minutes.
4. Put the dough in a clean buttered bowl and turn to butter the top. Cover and let rise in a warm place until doubled in bulk, about 1 hour.
5. Turn onto the floured board and knead again.
6. Divide and shape the dough into 2 loaves and place in well-oiled 9- by 5- by 3-inch loaf pans. Cover and let rise until doubled in bulk, about 45 minutes.
7. Preheat the oven to 400 degrees.
8. Bake for 5 minutes, lower the oven temperature to 350 degrees, and bake for 40 minutes longer, or until the loaves sound hollow when tapped on the bottom. Cool on wire racks. Brush the tops of loaves with butter for a soft crust.
Yield: Two loaves.

WHOLE WHEAT POTATO-ONION BREAD

1 cup unbleached white flour
1 package dry active yeast
1 tablespoon brown sugar
¾ teaspoon salt
2 teaspoons dried tarragon, crumbled
½ cup milk

1. Mix the white flour, yeast, brown sugar, salt, and tarragon in a bowl.
2. Heat the milk, water, and oil until very warm. Stir into the first mixture. Then beat at medium speed with an electric mixer for 2 minutes.
3. Stir in the potatoes, sour cream, onion, and enough whole wheat flour to make a

firm dough. Turn out onto a floured surface and knead for 10 minutes, or until elastic. Put in an oiled bowl, turning to oil the top of the dough. Cover with a sheet of plastic wrap, allowing the wrap to touch the dough.

4. Let rise in a warm place for 45 minutes, or until doubled.

5. Punch the dough down, shape into a loaf, and put in an oiled 9- by 5- by 3-inch loaf pan.

6. Let rise for 30 minutes, or until light.

7. Preheat the oven to 375 degrees.

8. Bake for 30 to 35 minutes, or until done. Turn out on a wire rack to cool.

Yield: One loaf.

¼ cup water
1 tablespoon vegetable oil
¾ cup unseasoned mashed potatoes
¼ cup sour cream
½ cup finely minced onion
1 to 1½ cups whole wheat flour, approximately

WHOLE WHEAT PIZZA CRUST

1. In a medium-sized bowl combine the water, yeast, honey, oil, and salt. Mix well and set in a warm place until it starts to bubble vigorously.

2. Stir in the whole wheat flour and dry milk. Gather together, kneading in enough of the extra flour to make a soft dough that can be kneaded on a lightly floured board.

3. Knead for 10 minutes, or until the dough is smooth and elastic. Divide in half and stretch or roll each half into a 12-inch circle to fit a pizza pan.

4. Bake on the bottom shelf of a 400-degree oven for 10 minutes. Top with sauce and toppings as desired and bake for 10 minutes longer, sprinkle with cheese and bake for 5 minutes longer.

Yield: Two pizzas; twelve servings.

Note: Use homemade tomato sauce (see page 397) and sautéed mushrooms, roasted peppers, mozzarella, and Parmesan cheese.

1 cup very warm water
1 envelope, or 1 tablespoon dry active yeast
1 teaspoon honey
1 tablespoon vegetable oil
1 teaspoon salt
1½ cups whole wheat flour
⅓ cup non-fat dry milk powder
½ cup whole wheat flour, approximately

ROUND ALMOND-CRACKED WHEAT LOAF

½ cup cracked wheat
Water
¾ cup (4 ounces) whole
  almonds
1 package dry active yeast
¼ cup non-fat dry milk
  powder
¾ teaspoon salt
2¼ to 2½ cups whole wheat
  flour
¼ cup vegetable oil
¼ cup unsulphured
  molasses

1. Combine the cracked wheat and 1 cup water in saucepan. Bring to a boil, cover, reduce heat, and cook, stirring occasionally, for 10 minutes, or until the wheat is tender and the water is absorbed. Set aside to cool.

2. Grind the almonds in blender or food processor or chop very fine.

3. In a medium-sized bowl mix the yeast, dry milk, salt, and 1 cup whole wheat flour. Add ½ cup very warm water, the oil, and molasses. Beat at medium speed with electric mixer for 2 minutes. Add 1¼ cups more flour and beat at high speed for 2 minutes. Stir in the almonds, cracked wheat, and enough additional flour to make a firm dough.

4. Turn out onto floured surface and knead for about 10 minutes. Put in an oiled bowl and turn to oil the top. Cover with a sheet of plastic wrap, allowing the wrap to touch the dough. Let rise in a warm place for 1½ hours or until light (bread will not double).

5. Turn out, punch down, and shape into a ball. Put on an oiled baking sheet and cover with the same sheet of plastic. Let rise for 30 minutes or until light. Slash across the top with a sharp knife in three places.

6. Preheat the oven to 400 degrees.

7. Bake for 20 minutes or until the loaf sounds hollow when tapped on the bottom. Cool on a wire rack. Delicious toasted.

Yield: One round loaf.

MIXED-GRAIN BREAD

1. Combine the milk and butter and set aside until lukewarm.

2. Sprinkle the dry active yeast over the warm water and stir to dissolve.

3. When the milk mixture is lukewarm, stir in the yeast mixture, egg, salt, honey, and molasses. Mix well.

4. Stir in the unbleached white flour, rye flour, and buckwheat flour and beat very hard for several minutes. Beat in the wheat germ, oats, and brewer's yeast and beat or knead well.

5. Add enough whole wheat flour to make a dough that can be kneaded on a board but is slightly sticky. Turn onto a floured board and knead until smooth and not sticky, about 15 minutes.

6. Put the dough in a clean, buttered bowl and turn to butter the top of the dough. Cover and let rise in a warm place until doubled in bulk, about 1½ hours.

7. Punch the dough down, knead briefly, then divide dough in half. Shape each half into a loaf and place in a well-oiled 8½- by 4½- by 2½-inch loaf pan. Cover and let rise until doubled in bulk, about 45 minutes.

8. Preheat the oven to 375 degrees.

9. Bake for 40 to 45 minutes, or until the loaves sound hollow when tapped on the bottom. Cool on a wire rack.

Yield: Two loaves.

1½ cups milk, scalded
2 tablespoons butter
1 tablespoon dry active yeast
¼ cup lukewarm water
1 egg, lightly beaten
2 teaspoons salt
2 tablespoons honey
2 tablespoons molasses
1 cup unbleached white flour
1 cup rye flour
½ cup buckwheat flour
¾ cup wheat germ
¾ cup rolled oats
3 tablespoons brewer's yeast
2 cups whole wheat flour, approximately

SWEET POTATO BREAD

1 cup unbleached white
  flour
1 package dry active yeast
1 teaspoon salt
½ cup milk
½ cup water
½ cup mashed cooked
  sweet potato
1 tablespoon vegetable oil
½ cup wheat germ
1½ cups whole wheat flour

1. Mix the white flour, yeast, and salt together.
2. Heat the milk, water, and sweet potato until very warm.
3. Add to the dry ingredients and beat with electric mixer at medium speed for 2 minutes.
4. Stir in the oil and wheat germ, then add enough whole wheat flour to make a firm dough.
5. Turn out onto a lightly floured surface and knead for 10 minutes, or until smooth and satiny.
6. Put in an oiled bowl, turning to oil the top. Cover with plastic wrap, allowing the wrap to touch the dough.
7. Let rise in warm place for 45 minutes, or until doubled.
8. Punch the dough down, then shape into a loaf and put in an oiled 8- by 4- by 2-inch loaf pan.
9. Let rise for 30 minutes, or until light.
10. Preheat the oven to 375 degrees.
11. Bake the bread for 35 minutes, or until done. Turn out and cool on a wire rack.
Yield: One loaf.

RAISIN PUMPERNICKEL

1. Stir the cold water into the cornmeal in a saucepan and heat, stirring, over medium heat until the mixture comes to a boil and thickens.

2. Remove from the heat and stir in the salt, molasses, and oil. Cool to lukewarm.

3. Sprinkle the yeast over the warm water and stir to dissolve. Add the honey and let stand in a warm place for 10 minutes.

4. Add the yeast mixture to the cornmeal mixture. Stir in 2 cups each whole wheat flour and rye flour to form a soft dough.

5. Turn the mixture onto a board dusted with some of the remaining flour. Knead the dough, gradually incorporating enough of the remaining flours to make a non-sticky dough. Knead for 10 minutes, or until very smooth and satiny.

6. Knead in the raisins. Place the dough in a clean oiled bowl, turn the dough to oil the top lightly. Cover and let rise in a warm place until doubled in bulk, about 1 hour.

7. Punch the dough down and divide in half. Shape each half into a well-rounded loaf and put on an oiled baking sheet dusted with cornmeal.

8. Cover and let rise until doubled in bulk, about 45 minutes.

9. Preheat the oven to 375 degrees.

10. Bake for 45 minutes, or until done. Rub the surface with butter for a soft crust or place in the draft from a window for a crisp crust. Cool on wire racks.

Yield: Two loaves.

2¼ cups cold water
¾ cup stoneground cornmeal
2 teaspoons salt
½ cup molasses
2 tablespoons vegetable oil
2 tablespoons dry active yeast
¼ cup lukewarm water
2 teaspoons honey
3 to 3½ cups whole wheat flour
3 to 3½ cups rye flour
1 cup raisins
Butter, optional

RYE BREAD

4⅓ cups stoneground whole wheat flour
1 cup rye flour
1 cup rye meal (coarsely ground rye flour)
⅓ cup soy flour
⅓ cup wheat germ
1 tablespoon salt
2 tablespoons caraway seeds
1 tablespoon dry active yeast
2½ cups lukewarm water
⅓ cup molasses
Soy oil

1. In a large bowl, combine the whole wheat flour, rye flour, rye meal, soy flour, wheat germ, salt, and caraway seeds. Mix very well.

2. Dissolve the yeast in ½ cup of water. Mix the remaining water with the molasses. Add the yeast mixture to the molasses mixture.

3. Add the yeast-molasses mixture to the dry ingredients and mix well. The mixture will appear sticky at first but as it is kneaded it will gradually leave the sides of the bowl clean.

4. Continue to knead the bread in the bowl, adding only a minimum of whole wheat flour, until the dough is smooth and satiny.

5. Remove the dough to a lightly floured board and knead for 3 to 4 minutes longer. (Long kneading is essential to success in all whole grain breads.)

6. Put dough in a clean buttered bowl and turn to butter the top of the dough. Cover and let rise in a warm place until doubled in bulk, about 1½ hours. Turn out onto a floured board and divide into 4 pieces.

7. Knead each portion and form into an oval-shaped loaf. Cut slashes at an angle on the top and place on oiled baking sheets. Brush the outside of the loaves with oil, cover, and place in a warm place to rise until doubled in bulk, about 1 hour.

8. Preheat the oven to 350 degrees.

9. Bake for 45 minutes, or until the loaves sound hollow when tapped on the bottom. Cool on wire racks.

Yield: Four loaves.

ONE-BOWL WHEAT GERM BREAD

1. In a bowl, mix together the rice flour, whole wheat flour, and unbleached flour very well.

2. In the large bowl of an electric mixer, mix 1 cup of the flour mixture with the salt, wheat germ, and dry yeast. Stir in the oil.

3. While beating at medium speed, gradually add the hot water and honey. Beat for 2 minutes at high speed, scraping the bowl occasionally.

4. Add ½ cup of the flour mixture, or enough flour mixture to make a thick batter. Beat for 2 minutes at high speed.

5. Stir in enough of the remaining flour mixture to make a stiff dough. Turn onto a floured broad and knead until the dough is smooth and elastic, about 10 minutes.

6. Split the dough into two pieces and form each into a round ball. Put on an oiled baking sheet. Cover and let rise in a warm place until doubled in bulk, about 1 hour.

7. Preheat the oven to 350 degrees.

8. Bake loaves for 20 to 25 minutes. Cool on wire racks.

Yield: Two small loaves.

Note: This bread has a texture much like that of shortcake.

1 cup brown rice flour
1 cup whole wheat flour
1 cup unbleached white flour or bread flour
2 teaspoons salt
½ cup wheat germ
2 tablespoons dry active yeast
2 tablespoons soy oil
1¼ cups very hot water
2 tablespoons honey

FOUR-GRAIN BREAD

¼ teaspoon dry active
  yeast
2 cups lukewarm water
3 to 4 cups whole wheat
  flour, approximately
½ cup rye flour
½ cup soy flour
½ cup cornmeal
½ cup buckwheat flour
2 teaspoons salt
1 tablespoon corn or soy
  oil

1. In the evening, sprinkle the yeast into ½ cup of the water and let stand.

2. In the meantime, place ½ cup whole wheat flour, the rye flour, soy flour, cornmeal, and buckwheat flour into a large enamel or glass bowl. Mix thoroughly.

3. Add the salt, oil, and remaining water. The mixture should form a heavy batter. Stir the yeast mixture and add it to the batter. Beat the mixture very well.

4. Cover with a cloth and a tight-fitting cover to prevent a crust from forming. Set in a warm place and let stand overnight.

5. Next day, stir down with a wooden spoon and stir in enough of the remaining whole wheat flour to form a dough that can no longer be stirred.

6. Turn onto a floured board and knead until smooth and elastic, using only enough flour to prevent sticking to the fingers. This will take at least 20 to 30 minutes. The dough should be smooth and have a consistency similar to your earlobe.

7. Shape the dough into a loaf and place in a well-oiled 9- by 5- by 3-inch loaf pan. Turn to oil the top. Prick three times with a fork, cover, and set in a warm place to rise for 1½ hours.

8. Preheat the oven to 275 degrees.

9. Bake for 1½ hours, or until bread comes out of the pan easily. Cool on a wire rack. For long storage, place in a plastic bag in the refrigerator. Then the bread will have to be toasted or fried.

Yield: One loaf.

Note: This is a heavy-textured bread.

THREE-GRAIN BREAD

1. In a large bowl mix 2 cups flour, corn-meal, salt, baking soda, and dry yeast. Add the butter.

2. Gradually add the hot water and honey and beat for 2 minutes at medium speed with an electric mixer. Add ½ cup more flour and beat for 2 minutes longer.

3. Stir in rice and enough extra flour to make a stiff dough. Turn out onto a lightly floured board and knead for 10 minutes, or until smooth and satiny. Put in an oiled bowl and turn to oil the top. Cover and let rise in a warm place until doubled in volume, about 1 hour.

4. Punch the dough down and turn onto floured board. Halve dough, cover, and let rest for 10 minutes. Roll each half into a 9-inch round. Put on an oiled baking sheet. Cover and let rise in a warm place until doubled in bulk, about 1¼ hours.

5. Preheat the oven to 375 degrees.

6. Using the handle of a wooden spoon, make deep indentations in the rounds at 1-inch intervals. Brush loaves with beaten egg. Bake for 35 minutes, or until the loaves sound hollow when tapped on the bottom. Cool on wire racks.

Yield: Two loaves.

6½ to 7½ cups unsifted unbleached flour
1 cup white cornmeal
2 teaspoons salt
¼ teaspoon baking soda
2 packages dry active yeast
¼ cup butter, softened
2 cups hot tap water (120 to 130 degrees)
½ cup honey
2 cups cooked brown rice, at room temperature (see page 228)
1 egg, beaten

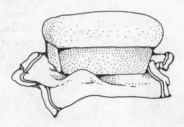

SEEDED HERB BRAID

1 cup wheat germ
2 to 2½ cups unbleached
white flour
1 package dry active yeast
2 tablespoons brown
sugar
¾ teaspoon salt
½ teaspoon dried
marjoram
½ teaspoon dried oregano
½ cup milk
½ cup water
¼ cup vegetable oil
3 eggs
½ cup whole wheat flour
Celery seed

1. Mix the wheat germ, 1 cup white flour, the yeast, brown sugar, salt, and herbs in a large bowl.
2. Heat the milk, water, and oil until very warm. Stir into first mixture. Add 2 eggs and beat at medium speed of an electric mixer for 2 minutes.
3. Stir in the whole wheat flour and enough additional white flour to make a firm dough. Turn out onto a floured surface and knead for 5 minutes, or until smooth and elastic.
4. Put in an oiled bowl, turning to oil the top. Cover with a sheet of plastic wrap, allowing the wrap to touch the dough. Let rise in a warm place for 45 minutes or until doubled.
5. Punch the dough down, cut off one-fourth and divide in three parts. Shape each into a 10-inch rope and braid.
6. Shape remaining dough into a loaf and put in an oiled 9- by 5- by 3-inch loaf pan.
7. Top with the braid and press down slightly. Cover and let rise until double in bulk. Brush with the remaining egg mixed with 1 tablespoon water. Sprinkle with celery seed.
8. Preheat the oven to 375 degrees.
9. Bake the bread for 25 to 30 minutes, or until done. If too brown cover with foil for the last 10 minutes. Turn out on a wire rack to cool.
Yield: One loaf.

CRACKED WHEAT BREAD

1. Put the cracked wheat in a very large bowl and cover with 4 cups of boiling water. Stir in the butter, brown sugar, and salt. Cool to lukewarm.

2. Dissolve the yeast in 1⅓ cups warm water and stir into the first mixture.

3. Gradually stir in enough whole wheat flour to make a firm dough.

4. Turn out onto a floured surface and knead for 10 minutes, or until elastic. Put in an oiled bowl, turning to oil the top. Cover with a sheet of plastic wrap, allowing the plastic to touch the dough.

5. Let rise in warm place for 1½ hours, or until doubled.

6. Turn the dough out and punch down. Let rest, covered with same sheet of plastic, for 15 minutes. Then shape into 4 loaves and put in oiled 8- by 4- by 2-inch loaf pans (9- by 5- by 3-inch pans can also be used).

7. Let rise for 30 minutes, or until light.

8. Preheat the oven to 375 degrees.

9. Bake for 30 minutes, or until well browned and done.

Yield: Four loaves.

3 cups cracked wheat
Water
3 tablespoons butter or vegetable oil
1 tablespoon brown sugar
1 tablespoon salt
3 packages dry active yeast
8 to 9 cups whole wheat flour

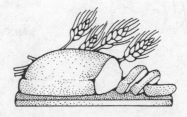

WHOLE WHEAT, RAISIN, AND OATS BREAD

2 envelopes dry active
yeast
3 cups very warm water
1 cup raisins
⅓ cup molasses
¼ cup vegetable oil
1 tablespoon salt
⅔ cup rolled oats
7 to 8 cups whole wheat
flour

1. Sprinkle the yeast into 2 cups very warm water in a large bowl. Stir until the yeast dissolves. Combine the remaining very warm water with the raisins in a small bowl.

2. Stir the molasses into the yeast mixture. Set in a warm place until mixture bubbles vigorously, about 15 minutes.

3. Stir in the raisins and water, oil, salt, rolled oats, and 4 cups flour. Beat until smooth and gradually stir in 3 more cups flour to make a stiff dough.

4. Turn the dough out onto a lightly floured board and knead until smooth and elastic, about 10 minutes.

5. Put dough in a greased or oiled bowl and turn to bring the oiled side up. Cover and let stand in a warm place for 1 hour, or until doubled in bulk.

6. Punch the dough down, turn onto a floured board, and knead a few times. Divide in half, cover with the bowl and let rest for 10 minutes. Shape into 2 loaves and place in oiled 9- by 5- by 3-inch loaf pans. Let rise in a warm place for 45 minutes, or until doubled in bulk.

7. Preheat the oven to 350 degrees.

8. Bake for 50 minutes, or until golden and hollow when tapped on the bottom. Cool on wire racks.

Yield: Two loaves.

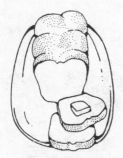

SPROUTED WHOLE WHEAT BREAD

1. Pour 1 cup water into a large mixing bowl. Sprinkle the yeast over the water and set aside for 5 minutes.

2. Stir to dissolve the yeast. Add the remaining water, the salt, honey, and oil and mix well.

3. Stir in the unbleached white flour and beat the dough until it is smooth and elastic. Cover and let rise in a warm place until doubled in bulk, about 45 minutes.

4. Stir in the ground sprouts and enough of the whole wheat flour to make a medium-soft dough. It will be slightly sticky.

5. Turn the dough out onto a floured board and knead until very smooth and elastic, about 10 minutes. Put in a clean oiled bowl and turn to oil the top of the dough. Cover and let rise in a warm place until doubled in bulk, about 1 hour.

6. Turn onto the floured board and knead briefly. Divide the dough in half and shape into two loaves. Put in well-oiled 9- by 5- by 3-inch loaf pans, cover, and let rise until doubled in bulk, about 45 minutes.

7. Preheat the oven to 375 degrees.

8. Bake for 25 minutes, lower the oven temperature to 300 degrees, and bake for 35 minutes longer, or until the loaves sound hollow when tapped on the bottom. Cool on wire racks.

Yield: Two loaves.

3 cups lukewarm water
2 tablespoons dry active yeast
1 tablespoon salt
¼ cup honey
3 tablespoons vegetable oil
3½ cups unbleached white flour or bread flour
2 cups wheat sprouts (see page 201), ground in a meat grinder
2 cups whole wheat flour, approximately

NO-KNEAD QUICK WHOLE WHEAT BREAD

2 tablespoons dry active yeast
3 cups lukewarm water
¼ cup molasses
¼ cup brown sugar
6 cups whole wheat flour
½ cup soy flour
¾ cup non-fat dry milk powder
3 tablespoons wheat germ
2 tablespoons brewer's yeast
2 teaspoons salt
¼ cup oil

1. Mix together the yeast and warm water. Add the molasses and sugar and let stand for 10 minutes, or until yeast dissolves and mixture starts to bubble.

2. Meanwhile, mix together the whole wheat flour, soy flour, dry milk, wheat germ, brewer's yeast, and salt.

3. Stir the yeast mixture and add half the flour mixture and the oil. Beat vigorously and add only as much additional flour mixture as can be beaten in easily.

4. Continue to beat the mixture until it is smooth and elastic, at least 10 minutes. With the spoon and the hands, work in the remaining flour mixture.

5. Turn into two well oiled 8½- by 4¼- by 2½-inch loaf pans. Cover and let rise until mixture has doubled in bulk, about 45 minutes.

6. Preheat the oven to 375 degrees.

7. Bake for 50 minutes, or until the loaves sound hollow when tapped on the bottom. Cool on wire racks.

Yield: Two loaves.

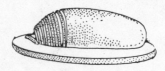

HEARTY BREAD

1. Dissolve the dry active yeast in the water. Stir in the molasses and oil. Stir in the rye flour and mix well. Stir in enough whole wheat flour to make a batter which can be beaten. Beat 300 strokes, or for 10 minutes. This develops the gluten and is very important.

2. Gradually work in, one at a time, the salt, dry milk, brewer's yeast, bulghur, cornmeal, oats, sesame seeds, sunflower seed kernels, whole wheat berries, and raisins. Mix well.

3. Add enough of the remaining whole wheat flour to make a moderately stiff dough that just pulls from the sides of the bowl.

4. Put the dough in a clean oiled bowl, cover, and let rise until doubled in bulk, about 2 hours. Punch down, turn onto a floured board, and knead lightly.

5. Divide the dough in half, shape each half into a loaf and put in well-oiled 9- by 5- by 3-inch loaf pans. Butter tops.

6. Let rise until doubled in bulk.

7. Preheat the oven to 375 degrees.

8. Bake for 50 minutes, or until the loaves sound hollow when tapped on the bottom. Cool on wire racks.

Yield: Two loaves.

3 tablespoons dry active yeast
4 cups lukewarm water
⅔ cup molasses
2 tablespoons vegetable oil
1 cup rye flour
6 to 8 cups whole wheat flour
1 tablespoon salt
1 cup non-fat dry milk powder
3 tablespoons brewer's yeast
½ cup fine bulghur wheat
½ cup stoneground yellow cornmeal
½ cup rolled oats
½ cup sesame seeds
½ cup sunflower seed kernels
½ cup whole wheat berries
1 cup raisins
Butter

GOLDEN BRAIDS

3 tablespoons dry active yeast
¾ cup lukewarm water
½ cup plus 2 tablespoons brown sugar
½ cup butter
1 cup boiling water
3 tablespoons vegetable oil
1 tablespoon salt
¼ cup honey
7 eggs
9 cups unbleached white flour or bread flour, approximately
1 cup wheat germ
1 tablespoon water
Sesame seeds or poppy seeds, optional

1. Dissolve the yeast in the warm water in a quart container. Add 2 tablespoons sugar and let stand in a warm place.

2. Meanwhile, put the butter in a large mixing bowl of an electric mixer and add the boiling water. When the butter is melted, add the oil, salt, remaining sugar, and the honey.

3. Add 6 eggs, one at a time, with the mixer set at low speed. Add the yeast mixture and beat.

4. Add 4 cups of flour and the wheat germ and mix well. Add enough of the remaining flour to make a cohesive dough that can be kneaded.

5. Turn out onto a floured board and knead, drawing in just enough flour to prevent sticking, until smooth and satiny, about 10 minutes.

6. Put the dough in a clean buttered bowl, turn to butter top, cover, and let rise in a warm place until doubled in bulk, about 1 hour.

7. Punch the dough down and divide it into 4 pieces. Divide each of the 4 pieces into 3 and form each of the thirds into a rope by rolling between the palms of the hands. Each rope should be about 12 inches long.

8. Form three ropes into a tight braid. Repeat with other ropes.

9. Place each braid in a greased and floured 9- by 5- by 3-inch loaf pan. Cover and let rise until dough reaches top of pan, about 1 hour.

10. Preheat the oven to 350 degrees.

11. Lightly beat the remaining egg with 1 tablespoon water.

12. Brush the tops of the braids with the egg mixture and sprinkle with the sesame

seeds, if desired. Bake for 30 minutes.
Rearrange the loaves during baking if they
are not browning evenly. Turn oven off
and wait 5 minutes before removing the
loaves from oven.

13. The loaves should shake free from the
pans. Put each loaf on a wire rack to cool.
When cool, put in a plastic bag to freeze.
Yield: Four loaves.

PANCAKES, WAFFLES, & CRÊPES

A good breakfast to start the day doesn't have to be bacon and eggs or come out of a package. Tempt the family into sitting down together with fruit-filled cottage cheese pancakes, nut-filled waffles, or baked French toast served with honey and real maple syrup.

CHUNKY APPLE PANCAKES

1. Mix the white flour, whole wheat flour, baking powder, salt, and brown sugar together.
2. Peel and core apples and cut in thin slices. Then cut the slices into ½-inch pieces.
3. Beat the eggs and milk and add with the oil to dry ingredients. Mix well. Fold in the apple pieces.
4. Bake on a preheated oiled griddle until browned on both sides (the apples will remain crisp). Serve hot with maple syrup.

Yield: Two dozen three-inch pancakes.

1 cup unbleached white flour
1 cup whole wheat flour
3 teaspoons baking powder
½ teaspoon salt
1 tablespoon brown sugar
2 medium-sized apples
2 eggs
1⅔ cups milk
3 tablespoons vegetable oil
Maple syrup

BREAD CRUMB PANCAKES

1. Heat milk and pour over crumbs. Let stand for 15 minutes.
2. Mix the flour, baking powder, and salt.
3. Add to the crumb mixture with the egg, honey, and oil. Beat until well blended and free of lumps.
4. Bake on a hot, oiled griddle until browned on one side. Turn and brown on other side. Serve hot with syrup.

Yield: Two to two-and-one-half dozen three-inch pancakes.

1½ cups milk
1½ cups soft crumbs from day-old whole wheat or other whole-grain bread, preferably homemade
½ cup whole wheat flour
2 teaspoons baking powder
½ teaspoon salt
1 egg, well beaten
2 tablespoons honey
1 tablespoon vegetable oil
Syrup or other preferred topping (see page 312)

BUTTERMILK CORN PANCAKES

½ cup whole wheat flour
¾ cup cornmeal
1 tablespoon brown
  sugar, optional
2 teaspoons baking
  powder
½ teaspoon baking soda
½ teaspoon salt
1¼ cups buttermilk
1 egg, lightly beaten
1 tablespoon vegetable oil
  Fruit butter, maple
  syrup, or honey

1. Combine the whole wheat flour, corn-meal, brown sugar, baking powder, baking soda, and salt in a medium-sized bowl. Add the buttermilk, egg, and oil and mix until smooth.
2. Spoon 3 tablespoons of the batter onto a hot (400-degree), oiled griddle, repeat to make 12 pancakes. Turn the pancakes when the underside is brown and then brown the second side. Serve with fruit butter, maple syrup, or honey.
Yield: Four servings.

DELICIOUS NUTRITIOUS PANCAKES

1 cup sifted whole wheat
  flour
1 cup sifted unbleached
  white flour
1 cup sifted soy flour
½ cup brown rice flour
½ cup peanut flour
1 cup non-fat dry milk
  powder
4 teaspoons baking
  powder
1 teaspoon salt
4 eggs
⅔ cup safflower oil
2 cups water,
  approximately
  Butter, maple syrup, or
  honey

1. Sift together twice the whole wheat flour, unbleached white flour, soy flour, rice flour, peanut flour, dry milk, baking powder, and salt.
2. Blend the eggs, oil, and 2 cups water in an electric blender, or beat well. Stir the liquid ingredients into the dry ingredients until the mixture is of heavy cream consistency, adding extra water as necessary.
3. Ladle onto a hot, oiled griddle and cook until browned. Turn and brown the second side. Serve with butter, maple syrup, or honey.
Yield: About twenty pancakes.

RAISED WHEAT PANCAKES

1. Dissolve the yeast in the warm skim milk. Add the molasses, eggs, and corn oil.
2. Add the remaining ingredients and mix until blended. Ladle onto a hot, oiled griddle and cook until bubbles form; turn and brown the second side.
Yield: About ten pancakes.

2 tablespoons dry active yeast
1½ cups lukewarm skim milk
1 tablespoon blackstrap or unsulphured molasses
2 eggs, lightly beaten
2 tablespoons corn oil
1 cup whole wheat flour
½ cup wheat germ
⅓ cup non-fat dry milk powder
1 teaspoon salt

BUCKWHEAT PANCAKES

1. In a bowl, mix together the buckwheat flour, wheat germ, whole wheat flour, sugar, and baking powder.
2. Stir in the eggs, oil, and enough water or milk to make a batter the consistency of thick heavy cream. Ladle the mixture onto a hot, oiled griddle. When holes appear on the surface of the pancakes, turn to brown second side.
Yield: About eight large pancakes.

¾ cup buckwheat flour
½ cup wheat germ
¼ cup whole wheat flour
3 tablespoons brown sugar
1¾ teaspoons double-acting baking powder
2 eggs, lightly beaten
3 tablespoons peanut oil
Milk or water

EASY WHEAT PANCAKES

1. In bowl, mix the milk, egg, sugar, flour, baking soda, salt, and oil together. Bake by ladleful on a hot, oiled griddle. Turn when bubbles form on top of the pancakes. Brown the second side.
2. Serve with syrup or honey.
Yield: About one dozen pancakes.

1 cup sour milk or buttermilk
1 egg
1 tablespoon brown sugar
1 cup whole wheat flour
1 teaspoon baking soda
½ teaspoon salt
1 tablespoon oil or melted butter
Maple syrup or honey

BARLEY FLOUR PANCAKES

1 egg, lightly beaten
⅓ cup sour cream
⅓ cup buttermilk
1 cup barley flour
1½ teaspoons baking powder
1 teaspoon salt
1 teaspoon brown sugar
Butter and honey

1. Beat the egg with the sour cream and buttermilk.
2. Sift together the barley flour, baking powder, salt, and sugar. Stir in the egg mixture and let stand for 2 minutes.
3. Ladle onto a hot, oiled griddle and cook until browned and puffy. Turn to brown the second side. Serve with butter and honey.
Yield: About eight pancakes.

WHEAT GERM PANCAKES

6 eggs
5 tablespoons cottage cheese
⅔ cup wheat germ
¼ teaspoon pure vanilla extract
1 tablespoon butter
Maple syrup or honey

1. Put the eggs, cheese, wheat germ, and vanilla into the container of an electric blender or food processor and blend or process for 30 seconds.
2. Melt the butter in a 10-inch skillet. Pour in the egg mixture and cook over medium heat until browned on the bottom; turn and brown on the other side. Serve with syrup or honey.
Yield: Four servings.

COTTAGE CHEESE PANCAKES

1 cup cottage cheese
2 eggs, lightly beaten
2 tablespoons whole wheat flour or unbleached white flour
¼ cup wheat germ
1 tablespoon butter, melted
Homemade applesauce (see page 328)
Ground cinnamon

1. Mix the cottage cheese, eggs, flour, wheat germ, and butter together until well blended.
2. Fry on a hot, oiled griddle until browned on one side. Turn and brown the other side.
3. Serve with applesauce, sprinkled with cinnamon.
Yield: About six pancakes.

STRAWBERRY PANCAKES

1. In a bowl, mix together the yogurt and eggs. Stir in the oil, salt, and flour.

2. Stir in enough milk to make a thick pancake batter consistency. Heat an oiled griddle and spoon quarter cups of the batter onto griddle. Cook until browned on one side; turn and brown the other side.

3. Slice the strawberries into a small saucepan. Add the honey and heat gently to warm but do not allow to come close to boiling.

4. For each serving, place a pancake on a warm plate, top with some strawberries, then another pancake; garnish with more strawberries.

Yield: Six servings.

1 cup plain yogurt (see page 324)
2 eggs, lightly beaten
3 tablespoons vegetable oil
¼ teaspoon salt
2 cups whole wheat flour
Milk
1 pint strawberries
Honey to taste

PUMPKIN CORNCAKES

1. Gradually add the cornmeal to the boiling water while stirring vigorously. Add the milk and stir until smooth.

2. Stir in the pumpkin. Sift together the flour, baking powder, and salt and stir into cornmeal mixture.

3. Stir in 1 tablespoon honey and the egg. Ladle the mixture onto a preheated and oiled griddle to form small cakes. Bake until bubbles form on the surface; turn and bake until second side is browned. Serve with syrup or honey.

Yield: Six servings.

½ cup stoneground cornmeal
1 cup boiling water
⅞ cup evaporated milk
¼ cup cooked pumpkin purée
1 cup whole wheat flour
2 teaspoons baking powder
¾ teaspoon salt
1 tablespoon honey
1 egg, beaten
Maple syrup or honey

LATKES OR POTATO PANCAKES

3 large potatoes
1 large onion
3 eggs
Salt to taste
2 tablespoons wheat germ
1 teaspoon unbleached
white flour
Vegetable oil
Sour cream

1. Grate the potatoes on a flat stainless steel grater. Grate the onion on a fine grater and add to the potatoes. Mix with the eggs. Alternately, the potatoes, onion, and eggs may be blended in an electric blender if divided into three batches.
2. Add salt, wheat germ, and flour to the potato mixture. Set aside while heating the oil. Add enough oil to just cover the bottom of a large, heavy skillet and heat.
3. Ladle the potato mixture by the tablespoon into the hot fat. Lower the heat slightly and fry quickly until browned; turn and brown other side. Drain on paper towels. Serve with sour cream.
Yield: Four servings.

POTATO PANCAKES

6 large potatoes, finely
grated into bowl of
water
3 eggs, lightly beaten
¼ cup soy grits
3 tablespoons chopped
parsley
2 small onions, finely
grated
1 teaspoon tamari (soy
sauce)
½ teaspoon salt
Vegetable oil for frying
Applesauce, cottage
cheese, and plain
yogurt (see page 324)

1. Squeeze the potatoes between the hands until dry. This removes the excess liquid and surface starch.
2. Combine the potatoes with the eggs, grits, parsley, onions, tamari, and salt and mix well.
3. Pour oil into a heavy skillet to a depth of ¼ inch. Heat the oil. Drop the potato mixture by ladles into the hot oil and fry until browned; turn to brown the second side. Drain on paper towels.
4. Serve with applesauce, cottage cheese, and yogurt.
Yield: Three or four servings.

WHOLE WHEAT PANCAKES

1. Wash the whole wheat thoroughly. Put the wheat and water in the container of an electric blender or food processor. Blend or process until smooth.
2. In a bowl, combine the dry milk, eggs, salt, sugar, corn oil, and baking powder. Mix well. Pour in the blended wheat mixture and stir to blend.
3. Bake on a preheated, lightly oiled griddle. Serve with honey or maple syrup. Yield: Four servings.

1 cup unground whole wheat
1⅓ cups water
1⅛ cups non-fat dry milk powder
2 eggs
1 teaspoon salt
1 tablespoon molasses
3 tablespoons corn oil
1 tablespoon baking powder
Honey or maple syrup

BAKED GERMAN PANCAKE

1. Preheat the oven to 450 degrees.
2. Put the eggs, milk, salt, and oil in the container of an electric blender or food processor and blend or process until well mixed.
3. In a bowl, combine the whole wheat flour, soy flour, and brewer's yeast. Pour in the egg mixture and beat until smooth. Pour into a cold, oiled 9- or 10-inch pie plate.
4. Bake for 10 minutes. Reduce the oven temperature to 350 degrees and bake for 10 minutes longer, or until done. Combine the remaining ingredients and spread over the top of the pancake. Yield: Four servings.

2 eggs
½ cup milk
⅛ teaspoon salt
1 tablespoon vegetable oil
1 cup whole wheat flour
½ teaspoon soy flour
1 teaspoon brewer's yeast
1 cup puréed cored peeled raw apples
¼ cup finely chopped walnuts
⅛ teaspoon grated nutmeg
¼ cup brown sugar
1 tablespoon honey or maple syrup

OLD-FASHIONED BUCKWHEAT HOT CAKES

2 cups lukewarm water
1 tablespoon dry active
  yeast
2 tablespoons brown
  sugar
2 cups buckwheat flour
1 cup unbleached white
  flour
1 cup milk, scalded and
  cooled to lukewarm
1 teaspoon salt

1. Mix together the warm water, yeast, and sugar and stir until dissolved.
2. Sift the buckwheat flour and unbleached flour together and add to the yeast mixture. Stir in the milk and salt. Beat until smooth.
3. Cover and set in a warm place to rise for 1 hour. The mixture will be light and fluffy. Stir well and bake on a hot, oiled griddle until browned; turn and brown the second side.

Yield: About two dozen hot cakes.

Note: To make the mixture overnight, use one-quarter of a cake of compressed yeast in place of the dry active yeast and add an extra ½ teaspoon salt.

WHOLE WHEAT CRÊPES I

½ cup whole wheat flour
½ teaspoon baking
  powder
⅛ teaspoon salt
1 egg
¾ cup milk, slightly
  warmed
1 tablespoon vegetable oil
  Additional oil for
  browning

1. Mix together the flour, baking powder, and salt.
2. Beat the egg until light. Gradually stir in the warm milk. Add the oil and beat until bubbly.
3. Stir into the dry ingredients to make a smooth batter.
4. Add a small amount of oil to a hot 6-inch skillet or crêpe pan.
5. Add about 3 tablespoons of the batter and swirl to cover skillet. Cook over medium heat until browned on one side. Turn and brown on the other side.
6. Repeat until all of batter is used. To serve, fill with creamed meat, fish, or vegetables.

Yield: Eight to ten crêpes.

WHOLE WHEAT CRÊPES II

1. Put all the ingredients, except the milk, in the container of an electric blender or food processor. Whirl or process until smooth. Chill for 30 minutes or longer.
2. Blend or whirl in enough milk to give the batter the consistency of heavy cream.
3. Test by heating a heavy 6-inch skillet. Oil the skillet lightly and add 3 to 4 tablespoons of batter. Swirl the pan to cover it evenly. (If the batter is too thick add more milk.) Cook until lightly browned on underside, flip, and brown the second side.

Yield: Twelve to sixteen crêpes.

Note: Fill crêpes with ratatouille (see page 147), creamed tuna, salmon, chicken, turkey, or mushrooms. Sprinkle with buttered whole wheat bread crumbs mixed with grated Parmesan and bake in a 375-degree oven for 20 minutes, or until hot.

1¼ cups buttermilk
¾ cup whole wheat flour
¼ cup wheat germ
1 egg
2 tablespoons vegetable oil
¼ teaspoon salt
½ cup milk, approximately

WHOLE WHEAT CRÊPES III

1. Put all the ingredients, with the exception of the oil for frying, in the container of an electric blender or food processor and blend or whirl until smooth. Let stand for 30 minutes or longer.
2. Heat a 6-inch skillet and oil well. Add 3 to 4 tablespoons batter and whirl skillet to give an even layer. If too thick, add water. Cook until lightly browned on bottom, flip and brown second side.

Yield: Twelve to sixteen crêpes.

1 cup skim milk
1 cup water
¼ cup non-fat dry milk powder
1 cup whole wheat flour
3 eggs
2 tablespoons vegetable oil
⅛ teaspoon salt
Vegetable oil for frying

FILLINGS FOR RAVIOLI AND CRÊPES

TOFU FILLING

1 tablespoon vegetable oil
1 medium-sized onion, finely chopped
2 cups (1 pound) crumbled tofu (see page 160)
1 tablespoon soy sauce
¼ cup chopped parsley
¼ cup freshly grated Parmesan cheese

1. In a small skillet, heat the oil and sauté the onion until tender but not browned.
2. Add the remaining ingredients and mix well.

Yield: Enough filling for sixteen crêpes or fifty ravioli.

RICOTTA FILLING

1 cup ricotta cheese
⅓ cup freshly grated Romano cheese
⅔ cup freshly grated Parmesan cheese
¼ cup chopped Italian parsley
1 egg yolk

Mix all ingredients together.

Yield: Enough filling for sixteen crêpes or fifty ravioli.

RICOTTA AND SPINACH FILLING

1 tablespoon vegetable oil
1 medium-sized onion, finely chopped
1 clove garlic, finely chopped
1 10-ounce package frozen chopped spinach, thawed and squeezed dry
1 cup ricotta cheese
1 tablespoon soy sauce
¼ teaspoon freshly ground black pepper
⅛ teaspoon grated nutmeg

In a small skillet, heat the oil and sauté the onion and garlic until tender but not browned. Place spinach in a medium-sized bowl. Add the onion, ricotta, soy sauce, pepper, and nutmeg.

Yield: Enough filling for sixteen crêpes or fifty ravioli.

WAFFLES

1. Sift into a bowl the flour, baking powder, and salt. Add the wheat germ.
2. Combine the egg yolks and oil and beat well. Gradually beat in the milk. Pour the milk mixture into the dry ingredients and mix lightly. Stir in the sunflower seed kernels and pumpkin seeds.
3. Beat the egg whites until stiff but not dry and fold into the batter. Drop the mixture onto a preheated and oiled waffle iron and bake until light brown. Serve with honey.
Yield: Four servings.

1¾ cups unbleached white flour
1 tablespoon baking powder
½ teaspoon salt
½ cup wheat germ
3 eggs, separated
¼ cup sunflower oil
1½ cups milk
½ cup chopped sunflower seed kernels
½ cup chopped pumpkin seeds
Honey

BLUEBERRY BRAN WAFFLES

1. Mix the white flour, whole wheat flour, bran, baking powder, and salt.
2. Beat the egg yolks with brown sugar, then stir in the milk and oil. Add the dry ingredients and mix just until moistened.
3. Beat the egg whites until stiff. Fold into the batter. Stir in berries.
4. Drop onto preheated, oiled waffle iron and bake until browned. Serve with syrup.
Yield: Four nine-inch square waffles.

⅔ cup unbleached white flour
⅔ cup whole wheat flour
¾ cup unprocessed bran
3 teaspoons baking powder
½ teaspoon salt
2 eggs, separated
¼ cup brown sugar
1½ cups milk
⅓ cup vegetable oil
½ cup blueberries
Syrup, honey, or other preferred topping (see page 312)

QUICK OAT WAFFLES

1 cup whole wheat flour
2 teaspoons baking
  powder
½ teaspoon salt
¾ cup quick rolled oats
2 eggs, separated
¼ cup vegetable oil
  Milk
  Syrup or honey

1. Mix the flour, baking powder, salt, and oats together.
2. Beat the egg yolks with the oil until blended. Add enough milk to make 1½ cups liquid.
3. Add to the dry ingredients and mix only enough to moisten.
4. Beat the egg whites until stiff and fold into batter.
5. Drop onto a preheated oiled waffle iron and bake until browned. Serve with syrup.
Yield: Three nine-inch square waffles.

WHOLE WHEAT WAFFLES

2 cups whole wheat flour
2 cups sifted soy flour
¾ cup cornmeal
2 teaspoons salt
1 cup wheat germ
6 eggs, well beaten
1 tablespoon plus 1
  teaspoon dry active
  yeast
1 cup lukewarm water
1 cup milk
1 cup vegetable oil
2 cups water,
  approximately
  Butter and maple syrup

1. In a large bowl, mix together the whole wheat flour, soy flour, cornmeal, salt, and wheat germ. Stir in the eggs.
2. Dissolve the yeast in the lukewarm water and add to flour mixture. Stir in the milk, oil, and enough water to make a waffle batter consistency. Let stand in a warm place until mixture shows signs of bubbling, about 15 minutes.
3. Cook the mixture in a lightly oiled, preheated waffle iron. Serve with butter and syrup.
Yield: Twenty large waffles.

RAISED WHOLE WHEAT WAFFLES

1. Put the water and yeast in a large mixing bowl and stir to dissolve the yeast. Let stand for 5 minutes in a warm place.
2. Add the milk, butter, salt, and sugar.
3. Beat in the flour and the eggs but do not overbeat (batter will be thin). Set the mixture in a warm place until mixture just begins to rise, about 15 minutes.
4. Cook the mixture in a preheated, oiled waffle iron.
Yield: About four large waffles.

½ cup lukewarm water
3 tablespoons dry active yeast
2 cups lukewarm water
¼ cup melted butter or vegetable oil
⅛ teaspoon salt
1 teaspoon brown sugar
2 cups whole wheat pastry flour
2 eggs, lightly beaten

OVEN FRENCH TOAST

1. Preheat the oven to 350 degrees.
2. Put the eggs, cottage cheese, and salt and pepper in the container of an electric blender or food processor. Blend or process until smooth.
3. Arrange the bread slices, buttered if you wish, in a buttered 13- by 9- by 2-inch baking dish or large shallow ovenproof dish.
4. Pour the egg-and-cheese mixture over bread and bake for 30 minutes, or until set and puffed. Serve with syrup or honey.
Yield: Six servings.

1 dozen eggs
1 pound cottage cheese
Salt and freshly ground black pepper to taste
6 slices homemade whole wheat cinnamon bread
Butter, optional
Maple syrup or honey

PANCAKE AND WAFFLE TOPPINGS

HONEY-ALMOND SPREAD

½ cup honey
¼ butter
½ cup heavy cream
½ cup ground unblanched almonds

Combine the honey, butter, and cream in a small saucepan and bring to a boil. Boil for 5 minutes or until mixture is consistency of thick syrup. Cool slightly. Stir in almonds.
Yield: About one and one-half cups.

HONEY-COCONUT SPREAD

¾ cup honey
2 tablespoons butter, melted
¾ cup unsweetened grated coconut, toasted (see note)

Combine all ingredients.
Yield: About one and one-quarter cups.
Note: To toast coconut, spread on a baking sheet and bake in a preheated 350-degree oven for 5 to 7 minutes, stirring or shaking often.

FRUITED HONEY SAUCE

3 pears or apples, peeled, cored, and finely diced
1 cup honey
1 teaspoon lemon juice
1 teaspoon butter
⅛ teaspoon ground cinnamon

Combine all ingredients in a small saucepan and cook slowly, stirring often, until fruit is tender.
Yield: About two cups.

MOLASSES AND ORANGE WAFFLE SAUCE

½ cup unsulphured molasses
¼ cup brown sugar
⅓ cup orange juice
¼ cup butter
1 tablespoon grated orange rind

Combine all the ingredients in a small saucepan and heat, stirring, until the mixture is smooth and well blended. Serve warm over waffles.
Yield: About one cup.

HONEY BUTTER

½ pound butter, softened
3 tablespoons honey

Mix honey and butter together until well blended. Pack into a crock or serving jar and chill. Use on pancakes, waffles, hot breads, and French toast.
Yield: About one cup.

PASTA & SAUCES

Homemade noodles and ravioli have always been the mark of a dedicated cook. Made with eggs and unbleached white flour or whole wheat flour, the noodles taste better, and cost less, than any store-bought product.

HOMEMADE PASTA

2 cups whole wheat flour,
    sifted if bran is not
    considered desirable
1 teaspoon salt
2 eggs
1 egg white
1 tablespoon olive oil
⅓ cup wheat germ
    Water
    Sifted whole wheat
    flour

1. Make a pile of 2 cups flour and the salt on a board. Make a well in the center and add the eggs, egg white, olive oil, and wheat germ.
2. With the fingers, gradually draw the flour into the wet ingredients, adding drops of water as it seems necessary to form the mixture into a ball of dough, or mix in a food processor.
3. Knead the dough, using a minimum of sifted flour on the board, until the dough is smooth and elastic, at least 10 minutes. Cover and let rest for 10 minutes.
4. Divide the dough in half and roll each half until it is very thin. Dust lightly with flour and let dry for 10 minutes.
5. Gently roll each rectangle of dough into a jelly roll shape and cut into ¼- to ½-inch widths. Unfold bundles and set aside to dry.
Yield: About one pound noodles.
Note: It is advisable to use unbleached white flour if making spaghetti, and the use of a pasta machine makes shaping the dough easier still. The whole wheat pasta can be shaped into ravioli and tortellini. Once they are dry, the whole wheat noodles can be frozen or can be stored for a short while in a closed container.

WHOLE WHEAT NOODLES

2 cups whole wheat flour
1 teaspoon salt
1 egg
2 egg yolks

1. Put the flour and salt in a pile on a board. Make a well in the center. Add egg, egg yolks, about 3 tablespoons water, and the oil to the well.

2. With the fingers, gradually mix the liquid ingredients into the flour, or mix in a food processor.

3. Add enough water to make a stiff dough that can be kneaded. Knead the dough on a lightly floured board very well. The dough should be satiny smooth.

4. Divide in half and roll each half into a rectangle about 12 by 24 inches. This is hard work, especially at the beginning, but it is important that the dough be rolled paper-thin. Let dry for 30 minutes. Dust lightly with flour.

5. Roll the rectangles from the long side like a jelly roll and cut into ⅛-inch-wide noodles. Cook immediately or spread the noodles out and let dry very well before storing.

Yield: About three-quarters pound noodles.

Note: If you are lucky enough to own a pasta machine, making noodles from this dough is a breeze.

3 to 4 tablespoons water, approximately
1 tablespoon vegetable oil

GREEN SAUCE AND NOODLES

1. Put the parsley and basil leaves in the container of an electric blender or food processor. Add the garlic, oil, butter, salt, and pepper and blend or process until smooth. Pour into a saucepan.

2. Warm, but do not allow to boil.

3. Pour over noodles or spaghetti. Sprinkle with cheese.

Yield: Four servings.

1 large bunch Italian parsley
1 large bunch fresh basil
3 cloves garlic
½ cup olive or vegetable oil
½ cup butter, melted
Salt and freshly ground black pepper to taste
1 pound homemade whole wheat noodles (see page 314) or spaghetti, cooked al dente and drained
Freshly grated Parmesan cheese

ANCHOVY SAUCE FOR PASTA

2 cups tightly packed
fresh basil leaves or
parsley
2 cloves garlic, crushed
⅓ cup olive oil
2 tablespoons walnut
pieces
1 28-ounce can tomatoes,
drained and chopped
1 2-ounce can anchovy
fillets, drained and
finely chopped
¼ teaspoon freshly ground
black pepper
3 tablespoons freshly
grated Parmesan cheese

1. Put the basil, garlic, oil, and walnuts in the container of an electric blender or food processor. Blend or process until smooth.
2. Transfer the basil mixture to a medium-sized saucepan. Add the tomatoes, anchovy fillets, and pepper. Bring to a boil, stirring, and simmer for 5 minutes. Serve over noodles with freshly grated Parmesan.

Yield: Enough sauce for 1 pound noodles or spaghetti. Four servings.

ASPARAGUS SAUCE

2 tablespoons butter
2 tablespoons olive or
vegetable oil
2 cloves garlic, finely
chopped
2 pounds asparagus
4 ripe tomatoes, peeled,
seeded, and chopped
½ teaspoon salt
¼ teaspoon freshly ground
black pepper
1½ teaspoons dried basil
¼ cup freshly grated
Parmesan cheese
¼ cup chopped parsley
½ cup pignoli nuts or
toasted walnuts
1 pound whole wheat
noodles (see page 314),
spaghetti, or macaroni,
cooked al dente and
drained

1. In a large heavy skillet heat the butter and oil and sauté the garlic and the stems of the asparagus, cut on the bias, into 1-inch lengths (reserve tips), until crisp-tender.
2. Add the tomatoes, asparagus tips, salt, pepper, and basil. Cook for 3 to 5 minutes.
3. Stir in the cheese, parsley, and nuts and toss with the pasta.

Yield: Four servings.

WHITE CLAM SAUCE

1. Heat the oil in a medium-sized saucepan and sauté the garlic until tender but not browned. Sprinkle with flour and cook for 1 minute.
2. Drain the clams and add the juice slowly to the garlic mixture, while stirring. Add the pepper and bring to a boil.
3. Add the reserved clams and parsley and reheat. Pour over the noodles and toss. Serve with Parmesan cheese, if you wish.
Yield: Four servings.

¼ cup olive or vegetable oil
1 clove garlic, finely chopped
1 tablespoon flour
2 7-ounce cans chopped clams
¼ teaspoon freshly ground black pepper
¼ cup chopped parsley
1 pound whole wheat noodles (see page 314), spaghetti, or macaroni, cooked al dente, drained

PARSLEY AND NUT SAUCE

1. Heat the oil in a small heavy skillet and sauté the onions until tender but not browned. Add the garlic and nuts and cook for 1 minute longer.
2. Put the onion mixture in the container of an electric blender or food processor. Add the cheese, parsley, and pepper and blend or process until smooth. Stir in the nuts. If sauce is too thick add a little more olive oil.
Yield: Four servings.

½ cup olive oil
2 medium-sized onions, finely chopped
2 cloves garlic, finely chopped
½ cup very finely ground toasted walnuts, pecans, cashews, or peanuts
¼ cup freshly grated Parmesan cheese
¼ cup finely chopped Italian parsley
¼ teaspoon freshly ground black pepper
½ cup finely chopped roasted walnuts, pecans, cashews, or peanuts
1 pound whole wheat noodles (see page 314), spaghetti, or macaroni, cooked al dente and drained

PESTO SAUCE

¼ cup olive or vegetable
 oil
1 clove garlic, crushed
½ teaspoon salt
¼ teaspoon freshly ground
 black pepper
2 teaspoons dried basil
3 cups parsley sprigs
¼ cup pignolis or walnuts
1 cup shredded
 mozzarella cheese
¼ cup freshly grated
 Parmesan cheese
1 pound whole wheat
 noodles (see page 314),
 spaghetti, or macaroni,
 cooked al dente and
 drained

1. Put the oil, garlic, salt, pepper, basil, and parsley in the container of an electric blender or food processor. Blend or process until smooth. Add the nuts and cheeses, and blend or process until smooth. Blend with ¼ cup pasta cooking water.

2. Pour the sauce over the pasta and toss. Yield: Four servings.

SAUCE PRIMAVERA

2 sweet red peppers
2 green peppers
¼ pound green beans
2 cups broccoli flowerets
1 medium-sized zucchini,
 sliced
1 cup cauliflower
 flowerets
1½ cups sugar snap peas or
 snow peas or 1 7-ounce
 package frozen snow
 peas
¼ cup olive or vegetable
 oil
½ pound mushrooms,
 sliced
 Salt and freshly ground
 black pepper

1. Roast the red and green peppers over a charcoal fire, under the broiler, or in a hot oven until well charred, turning often. Put in a paper bag until cool enough to handle. Peel, seed, and dice the peppers.

2. Steam the green beans, broccoli, zucchini, and cauliflower for 3 minutes, adding the sugar snap peas for the last 15 seconds.

3. Heat the oil in a heavy skillet. Add the mushrooms, peppers, and steamed vegetables and stir-fry until hot. Season with salt and pepper to taste.

Yield: Enough to toss with 1 pound noodles or spaghetti. Four servings.

PASTA WITH YOGURT-PRIMAVERA SAUCE

1. Melt the butter in a large skillet and sauté the scallions and garlic until tender but not browned. Sprinkle with the flour and cook for 2 minutes.

2. Stir in the salt, pepper, oregano, and light cream, and bring to a boil, stirring, and cook until thickened. Whisk in the yogurt cheese.

3. Stir in the vegetables. Check the seasonings and add salt and pepper if necessary. Serve over noodles with freshly grated Parmesan cheese, if you wish.

Yield: Four servings.

3 tablespoons butter
1 bunch scallions, including some green part, finely chopped
1 clove garlic, finely chopped
2 tablespoons whole wheat flour
½ teaspoon salt
¼ teaspoon freshly ground black pepper
½ teaspoon dried oregano
1 cup light cream
1 cup yogurt cheese (see page 14)
2 cups blanched or leftover cooked vegetables (carrots, broccoli, cut beans, peas, cut asparagus)
1 pound whole wheat noodles (see page 314), cooked al dente and drained

"SAUSAGE" SAUCE FOR PASTA

1 recipe for turkey
sausage (see page 88)
¼ cup olive or vegetable
oil
1 clove garlic, finely
chopped
1 6-ounce jar roasted
peppers, drained and
chopped
1 2-pound, 3-ounce can
Italian plum tomatoes,
drained and chopped
¼ cup chopped parsley
1 teaspoon dried basil
1 teaspoon dried oregano
½ teaspoon salt
1 pound whole wheat
noodles (see page 314),
spaghetti, or macaroni,
cooked al dente and
drained

1. Put turkey sausage mixture, before it is
made into patties, into a large heavy
skillet with the olive oil and garlic. Cook,
stirring, until no hint of pink remains and
the sausage is cooked.
2. Add the roasted peppers, tomatoes,
parsley, basil, oregano, and salt. Bring to
a boil, lower the heat, and simmer for 15
minutes.
Yield: Four servings.

ZUCCHINI SAUCE

¼ cup olive or vegetable
oil
2 cloves garlic, finely
chopped
2 medium-sized zucchini,
cut into matchstick
pieces
1 pound whole wheat
noodles (see page 314),
spaghetti, or macaroni
1 cup ricotta cheese
½ cup freshly grated
Parmesan cheese
⅓ cup chopped parsley
½ teaspoon salt
⅛ teaspoon hot red pepper
flakes

1. Heat the oil in a medium-sized skillet
and sauté the garlic and zucchini until
crisp-tender.
2. Cook the pasta al dente, drain, and
return to the hot kettle. Stir in the ricotta
and Parmesan.
3. Add the parsley, salt, and pepper
flakes to the zucchini mixture and pour
over the pasta. Toss.
Yield: Four servings.

TUNA SAUCE

1. Put the eggplant in a colander and sprinkle with salt. Let stand for 30 minutes. Rinse well, drain, and pat dry.
2. Heat half the oil in a large skillet and sauté the eggplant in batches until lightly browned. Reserve. Add the garlic to the skillet and sauté for 1 minute.
3. Add the tomatoes with their juice, pepper, oregano, basil, and reserved eggplant. Cook, stirring and breaking up the tomatoes, until the eggplant is tender, about 8 minutes. Stir in the tuna and parsley. Serve over pasta.
Yield: Four servings.

1 large eggplant, pared and cubed
Salt
⅓ cup vegetable oil, approximately
2 cloves garlic, finely chopped
1 16-ounce can plum tomatoes
¼ teaspoon freshly ground black pepper
½ teaspoon dried oregano
1 teaspoon dried basil
1 6½- to 7-ounce can tuna, drained and flaked
¼ cup chopped parsley
1 pound whole wheat noodles (see page 314), spaghetti, or macaroni

YOGURT SAUCE

1. Heat the oil in a medium-sized skillet and sauté the garlic and scallions until tender but not browned.
2. Stir in the yogurt, walnuts, salt, pepper, parsley, and dill. Reheat while stirring but do not boil. Serve with pasta.
Yield: Four servings.

¼ cup vegetable oil
2 cloves garlic, finely chopped
1 bunch scallions, chopped with some green
2 cups plain yogurt (see page 324)
1 cup chopped walnuts
½ teaspoon salt
¼ teaspoon freshly ground black pepper
½ cup chopped parsley
2 tablespoons snipped fresh dill weed
1 pound whole wheat noodles (see page 314), spaghetti, or macaroni

BROCCOLI SAUCE

2 tablespoons red wine
vinegar
⅓ cup olive or vegetable
oil
½ teaspoon salt
1 clove garlic, finely
chopped
¼ teaspoon freshly ground
black pepper
4 ripe tomatoes, peeled,
seeded and chopped
3 cups small broccoli
flowerets, steamed for 3
minutes
2 teaspoons dried basil
½ cup chopped scallions,
including green parts
2 hard-cooked eggs,
chopped
1 cup shredded
mozzarella cheese
1 pound whole wheat
noodles (see page 314),
spaghetti, or macaroni,
cooked al dente and
drained

1. In bowl combine the vinegar, oil, salt, garlic, pepper, tomatoes, broccoli, basil, scallions, and eggs.
2. Add the mozzarella cheese to the hot pasta and stir to melt the cheese. Top with the broccoli mixture. Toss and serve with freshly grated Parmesan cheese. This is a cold sauce for hot pasta.
Yield: Four servings.

CHICK-PEA SAUCE

1 cup dried chick-peas
Cold water
¼ cup lemon juice
Salt

1. Pick over and wash the chick-peas and put them in a bowl. Pour in water to cover. Let soak overnight.
2. Add lemon juice and blend in an electric blender or process in a food processor until smooth, adding more water if necessary. Season with salt to taste. Serve cold over salads or warm over vegetables.
Yield: About two and one-half cups sauce.

YOGURT

Yogurt is a cultured milk product, made with cultures such as lactobacillus bulgaricus and streptococcus thermophilus, that have been known to man since Biblical times. It is a staple in the diets of many Middle Eastern countries, especially Lebanon and Syria, as well as in Bulgaria, Yugoslavia, and India. Compared with the milk from which it is made, which may come from a cow, goat, buffalo, reindeer, mare, or ewe, yogurt has a slightly lower sugar content and protein that is more finely divided and readily digestible. In the human intestinal tract, the bacteria in yogurt produce lactic acid which controls, or in some instances may destroy, putrefying bacteria present which left unchecked can cause discomfort and often illness. Despite some historians' and health enthusiasts' claims, yogurt is neither a panacea for all ills nor the long-sought-after elixir of life.

PANIR OR FRESH CURDS

1 pint whole milk
½ cup plain yogurt (see below)

1. Bring the milk to a boil. Add the yogurt and bring to a boil again. The milk will curdle.
2. Strain it through a double thickness of muslin and tie to the water faucet or some other place where it can drain for 1 to 2 hours depending on how dry, or moist, you want the curds.
3. For a more solid product, lay the muslin-wrapped curds on a board, weight heavily, and leave overnight. The solid curds can be cut into small squares and fried to a light golden brown color for adding to curry dishes such as a curry of peas and tomatoes.
4. Crumbly or solid, the cheese can be used in sandwiches and salads.
Yield: About one-half cup.

PREPARATION OF HOMEMADE YOGURT

1 quart raw or pasteurized and homogenized whole, skim, goat, soy, or reconstituted dry milk powder
½ cup non-fat dry milk powder
2 tablespoons plain yogurt, homemade or store-bought, or ⅓ ounce dry Bulgarian culture, approximately

1. Combine the liquid milk product with the extra ½ cup dry milk powder in a heavy saucepan. Heat until the mixture reaches 190 degrees. A thermometer is a great help in uniformly good-quality yogurt.
2. Cover the pan and allow the milk mixture to cool down to about 110 degrees or lukewarm.
3. Mix the plain yogurt or the culture with a little of the warm milk and add back to the bulk of the mixture. Mix well.
4. Pour into a warm, sterilized quart jar with a wide mouth. Cover with clear plastic wrap and set in a warm place (105 to 110 degrees) such as those listed below.

(a) Set the jar in an insulated picnic cooler, warmed by 2 quart jars of hot water. Set the cooler in a place where it will not be disturbed for several hours and replenish the hot water jars if the temperature in the cooler goes below about 106 degrees.

(b) Set the quart jar in a pan of medium-hot water over a pilot light on the stove and cover with a blanket. Do not disturb for several hours. *Or*, an oven with a pilot light is usually warm enough.

(c) Line a kettle with thick foam rubber sheets and place in it the jar of milk mixture and one of hot water. Do not disturb.

(d) Pour the milk mixture into a very clean, warmed thermos and set aside undisturbed.

(e) Fill a box with green hay. Bury the jar of milk mixture in it, cover, and set in the sun.

(f) The warmth necessary for growth of the culture can often be maintained by merely wrapping the jar of warm milk in insulating material, such as a blanket or newspaper.

(g) Campers have been known to place jars of the milk mixture in the dying ashes of a campfire or to bury the jars under pine boughs with success.

(h) A container warmed by a 15-watt light bulb or a night light makes an excellent place to leave the jar of milk mixture for the culture to grow undisturbed.

(i) Many commercial electric and non-electric yogurt makers are available.

5. The finished product should be thick, creamy, and custardy in texture with a mild flavor and pleasant degree of acidity.

The yogurt will keep in the refrigerator for six to seven days. However, batches to be used as starters for culturing new jars of yogurt should not be more than three to five days old for best results. Successive batches of yogurt made with yogurt starter can be made for a month before flavor and texture deteriorate. It is then advisable to use another purchased dry culture or a small quantity of store-purchased yogurt.

Scrupulous cleanliness is essential to successful yogurt.

For flavored yogurts stir in fruit preserves, pureed fruits or honey and carob.

For thicker, creamier yogurt put the yogurt in a double thickness of cheesecloth set in a strainer over a bowl and allow to drain for 30 minutes.

For yogurt cheese, 1 recipe yogurt (see page 324) or 4 large containers (16-ounce) plain yogurt.

Line a strainer with a double thickness of cheesecloth, place strainer over a big bowl. Add the yogurt to the strainer. Gather up corners of cheesecloth to make a tight package. Place a small plate on top of the bag and weight down with cans. Let drain in the refrigerator for 8 hours or overnight.

Yield: About 3 cups.

Note: Yogurt cheese can be used in place of dry cottage cheese, farmer cheese and part-skim ricotta.

For mock crème fraîche add 1 to 2 teaspoons plain yogurt to 1 cup heavy cream and let stand at room temperature until it thickens. Refrigerate.

In general, plain yogurt can be substituted for sour cream in all but a few critical baking recipes with the benefit of fewer calories. Baking recipes often have to be adjusted and where yogurt is used in place of milk add ½ teaspoon baking soda for each cup yogurt.

Yogurt adds zip, tartness, and creaminess to salad dressing, sauces, dips, gravies, marinades, soups, and beverages. For recipes in this book, see the index.

DESSERTS

Fresh and dried fruits are probably the most desirable desserts and between-meal snacks, providing an abundance of natural nutrients and few empty calories. However, because of the habits of generations of America's cooks, people have come to expect and enjoy pies, cakes, puddings, and cookies. It's hard to eliminate them from a family's diet suddenly. The children may be satisfied with a banana or date chips once in a while, but will insist on their favorite cookie or cake when a special occasion comes around. So in this book there's a fairly large offering of dessert recipes, all of which attempt to cut down on the amount of sugar used and concentrate on whole grains, unbleached white flour, and nutritious additions to contribute essential nutrients and a minimum of empty calories. Use of some sweetening product is necessary to make desserts palatable. The sweetening product best able to create an emulsion, the basis for texture in many familiar cakes and cookies, is sugar. A homemade raisin, oatmeal, and whole wheat flour cookie with a small percentage of sugar contributes essential nutrients to a child's lunch box, or is a good after-school snack, when an apple or an orange will not satisfy the acquired sweet tooth. Established food patterns are hard to change for parents, too, so when switching from a highly refined and processed diet including many convenience foods, these desserts are good-tasting, beneficial alternatives.

HOMEMADE APPLESAUCE I

2 pounds tart cooking
  apples, washed
½ cup boiling water
  Honey to taste
  Maple syrup to taste
¼ cup wheat germ
½ cup unsulphured raisins
2 tablespoons ground
  sunflower seed kernels
⅛ teaspoon grated nutmeg
⅛ teaspoon ground
  cinnamon
1 teaspoon lemon juice or
  grated lemon rind

1. Do not peel or core the apples. Quarter them and place the quarters in the boiling water. Cook, covered, until barely tender, about 15 minutes.
2. Press the apples through a colander or food mill and add honey and maple syrup.
3. Add remaining ingredients.
Yield: Six servings.

HOMEMADE APPLESAUCE II

8 cups peeled and cored
  apple slices (even
  apparently wormy
  apples from a neglected
  orchard can be used if
  you're willing to pare
  away the bad parts)
2 cups water
2 teaspoons lemon juice
1 teaspoon ground
  cinnamon
½ teaspoon ground ginger
½ teaspoon ground cloves
¼ teaspoon grated nutmeg
¼ teaspoon ground
  allspice
¼ teaspoon ground mace
  Honey

1. Put the apple slices, water, and lemon juice in a 6-quart kettle. Bring to a boil and simmer until half the apples are mushy.
2. Add the remaining ingredients including enough honey to sweeten to taste. Press the apple mixture with a potato masher, leaving some chunks for texture. Alternately, the mixture can be puréed in a food mill, electric blender, or food processor.
Yield: Six servings.
Note: This same recipe can be used to cook homegrown peaches and pears.

CITRUS MOLD

1. Soak the gelatin in ½ cup water for 5 minutes. Heat the remaining water and honey to boiling and add to the soaked gelatin. Stir to dissolve gelatin.

2. Add the grapefruit juice, lemon juice, and orange juice. Mix well and chill until the mixture just shows signs of setting.

3. Fold in the fruit sections, nuts, apple, and banana. Pour into a lightly oiled 1½- to 2-quart mold or serving dish. Chill well.

4. Serve from the dish, or unmold, and serve with yogurt.

Yield: Six servings.

1½ tablespoons unflavored gelatin
1 cup water
½ cup honey
¾ cup fresh or unsweetened canned grapefruit juice
2 tablespoons lemon juice
¼ cup orange juice
1½ medium-sized grapefruit, sectioned
2 medium-sized oranges, sectioned
½ cup chopped almonds or walnuts
2 unpeeled apples, cored, and chopped
1 banana, sliced and dipped in lemon juice
Plain yogurt (see page 324)

COLD FRUIT PUDDING

1. Wash the dried fruit in warm water, drain, and put in a bowl with the raisins and apples. Pour the water over all. Add sugar and stir well. Let stand overnight.

2. Transfer fruit and liquid to a pan, add the cinnamon stick, and bring to a boil. Simmer slowly until the fruit is tender but not mushy.

3. Strain off the cooking liquid into a second pan. Mix the potato starch with the cold water and stir into fruit liquid. Bring to a boil, stirring until the mixture thickens and is clear, about 3 minutes.

4. Put the fruit in a serving bowl, pour the hot pudding over all, cool, and chill. Serve with yogurt.

Yield: Six servings.

20 to 24 ounces (1½ boxes) mixed dried unsulphured fruit
1 cup unsulphured raisins
3 tart apples, peeled, cored, and quartered
1½ quarts water
½ cup brown sugar
1 cinnamon stick
¼ cup potato starch
3 tablespoons cold water
Plain yogurt (see page 324)

COEUR À LA CRÈME

1 pound goat cottage
cheese or cottage
cheese, at room
temperature
1 pound goat cream
cheese or cream cheese,
at room temperature
¼ teaspoon salt
2 cups heavy goat's cream
or heavy cream
1 pint strawberries

1. Line 6 coeur à la crème wicker baskets with a double thickness of muslin moistened in water.
2. Beat together the cottage cheese, cream cheese, and salt until smooth.
3. Gradually beat in the cream. Pour the mixture into the prepared baskets. Draw the muslin over the top of the cheese mixture and place a small weight on each basket. Place the baskets on a rack, over a platter, and let stand at cellar or refrigerated temperature overnight.
4. Unmold the baskets onto serving plates and garnish with strawberries.
Yield: Six servings.

NO-BAKE LEMON CHIFFON

8 eggs, separated
1 cup brown sugar
⅔ cup lemon juice, about
4 lemons
2 tablespoons unflavored
gelatin
¼ cup cold water
1 teaspoon grated lemon
rind
⅓ cup graham cracker
crumbs

1. Put the egg yolks in the top of a double boiler with the sugar and lemon juice.
2. Heat over simmering water, stirring, until the mixture thickens. Do not boil.
3. Soak the gelatin in the cold water. Add to the hot egg mixture and stir to dissolve the gelatin. Cool until the mixture starts to thicken and is the consistency of unbeaten egg white.
4. Beat the egg whites until stiff but not dry and fold into the cooled mixture. Fold in the rind. Pour the mixture into a well-buttered deep pie plate sprinkled with graham cracker crumbs on bottom and sides. Chill several hours before serving.
Yield: Six servings.

FRUIT PUDDING

1. Combine the butter, carob powder, and vanilla.
2. Put eggs in the container of an electric blender or food processor and blend or process until frothy.
3. Add the butter mixture and honey and blend or process until well mixed.
4. Add the ricotta and blend or process until smooth. Stir in one of the optional ingredients. Pour into a serving bowl and chill.
Yield: Eight servings.

1 cup butter, melted
1 cup carob powder
1 teaspoon pure vanilla extract
2 eggs
2 tablespoons honey
1 pound whole-milk ricotta cheese
1 cup chopped dates, pecans, walnuts, or coconut, or ¼ cup sesame seeds or sunflower seed kernels, optional

HOMEMADE STRAWBERRY ICE CREAM

1. Combine the strawberries and honey, cover and chill in the refrigerator for at least 1 hour.
2. Put the water and soy milk powder in the container of an electric blender or food processor. Blend until smooth and thick. Add the egg yolks and blend well again.
3. Add the oil slowly while blending on low speed or processing. Blend or process at high speed until smooth and thick.
4. Add the strawberry mixture and blend again. Pour into chilled ice cube trays and freeze until the mixture is solid around the edges and slightly mushy in the middle. Turn into the blender or food processor and blend or process until smooth. Return to the trays; freeze again.
5. Repeat the freezing and blending or processing twice more, and serve frozen. Store any leftover ice cream in covered containers in the freezer.
Yield: Four servings.

2 cups strawberries, washed and sliced if large
1 cup honey
1 cup ice-cold water
1 cup soy milk powder
2 egg yolks
½ cup chilled vegetable oil

RAW NUT ICE CREAM

2 cups soy milk or half-
  and-half
1 cup almonds
1 cup pecans
½ cup sunflower seed
  kernels
½ cup sesame seeds
¼ cup flax seeds
½ cup honey
¼ cup vegetable oil
1 teaspoon pure vanilla
  extract

Mix all the ingredients together and blend in the container of an electric blender or process in a food processor in batches until smooth. Pour into ice cube trays and freeze until solid.
Yield: Six to eight servings.

QUICK FROZEN FRUIT DESSERT

1 pint plain yogurt (see
  page 324)
1 tablespoon honey
1 pound frozen
  strawberries,
  raspberries, peaches, or
  cherries

1. Put the yogurt in the container of an electric blender or food processor. Add the honey.
2. Slowly add pieces of the frozen fruit while blending on medium speed or processing until mixture is like slush, partly frozen but still able to flow. Add as much of the fruit as possible.
Yield: Four servings.

TOFU FRUIT PUDDING

1 10-ounce package
  frozen strawberries,
  thawed
½ pound tofu (see page
  160), drained and
  crumbled
2 tablespoons honey
2 tablespoons
  unsweetened coconut

Put all the ingredients in the container of an electric blender or food processor and blend or process until smooth. Chill well before serving.
Yield: Four servings.

ORANGE-MILLET DESSERT

1. In the top of a double boiler, mix the millet with ½ cup of the milk. Scald the remaining milk and stir into the millet.
2. Add the grated rind of the orange and the honey. Cook over boiling water, stirring occasionally, until the millet is tender and has absorbed about three quarters of the liquid, about 45 minutes.
3. Beat the egg yolks lightly, stir into the millet mixture, and cook, stirring, until the mixture thickens slightly. Cool to room temperature. Chill.
4. Beat the egg whites until stiff but not dry and fold into the dessert. Fold in the almonds. Section the orange and use as a garnish.
Yield: Four servings.

¼ cup whole hulled millet
2 cups milk
1 orange
¼ cup honey
2 eggs, separated
¼ cup slivered almonds

SOFT FROZEN YOGURT

1. Drain the yogurt through 2 thicknesses of cheesecloth for 30 minutes.
2. Sprinkle the gelatin over the water and let soften for 5 minutes. Add the honey and heat the mixture while stirring until the gelatin dissolves. Pour into a large bowl and cool to lukewarm.
3. Beat the drained yogurt into the gelatin mixture until smooth. Chill. Pour into a 9-inch square pan and freeze, stirring several times to ensure even freezing.
4. Break the frozen mixture into chunks and beat with an electric mixer until smooth.
Yield: About one quart.
Note: A thick creamy, non-icy frozen yogurt can be made easily from the chilled mixture in an ice cream maker following manufacturer's directions. Pack into containers and freeze for about 30 minutes.

2 16-ounce containers or homemade plain yogurt (see page 324)
1 envelope unflavored gelatin
½ cup water
¾ cup honey

MAPLE ELEGANCE

5 extra-large eggs, lightly
  beaten
1¼ cups hot pure maple
  syrup
2 cups heavy cream,
  whipped

1. Put the eggs in the top of a double boiler.
2. Gradually pour the hot syrup into the eggs while beating vigorously. Cook the mixture over simmering hot water until the mixture thickens, stirring constantly. Cool.
3. Fold in the cream and spoon into parfait goblets, individual soufflé dishes, or a mold. Freeze. Serve frozen, unmolded if frozen in a mold.
Yield: Six servings.

YOGURT COEUR À LA CRÈME

3 cups yogurt cheese (see
  page 14)
1 cup heavy cream
  Fresh strawberries

1. Combine the yogurt cheese with the heavy cream and mix very well. Turn into a cheesecloth-lined 1-quart heart-shaped basket or two small ones. Fold the ends of the cheesecloth over the cheese mixture and weight with cans. Place over a bowl and refrigerate overnight.
2. Unmold onto a plate and surround with fresh berries.
Yield: Six servings.

GRAPES, YOGURT, AND BROWN SUGAR

4 small bunches seedless
  grapes
2 cups plain yogurt (see
  page 324), drained
  through 2 thicknesses
  of cheesecloth for 30
  minutes
¼ cup light brown sugar
2 tablespoons chopped
  crystallized ginger

1. Wash the grapes and put them in four individual serving dishes.
2. Combine the drained yogurt, brown sugar, and ginger and spoon over the grapes. Chill.
Yield: Four servings.

BANANA ICE CREAM

1. Beat the milk into the eggs. Add the honey and mix well.
2. Stir in the vanilla. Fold in the cream and then the banana. Turn into an ice cube tray and freeze until solid about 1 inch from the edges.
3. Turn into a mixing bowl and beat until smooth. Return to the tray and freeze again.

Yield: Six servings.

Note: Frozen strawberries can be used in place of the banana if desired.

1 cup milk
2 eggs, lightly beaten
⅔ cup honey
2 teaspoons pure vanilla extract
1 cup heavy cream, whipped
1 ripe banana, mashed

BLENDER BAKED RAISIN CUSTARD

1. The day before the custard is to be served, put the milk and raisins in a jar, cover, and store in refrigerator overnight.
2. Next day, put the raisin mixture in the container of a blender or food processor and whirl or process until the raisins are finely chopped.
3. Stir in the eggs, vanilla, salt, and ⅛ teaspoon nutmeg.
4. Pour into custard cups, stirring while pouring to keep the raisin bits evenly distributed.
5. Sprinkle the custards with nutmeg.
6. Preheat the oven to 300 degrees.
7. Set the cups in a pan of hot water, having the water come up to a depth of 1 inch around the cups.
8. Bake for 1 hour or until a knife inserted comes out clean.
9. Remove from the pan, cool, then chill.

Yield: Six four-ounce custards.

1⅔ cups milk
⅔ cup raisins
3 large eggs, lightly beaten
½ teaspoon pure vanilla extract
⅛ teaspoon salt
Grated nutmeg

APPLE CRUNCH

1½ cups sifted whole wheat flour
1 cup rolled oats
1 cup brown sugar
½ teaspoon baking soda
½ cup butter

FILLING I
6 to 8 apples, peeled, cored, and sliced
¼ cup brown sugar
1 teaspoon ground cinnamon
1 teaspoon lemon juice

FILLING II
3 cups rhubarb, cut into ½-inch slices
¼ cup brown sugar
2 tablespoons tapioca
1 egg

FILLING III
1 pint blueberries
⅛ teaspoon ground mace or grated nutmeg
1 tablespoon quick tapioca
Ice cream, optional

1. Preheat the oven to 350 degrees.
2. Put the flour, oats, sugar, and baking soda in a large bowl. With two knives or a pastry blender, work the butter into the dry ingredients until pieces are uniform and quite small.
3. If apple filling is being used, mix apples, sugar, cinnamon, and lemon juice and put in bottom of a buttered 9-inch square baking pan.
4. Cover with oats mixture.
5. If rhubarb or blueberry filling is to be used, pat half the oats mixture into a buttered 9-inch square baking pan.
6. Combine the fruit with other ingredients indicated and place on top of the oats mixture. Put remaining oats mixture on top of fruit and bake for 50 minutes, or until done. Serve warm or cold, with ice cream if desired.
Yield: Six servings.

HONEY PECAN ICE CREAM

1. Put the egg yolks, honey, and vanilla in the small bowl of an electric mixer. Beat until well blended and very smooth.
2. Fold egg-and-honey mixture into cream.
3. Beat the egg whites with the salt until stiff but not dry and fold into the cream mixture. Fold in the nuts.
4. Pour into three ice cube trays and set in the freezer. When solid, remove and pack into a quart container.
Yield: One quart.

4 **eggs, separated**
¾ **cup honey**
3 **teaspoons pure vanilla extract**
2 **cups heavy cream, whipped**
⅛ **teaspoon salt**
1 **cup chopped pecans**

APPLE-OAT CRISP

1. Preheat the oven to 300 degrees.
2. Oil a large heavy iron skillet. Place the unpeeled apple slices in the skillet and sprinkle with 2 tablespoons of the sugar and the cinnamon.
3. In a bowl, combine the cornmeal, oats, and the remaining sugar. Pour in the oil and work with the fingers through the dry mixture. Mixture will be crumbly. Sprinkle over apples. Bake for 40 minutes, or until the topping is brown. Do not overcook. Serve warm.
Yield: Six to eight servings.

6 **medium-sized Red Delicious, Cortland, or Rome apples, washed, cored, and thinly sliced**
¾ **cup plus 2 tablespoons dark brown sugar**
½ **teaspoon ground cinnamon**
½ **cup stoneground cornmeal**
¾ **cup rolled oats**
½ **cup peanut oil**

BANANA-SWEET POTATO PUDDING

1. Preheat the oven to 300 degrees.
2. Combine all the ingredients in a large bowl and mix well. Turn into a well-buttered 1-quart baking dish or casserole and bake for about 45 minutes, or until set and browned on top.
Yield: Four servings.

2 **ripe bananas, mashed**
1 **cup light cream**
⅛ **teaspoon salt**
¼ **cup chopped raisins**
1 **cup mashed cooked sweet potatoes**
2 **tablespoons brown sugar**
2 **egg yolks, lightly beaten**

YOGURT LIME PIE

1 cup yogurt cheese (see page 14)
1 envelope unflavored gelatin
½ cup light cream
¾ cup brown sugar
3 eggs, lightly beaten
1 cup plain yogurt (see page 324), drained through 2 layers of cheesecloth for 30 minutes
⅓ cup lime juice
1 tablespoon grated lime rind
1 baked 9-inch Whole Wheat Pastry I pie shell (see page 344)

1. Put the cheese in the container of an electric blender or food processor and whirl or process until smooth.

2. In a small heavy pan sprinkle the gelatin over the cream and let soften for 5 minutes. Add the sugar and heat, stirring, until the sugar and gelatin are dissolved.

3. Stir some of the hot mixture into the eggs. Return to the saucepan and heat, stirring, until mixture thickens. Do not boil.

4. Add the yogurt, yogurt cheese, lime juice, and rind. Mix well and pour into the pie shell. Refrigerate for several hours or overnight.

Yield: Six servings.

APRICOT BETTY

1 cup dried apricots
1 cup water
2 cups bread crumbs from day-old whole wheat or other whole-grain bread, preferably homemade (see page 294)
¼ cup butter, melted
⅓ cup brown sugar
1 teaspoon ground cinnamon
1 teaspoon grated lemon rind
2 tablespoons lemon juice
Plain yogurt (see page 324) or half-and-half

1. Put the apricots in a saucepan and add the water. Bring to a boil, cover, and simmer for 10 minutes, or until apricots are tender. Drain, reserving the cooking water.

2. Mix the crumbs and butter and put half in a 1-quart casserole.

3. Cover the crumbs with the apricots. Mix the sugar, cinnamon, grated rind, and lemon juice and pour over the apricots. Add the remaining crumbs. Pour the reserved cooking water over top.

4. Preheat the oven to 350 degrees.

5. Cover the casserole and bake for 15 minutes. Uncover and bake for 15 minutes longer. Serve with yogurt.

Yield: Four servings.

BLUEBERRY COBBLER

1. Preheat the oven to 350 degrees.
2. Combine the berries, water, ¾ cup sugar, and the rind in an ovenproof casserole. Bring to a boil and simmer for 2 minutes.
3. Meanwhile, combine the remaining sugar with the flour, salt, and baking powder. Cut in the butter until the mixture is crumbly.
4. Sprinkle the crumbs over fruit. Bake for about 25 minutes, or until browned. Serve warm.
Yield: Four servings.
Note: Other berries can be used in place of the blueberries.

1 pint blueberries
⅓ cup water
1½ cups brown sugar
1 teaspoon grated lemon rind
1 cup whole wheat flour
½ teaspoon salt
1 teaspoon baking powder
⅓ cup butter

COTTAGE CHEESE BERRY SOUFFLÉ

1. Beat together the eggs, wheat germ, milk, and salt. Turn into a well-buttered 2-cup ceramic or glass bowl. Cover the bowl with aluminum foil. Set on a rack in a pan of boiling water, with the water extending at least two thirds the way up the bowl. Cover the pan and simmer very gently for 15 minutes, or until the mixture is set. Cool, and chill if desired. The dessert may be eaten warm or cold.
2. Turn the mixture out onto a serving plate. Cover the outside of the mold with cottage cheese. Sweeten the fruit with honey and pour over the cottage cheese.
3. Serve with yogurt.
Yield: Four servings.

4 eggs, well beaten
2 tablespoons wheat germ, or whole wheat bread crumbs
½ cup milk
¼ teaspoon salt
½ pound cottage cheese
2 cups sliced strawberries, blueberries, sliced peaches, or applesauce
Honey to taste
Plain yogurt (see page 324)

CRANAPPLE COBBLER

3 large apples, cored and
cut into small pieces
2 cups cranberries
2 teaspoons pure almond
extract
¾ cup honey
½ cup finely chopped
orange peel
1 cup wheat germ
1 teaspoon ground
cinnamon
¼ teaspoon salt
¼ cup sweet butter
Plain yogurt (see page
324)

1. Preheat the oven to 425 degrees.
2. Mix together the apples, cranberries, almond extract, honey, and peel. Put in the bottom of a well-buttered 1½- to 2-quart baking dish or casserole.
3. Combine the wheat germ, cinnamon, and salt and sprinkle over the fruit mixture. Dot with the butter and bake for 40 minutes, or until bubbly and brown. Serve warm with yogurt.
Yield: Six servings.

CRANBERRY CRUNCH

1 pound fresh cranberries
Honey to taste
1 cup rolled oats
½ cup whole wheat flour
1 cup brown sugar
½ cup butter
Homemade vanilla ice
cream or plain yogurt
(see page 324)

1. Preheat the oven to 350 degrees.
2. Put the berries in a saucepan and cook until they pop and then a minute or two longer. Do not let them get mushy. Sweeten very lightly with honey. Cool slightly.
3. Put the oats, flour, and sugar in a bowl. Cut in the butter with two knives, or a pastry blender, until the mixture is crumbly.
4. Put half the oat mixture in the bottom of a buttered 8-inch square baking pan. Cover with the cranberry mixture. Top with the remaining oat mixture. Bake for 45 minutes, or until done. Serve warm with ice cream or yogurt.
Yield: Six to eight servings.

INDIAN PUDDING

1. Preheat the oven to 325 degrees.
2. Pour the milk over the cornmeal in a saucepan and bring to a boil, stirring. Cook over low heat, stirring constantly, until thick, smooth, and creamy, about 15 minutes.
3. Pour the cornmeal mixture over the eggs. Add the salt, ginger, nutmeg, butter, molasses, and raisins and pour into a greased baking dish. Bake for 1½ hours. Serve warm with ice cream or yogurt.
Yield: Six servings.

1 quart milk, scalded
5 tablespoons stoneground cornmeal
2 eggs, well beaten
½ teaspoon salt
½ teaspoon ground ginger
½ teaspoon grated nutmeg
2 tablespoons butter
½ cup unsulphured molasses
½ cup unsulphured raisins
Ice cream or plain yogurt (see page 324)

OLD-FASHIONED TAPIOCA CREAM

1. Put the tapioca in the top of a double boiler. Add water to cover and let stand for 2 hours.
2. Drain off the excess water. Add the milk and cook, covered, over boiling water until the tapioca is transparent, about 1 hour.
3. Beat together the eggs, sugar, and salt. Gradually beat in the tapioca. Return to the double boiler and cook, stirring constantly, until the mixture thickens. Do not allow to boil or it will curdle. Stir in the vanilla and serve warm.
Yield: Six servings.

1 cup large pearl tapioca
Water
4 cups milk
4 eggs, lightly beaten
¾ cup brown sugar
¼ teaspoon salt
1 teaspoon pure vanilla extract

BAKED BROWN RICE WITH DATES

1 quart milk
½ cup raw brown rice
½ cup brown sugar
⅛ teaspoon salt
½ cup chopped dates
Plain yogurt (see page 324)

1. Preheat the oven to 300 degrees.
2. Put the milk, rice, sugar, salt, and dates in a 1½-quart buttered casserole or baking dish. Stir to mix. Bake until a light brown skin forms over the surface. Stir the skin into the pudding and bake until another skin forms and stir that in. Continue stirring in the skins for 2 to 2½ hours.
3. Bake, without stirring, until the rice is tender and the top is well browned. Serve with whipped cream.
Yield: Four servings.

CURRANT AND RICE PUDDING

3 cups milk
3 eggs, lightly beaten
½ teaspoon pure vanilla extract
½ cup brown sugar
⅛ teaspoon salt
2 cups cooked brown rice (see page 228)
½ cup chopped nuts
2 tablespoons currants
¼ teaspoon grated nutmeg
½ teaspoon ground cinnamon, or to taste

1. Preheat the oven to 325 degrees.
2. Beat the milk, eggs, vanilla, sugar, and salt together. Add the rice, nuts, currants, nutmeg, and cinnamon. Turn into a buttered casserole and bake for 30 minutes, or until pudding is the desired consistency. The longer the pudding bakes, the drier it will become.
Yield: Four servings.

SWEET PELLAO

4 cups cooked brown rice (see page 228)
½ cup raisins

1. Mix together the rice, raisins, almonds, salt, cinnamon, mace, and cardamom.
2. Melt the butter in a heavy skillet and

add the brown sugar. Heat, stirring, until the sugar dissolves. Add the rice mixture, spreading it over the pan, and heat over medium heat until mixture is warmed through and brown on the bottom.
Yield: Six servings.

¼ cup almonds, left whole or roughly chopped
¼ teaspoon salt
½ teaspoon ground cinnamon
⅛ teaspoon ground mace
Seeds from one whole cardamom pod, lightly crushed
6 tablespoons butter
3 tablespoons brown sugar

COTTAGE CHEESE PUDDING

1. Preheat the oven to 350 degrees.
2. Put all the ingredients, with the exception of the nutmeg, in the container of an electric blender or food processor and blend or process until smooth.
3. Pour into six buttered or oiled custard cups. Sprinkle with nutmeg if desired. Place cups in a pan of hot water and bake until pudding is firm or until a silver knife inserted comes out clean, about 35 to 40 minutes. Cool and chill.
Yield: Six servings.

2 cups fresh goat's milk cottage cheese or cottage cheese
2 cups well-drained fresh, frozen thawed or canned pumpkin or squash pulp
4 eggs
½ cup brown sugar
⅛ teaspoon salt
¼ teaspoon grated nutmeg, optional

WHEAT GERM PIE CRUST

1. Preheat the oven to 325 degrees.
2. Put all the ingredients in a bowl and cut mixture with a knife to blend. Turn into a 10-inch pie plate and press evenly over bottom and sides.
3. Bake for 30 minutes or until done.
Yield: One baked pie shell.

1 cup wheat germ
1 cup whole wheat pastry flour
1 teaspoon salt
1 tablespoon blackstrap molasses
½ cup cold-pressed sesame or corn oil
3 tablespoons cold water

WHOLE WHEAT PASTRY I

1 cup whole wheat flour
(whole wheat pastry
flour makes the most
tender crust)
½ teaspoon salt
¼ cup vegetable oil
3 tablespoons ice water,
approximately

1. Put the flour and salt in a small bowl. Stir in the oil and enough water to make a very stiff dough. On a lightly floured board or between sheets of wax paper, roll out to a 12-inch circle and fit into a 9- or 10-inch pie pan. Turn under the edge and flute. Prick bottom with a fork.
2. Bake in a 375-degree oven for 20 minutes, or until set and lightly browned.
Yield: One nine- or ten-inch pie shell.

WHOLE WHEAT PASTRY II

1½ cups whole wheat flour
⅛ teaspoon salt
½ cup butter, softened
Ice water

1. Mix the flour and salt in a bowl. Add the butter and cut in with a pastry blender.
2. Stirring with a fork, add the ice water a few drops at a time until particles hold together. Shape in a ball and use as directed in individual recipe.
Yield: One nine- or ten-inch pie shell.

OIL PASTRY

2 cups soya-carob flour
½ teaspoon baking
powder
½ teaspoon salt
⅔ cup oil
⅓ cup chilled water

1. Sift together the flour, baking powder, and salt. Blend the oil and water together and immediately pour into the dry ingredients, stirring with a fork to distribute. Pour half of the mixture into a pie pan and press into place for bottom crust.
2. For top crust, flour wax paper, pour the remaining mixture onto the paper, place another sheet of wax paper on top, and roll out.
Yield: Enough for a two-crust pie.

WHOLE WHEAT-RICE PASTRY

1. Preheat the oven to 400 degrees.
2. Sift the flour before it is measured and discard or reserve any solids (bran husks) left in sieve to enrich another dish.
3. Place the whole wheat flour, rice flour, salt, and wheat germ in a bowl. Stir in the oil and milk to make a dough.
4. Roll out the dough between pieces of wax paper to a 10-inch round. Remove the top piece of paper. Turn the pastry side down into a 9-inch pie plate. Remove the second piece of wax paper and fit the pastry gently into the pan. Trim the edges and decorate. Bake for 20 minutes, or until set and lightly browned.
Yield: One pie shell.

1 cup whole wheat pastry flour (see step 2)
1 cup brown rice flour
1 teaspoon salt
2 tablespoons wheat germ
⅓ cup vegetable oil
¼ cup plus 1 tablespoon cold milk

APPLE DUMPLINGS

1. Divide pastry into six equal portions. Roll each on a floured surface or between sheets of wax paper to form a 7-inch square.
2. Roll the apples in brown sugar and put one in the center of each square. Fill with brown sugar and add a dash of cinnamon. Bring the pastry up to enclose the apple, pinching the edges together (do not be concerned if the pastry breaks; simply push back together).
3. Arrange the dumplings on a jelly roll pan or baking sheet.
4. Preheat the oven to 400 degrees.
5. Bake for 30 minutes, or until the apples are tender and the crust is browned. Serve slightly warm or cool, with half-and-half, if you wish.
Yield: Six servings.

Double recipe of Whole Wheat Pastry II (see page 344)
6 small tart apples, left whole, peeled and cored
Brown sugar
Ground cinnamon
Half-and-half, optional

WHOLE WHEAT-RICE PASTRY APPLE PIE

CRUST
1 cup whole wheat pastry
flour (see step 2)
1 cup brown rice flour
1 teaspoon salt
½ cup plus 2 tablespoons
butter
Ice water

APPLE FILLING
4 cups sliced tart apples
⅔ cup brown sugar
½ teaspoon ground
cinnamon
1½ tablespoons whole
wheat flour
Grated lemon rind to
taste

1. Preheat the oven to 400 degrees.
2. Sift the flour before it is measured and discard or reserve any solids (bran husks) left in sieve to enrich another dish.
3. Put the whole wheat flour, rice flour, and salt in a bowl. With a pastry blender, or the fingertips, work the butter into the flours until mixture resembles course oatmeal.
4. Mixing with a fork, add enough ice water to make a dough. Roll out half the dough on a rice-floured board or between sheets of wax paper into a circle to fit a 9-inch pie pan. Fit the dough into the pan.
5. Combine all the ingredients for the filling and turn into the pastry-lined pie pan.
6. Roll out the remaining pastry to cover the top of the pie. Place on pie, seal edges, and decorate. Make steam holes. Bake for 40 to 50 minutes, or until filling is tender and pastry is done and slightly browned. Place aluminum foil over the pie if it tends to over-brown.

Yield: Six to eight servings.

GRAHAM-NUT PIE SHELL

¾ cup finely crushed
graham crackers
¾ cup finely chopped
almonds, pecans, or
walnuts
¼ cup light brown sugar
⅓ cup butter, melted

Mix together the crackers, nuts, sugar, and butter in a medium-sized bowl. Press into a 9-inch pie plate. Chill.

Yield: One nine-inch pie shell.

APPLE RAISIN WALNUT PIE

1. Prepare pastry and press evenly in 10-inch pie plate. Flute edges with fork.
2. Blend the arrowroot with the apple juice in a large saucepan.
3. Add apples, spices, salt, lemon juice, honey, raisins, and walnuts.
4. Bring to a boil and cook, stirring occasionally, until fairly thick.
5. Preheat the oven to 350 degrees.
6. Pour the filling into pie shell and bake below the center of the oven for about 40 minutes, or until crust is browned and apples are tender.
7. Serve slightly warm or cool.
Yield: One ten-inch pie.
Note: To use a 9-inch pie plate, press pastry into plate and build up a high edge. Flute with fingers and proceed as directed.

1 recipe Whole Wheat Pastry II (see page 344)
2 tablespoons arrowroot or cornstarch
¾ cup apple juice
4 cups thinly sliced peeled tart apples (6 to 8)
1 teaspoon ground cinnamon
½ teaspoon ground allspice
½ teaspoon grated nutmeg
⅛ teaspoon salt
1 tablespoon lemon juice
¾ cup honey
¾ cup raisins
¾ cup broken walnuts

APPLE PIE

1. Put the apples in a medium-sized saucepan and add the apple juice, salt, cinnamon, allspice, and cloves. Mix the cornstarch with apple juice and lemon juice and stir into the apple mixture. Add the honey and bring mixture to a boil. Cook, stirring, until thick.
2. Stir in raisins and nuts. Cool. Preheat the oven to 350 degrees.
3. Pour the cooled mixture into the pie shell and bake below the center of the oven for 40 minutes, or until the pastry is done and apples are tender.
Yield: One ten-inch pie.

2 cups peeled and thinly sliced tart apples
¾ cup apple juice
⅛ teaspoon salt
1 teaspoon ground cinnamon
½ teaspoon ground allspice
¼ teaspoon ground cloves
2 tablespoons cornstarch
3 tablespoons apple juice
1 tablespoon lemon juice
¾ cup honey
¾ cup raisins
¾ cup chopped walnuts
1 chilled 10-inch Whole Wheat Pastry I pie shell (see page 344)

BAKED APPLE DESSERT

6 to 7 baking apples, peeled, cored, and thickly sliced
1 teaspoon ground cinnamon
2 tablespoons dark brown sugar
¾ cup unsweetened pineapple juice
½ cup finely chopped fresh pineapple or canned crushed pineapple, optional
⅓ cup chopped walnuts

1. Preheat the oven to 350 degrees.
2. Place the apple slices in a well-buttered deep pie plate. Sprinkle the cinnamon and sugar over all. Pour the juice over the apples and spoon the pineapple over all.
3. Sprinkle the walnuts over the top and bake for 40 minutes. Cool and chill.
Yield: Six servings.

PEACH CUSTARD PIE

1 recipe Whole Wheat Pastry II (see page 344)
2 cups sliced peeled peaches
4 large eggs
1 cup sour cream
¾ cup honey
1 teaspoon ground cinnamon
1 teaspoon pure vanilla extract
⅛ teaspoon salt

1. Prepare the pastry and press on bottom and sides of a 10-inch pie plate. Flute the edges with a fork.
2. Preheat the oven to 400 degrees.
3. Arrange the peaches in the pie shell. Beat together the eggs, sour cream, honey, cinnamon, vanilla, and salt. Pour over the peaches and bake below the center of the oven for 10 minutes. Reduce the oven temperature to 300 degrees and bake for 40 to 45 minutes longer, or until golden brown and firm.
4. Cool to room temperature before cutting. Best served the same day.
Yield: One ten-inch pie.
Note: Other fruits can be substituted for peaches. For strawberry pie, arrange 2 cups clean hulled berries pointed end up in pie shell. Omit the cinnamon from filling. Or use 2 cups sliced bananas or thinly sliced peeled apples. Proceed as directed for peach pie.

PEACH YOGURT PIE

1. Preheat the oven to 400 degrees.
2. Arrange the peaches over the bottom of the pie shell.
3. Put the eggs, yogurt, honey, vanilla, and salt in the container of an electric blender or food processor and whirl or process until smooth. Pour over the peaches. Bake below the center of the oven for 10 minutes. Reduce the oven temperature to 300 degrees and bake for 40 minutes longer, or until the pie is golden and almost set. Cool on a wire rack.
Yield: Eight servings.

2 cups peeled, sliced, ripe peaches
1 9- or 10-inch chilled Whole Wheat Pastry I pie shell (see page 344)
4 eggs, lightly beaten
1 cup plain yogurt (see page 324)
¾ cup honey
1 teaspoon pure vanilla extract
⅛ teaspoon salt

GOLDEN PINEAPPLE PIE

1. In a small saucepan, combine the pineapple, ½ cup honey, 2 tablespoons arrowroot, and the water. Bring to a boil, stirring, and cook for 1 minute. Cool.
2. Preheat the oven to 450 degrees.
3. Beat together the butter, cottage cheese, vanilla, salt, eggs, milk, remaining honey, and remaining arrowroot until smooth.
4. Pour the cooled pineapple mixture into the pie shell. Pour cottage cheese mixture over the pineapple mixture and bake for 15 minutes. Lower the oven temperature to 325 degrees and bake for 45 minutes longer, or until set. Cool and chill.
Yield: Six servings.

2 cups very finely chopped fresh pineapple or canned crushed unsweetened pineapple
1 cup crystallized honey
5 tablespoons arrowroot
2 tablespoons water
1 tablespoon butter
1 cup cottage cheese
1 teaspoon pure vanilla extract
¼ teaspoon salt
2 eggs, lightly beaten
1¼ cups milk
1 unbaked 10-inch pie crust (see pages 344–346)

PUMPKIN PIE

CRUST

1½ cups unbleached white
    flour
¼ teaspoon salt
½ cup butter
    Ice water

FILLING

2 eggs
1¾ cups pumpkin pulp or
    purée
¾ cup honey
¼ teaspoon salt
1 teaspoon ground
    cinnamon
½ teaspoon ground ginger
⅛ teaspoon ground cloves
1 cup evaporated milk
½ cup skim milk

TOPPING

Plain yogurt (see page
    324), sweetened with
    honey

1. To prepare the crust, put the flour and salt in a bowl. Cut in the butter with two knives until the mixture resembles coarse oatmeal.

2. With a fork, stir in 3 tablespoons ice water. Very slowly stir in enough extra ice water until dough hangs together loosely. Turn onto a well-floured board and roll to fit a 9-inch pie plate. Fit into the pie plate and decorate the edges.

3. Meanwhile, preheat the oven to 425 degrees.

4. Put all the filling ingredients in the container of an electric blender or food processor and blend or process until smooth. Pour into the prepared pie shell and bake for 15 minutes. Reduce the oven temperature to 350 degrees and bake for 45 minutes longer, or until pie is set.

5. Serve warm or cold, with yogurt.
Yield: Six servings.

YOGURT CHEESE PIE

½ cup rolled oats
½ cup pitted dates
2 tablespoons safflower
    oil
8 ounces cream cheese,
    softened
⅔ cup plain yogurt (see
    page 324)
1 teaspoon pure vanilla
    extract
2 tablespoons honey
6 dates, cut up

1. Put the oats and pitted dates through the fine blade of a food grinder. Mix with the oil and press into an 8-inch pie plate to make a pie shell.

2. Beat together the cream cheese, yogurt, vanilla, and honey until very smooth. Stir in the cut-up dates and pour into the pie shell. Refrigerate for several hours, or overnight, before serving.
Yield: Six servings.
Note: This is an unbaked pie.

HONEY YOGURT PIE

1. Soften the gelatin in the water for 5 minutes. Heat the gelatin over low heat, stirring to dissolve. Cool.

2. Combine the honey, vanilla, and lemon rind in a bowl. Add the gelatin mixture slowly and then stir in the yogurt cheese until smooth. Stir in the fruit and pour into the pie shell. Chill overnight. Garnish with fresh fruits.

Yield: One nine-inch pie.

1 teaspoon unflavored gelatin
⅓ cup water
⅓ cup honey
1 teaspoon pure vanilla extract
1 teaspoon grated lemon rind
3 cups yogurt cheese (see page 14)
1 cup mashed banana, puréed peaches, nectarines, blueberries, strawberries, or raspberries
1 baked 9-inch Whole Wheat Pastry I pie shell (see page 344) or 1 9-inch Graham-Nut Pie Shell (see page 346)

BANANA CAKE

1. Preheat the oven to 350 degrees.

2. In a medium-sized bowl beat together the bananas, butter, honey, vanilla, and salt. Stir in the egg.

3. Mix together the whole wheat flour, baking soda, cinnamon, dates, and nuts. Stir the flour mixture into the banana mixture. Turn into an oiled 9-inch square baking pan.

4. Bake for 45 minutes, or until the cake tests done. Cool on a wire rack and serve from the pan.

Yield: Nine servings.

1 cup mashed banana (2 to 3 medium)
½ cup butter, softened
¾ cup honey
1 teaspoon pure vanilla extract
½ teaspoon salt
1 egg, lightly beaten
1¾ cups whole wheat flour
1 teaspoon baking soda
½ teaspoon ground cinnamon
1 cup chopped pitted dates
½ cup chopped pecans or walnuts

YAM PRALINE PIE

1 recipe Whole Wheat
  Pastry II (see page 344)
2 eggs
½ cup brown sugar
½ cup granulated sugar
1 teaspoon ground
  cinnamon
½ teaspoon grated nutmeg
½ teaspoon ground ginger
¼ teaspoon salt
2 cups mashed peeled
  cooked yams (3
  medium)
¾ cup milk
1 cup light cream
  Praline topping (see
  below)

1. Prepare the pastry and press into a 10-inch pie plate.
2. Beat the eggs, then beat in the sugars, spices, and salt. Stir in the yams. Gradually stir in the milk and cream.
3. Preheat the oven to 400 degrees.
4. Pour the filling into the pie shell and bake below the center of the oven for 10 minutes. Reduce the oven temperature to 350 degrees and bake for 20 minutes.
5. Remove the pie from oven and sprinkle with the praline topping. Bake for 25 minutes or until a knife inserted in center comes out clean.
6. Cool completely before serving.

PRALINE TOPPING: Mix ⅓ cup chopped pecans or walnuts, ⅓ cup brown sugar and 3 tablespoons softened butter.
Yield: One ten-inch pie.
Note: To bake in a 9-inch pie plate, press the pastry into plate, build up high edges, and flute with your fingers.

BANANA-DATE NUT CAKE

1¾ cups whole wheat flour
1 teaspoon baking soda
½ teaspoon salt
½ teaspoon ground
  cinnamon
1 cup snipped pitted
  dates
½ cup chopped walnuts
½ cup butter, softened
¾ cup honey
1 egg
1 cup mashed very ripe
  banana (2-3 medium)

1. Preheat the oven to 350 degrees.
2. Mix the whole wheat flour, baking soda, salt, cinnamon, dates, and nuts.
3. Cream the butter and honey until well blended. Beat in the egg and banana. Stir in dry ingredients.
4. Turn into an oiled and lightly floured 9-inch square pan.
5. Bake for 45 to 50 minutes, or until a toothpick inserted in the center comes out clean.
6. Turn out on a wire rack to cool.
Yield: One nine-inch cake.

APPLE CRUMB CAKE

1. Preheat the oven to 400 degrees.
2. Mix the apples, ⅓ cup brown sugar, 2 tablespoons flour, and the cinnamon together.
3. With a pastry blender, mix the remaining sugar, flour, and the butter to make crumbs.
4. Press half the crumbs on bottom of 9-inch springform pan and ¾-inch up sides. Reserve the remaining crumbs. Spoon apples into pan.
5. Bake for 20 minutes. Remove from oven and sprinkle with reserved crumbs. Bake for 30 minutes longer, or until the apples are tender.
6. Cool cake to room temperature, then remove the sides of the pan and cut the cake in wedges to serve. Best served same day.
Yield: Eight servings.

5 cups peeled and thinly sliced tart apples (8 or 9 medium)
⅔ cup brown sugar
1½ cups plus 2 tablespoons whole wheat flour
1 teaspoon ground cinnamon
½ cup butter, softened

DATE AND NUT CAKE

1. Beat the eggs, sugar, and oil together very well.
2. Stir in the remaining ingredients until thoroughly blended. Put in an oiled and floured 9- by 5- by 3-inch loaf pan and put in a cold oven. Set the temperature at 300 degrees, light the oven, and bake for 2 hours, or until done.
Yield: Ten servings.

4 eggs, at room temperature
1 cup brown sugar
½ cup oil
1 cup whole wheat flour
1 teaspoon salt
3 cups chopped dates
3 cups chopped pecans
1 teaspoon pure vanilla extract

APPLESAUCE CAKE WITH BROILED TOPPING

CAKE

1½ cups whole wheat flour
⅔ cup unprocessed bran
2 teaspoons baking powder
½ teaspoon baking soda
½ teaspoon salt
1 teaspoon ground cinnamon
½ teaspoon grated nutmeg
¼ teaspoon ground cloves
¼ teaspoon ground allspice
1 cup raisins
1 cup finely chopped nuts
½ cup butter, softened
1 cup brown sugar
2 eggs
1½ cups thick homemade applesauce (see page 328)

TOPPING

½ cup butter, melted
½ cup brown sugar
½ cup milk
⅓ cup unprocessed bran
¾ cup unsweetened flaked coconut
½ cup finely chopped nuts
1 teaspoon pure vanilla extract

1. Preheat the oven to 350 degrees.
2. Mix the flour, bran, baking powder, baking soda, salt, spices, raisins, and nuts together.
3. Cream the butter and sugar until well blended. Add the eggs and beat well. Add the dry ingredients alternately with the applesauce, mixing well.
4. Turn into an oiled and lightly floured 9-inch square pan.
5. Bake for 30 to 35 minutes, or until a toothpick inserted in center of cake comes out clean.
6. To make the topping, mix the butter, brown sugar, and milk and boil, stirring, for 1 minute. Stir in the bran, coconut, nuts, and vanilla. Spread over the hot cake.
7. Put under the broiler for 2 to 3 minutes or until bubbly.
8. Serve the cake warm or cool from pan.
Yield: Nine servings.

WHOLE WHEAT APPLE CAKE

1. Preheat the oven to 350 degrees.
2. Combine the nuts, ¼ cup of the sugar, the cinnamon, wheat germ, apple slices, and lemon juice in a small bowl and set aside.
3. Cream the butter and remaining sugar very well. Beat in the eggs, one at a time.
4. Sift together the flour, baking powder, and baking soda. Combine the sour cream and the milk. Stir the sifted dry ingredients into the creamed mixture alternately with the sour cream mixture.
5. Pour half the batter into a well-buttered 9- by 5- by 3-inch glass loaf pan, spread the apple mixture over, and top with remaining batter. Bake for 50 minutes, or until done. Serve warm with yogurt.
Yield: Six servings.

½ cup finely chopped nuts
¾ cup brown sugar
1 teaspoon ground cinnamon
2 teaspoons wheat germ
1½ cups thin peeled apple slices
½ teaspoon lemon juice
½ cup butter
2 eggs
1¼ cups sifted whole wheat flour
1½ teaspoons baking powder
½ teaspoon baking soda
½ cup sour cream
½ tablespoon milk
Plain yogurt (see page 324)

STRAWBERRY SHORTCAKE

1. Preheat the oven to 450 degrees.
2. Sift the flour with the baking powder. Add the sugar and salt and cut in 4 tablespoons of the butter until the mixture resembles coarse oatmeal. Combine the eggs and milk and stir into the dry ingredients.
3. Mix well. The dough will be soft. Place in a well-buttered, or oiled, 9- or 10-inch layer pan and bake for 20 minutes, or until done.
4. Remove from the pan, split, and butter the cut sides with remaining butter. Cover the bottom half with sliced strawberries.
5. Place top half in position, cover with remaining berries, and top with whipped cream.
Yield: Eight servings.

2 cups whole wheat pastry flour
1 teaspoon baking powder
2 tablespoons brown sugar
¼ teaspoon salt
6 tablespoons butter
2 eggs, lightly beaten
⅔ cup milk
1 quart strawberries, sliced
1 cup heavy cream, whipped

GINGERBREAD

2⅓ cups sifted whole wheat pastry flour
1 teaspoon baking powder
¼ teaspoon salt
½ teaspoon baking soda
1 teaspoon ground ginger
½ teaspoon ground cinnamon
½ teaspoon grated nutmeg
½ teaspoon ground allspice
½ cup butter, softened
1 cup brown sugar
2 eggs
½ cup unsulphured molasses
¾ cup hot water

1. Preheat the oven to 350 degrees.
2. Sift together the flour, baking powder, and salt.
3. Blend together the baking soda, ginger, cinnamon, nutmeg, allspice, and butter. Stir in the sugar. Beat in the eggs. Stir in the molasses and add the hot water alternately with the flour mixture. Pour into well-buttered 9-inch square pan and bake for 45 minutes.
Yield: Nine servings.

COFFEE LAYER CAKE

1 cup honey
1 cup butter, softened
3 eggs, separated
1 teaspoon pure vanilla extract
½ cup strong coffee or coffee substitute
2¼ cups whole wheat flour (pastry flour works best)
1 teaspoon baking soda
¼ teaspoon salt
¾ cup buttermilk
3 egg whites
Cream Cheese Frosting

1. Preheat the oven to 300 degrees.
2. Line three 9-inch layer pans with wax paper and oil the sides and bottoms.
3. Beat together the honey, butter, egg yolks, and vanilla. Add the coffee. Sift together the whole wheat flour, baking soda, and salt and stir in alternately with the buttermilk.
4. Beat the 6 egg whites until stiff but not dry and fold into the cake batter. Divide among the three pans and bake for 30 minutes or until cake tests done. Cool on wire racks.

CREAM CHEESE FROSTING: Beat 2 packages (8 ounces each) softened cream cheese with ½ cup butter, softened, 1 cup honey and ⅓ cup strong coffee or coffee substitute. Stir in 1 cup chopped walnuts. Use to fill between layers and frost top.
Yield: Ten to twelve servings.

QUICK SOUR CREAM COFFEE CAKE

1. Preheat the oven to 350 degrees.
2. Mix 1⅓ cups whole wheat flour, the baking soda, and salt.
3. Heat ½ cup honey until warmed. Add to the butter and beat until fluffy. Beat in eggs.
4. Stir in dry ingredients, sour cream, and vanilla.
5. In a small bowl, mix 2 tablespoons flour, 2 tablespoons honey, the cinnamon, and nuts.
6. Turn half the batter into an oiled 9-inch square pan. Drizzle half the honey mixture over top. Repeat with the remaining batter and honey mixture.
7. Bake for 45 minutes, or until a pick inserted in the center of cake comes out clean. Serve warm or cold, cut in squares. Yield: Nine servings.

1⅓ cups plus 2 tablespoons whole wheat flour
1 teaspoon baking soda
¼ teaspoon salt
Honey
½ cup butter, softened
2 eggs
1 cup sour cream
1 teaspoon pure vanilla extract
2 teaspoons ground cinnamon
¾ cup chopped nuts

RAW FRUIT "CAKE"

1. On a small 6-inch plate or dish, spread a layer of 1 cup of the figs. Top with a layer of 1 cup nuts, then 1 cup dates, and 1 cup coconut.
2. Repeat the four layers three more times. Apply light pressure to top of "cake" and let stand overnight. Cut in small wedges to serve.
Yield: Ten servings.

4 cups ground figs
4 cups grated nuts
4 cups chopped dates
4 cups unsweetened shredded fresh coconut

PUMPKIN CAKE

2 cups honey
1 cup vegetable oil
2 cups sieved cooked
  pumpkin
4 eggs, lightly beaten
3 cups whole wheat flour
2 tablespoons ground
  cinnamon
3 teaspoons baking
  powder
2 teaspoons baking soda
2 teaspoons pure almond
  extract
1 teaspoon salt
1 cup chopped nuts or
  seeds
1 cup raisins or chopped
  figs

1. Preheat the oven to 350 degrees.
2. Mix all the ingredients together in a large bowl. Pour into two well-oiled or buttered 9-inch layer pans or one oiled 9-inch tube cake pan. Bake the layers for 50 minutes and the tube pan for 1 hour and 25 minutes, or until done.
Yield: Two layers or one cake; about twelve servings.

SOUR CREAM CHEESECAKE

1 pound cottage cheese
1 pound cream cheese,
  softened
1½ cups brown sugar
4 eggs
3 tablespoons
  stoneground whole
  wheat flour
3 tablespoons arrowroot
1½ teaspoons pure vanilla
  extract
2 tablespoons lemon juice
½ cup butter, melted and
  cooled
2 cups sour cream

1. Preheat the oven to 325 degrees.
2. Sieve the cottage cheese and whip, or beat, with the cream cheese for 5 minutes. Still beating, gradually add the sugar.
3. Beat in the eggs, one at a time. Add the flour, arrowroot, vanilla, and juice. Mix well.
4. Fold in the butter and sour cream and pour into an oiled 9- or 10-inch springform pan. Bake for 1 hour. Turn the heat off and leave the cake in the oven for 1 hour longer without opening the oven door.
Yield: Twelve servings.

QUICK UPSIDE-DOWN CAKE

1. Preheat the oven to 350 degrees.
2. Drain the fruit, reserve liquid, and place fruit in a buttered 13- by 9- by 2-inch baking pan.
3. Measure 1¼ to 1½ cups reserved liquid into a small saucepan. Add honey to sweeten (¼ cup, or to taste) and stir in the 2 tablespoons whole wheat flour. Bring to a boil and simmer for 1 minute. Pour over the fruit and set pan in oven.
4. Beat together the eggs, oil, vanilla, and ½ cup honey.
5. Sift together three times the pastry flour, baking powder, and salt. Add alternately with the milk to the egg mixture. Pour over the fruit mixture and bake for 35 to 45 minutes, or until the cake is done (fruit bubbles up all over). Serve warm with yogurt.

Yield: Ten servings.

1 quart home-canned peaches, apples, pineapple, or cherries
Honey
2 tablespoons whole wheat flour
2 eggs
½ cup vegetable oil
1 teaspoon pure vanilla extract
1¾ cups whole wheat pastry flour
2 teaspoons baking powder
¼ teaspoon salt
¾ cup milk
Plain yogurt (see page 324)

CREAMY CHEESY CAKE

1. Preheat the oven to 350 degrees.
2. Mix together the wheat germ and cinnamon and sprinkle over a very well-buttered 9-inch springform pan. Roll pan until the inside is evenly coated with the mixture. Chill in the refrigerator.
3. Beat the eggs until very thick and creamy. Gradually beat in the cottage cheese. Stir in the lemon juice, yogurt, honey, and flour. Mix well.
4. Pour into the prepared pan and bake for 1 hour. Turn the oven off but leave the cake in the oven for 1½ hours longer (do not open oven door). Chill overnight in refrigerator.

Yield: Ten servings.

¼ cup wheat germ
1 teaspoon ground cinnamon
8 eggs, at room temperature
2 pounds (4 cups) cottage cheese)
3 tablespoons lemon juice
1 cup plain yogurt (see page 324)
1 cup honey
¼ cup whole wheat flour

SPICY RAISIN LOAF CAKE

1 cup cornmeal
1 cup rye flour
2 teaspoons baking
  powder
½ teaspoon baking soda
¼ teaspoon salt
1 teaspoon ground
  cinnamon
½ teaspoon grated nutmeg
¼ teaspoon ground cloves
¼ teaspoon ground
  allspice
1 cup brown sugar
⅓ cup butter or vegetable
  oil
1½ cups water
1 cup raisins

1. Mix the cornmeal, rye flour, baking powder, baking soda, salt, and spices together.
2. Put the sugar, butter, water, and raisins in a saucepan. Bring to a boil. Remove from the heat and cool.
3. Preheat the oven to 350 degrees.
4. Stir the dry ingredients into mixture in saucepan. Turn into an oiled 9- by 5- by 3-inch loaf pan.
5. Bake for 45 minutes, or until a toothpick inserted in the center comes out clean.
6. Let stand in the pan for 10 minutes, then turn out on a rack to cool.
Yield: One loaf.

WHOLE WHEAT SPONGECAKE

12 eggs, separated
1½ cups brown sugar
¼ teaspoon salt
1½ teaspoons cream of
  tartar
¼ cup honey
1½ cups whole wheat flour
  or unbleached white
  flour
1½ teaspoons pure vanilla
  extract
1 teaspoon grated lemon
  rind

1. Preheat the oven to 300 degrees.
2. Beat the egg whites at highest speed on an electric mixer until soft peaks form. While still beating, gradually add 1 cup of the sugar, the salt, cream of tartar, and honey. Continue to beat until stiff peaks form, or until the mixture clings to the bowl.
3. Beat the egg yolks with the same beaters in a second bowl. Gradually add the remaining sugar and beat until thick and light in color.
4. Fold the yolk mixture into the whites mixture gently but quickly. Fold in the flour, vanilla, and lemon rind. Turn into an ungreased 9-inch tube cake pan and bake for 1 hour. Increase the oven temperature to 350 degrees and bake for 15 minutes longer. Invert the pan to cool the cake. Loosen with a spatula.
Yield: Ten servings.

SUNSHINE CAKE

1. Preheat the oven to 325 degrees.
2. To prepare the cake, beat the egg yolks until very light and thick. Gradually beat in the honey. Add the vanilla and lemon rind.
3. Sift the baking powder with ½ cup of the flour. Combine remaining flour with the carob powder.
4. Fold the carob mixture alternately with the water into the egg yolk mixture. Stir in the baking powder mixture.
5. Beat the egg whites until stiff but not dry and fold into batter. Pour the mixture into a buttered 9-inch tube pan and bake for 45 minutes, or until done. Invert the pan and cool cake in pan.
6. To prepare the frosting, cream together the butter and dry milk. Stir in the carob powder. Beat in remaining ingredients and use to frost cooled cake.
Yield: Eight servings.

CAKE
4 eggs, separated
½ cup honey
3 teaspoons pure vanilla extract
1 teaspoon grated lemon rind
3 teaspoons baking powder
1¼ cups whole wheat pastry flour
¼ cup carob powder
⅓ cup water

FROSTING
2 tablespoons butter, softened
⅔ cup non-fat dry milk powder
⅓ cup carob powder
¼ cup honey
¼ cup heavy cream
1 teaspoon pure vanilla extract

UNCOOKED HONEY FROSTING

1. Using a rotary beater, beat the egg white with the salt until peaks form. While still beating, add the honey in a slow constant stream.
2. Add the almond extract and continue to beat until mixture is thick and fluffy.
Yield: Enough to cover a nine-inch layer cake.

1 egg white
⅛ teaspoon salt
½ cup warm honey
¼ teaspoon pure almond extract

FRESH PLUM COFFEE CAKE

1 package dry active yeast
½ cup granulated sugar
¼ teaspoon salt
1½ cups unbleached white flour
¾ cup water
1 cup butter, divided
2½ cups whole wheat flour
1 teaspoon grated lemon rind
1 egg
1½ pounds fresh prune plums
½ cup brown sugar
½ cup wheat germ
1 teaspoon ground cinnamon
½ teaspoon ground cloves

1. Mix the yeast, granulated sugar, the salt, and white flour in a large bowl.
2. Heat the water and ½ cup butter until very warm and butter is melted. Add to dry ingredients and beat at medium speed with electric mixer for 2 minutes.
3. Add 1 cup whole wheat flour, the lemon rind, and egg and beat at high speed for 2 minutes. Stir in 1½ cups whole wheat flour or enough to make a firm dough.
4. Turn out and knead a few turns or until smooth. Cover with a sheet of plastic wrap and let rest for 15 minutes.
5. Roll dough to form a 15- by 10-inch rectangle and press into a jelly roll pan, building up sides about ½ inch.
6. Halve the plums, remove the pits, and cut the plums in ½-inch-thick slices. Arrange in even rows on dough. Let cake rise for 20 minutes.
7. Preheat the oven to 350 degrees.
8. Mix the brown sugar, wheat germ, cinnamon, and cloves. Cut in the remaining butter until the mixture resembles large peas. Sprinkle over the plums.
9. Bake for 40 to 50 minutes, or until browned around the edges and the fruit appears dry.
Yield: Sixteen servings.

EASY TROPICAL FRUITCAKE

¾ cup whole wheat flour
¼ teaspoon baking powder
¼ teaspoon baking soda
¼ teaspoon salt

1. Preheat the oven to 250 degrees.
2. Line an 8- by 4- by 2-inch loaf pan with waxed paper.
3. Mix the whole wheat flour, baking powder, baking soda, and salt. Add fruits

and nuts and mix to coat.

4. Beat the eggs until light. Add honey and beat well. Add the vanilla. Then add to the dry ingredients and mix well.

5. Turn the batter into the prepared pan, pressing down with a spoon to pack.

6. Bake for 60 to 75 minutes, or until done (time may vary with fruits used and degree of dryness).

7. Turn out of pan onto a wire rack and peel off the paper. Cool, then store airtight. Cut in thin slices to serve. Stored cake will keep for 1 to 2 weeks, or for several months in the freezer.

Yield: One loaf.

2 cups total: dried apricot halves, whole pitted prunes, raisins, unsweetened flaked coconut, pitted dates, dried figs (choose as desired; not all need be used)
3 cups walnut or pecan halves
3 eggs
½ cup honey
1 teaspoon pure vanilla extract

CAROB CAKE

1. Preheat the oven to 325 degrees.

2. Mix the whole wheat flour, white flour, sugar, baking powder, baking soda, salt, 2 tablespoons carob powder, and the spices.

3. Mix the applesauce, oil, egg, dates, and orange peel. Add to dry ingredients and mix well.

4. Oil well a 9-inch square pan and dust lightly with carob powder. Turn batter into the pan and bake for 1 hour, or until a toothpick inserted in the center comes out clean.

5. Cool in the pan on a wire rack and cut in squares to serve.

Yield: Nine servings.

Note: One-half cup chopped nuts or sunflower seeds can be added to the cake batter, if you wish.

1 cup whole wheat flour
1 cup unbleached white flour
1 cup brown sugar
2 teaspoons baking powder
½ teaspoon baking soda
¼ teaspoon salt
Carob powder or unsweetened cocoa
1 teaspoon ground cinnamon
½ teaspoon ground cloves
½ teaspoon grated nutmeg
1½ cups chunky unsweetened homemade applesauce (see page 328)
½ cup vegetable oil
1 large egg, lightly beaten
½ cup finely snipped pitted dates
1 teaspoon grated orange or lemon rind

SPICY PRUNE-NUT CUPCAKES

1¾ cups whole wheat flour
1½ teaspoons baking
powder
¼ teaspoon baking soda
¼ teaspoon salt
1 teaspoon ground
cinnamon
¼ teaspoon ground cloves
½ cup butter, softened
1 cup brown sugar
1 teaspoon pure vanilla
extract
2 eggs
½ cup milk
1 cup snipped soft pitted
prunes
½ cup chopped nuts

1. Preheat the oven to 350 degrees.
2. Mix the whole wheat flour, baking powder, baking soda, salt, and spices.
3. Cream the butter and sugar until well blended. Beat in the vanilla and eggs. Stir in the dry ingredients, milk, prunes, and nuts.
4. Spoon into oiled cupcake tins, filling three-fourths full.
5. Bake for 20 minutes, or until browned and done.
6. Turn out of pans on wire racks to cool.
Yield: Sixteen cupcakes.

PUMPKIN APPLE BUNDT CAKE

1 cup unbleached white
flour
1 cup whole wheat flour
1 teaspoon baking
powder
¾ teaspoon baking soda
½ teaspoon salt
1 teaspoon ground
cinnamon
¼ teaspoon grated nutmeg
¼ teaspoon ground cloves
¼ teaspoon ground ginger
½ cup butter, softened
¾ cup brown sugar
¾ cup granulated sugar
2 teaspoons grated orange
rind
2 eggs
1 cup pumpkin purée
1½ cups shredded peeled
apples (2 medium)

1. Preheat the oven to 350 degrees.
2. Mix the white flour, whole wheat flour, baking powder, baking soda, salt, and spices.
3. Cream the butter, sugars, and orange rind until fluffy. Beat in the eggs. Stir in the pumpkin and apples.
4. Add the dry ingredients and mix well. Turn into an oiled and lightly floured 9-inch Bundt pan.
5. Bake for 50 to 60 minutes, or until a toothpick inserted in the center comes out clean. Cool in the pan for 10 minutes, then turn out on a wire rack to cool completely.
Yield: Twelve servings.

FRESH PEAR KUCHEN

1. Mix together 1 cup flour, the wheat germ, yeast, and salt.
2. Heat the milk, water, granulated sugar, and ¼ cup butter until very warm. Add to dry ingredients and beat at medium speed with an electric mixer for 2 minutes.
3. Add the egg and enough additional flour to make a firm dough. Turn out on a lightly floured surface and knead until smooth and elastic. Put in an oiled bowl, turning to oil the top. Cover with a sheet of plastic wrap, allowing the wrap to touch the dough. Let rise for 1 hour or until doubled.
4. Punch the dough down and let rest for 10 minutes. Pat onto bottom of an oiled 13- by 9- by 2-inch pan. Brush the dough with melted butter.
5. Arrange the pear slices in even rows on the dough. Mix the brown sugar and allspice and sprinkle on the pears. Let rise for 30 minutes.
6. Preheat the oven to 350 degrees.
7. Bake for 45 minutes, or until well browned and the pears are tender. Serve warm or cold, cut in squares.
Yield: Twelve servings.

2 to 2½ cups unbleached white flour
½ cup wheat germ
1 package dry active yeast
½ teaspoon salt
½ cup milk
¼ cup water
¼ cup granulated sugar
¼ cup butter
1 egg
Melted butter
2 fresh winter pears, cored and sliced
½ cup brown sugar
1 teaspoon ground allspice

FIG FILLING

1. Combine all the ingredients in a saucepan. Bring to a boil and simmer, stirring constantly, for 15 minutes. Cool.
2. Use as a filling for yeast or layer cakes.
Yield: About two and one-half cups, enough for two cakes.

2 cups ground unsulphured figs
½ cup honey
2 tablespoons unsweetened prune juice
1 tablespoon lemon juice
1 tablespoon orange juice

COFFEE WALNUT LAYER CAKE

CAKE

2¼ cups whole wheat flour
1 teaspoon baking soda
¼ teaspoon salt
1 cup butter, softened
1 cup honey
3 egg yolks
1 teaspoon pure vanilla extract
½ cup strong liquid coffee or coffee substitute
¾ cup buttermilk
6 egg whites

FROSTING

2 8-ounce packages cream cheese, softened
½ cup butter, softened
1 cup honey
½ cup strong liquid coffee or coffee substitute
Chopped nuts

1. Preheat the oven to 300 degrees.
2. Mix the whole wheat flour, baking soda, and salt.
3. Cream the butter, honey, egg yolks, and vanilla until fluffy. Add coffee and buttermilk alternately with the dry ingredients and mix well.
4. Beat the egg whites until stiff and fold into the batter.
5. Line the bottoms of three 9-inch layer cake pans with wax paper and oil the sides of the pans.
6. Turn the batter into the pans, spreading it evenly.
7. Bake for 30 minutes, or until browned and the edges pull away from the sides of the pans. Let stand for about 5 minutes, then turn out on racks to cool. Peel off the paper.
8. To make the frosting, beat the cream cheese, butter, and honey until well blended. Beat in the coffee. Refrigerate until ready to use.
9. When the cakes are thoroughly cooled, spread the frosting between layers and on top of the cake, sprinkling each layer with walnuts, including the top layer.

NUTRITIOUS BITES

3 eggs, well beaten
1 cup brown sugar
1 cup chopped walnuts
1 cup unsweetened shredded coconut
1 cup chopped dates
¾ cup whole wheat flour
¼ cup wheat germ

1. Preheat the oven to 350 degrees.
2. Combine all the ingredients and press down into a well-oiled 9-inch square baking pan. Bake for 20 minutes or until done. Cut while warm into squares or bars.
Yield: About sixteen squares.

SWEET APPLE SNITZ AND DUMPLINGS

1. Soak the dried apples in the water for 30 minutes. Bring to a boil and simmer for 30 minutes, or until tender. Sweeten with honey.
2. Combine the flour, baking powder, salt, and sugar in a bowl. Stir in enough milk to make a stiff dumpling batter.
3. Drop the batter by the tablespoon onto the top of the simmering apple mixture. Cover tightly and cook for 15 minutes. Yield: Eight servings.

4 cups (about 1 pound) dried apples
4 cups water
Honey to taste
1 cup sifted whole wheat flour
1¼ teaspoons baking powder
¼ teaspoon salt
1 tablespoon brown sugar
Milk

WHOLE WHEAT POUNDCAKE

1. Preheat the oven to 325 degrees.
2. Cream the butter until light. Gradually beat in the sugar. Beat in the eggs very well one at a time. Add the remaining ingredients and blend with an electric mixer at low speed. Beat for 3 minutes at medium speed, scraping the bowl occasionally.
3. Pour the batter into a well-buttered and floured 10-inch tube cake pan. Bake for 65 minutes, or until done. Cool in the pan for 15 minutes before transferring to a wire rack.
Yield: Twelve servings.

1 cup butter
2 cups brown sugar
1 teaspoon grated lemon rind
3 eggs
2¼ cups sifted whole wheat flour
¼ teaspoon baking soda
¼ teaspoon salt
1 cup plain yogurt (see page 324)

BLUEBERRY SQUARES

2 cups whole wheat flour
1 teaspoon baking powder
½ teaspoon baking soda
¼ teaspoon salt
½ cup butter, softened
1 cup brown sugar
2 teaspoons grated orange rind
1 teaspoon pure vanilla extract
2 eggs
½ cup milk
1½ cups blueberries

1. Preheat the oven to 350 degrees.
2. Mix together the whole wheat flour, baking powder, baking soda, and salt.
3. Cream the butter, sugar, and orange rind until fluffy. Add the vanilla and eggs and beat well.
4. Add the dry ingredients and milk, and mix well. Fold in berries and spread in an oiled 13- by 9- by 2-inch baking pan.
5. Bake for 40 minutes, or until a toothpick inserted comes out clean. Cool in the pan on a wire rack, then cut in squares to serve.

Yield: Eighteen squares.

Note: If you wish, sprinkle the squares with confectioners' sugar before cutting.

DUTCH BUTTER COOKIES

1 cup butter
¾ cup brown sugar
1 egg, separated
1 teaspoon pure vanilla extract
¼ teaspoon salt
1½ cups whole wheat pastry flour
1 cup unbleached white flour
½ cup chopped pecans

1. Preheat the oven to 375 degrees.
2. Cream the butter and sugar together very well. Beat in the egg yolk, vanilla, and salt.
3. Stir in the whole wheat flour and unbleached white flour. Press the mixture into a well-buttered 15- by 10- by 1-inch jelly roll pan. Sprinkle with the nuts and press them in. Beat the egg white lightly and brush over the top.
4. Bake for 20 minutes or until well browned and done. Cut into bars or squares while hot. Cool in the pan.

Yield: About five dozen squares.

JELLY CAKES

1. Preheat the oven to 350 degrees.
2. To make the dough, combine the oil, water, and eggs in a bowl and gradually work in enough of the flour to make a dough that is soft but not sticky. Divide into three balls, cover and let rest while peeling the apples.
3. Oil the bottom of a large baking sheet with ¼- to ½-inch-high sides.
4. Roll out one ball of dough between sheets of wax paper, or on a lightly floured board, into an ⅛-inch-thick rectangle. Transfer the rolled-out dough to the baking sheet.
5. Cover with the apples, dot with ¼ cup honey, and sprinkle with cinnamon.
6. Roll out the second ball of dough to the same size as the first and lay it over the apples. Spread this layer with jam and sprinkle with raisins.
7. Roll out the remaining ball of dough and lay it over the jam layer. Drizzle the remaining honey over the top and sprinkle with cinnamon. Bake for 1 hour, or until the pastry is brown and the filling bubbly. Cool slightly, cut into squares, and serve warm or at room temperature.
Yield: Eighteen squares.

DOUGH
⅔ cup safflower oil
⅓ cup cold water
3 eggs, lightly beaten
3 to 4 cups whole wheat pastry flour

FILLING
4 to 6 tart apples, peeled, cored, and sliced
¼ cup plus 2 tablespoons honey
Ground cinnamon to taste
½ cup jam or marmalade
½ cup raisins

NUT SQUARES

1. Preheat the oven to 350 degrees.
2. Beat the eggs and honey together. Stir in the remaining ingredients and turn into an oiled 9-inch square baking pan. Bake for 20 to 25 minutes, or until done. Cool in the pan and cut into squares.
Yield: One dozen squares.

2 eggs, lightly beaten
⅔ cup honey
6 tablespoons whole wheat flour
¼ teaspoon salt
1 cup chopped nuts
½ cup sesame seeds

PEANUT BUTTER AND BANANA BARS

2 eggs, well beaten
⅓ cup peanut butter
¼ cup molasses
½ cup brown rice flour
½ cup chopped walnuts or peanuts
1 ripe banana, chopped
½ teaspoon ground cinnamon
¼ teaspoon salt

1. Preheat the oven to 350 degrees.
2. Combine all the ingredients and mix well. Turn into a buttered 8-inch square baking pan and bake for 15 minutes.
3. Cut into bars while still warm.
Yield: Twelve to eighteen bars.

OAT SHORTBREAD

3½ cups rolled oats
⅔ cup brown sugar
¼ cup unbleached white flour
¾ cup butter, softened
½ teaspoon salt
1 teaspoon pure vanilla extract

1. Preheat the oven to 325 degrees.
2. Place all the ingredients in a bowl and work together lightly with a wooden spoon or the fingertips. Press into a well-buttered 13- by 9- by 2-inch baking pan. Bake for 30 minutes, or until done. Cool for 10 minutes. Cut into squares.
Yield: Two dozen.

EASY BAR COOKIES

1 cup graham cracker crumbs
1 tablespoon butter, melted
1 small 5⅓-ounce can evaporated milk
1½ tablespoons honey
¼ cup wheat germ
¼ cup soy grits
½ cup unsweetened shredded coconut
¼ cup sesame seeds
½ cup chopped nuts

1. Preheat the oven to 350 degrees.
2. Combine all the ingredients in a bowl and mix well. Pat into an oiled 8-inch square baking pan and bake for 20 minutes, or until done.
3. Cool in the pan and cut into bars while still slightly warm.
Yield: One dozen bars.

WHEAT GERM-JAM BARS

1. Preheat the oven to 350 degrees.
2. Mix together the flour, salt, and ½ cup wheat germ in large bowl.
3. Beat together the butter, ¼ cup sugar, egg yolks, rind, and vanilla.
4. Stir in dry ingredients. With your hands press mixture into 13- by 9- by 2-inch baking pan, building up the edges to about ½ inch.
5. Bake for about 12 minutes.
6. Beat the egg whites until foamy throughout. Gradually add the remaining sugar and beat until stiff. Fold in the nuts and remaining wheat germ.
7. Spread jam on the baked crust, then spread the egg white mixture over jam. Bake for 15 to 18 minutes longer, or until golden brown. Remove from the oven and cool on a wire rack. Cut in small bars.
Yield: About thirty bars.

1¼ cups whole wheat flour
¼ teaspoon salt
¾ cup wheat germ
6 tablespoons butter, softened
½ cup brown sugar
2 eggs, separated
2 teaspoons grated lemon or orange rind
1 teaspoon pure vanilla extract
¼ cup finely chopped walnuts
¾ cup seedless raspberry jam, apricot preserve, or other jam

APPLE-OATMEAL COOKIES

1. Preheat the oven to 350 degrees.
2. Cream the butter with the sugar. Beat in the eggs very well.
3. Combine all the remaining ingredients and stir into the creamed mixture. Drop by teaspoons onto an oiled baking sheet and bake for 12 to 15 minutes, or until done. Cool on a wire rack.
Yield: Three to four dozen cookies.

½ cup butter
1 cup brown sugar
2 eggs
1¾ cups whole wheat pastry flour
½ cup rolled oats
½ teaspoon salt
2 teaspoons baking powder
½ teaspoon ground cinnamon
1 cup chopped raisins
1 cup chopped walnuts
1½ cups finely chopped apples

APPLE SPICE COOKIES

1¾ cups whole wheat flour
1 cup quick rolled oats
½ teaspoon baking powder
½ teaspoon baking soda
¼ teaspoon salt
½ teaspoon ground cinnamon
½ teaspoon ground cloves
½ cup butter, softened
¾ cup honey
1 teaspoon pure vanilla extract
2 eggs
1¾ cups grated unpeeled eating apples (6 or 7 medium)
½ cup raisins
½ cup snipped pitted dates
½ cup chopped walnuts

1. Preheat the oven to 350 degrees.
2. Mix the flour, oats, baking powder, baking soda, salt, and spices in a large bowl.
3. Cream the butter and honey until well blended. Beat in the vanilla and eggs. Stir in the apples and dry ingredients. Add the raisins, dates, and nuts. Drop by teaspoons 2 inches apart onto oiled baking sheets.
4. Bake for 12 to 15 minutes, or until well browned. Remove to racks to cool.
Yield: Three and one-half to four dozen cookies.

APPLESAUCE COOKIES

1 cup brown sugar
¾ cup vegetable oil
1 cup thick homemade applesauce (see page 328)
½ cup chopped nuts
½ teaspoon salt
1 teaspoon pure vanilla extract
4 cups rolled oats
½ cup chopped dates

1. Preheat the oven to 375 degrees.
2. Beat the brown sugar and oil together until well blended.
3. Add the remaining ingredients and mix well. Drop from a teaspoon onto an oiled baking sheet. Bake for 25 minutes, or until well browned and done. Cool on a wire rack.
Yield: About five dozen cookies.

OLD-FASHIONED SOFT SPICY APPLE COOKIES

1. Preheat the oven to 350 degrees.
2. In a medium-sized bowl combine the flour, salt, baking powder, baking soda, cinnamon, nutmeg, cloves, and oats.
3. In another bowl beat together the butter, honey, and vanilla. Beat in the eggs, stir in the dry ingredients and mix to moisten.
4. Stir in the apples, raisins, dates, and nuts. Drop by teaspoons 2 inches apart onto an oiled baking sheet. Bake for 12 minutes, or until lightly browned.

Yield: Three to four dozen cookies.

1¾ cups whole wheat flour
¼ teaspoon salt
½ teaspoon baking powder
½ teaspoon baking soda
½ teaspoon ground cinnamon
¼ teaspoon grated nutmeg
¼ teaspoon ground cloves
1 cup quick cooking oats
½ cup butter, softened
¾ cup honey
1 teaspoon pure vanilla extract
2 eggs, lightly beaten
1 cup grated apple (6 to 7 medium)
½ cup raisins
½ cup chopped pitted dates
½ cup chopped pecans or walnuts

CAROB CHIP COOKIES

1. Preheat the oven to 350 degrees.
2. Mix together the oils, sugar, eggs, dry milk, salt, and vanilla.
3. Combine the baking powder, flour, and cara-coa nuggets. Stir into the batter. Drop by teaspoons 2 inches apart onto a buttered baking sheet. Bake for 8 to 10 minutes, or until done.

Yield: About four dozen cookies.

½ cup mixed peanut and safflower oils
¾ cup packed dark brown sugar
2 eggs
½ cup non-fat dry milk powder
½ teaspoon salt
1 tablespoon pure vanilla extract
2 teaspoons baking powder
1½ cups wheat germ flour or whole wheat flour with wheat germ
1 cup cara-coa nuggets

FINNISH CARDAMOM COOKIES

2 cups whole wheat flour
½ cup brown sugar
½ teaspoon baking soda
½ cup dark corn syrup
½ cup butter
2 teaspoons grated orange rind
1 teaspoon ground cardamom
¼ teaspoon ground ginger
¼ teaspoon ground cloves
1 egg

1. Preheat the oven to 350 degrees.
2. Mix the flour, brown sugar, and baking soda in a large bowl.
3. In a 1-quart saucepan mix the corn syrup, butter, orange rind, and spices. Bring to a boil over medium heat, stirring constantly. Remove from the heat. Cool.
4. In a large bowl beat the egg until thick and lemon-colored. Slowly stir in the syrup mixture. Add the dry ingredients and mix well. Drop by teaspoons 2 inches apart onto well-oiled cookie sheets.
5. Bake for 8 to 10 minutes, or until lightly browned. Remove *at once* from the cookie sheets and cool on wire racks.

Yield: About four and one-half dozen two-and-one-half-inch cookies.

CAROB BROWNIES

1 cup brown sugar
⅔ cup peanut oil
2 eggs
½ teaspoon pure vanilla extract
½ cup unsifted unbleached white flour
½ cup unsifted full fat soy flour
1 teaspoon baking powder
½ teaspoon salt
3 tablespoons carob powder

1. Preheat the oven to 350 degrees.
2. Mix together the sugar and the oil. Beat in the eggs and vanilla. Sift together the unbleached flour, soy flour, baking powder, salt, and carob powder.
3. Combine the egg mixture with the sifted dry ingredients. Mix well. Pour into a well-buttered 9-inch square baking pan and bake for about 30 minutes, or until done. Cut into squares or bars while still slightly warm.

Yield: Sixteen to twenty squares or bars.

CAROB-NUT BROWNIES

1. Preheat the oven to 350 degrees.
2. Cream the butter with the honey and the sugar until light and fluffy. Beat in the egg, salt, vanilla, and coriander. Mix the carob powder with the oil and beat into the butter mixture.
3. Sift the flour with the baking powder and stir into the carob mixture. Stir in the nuts. Spread the batter in a 9-inch square pan lined with wax paper. Bake for 30 minutes.
4. Cool in the pan and cut into squares while still warm.
Yield: Sixteen brownies.

½ cup butter
⅓ cup honey
⅓ cup brown sugar or date sugar
1 egg
½ teaspoon salt
1 teaspoon pure vanilla extract
1 teaspoon ground coriander, optional
½ cup carob powder
1 tablespoon vegetable oil
⅔ cup whole wheat pastry flour
1 teaspoon baking powder
1 cup chopped nuts

MOLLIE COOKIES

1. Preheat the oven to 375 degrees.
2. Cream the butter and sugar together until very light and fluffy.
3. Beat in the eggs. Sift together the flour, baking powder, and salt and stir with the vanilla into the creamed mixture.
4. Drop by teaspoons, at least 2 inches apart, onto an oiled baking sheet. Bake for 8 to 12 minutes, or until lightly browned and done.
Yield: About four dozen cookies.

½ cup butter
1 cup brown sugar
2 eggs
1½ cups whole wheat pastry flour
1 teaspoon baking powder
¼ teaspoon salt
1 teaspoon pure vanilla extract

CAROB OR CAROB-RAISIN CHIP COOKIES

2½ tablespoons butter
1 cup honey
1 teaspoon pure vanilla extract
2 eggs, lightly beaten
3 cups whole wheat flour or unbleached white flour, or 1½ cups whole wheat flour, 1¼ cups unbleached white flour, and ¼ cup soy flour
1 teaspoon baking powder
1 10-ounce bag cara-coa nuggets, or equivalent amount of carob-covered raisins

1. Preheat the oven to 350 degrees.
2. Melt the butter over low heat. Add the honey, vanilla, and eggs and mix well. Cool.
3. Combine the flour and baking powder. When the honey mixture is cool, gradually add the flour mixture. Fold in the cara-coa nuggets.
4. Drop by teaspoons at least 2 inches apart onto an oiled baking sheet. Bake for 15 minutes, or until done. Cool on a wire rack.

Yield: About two dozen cookies.

COCONUT WHEAT GERM JUMBOS

¾ cup whole wheat flour
¾ cup wheat germ
1 teaspoon baking powder
¼ teaspoon salt
½ cup unsweetened flaked coconut
¼ cup quick rolled oats
½ cup butter, softened
½ cup brown sugar
½ cup granulated sugar
1 egg
1 teaspoon pure vanilla extract

1. Preheat the oven to 375 degrees.
2. Mix the flour, wheat germ, baking powder, salt, coconut, and oats.
3. Cream the butter, sugars, egg, and vanilla until fluffy. Add the dry ingredients and mix well.
4. Put the dough by ¼ cupfuls on ungreased baking sheets about 6 inches apart (cookies spread to form 4-inch circles).
5. Bake for 17 minutes, or until golden brown and centers are firm. Cool for 2 to 3 minutes, then carefully remove to wire racks to cool.

Yield: Sixteen crisp cookies.

HONEY COOKIES

1. Preheat the oven to 375 degrees.
2. Combine the butter and honey. Stir in the eggs and milk.
3. Sift together the flour, baking powder, baking soda, salt, cinnamon, and allspice. Add the fruits and kernels to the flour mixture and stir into the honey mixture.
4. Place by teaspoons on an oiled or buttered baking sheet.
5. Bake for 12 to 15 minutes, or until done. Cool on a wire rack.

Yield: About five dozen cookies.

⅓ cup butter, melted
1 cup honey
2 eggs
½ cup milk
3½ cups unbleached white flour
2 teaspoons baking powder
½ teaspoon baking soda
¼ teaspoon salt
1 teaspoon ground cinnamon
½ teaspoon ground allspice
1 cup chopped mixed dried fruits, such as raisins, dates, apricots, and dried apples
½ cup sunflower seed kernels

CASHEW-COCONUT COOKIES

1. Preheat the oven to 350 degrees.
2. In a large bowl, combine all the ingredients and mix well.
3. Drop by teaspoons onto an oiled baking sheet and bake for 10 to 12 minutes. Cook on a wire rack.

Yield: About five dozen cookies.

1 cup vegetable oil
1 cup honey
1 cup soy milk
2 cups unsweetened shredded coconut
⅛ teaspoon salt
1 cup raw unsalted cashews, roughly chopped
1 cup whole wheat flour
1 cup full fat soy flour
3 cups rolled oats
4 teaspoons pure vanilla extract

MOLASSES-OATMEAL COOKIES

⅓ cup vegetable oil
½ cup molasses
3 tablespoons honey
2 eggs, lightly beaten
½ cup whole wheat flour
½ cup unbleached white
   flour
1 teaspoon baking
   powder
1 teaspoon ground
   cinnamon
⅛ teaspoon salt
½ teaspoon ground cloves
½ teaspoon ground ginger
½ teaspoon ground
   allspice
2 tablespoons brewer's
   yeast
½ cup wheat germ
2 cups rolled oats
½ cup raisins

1. Preheat the oven to 375 degrees.
2. Beat together the oil, molasses, honey, and eggs.
3. Sift together the whole wheat flour, unbleached white flour, baking powder, cinnamon, salt, cloves, ginger, and allspice. Stir in the brewer's yeast, wheat germ, rolled oats, and raisins.
4. Add the oil mixture to the dry ingredients and mix well. Drop by teaspoons onto an oiled baking sheet and bake for 8 to 10 minutes, or until done. Cool on a wire rack.

Yield: About four dozen cookies.

MOLASSES CRINKLES

2 cups whole wheat flour
1 teaspoon baking
   powder
1 teaspoon baking soda
¼ teaspoon salt
1 teaspoon ground
   cinnamon
1 teaspoon ground ginger
½ teaspoon ground cloves
¾ cup butter, softened
1 cup brown sugar
1 egg
¼ cup molasses
   Granulated sugar

1. Mix the whole wheat flour, baking powder, baking soda, salt, and spices together.
2. Cream the butter, brown sugar, egg, and molasses until fluffy. Add the dry ingredients and mix well. Chill until firm enough to handle.
3. Preheat the oven to 375 degrees.
4. Roll the dough into 1-inch balls.
5. Dip in granulated sugar and put 3 inches apart on lightly oiled cookie sheets. Sprinkle each cookie with 2 or 3 drops of water (this causes the crinkling).
6. Bake for 8 to 10 minutes. Remove to wire racks to cool.

Yield: About four dozen cookies.

MOLASSES FRUIT BALLS

1. Preheat the oven to 350 degrees.
2. Force the raisins, dates, figs, and walnuts through the medium blade of a food chopper.
3. Mix together the flour, baking powder, spices, and salt.
4. Cream the butter, sugar, lemon rind, and molasses until well blended. Stir in fruit-nut mixture and dry ingredients.
5. Shape the mixture into 1-inch balls and arrange on lightly oiled baking sheets (balls do not spread).
6. Bake for 10 to 12 minutes, or until lightly browned on the bottom. Cool on wire racks, then roll in sugar.
Yield: About three and one-half dozen cookies.

2 cups total: raisins, pitted dates, and dried figs
1 cup walnuts
¼ cup whole wheat flour
½ teaspoon baking powder
½ teaspoon ground cinnamon
½ teaspoon grated nutmeg
¼ teaspoon salt
¼ cup butter, softened
2 tablespoons brown sugar
¾ teaspoon grated lemon rind
¼ cup molasses
Additional brown sugar for rolling

OATMEAL DROP COOKIES

1. Preheat the oven to 400 degrees.
2. Cream the sugar with the oil until light and fluffy. Beat in the eggs and then the molasses.
3. Sift the rice flour with the cinnamon, baking soda, and salt and stir into the sugar mixture. Stir in the remaining ingredients. Drop by teaspoons onto an oiled baking sheet. Bake for 8 to 10 minutes, or until done. Cool on a wire rack.
Yield: Three dozen cookies.

1¼ cups brown sugar
½ cup safflower oil
2 eggs
6 tablespoons unsulphured molasses
1¾ cups brown rice flour
1 teaspoon ground cinnamon
1 teaspoon baking soda
½ teaspoon salt
2 cups rolled oats
½ cup chopped nuts
1 cup unsulphured raisins

FILLED SAND DOLLARS

1 cup butter, softened
1½ cups whole wheat flour
1 cup wheat germ
1 cup brown sugar
⅛ teaspoon salt
1 cup packed finely
  snipped dates
1 teaspoon grated orange
  rind
⅔ cup orange juice
½ cup chopped walnuts or
  almonds

1. Preheat the oven to 350 degrees.
2. For the dough, cut the butter into the flour until crumbly. With your hands, work in the wheat germ, ¾ cup sugar, and the salt.
3. For the filling, work the dates, orange rind, juice, nuts, and remaining sugar with spoon until most of juice has been absorbed.
4. Roll the dough to a ⅛-inch thickness on a lightly floured surface. Cut with a floured 2½-inch cutter.
5. Arrange half of the rounds on an ungreased baking sheet. Divide the filling among the rounds and top with remaining cookie rounds, pressing the edges together. Cut five small slits in the top of each cookie so that they resemble sand dollars.
6. Bake for 12 to 15 minutes, or until golden brown. Remove carefully to wire racks to cool (cookies are fragile).
Yield: Two dozen cookies.

BIG SUR COCONUT COOKIES

¾ cup butter
¾ cup brown sugar
2 eggs
1 teaspoon pure vanilla
  extract
2 cups whole wheat
  pastry flour
2 tablespoons milk
½ cup unsweetened
  shredded coconut
½ cup raisins

1. Preheat the oven to 350 degrees.
2. Cream the butter with the sugar until light and fluffy. Beat in the eggs and the vanilla. Sift the flour and stir in with the milk, coconut, and raisins.
3. Drop by teaspoons onto an oiled baking sheet. Bake for 8 to 10 minutes, or until done.
Yield: About four dozen cookies.

PEANUT BUTTER-WHEAT GERM CRISPS

1. Preheat the oven to 350 degrees.
2. Mix the flour, wheat germ, oats, baking soda, and salt in a medium-sized bowl.
3. Cream the butter, peanut butter, brown sugar, and egg until fluffy.
4. Stir in the vanilla and dry ingredients.
5. Shape level tablespoons of dough in balls and arrange on ungreased baking sheets.
6. Flatten the balls to about ¼-inch thickness with the bottom of a glass dipped in granulated sugar.
7. Bake for 8 to 10 minutes. Remove the cookies from the sheets to wire racks to cool.
Yield: About four dozen cookies.

1 cup unbleached white flour
1 cup wheat germ
¼ cup quick rolled oats
1 teaspoon baking soda
¼ teaspoon salt
¾ cup butter, softened
½ cup crunchy peanut butter
1 cup brown sugar
1 egg
1 teaspoon pure vanilla extract
Granulated sugar

RAISIN-NUT OATMEAL COOKIES

1. Preheat the oven to 350 degrees.
2. Mix together the flour, oats, baking powder, salt, and spices.
3. Cream the butter and sugar until fluffy. Beat in the egg. Add the dry ingredients and milk and mix well. Stir in the nuts and raisins.
4. Drop by teaspoons onto oiled baking sheets.
5. Bake for 12 to 15 minutes, or until well browned. Remove to wire racks to cool.
Yield: Two dozen cookies.

½ cup whole wheat flour
1½ cups quick rolled oats
½ teaspoon baking powder
¼ teaspoon salt
½ teaspoon ground cinnamon
⅛ teaspoon grated nutmeg
6 tablespoons butter, softened
½ cup brown sugar
1 egg
3 tablespoons milk
½ cup chopped walnuts
½ cup raisins

RAISIN COOKIES

1 cup water
2 cups raisins
1 cup soy or safflower oil
1½ cups honey
3 eggs
1 teaspoon pure vanilla
extract
4 cups whole wheat
pastry flour
1 teaspoon baking
powder
1 teaspoon baking soda
1 teaspoon ground
cinnamon
¼ teaspoon grated nutmeg
¼ teaspoon ground
allspice
½ teaspoon salt
1 cup chopped nuts
1 cup wheat germ,
approximately

1. Put the water and raisins in a saucepan and simmer for 5 minutes. Cool.
2. Preheat the oven to 400 degrees.
3. Mix together the oil, honey, eggs, and vanilla. Beat well. Add cooled raisin mixture and the remaining ingredients, including enough of the wheat germ to make a batter that can be dropped by teaspoons onto an oiled and floured baking sheet and maintain shape. Bake 2 cookies to test.
4. Bake for 12 to 15 minutes, or until done. Cool on a wire rack.
Yield: About eight dozen cookies.

RAISIN-NUT OAT COOKIES

½ cup brown sugar
1 egg
1 teaspoon safflower oil
⅛ teaspoon salt
½ cup rolled oats
½ cup unsweetened
shredded coconut
½ cup chopped nuts
½ cup raisins
½ teaspoon pure vanilla
extract

1. Preheat the oven to 375 degrees.
2. Beat the sugar and egg together until light and fluffy. Add the remaining ingredients and mix well.
3. Drop by teaspoons 2 inches apart on an oiled baking sheet and bake for 10 minutes, or until tops are golden. Cool on the baking sheet several minutes, then carefully remove to a wire rack.
Yield: About eighteen cookies.

HONEY-SESAME BITES

1. Preheat the oven to 325 degrees.
2. Beat the egg whites until soft peaks form. Gradually beat in the sugar and then the honey until mixture is very stiff and holds stiff peaks.
3. Fold in the wheat germ, coconut, rice polishings, and sesame seeds. Stir in the vanilla.
4. Drop the mixture by the teaspoonful onto a buttered and floured baking sheet. Bake for about 20 minutes, or until lightly browned.

Yield: About three dozen.

2 egg whites, at room temperature
¾ cup brown sugar
2 tablespoons honey
1 cup raw wheat germ
½ cup unsweetened shredded coconut
1 tablespoon rice polishings
½ cup toasted sesame seeds
½ teaspoon pure vanilla extract

SESAME SEED CRISPS

1. Preheat the oven to 375 degrees.
2. Place the seeds in a dry skillet and toast over medium heat, shaking occasionally, until light golden in color. Cool.
3. Cream together the sugar, butter, and egg until very light and fluffy. Sift together the flour, baking powder, and salt.
4. Stir the sifted dry ingredients, cream, vanilla, and seeds into the creamed mixture.
5. Place by the teaspoon at least 2 inches apart on an oiled baking sheet. Bake for 10 to 12 minutes, or until lightly browned around the edges and done. Cool on a wire rack.

Yield: About thirty cookies.

½ cup sesame seeds
½ cup brown sugar
½ cup butter, softened
1 egg
¾ cup unbleached white flour
¼ teaspoon single-acting baking powder (Royal brand)
¼ teaspoon salt
2 tablespoons heavy cream
1 teaspoon pure vanilla extract

SESAME STRIPS

¾ cup brown sugar
½ cup oil
2 tablespoons non-fat dry milk powder
2 eggs
½ teaspoon grated orange rind
1½ teaspoons pure vanilla extract
2 tablespoons wheat germ
1¼ cups toasted sesame seeds
¼ cup toasted cashews, coarsely chopped
½ cup raisins
3 cups unbleached white flour or whole wheat pastry flour, approximately

1. Preheat the oven to 300 degrees.
2. Put the sugar, oil, and dry milk in a mixing bowl and mix with an electric mixer on medium speed for 2 minutes. Add 1 egg, the orange rind, and vanilla and mix for 2 minutes longer.
3. Stir in the wheat germ, ¼ cup of the sesame seeds, the cashews, and raisins and mix well. Stir in enough flour to make a dough that can be rolled. Shape into a ball. Cover and let the dough rest for 10 minutes; divide into two.
4. Roll out half of the dough into an approximate 16- by 5-inch strip. Transfer carefully to an oiled baking sheet, using wide spatulas if necessary to prevent breaking. Beat the remaining egg lightly and brush over the dough strip. Sprinkle with half of the remaining sesame seeds.
5. Repeat rolling, brushing, and sprinkling with second half of the dough. Bake the strips for 45 minutes, or until lightly browned and done.
6. Cut into 1-inch strips, on the diagonal if desired, while still hot.
Yield: Thirty-two strips.

WHOLE WHEAT-FRUIT COOKIES

1. Preheat the oven to 375 degrees.
2. Blend the honey with the oil. Beat in the eggs and vanilla.
3. Stir in the remaining ingredients and mix well. The batter should be stiff but soft enough to place by the teaspoonful on an oiled baking sheet. If the batter is too thick, add a small quantity of unsweetened fruit juice. If too thin, add a little more flour. (This is a necessary precaution as the water absorption of different whole wheat flours varies so much.) Put on baking sheets.
4. Flatten the teaspoons of dough with the bottom of a tumbler dipped in water. Bake for 12 to 15 minutes, or until done.
Yield: About four and one-half dozen cookies.

½ cup honey
½ cup vegetable oil
2 eggs, well beaten
1 teaspoon pure vanilla extract
⅛ teaspoon salt
2 cups whole wheat flour
½ cup raisins
½ cup chopped nuts
¼ cup chopped dates
¼ cup chopped figs

WHEAT GERM SNICKER-DOODLES

1. Preheat the oven to 400 degrees.
2. Cream the butter and brown sugar together until light and fluffy. Beat in the eggs, one at a time.
3. Blend in the vanilla and wheat germ.
4. Sift together the flour, baking powder, and salt and stir into the creamed mixture. Combine the sugar and cinnamon in a small bowl.
5. Form the dough into balls the size of a small walnut; roll in the cinnamon-sugar mixture. Place 2 inches apart on an ungreased baking sheet. Bake for 8 to 10 minutes. Cool on a wire rack.
Yield: About six dozen cookies.

1 cup butter, softened
1½ cups brown sugar
2 eggs
1 teaspoon pure vanilla extract
½ cup wheat germ
2½ cups whole wheat flour
2 teaspoons baking powder
½ teaspoon salt
½ cup brown sugar
1 teaspoon ground cinnamon

COCONUT SHORTBREAD

1 cup butter
½ cup less 2 tablespoons
  brown sugar
2 cups unbleached white
  flour
1 teaspoon pure vanilla
  extract
1 cup unsweetened
  shredded coconut
⅛ teaspoon salt

1. Cream the butter and sugar together very well.
2. Add the remaining ingredients and, with a wooden spoon or the fingers, work into a dough. Form into a roll about 9 inches long and 1 inch in diameter. Wrap in wax paper and chill for several hours, or overnight.
3. Preheat the oven to 350 degrees.
4. Cut the rolls into ¼-inch-thick rounds and place on ungreased baking sheets. Bake for 10 minutes, or until lightly browned and done.

Yield: About three dozen cookies.

WHEELS OF STEEL

½ cup butter
½ cup raw peanut butter
1 cup brown sugar
1 egg
1 teaspoon pure vanilla
  extract
¾ cup whole wheat flour
¼ cup wheat germ
½ cup non-fat dry milk
  powder
½ teaspoon salt
¼ teaspoon baking
  powder
¼ teaspoon baking soda
3 tablespoons milk
1 cup quick-cooking
  rolled oats
1 cup raisins, chopped
3 tablespoons sesame
  seeds

1. Preheat the oven to 375 degrees.
2. Cream the butter, peanut butter, and sugar together until light. Beat in the egg and vanilla.
3. Combine the flour, wheat germ, dry milk, salt, baking powder, and baking soda. Stir into the creamed mixture.
4. Add the milk, oats, and raisins and mix well. Place a heaping tablespoon of the batter on an oiled baking sheet and spread into a circle about 4½ inches in diameter. Sprinkle with 1 teaspoon sesame seeds.
5. Leave ample room for the cookies to spread. It may be wise to have only two on one large sheet. Make more circles with the remaining batter and seeds. Bake for about 12 minutes, or until done. Cool on pan for 5 minutes and then, using a wide spatula, transfer carefully to a wire rack.

Yield: About nine giant cookies.

GINGER COOKIES

1. Preheat the oven to 350 degrees.
2. Cream the butter and ½ cup sugar together until light and fluffy. Beat in the molasses and egg.
3. Sift together the unbleached white flour, whole wheat flour, soy flour, yeast, dry milk, salt, baking soda, ginger, and cinnamon.
4. Stir the sifted dry ingredients into the creamed mixture. Stir in the wheat germ. Mix until the ingredients are well blended.
5. Form the dough (it's fairly soft) into balls the size of a walnut. Roll in sugar and place 2 inches apart on an oiled baking sheet.
6. Bake for about 15 minutes, or until lightly browned and the tops are crackled. Cool on a wire rack.

Yield: About four dozen cookies.

½ cup butter
½ cup brown sugar
½ cup molasses
1 egg
½ cup unbleached white flour
1 cup whole wheat flour
¼ cup soy flour
2 tablespoons brewer's yeast
½ cup non-fat dry milk powder
¼ teaspoon salt
2 teaspoons baking soda
3 teaspoons ground ginger, or to taste
1 teaspoon ground cinnamon
¼ cup wheat germ
Brown sugar

HOMEMADE GRAHAM CRACKERS

1. Preheat the oven to 350 degrees.
2. Put the whole wheat flour in a bowl. Cut in the butter until the mixture is the consistency of coarse oatmeal. Add the sugar, baking soda, cream of tartar, egg, and enough hot water to make a dough that can be rolled like pastry.
3. Roll out the dough to ⅛- to ¼-inch thickness on a floured pastry cloth or board (use unbleached flour for rolling). Cut into 3-inch squares. Place on an ungreased baking sheet and bake for 15 to 20 minutes, or until done. Cool on a wire rack.

Yield: About two dozen crackers.

4 cups whole wheat flour
1 cup butter
1 cup brown sugar
1 teaspoon baking soda
1 teaspoon cream of tartar
1 egg, lightly beaten
½ cup hot water, approximately
Unbleached white flour

THREE-WAY COOKIES

1 cup butter
¼ cup carob powder
1 teaspoon pure vanilla
extract
2 eggs
2 tablespoons honey
1 cup almond meal
Unsweetened shredded
coconut
1 cup quick-cooking oats
½ cup wheat germ
1 cup slivered or sliced
almonds

1. Melt the butter in a small saucepan and stir in the carob powder and vanilla.
2. Put the eggs in the container of an electric blender and blend for 1 second. Add the butter mixture while blending and add the honey.
3. In a large bowl, mix together the almond meal, 1 cup coconut, the oats, wheat germ, and almonds. Pour in the butter mixture and mix well. Form into 1-inch balls. Roll in coconut.
4. Now, pick your choice
   a. eat the cookies raw
   b. freeze them and serve frozen, or
   c. place them on a lightly oiled baking sheet and bake for 10 minutes in a 350-degree oven.

Yield: About forty cookies.
Note: Dry ingredients may be varied with the use of chopped dates, pecans, walnuts, raisins, and sunflower seed kernels.

ZUCCHINI COOKIES

1½ cups whole wheat flour
1¾ cups quick rolled oats
⅛ teaspoon salt
½ teaspoon baking soda
1 teaspoon ground
cinnamon
½ cup raisins
½ cup unsweetened flaked
coconut
½ cup butter, softened
¾ cup brown sugar
1 egg
½ teaspoon pure vanilla
extract
1 cup grated raw zucchini

1. Preheat the oven to 375 degrees.
2. Mix together the flour, oats, salt, baking soda, cinnamon, raisins, and coconut.
3. Cream the butter and sugar until blended. Beat in the egg. Stir in the vanilla.
4. Stir in the dry ingredients and zucchini, mixing well.
5. Drop by rounded teaspoons about 2 inches apart onto oiled baking sheets (cookies do not spread).
6. Bake for 10 to 12 minutes, or until well browned. Remove to wire racks to cool.

Yield: About three dozen cookies.

APRICOT BAR COOKIES

1. Preheat the oven to 375 degrees.
2. Beat together the honey, molasses, and oil very well in an electric mixer, electric blender, or food processor.
3. In a large bowl, combine the oats, whole wheat flour, wheat germ, soy flour, and salt. Pour in the honey mixture and stir to moisten the dry ingredients.
4. Add the apricots, raisins, and sunflower seed kernels and mix well. If the mixture is very stiff, add a small amount of orange juice. Press the mixture into a well-oiled 9-inch square baking pan. Bake for 20 minutes. Cool in the pan. Cut into squares.
Yield: Sixteen squares.

⅓ cup honey
⅓ cup molasses
½ cup vegetable oil
1½ cups steel cut oats
1 cup whole wheat flour
½ cup wheat germ
3 tablespoons soy flour
⅛ teaspoon salt
1 cup cut-up unsulphured apricots
1 cup raisins
½ cup sunflower seed kernels or pumpkin seeds
Orange juice, if necessary

SUNFLOWER SEED COOKIES

1. Preheat the oven to 375 degrees.
2. Cream the butter with brown sugar until light and fluffy. Beat in the eggs and the vanilla.
3. Sift together the flour, salt, and baking soda and stir into creamed mixture.
4. Fold in the oats, sunflower seed kernels, and wheat germ.
5. Place teaspoonsful of batter 2 inches apart on ungreased baking sheets. Bake for 10 to 12 minutes. Cool on wire racks.
Yield: About five dozen cookies.

1 cup butter
1¼ cups packed brown sugar
2 eggs, lightly beaten
2 teaspoons pure vanilla extract
1⅓ cups unbleached white flour
½ teaspoon salt
1 teaspoon baking soda
3 cups old-fashioned rolled oats
¾ cup sunflower seed kernels
½ cup wheat germ

SOYA COOKIES

¼ cup butter
½ cup brown sugar
¾ cup unbleached white
flour
1 teaspoon single-acting
baking powder (Royal
brand)
1 teaspoon ground
cinnamon
⅛ teaspoon salt
1 egg, lightly beaten
½ teaspoon pure vanilla
extract
¼ cup soy grits
18 walnut halves,
approximately

1. Preheat the oven to 375 degrees.
2. Cream the butter and sugar together until light and fluffy.
3. Sift together the flour, baking powder, cinnamon, and salt. Mix the egg with the vanilla. Add the flour mixture alternately with the egg mixture to the creamed mixture.
4. Stir in the soy granules. Place rounded teaspoons of the mixture on oiled baking sheets and decorate each cookie with a walnut half. Bake for 12 minutes, or until lightly browned.

Yield: About eighteen cookies.

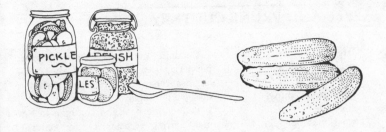

PRESERVES &
RELISHES

Beautiful homebaked breads should be lovingly spread with good-tasting, unadulterated, and nutritious fillings such as those given in this chapter. Picnickers and the lunch box crowd become the center of attention and envy when they set out something different and they know it's worth talking about. A cupboard full of homemade preserves, pickles, and relishes gives a feeling of security. You know they taste good and that nothing unnecessary has been added.

APPLE AND PRUNE CHUTNEY

2 large tart apples,
  peeled, cored, and
  diced
1 large onion, thinly
  sliced
1 small green pepper,
  seeded and diced
1 clove garlic, crushed
¾ cup white vinegar
¾ cup brown sugar
1 12-ounce package pitted
  prunes, halved
1 teaspoon dry mustard
½ teaspoon salt
½ teaspoon ground ginger
¼ teaspoon freshly ground
  black pepper

1. Combine the apples, onions, green pepper, garlic, vinegar, and sugar in a large saucepan. Bring to a boil, stirring to dissolve the sugar.
2. Reduce the heat and continue to simmer, stirring occasionally, for about 15 minutes, or until the onion is tender.
3. Add the remaining ingredients and simmer for 10 minutes, stirring often, until the mixture is thick like jam. Pour into canning jars, seal, and process in a boiling water bath for 15 minutes. Cool, test the seal, and store in a cool dark place. Great with pork, ham, roast turkey, and chicken.
Yield: About two pints.

BARBECUE SAUCE

2½ cups homemade chili
   sauce (see page 393)
 1 teaspoon seeded and
   chopped hot green
   peppers
½ cup vegetable oil
⅓ cup lemon juice
 2 tablespoons red wine
   vinegar
 1 large onion, finely
   chopped
 1 tablespoon brown sugar
 1 bay leaf, crumbled
 1 teaspoon dry mustard
 1 teaspoon salt
½ cup water
   Liquid red pepper
   seasoning to taste

Combine all the ingredients in a heavy enameled or stainless steel pan. Bring to a boil and simmer for 20 minutes.
Yield: About four cups.

CHILI SAUCE

1. Put the tomatoes, peppers, celery, onions, and garlic in a large enamel or stainless steel kettle. Tie the allspice, mustard seeds, and cloves in a cheesecloth bag. Add to the kettle, bring to a boil, and simmer for 45 minutes.

2. Add the remaining ingredients and boil, uncovered, until thick. Discard the spice bag. Pour the sauce into 8 hot sterilized pint jars. Cap and process in a boiling water bath for 10 minutes. Cool, check the seals, and store in a cool dark, dry place.

Yield: Eight pints.

8 pounds ripe tomatoes, peeled and chopped
3 sweet red peppers, seeded and chopped
3 green peppers, seeded and chopped
1 celery stalk, chopped
6 medium-sized onions, finely chopped
3 cloves garlic, finely chopped
1½ teaspoons whole allspice
1½ teaspoons mustard seeds
1½ teaspoons whole cloves
1½ cups brown sugar
2 tablespoons salt
1 teaspoon freshly ground black pepper
1 teaspoon dry mustard
2 dried hot red peppers, crushed
2 cups cider vinegar

PLUM CONSERVE

1. Grind the oranges through the fine blade of a meat grinder.

2. Combine the oranges, plums, sugar, and raisins in a heavy saucepan. Cook, stirring occasionally, until the mixture is very thick, about 1½ hours.

3. Stir in the nuts and cook for 20 minutes longer. Pour into hot sterilized jars. Cover and cool. Store in the refrigerator.

Yield: About two quarts.

2 thin-skinned Florida oranges, seeds removed
3 pounds fresh plums, pitted and quartered
3 pounds brown sugar
1 pound raisins
½ pound chopped walnuts

UNCOOKED JAM FOR THE FREEZER

3 cups crushed fruit, such as strawberries, blueberries, blackberries, peaches, apricots
5 cups brown sugar
1 package powdered pectin
1 cup water

1. Combine the fruit and sugar, stir well, and let stand for 20 minutes.
2. Dissolve the powdered pectin in the water, bring to a boil, and boil for 1 minute. Add to the fruit-and-sugar mixture and stir for 2 minutes. Let stand for 24 hours and then freeze. The jam can be served directly from the freezer.
Yield: About three pounds.
Note: This is good over homemade ice cream. If only liquid pectin is available, follow the directions for uncooked jam in the liquid pectin brochure and freeze.

GREEN RELISH

6 medium-sized green tomatoes, stems removed, cut roughly
3 medium-sized yellow onions, quartered
¼ small head cabbage, cut roughly
3 green peppers, seeded and cut roughly
3 sweet red peppers, seeded and cut roughly
1½ tablespoons salt
¾ cup light brown sugar
2 cups cider vinegar
1 tablespoon mustard seeds
2 teaspoons celery seeds
1 tablespoon mixed pickling spices, tied in a muslin bag

1. Grind the tomatoes, onions, cabbage, and peppers through the coarse blade of a food grinder. Sprinkle with the salt, cover and let stand for 3 hours. Transfer to a colander and rinse well under cold water. Squeeze out as much liquid as possible.
2. In a large stainless steel or enamel kettle combine the sugar, vinegar, mustard seed, celery seed, and pickling spices. Heat to boiling, stirring to dissolve the sugar.
3. Add the well drained vegetables and simmer for 15 minutes.
4. Ladle the relish into hot sterilized jars, seal, and process in a boiling water bath for 10 minutes. Cool. Check the seals and store in a cool dry place.
Yield: Four pints.

QUINCE CHUTNEY

1. Combine all the ingredients in a heavy kettle and bring to a boil.
2. Cook gently, stirring occasionally, for about 3 hours, or until the mixture is quite thick.
3. Pour the hot chutney into hot sterilized jars. Seal and process in a boiling water bath for 10 minutes. Cool and store in a cool, dark, dry place.
Yield: About seven pints.
Note: It is recommended that this chutney be boiled in a well-ventilated kitchen because the mixture emits a strong odor while cooking.

3 onions, sliced
2 pounds quinces, peeled, cored, and diced
3 pounds apples, peeled, cored, and sliced
1½ pounds raisins
½ teaspoon cayenne pepper
4 cloves garlic, finely chopped
2 quarts cider vinegar
½ pound candied ginger, chopped
1 teaspoon ground mace
1 teaspoon ground cinnamon
1 teaspoon ground cloves
3 tablespoons ground ginger
2 tablespoons paprika
2 ounces kosher salt
4 pounds honey

PEPPER RELISH

1. Preheat the oven to 450 degrees.
2. Put the green peppers and hot chili pepper in a shallow pan and bake until browned, about 20 minutes.
3. Using pot holders, transfer the peppers to a bowl of cold water.
4. Skin the peppers, remove the stems and seeds, and chop the peppers finely.
5. Add enough olive oil to give a spreading consistency. Season with salt and cumin to taste. Store in a jar in the refrigerator and serve as a relish or spread.
Yield: About three pints.

3 large green peppers
1 small fresh hot chili pepper
Olive oil
Salt
Ground cumin

MUSHROOM AND ARTICHOKE RELISH

1 cup button mushrooms,
  or large mushrooms cut
  into quarters
1½ cups 1-inch lengths
  celery
2 cups peeled and diced
  Jerusalem artichokes
½ cup lemon juice
1 teaspoon sugar
  Cold water

1. Put the mushrooms and celery in a colander and steam over boiling water for 5 minutes. Turn into a bowl.
2. Put the artichokes in the colander and steam over the boiling water until barely tender, about 12 minutes. Add to the mushroom mixture.
3. Stir in the remaining ingredients, including enough water to cover the vegetables. The relish will keep for a week or more in the refrigerator.
Yield: Six servings.

FRUITY TOMATO RELISH

3 pounds ripe tomatoes,
  cored, peeled, and cut
  into wedges
3 pounds ripe pears,
  pared, cored, and cubed
2 large onions, coarsely
  chopped
2 large green peppers,
  seeded and coarsely
  chopped
2 large sweet red peppers,
  seeded and coarsely
  chopped
1 cup raisins
1 cup brown sugar
1½ cups light corn syrup
1½ cups cider vinegar
1½ teaspoons salt
1 teaspoon dry mustard
1 teaspoon ground ginger
¼ cup diced crystallized
  ginger
¼ teaspoon ground cloves
¼ teaspoon crushed hot
  red pepper flakes

1. Put tomatoes, pears, onions, peppers, and raisins in a large stainless steel or enamel pan. Stir in the sugar, corn syrup, vinegar, salt, mustard, ginger, cloves, and red pepper flakes. Bring to a boil and boil, uncovered, for about 1 hour, or until thick, stirring occasionally.
2. Ladle the relish into hot clean canning jars. Seal and process in a boiling water bath for 10 minutes. Cool. Check the seals and store in a cool dry place.
Yield: About nine half-pints.

ZIPPY TOMATO SAUCE

1. Chop the tomatoes coarsely. Heat the oil in a large kettle and sauté the hot pepper and onion until the onion is tender but not browned. Add the garlic and pepper and cook for 3 minutes.
2. Add the tomatoes, salt, pepper, basil, oregano, and parsley. Bring to a boil and cook, stirring occasionally, for 30 minutes. Yield: About three cups.

6 medium-sized tomatoes, peeled and quartered
1½ tablespoons vegetable oil
1 long hot pepper, seeded and chopped
1 large onion, finely chopped
1 clove garlic, finely chopped
1 small green pepper, seeded and chopped
¾ teaspoon salt
¼ teaspoon freshly ground black pepper
½ teaspoon dried basil
½ teaspoon dried oregano
2 tablespoons chopped parsley

BASIC TOMATO SAUCE

1. Combine all the ingredients in a stainless steel, or porcelainized steel, pan or casserole. Bring to a boil and simmer, uncovered, for 45 minutes. Purée (in a blender or food processor), if desired. Season with salt and pepper to taste.
2. Refrigerate overnight before using or freezing for future use.
Yield: About two quarts.

12 large ripe tomatoes, peeled and chopped
2 green peppers, seeded
2 onions, chopped
2 carrots, chopped
6 celery stalks, diced
2 tablespoons snipped fresh chives
2 tablespoons chopped parsley
2 tablespoons chopped fresh basil
2 cloves garlic, finely chopped
Salt and freshly ground black pepper

RAW REFRIGERATOR RELISH

1 dozen red and green
  sweet peppers, seeded
  and diced
6 pounds cabbage,
  shredded
6 medium-sized carrots,
  shredded
6 medium-sized onions,
  sliced
  Vegetable salt to taste
6 cups cider vinegar
3 to 4 cups honey, or to
  taste
1 tablespoon celery seeds
1 tablespoon mustard
  seeds

Combine all the ingredients in a large bowl and mix very well.

Ladle into jars and store in the refrigerator for several days before using.

Yield: About six quarts.

Note: Alternately, the ingredients can be brought to a boil in a kettle and boiled for 20 minutes before being poured into hot sterilized jars. Cool and store in the refrigerator.

APPLE BUTTER

10 pints apples, peeled
  and sliced
1 quart fresh cider
5 cups brown sugar
1 tablespoon ground
  cinnamon
1 teaspoon ground cloves
1 teaspoon ground
  allspice

1. Combine the apples and cider in a large kettle, bring to a boil, and simmer, covered, until the apples are soft. Pass through a food mill.

2. Combine the strained applesauce with the remaining ingredients in a clean kettle. Bring to a boil, stirring until the sugar is dissolved.

3. Cook gently, uncovered, until the mixture becomes quite thick, at least 2½ hours. Stir often. Pour into hot sterilized jars and seal. Process in a boiling water bath for 15 minutes. Store in a cool dry place.

Yield: About two quarts.

BABY FOOD

Preparing natural foods for babies is not much different than cooking from scratch for children and adults. Use the freshest, best-quality ingredients you can grow or purchase, choose the best nutrient and flavor-saving techniques, eliminate salt and spices, and use sweeteners sparingly.

All decisions on when, what, and how to feed a baby should be made in consultation with a pediatrician, physician, or nutritionist.

Six Basic Steps

1. Mother's milk (or formula) until baby is ready for solid food (see signs to look for below).
2. Mother's milk (or formula) plus small amounts of cereal mixed with strained juice, formula, or mother's milk.
3. Mother's milk (or formula); cereal; plus strained single vegetables, fruits, and meat.
4. Mother's milk (or formula); cereal; plus strained combination foods; meat and vegetable; fruit and cereal.
5. Mother's milk (or formula); cereal; plus finely textured foods.
6. Gradually replace mother's milk (or formula) with pasteurized cow's milk; cereal; finely divided regular family foods. There's no set age to begin solid feeding. The signs to look for, usually at the age of three to four months:

- baby's weight has almost doubled since birth, or about 13 pounds
- baby drinks more than 1 quart of formula a day
- breast-fed baby demands feeding every 3 hours or less
- baby often seems hungry

Making your own baby's food may not be as easy as opening up all those little jars, but once you develop a cook-and-freeze-ahead routine it can be painless. One of the best methods involves cooking and puréeing a selection of fruits, vegetables, and meats in adult quantities, and freezing in ice cube trays or in freeform baby-meal-sized dollops. The frozen cubes or dollops are placed in freezer bags, labeled, and sealed, ready for quick thawing and reheating.

One of the main reasons for preparing baby food at home is that you can control every ingredient and process to ensure high nutrient content. To preserve maximum nutrients, steam or bake scrubbed unpeeled fruits and vegetables. Boiling is faster, but more nutrients are lost in the process. Whichever cooking method you choose, use as little water as possible, and reserve the cooking liquid to use in puréeing the food.

First Solids

Cereal is usually added in the third or fourth month with rice cereal first. Fruits and vegetables are next in acceptability with mashed ripe banana first. Introduce one new food at a time and check for adverse reactions before proceeding to the next.

From about five months of age, most babies will tolerate puréed ripe, raw fruits, which are easiest to prepare and provide the most nutrients.

Babies will enjoy the tart-sweet taste of ripe fruit, so do not automatically add sugar. If home-prepared fruits seem unnaturally tart, very small amounts of corn syrup can be added *after* cooking. Use no more than 1 tablespoon per cup of fruit purée. Honey should never be given to babies under one year, since it can cause a kind of infant botulism, a serious and sometimes fatal form of food poisoning.

Little attention is necessary to seasoning baby foods, but texture is important. Besides the basic taste, the smoothness or thickness of a food concerns your baby most. To thin purées, use cooking liquid, milk, or formula, or juices the baby normally drinks. When purées need thickening, use small amounts of wheat germ, enriched unbleached or whole wheat flour, or cereals which the baby is already eating. If your baby is fond of puréed potatoes, winter squash, carrots, or peas, these vegetables make great "natural" thickeners.

Equipment

Modern kitchen equipment, such as food processors, blenders, grinders, graters, and food mills, simplify baby food preparation. A simple metal collapsible steamer basket is ideal, but if you only have a Chinese bamboo steamer, use it for steam-cooking baby foods.

If a microwave oven is available, use it for preparing baby meals, and for the cleanest, speediest warm-ups, too.

The only other equipment you will need, besides a hungry baby at meal times, are some small unbreakable bowls, a supply of small-bowled feeding spoons (demi-tasse spoons are perfect), and a two-handled weighted cup for drinking lessons. Solid food should never be mixed with liquid and fed from a bottle; it may cause choking and eliminates the spoon feeding experience. An infant seat will support the baby until five or six months, when he or she can sit up in a high chair. And, especially at the beginning, a selection of bibs is essential not just for the baby, but for the feeder, too.

Traveling and Visiting

It is not necessary for babies to consistently dine on perfectly planned, pre-cooked foods at every meal. Keep a selection of enriched cereals or finely ground whole grains, plain yogurt and cottage cheese, eggs, fresh fruits, and fresh or frozen vegetables to prepare almost-instant natural baby meals, anytime.

These kinds of "people" foods will also serve when traveling or visiting when more elaborate baby food cooking isn't feasible. Also, don't overlook the possibility of turning simply cooked lightly seasoned, low-fat family foods or leftovers into healthy baby meals. Purée, thin, or thicken accordingly, and serve, or freeze in baby meal-size portions.

How to Prepare Whole Grain Cereals for Babies

After rice has been accepted, move on to barley, oatmeal, millet, and other grains, reserving wheat for last. Below are two simple methods of preparing whole grain and refined enriched cereals for babies.

Pre-ground Method: Place a cup of any whole grain or refined enriched cereal in a blender, food processor, or grain mill and process until the grain forms a fine powder. In a small saucepan combine 2 tablespoons grain and 6 tablespoons formula, milk, or water and bring to a boil. Simmer the cereal, stirring often, until thickened and smooth. Thin with additional water before serving. Makes 1 to 2 servings.

Purée Method: Cook any whole grain or refined enriched cereal according to package directions without adding salt, sugar, or butter. Purée in the container of a food processor or blender, or push through a food mill until uniformly smooth, then stir in milk to thin. Using this second method, unseasoned cereals prepared for the family can easily be adjusted for the baby.

Fruit

Bananas: The First Fruit

Bananas may be the ultimate instant natural baby food. It is often the first food fed to babies for its taste as well as digestability. Select very ripe bananas, mash or purée, until very smooth, thinning if needed with a little milk, juice, or water. If several bananas ripen at the same time, they will keep from further ripening in the refrigerator for 3 or 4 days. Bananas can also be frozen with or without skins and puréed just before serving.

COOKED FRUIT SAUCE

Combine the fruit and water in a small saucepan and bring to a boil. Reduce the heat and simmer for 10 to 40 minutes, depending on the kind of fruit used, until fruit is very tender, but still holds its shape. Purée the fruit with the cooking liquid until smooth. Taste the sauce and sweeten very slightly—only if sauce is unnaturally tart. Refrigerate up to 4 days or freeze up to 1 year.
Yield: Two cups sauce.

2 cups peeled, cored, or pitted apples, pears, peaches, plums, apricots, or nectarines
¼ cup water

Uncooked Fruit Purée

Except for bananas, start raw fruits at around four to five months. Puréed raw fruits can be served at once, refrigerated for one day, or frozen for up to one year.

FRESH APPLESAUCE

Put the fruit and juice in the container of a blender or food processor and blend or process until smooth. Quantities can be increased to freeze in larger amounts.
Yield: One-half cup.

1 sweet apple, peeled, cored, and cut in chunks
1 teaspoon lemon juice

Citrus Combinations

Raw orange, grapefruit, or tangerine can be started at five months. As citrus fruits are so juicy, they are especially good combined with sturdier fruits like bananas or apples.

ORANGEY APPLESAUCE

In the container of a blender or food processor combine 1 apple and 1 orange, both peeled, seeded, and cored, and whirl or process until smooth. Serve at once or freeze.

Yield: Three-fourths cup.

BANANA GRAPEFRUIT PURÉE

In the container of a blender or food processor combine 1 peeled banana and ½ grapefruit, skinned and seeded, and process until smooth.

Yield: One cup.

Note: One whole, skinned, and seeded orange can be substituted for grapefruit.

MELON MUSH

Purée any very ripe seeded melon except watermelon with half as much banana, apple, ripe pear, or peach.

SPOONABLE PEACHES

1 pound ripe peaches, nectarines, apricots, or plums
1 teaspoon lemon juice

Bring a large saucepan filled with water to a boil. Put the fruit in the boiling water for 1 minute. Remove the fruit and slip off the skins under cold running water. Halve the fruit and discard the pits. Purée with the lemon juice in the container of a food processor or blender, or push through a food mill.

Yield: Two cups.

Note: Serve this purée blended with an equal quantity of cottage cheese or yogurt. Add 1 tablespoon of wheat germ for breakfast-in-a-bowl.

Dried Fruit "Compote"

Introduce cooked dried fruit the way you do fresh—a small amount, one fruit at a time. Try to find dried fruits that are packaged without preservatives. Babies seem to like the intense flavor of cooked dried fruit purées, so after they've had each fruit individually, try combining two different dried fruits or a dried fruit with fresh.

Combine fruit with water to cover in a large saucepan. Bring to a boil and simmer for 30 to 40 minutes, or until fruit is very soft. Purée the fruit with some of the cooking liquid. Taste and add up to 1 tablespoon corn syrup or sugar per cup of purée. Refrigerate for up to four days or freeze up to two months.

1 cup preservative-free dried apricots, peaches, pears, apples, or prunes*
Water

Vegetables

Vegetables should be steamed or baked to retain the highest proportion of nutrients. If you are in a hurry, boiling is quicker, but use as little water as possible. Whichever method you use, save the cooking liquid to use in puréeing the vegetables.

FIRST TIME CARROTS

Steam the carrots for 30 to 40 minutes, or until very tender. Cool slightly and rub off the skins. Purée the carrots in the container of a food processor or blender, or push through a food mill with some of the steaming water or fruit juice until smooth. Yield: Two cups purée.

1 pound whole carrots, scrubbed

---

*Since they have a laxative effect, prunes should only be served in very small portions of a teaspoon or less, or combined in a small proportion with other fruits.

BABY GREEN BEANS

1 pound whole green
beans, washed and
trimmed

Steam the green beans for 10 to 15 minutes, or until very tender. Purée with the steaming liquid.
Yield: Two cups.

Veggie Combinations

Once your baby has had any of these vegetables individually, try combining them in equal quantities.

peas and carrots
peas and potatoes
potatoes and spinach
winter squash and apples
summer squash and
white or sweet potato

broccoli and winter squash
cauliflower and peas
green beans and potatoes
celery and carrots

POPEYE JUICE

Freshly made vegetable* juice (with or without a juicer**) makes a vitamin-and-mineral-packed juice break for a baby.

1 cup cut-up carrots,
celery, or beets
½ cup water
Small handful seedless
grapes

Put the vegetables, water, and grapes in the container of a blender or food processor and process until the vegetables are pulverized. Strain the pulp, reserving juice.
Yield: About ½ cup juice.

*Fresh fruit juices can be prepared in the same way, using cut up washed fruits. Peeling and coring is not necessary since the fruits will be strained.
**If a juicer is used, follow manufacturer's directions.

Dried Beans, Peas, and Lentils

Dried beans, peas, and lentils can be cooked according to a standard recipe, and puréed to the consistency of cereal. Serve them in place of starchy vegetables or cereal grains. The purée can be refrigerated for up to 3 days and frozen for 1 month. To augment the incomplete protein in legumes, combine with milk, yogurt, cheese, or small amounts of meat for an inexpensive high-quality protein source.

Vegetables to Avoid

Corn is the only vegetable to avoid in the first year. The tough outer skin is difficult for babies to digest, and once it is removed, there really isn't much of anything left to eat. Cornmeal cereal, however, is acceptable.

Meats, Poultry, and Fish

You can start introducing liver to babies around five months, followed a few months later with veal and chicken. No shellfish should be given before one year, but plain, lean fish fillets, very carefully checked for bones, can be started around seven months.

The Palatability Principle

The first spoonful of meat, poultry, or fish may elicit the most quizzical look from your baby of any food given thus far. It's not sweet, it's not as "swallowable" as cereal . . . let's face it, it's definitely different. If you find your baby just isn't eating up all his/her perfectly poached liver try adjusting your recipes. Cook meats with half their weight in sliced carrots (added during the final 20 minutes cooking time) and purée together. Thicken or "smooth out" meat purées with cereals or puréed sweeter vegetables, such as sweet potato, winter squash, green peas, beets, or carrots. Try to make the texture of puréed meat, fish, or poultry similar to that of the cereal he or she usually enjoys.

The Meat Machines

The machines that do the best job puréeing meats are the electric baby food grinder, the food processor, and the manual or electric meat grinder. The electric blender tends to shred rather than purée most meats, though it does a good job with liver. Most meats can be puréed in a food mill, but it will take considerable muscle power.

VEAL STEW

1 pound veal shoulder,
cubed
½ cup sliced, scrubbed
carrots
2 onion slices, for babies
older than six months
1½ cups water

Combine all ingredients in a saucepan and bring to a boil. Reduce the heat, cover, and simmer for about 40 minutes, or until the meat is very tender. Purée with about 1 cup of the cooking liquid.
Yield: About 2½ cups.

BABY BURGERS

1 pound fresh lean
ground turkey,* thawed
if frozen
1 cup water

Put the turkey and water in a skillet and bring to a boil. Reduce the heat and simmer for 10 minutes or until the meat loses its pink color and is thoroughly cooked. Purée the meat using all of the cooking liquid.
Yield: Two cups.

BABY SHEPHERD'S PIE

Purée cooked turkey with 1 cup cooked sliced carrots or potatoes.

CHICKEN PURÉE

1 2½- to 3-pound chicken,
cut up
2 cups water

Combine the chicken and water in a skillet and bring to a boil. Reduce the heat, cover, and simmer for 45 minutes, or until the chicken is done. Cool the chicken in the broth. Remove the skin and bones and purée the meat with 1 to 1½ cups of the cooking liquid. For a creamier texture, cook 1 tablespoon finely ground cereal in 4 tablespoons of the cooking liquid and add it to the chicken purée.
Yield: About 2 cups.

*Do not refreeze ground turkey that has been made from frozen meat.

SUPER-QUICK CHICKEN

Cut the chicken into 1-inch cubes and combine in a saucepan with the water and oats. Bring to a boil, reduce the heat, and simmer for 3 minutes. Pour into the container of a food processor and purée.
Yield: One cup.
Note: Chicken purée seems to pass the palatability test best when blended with or served with fruit or a sweet vegetable.

1 whole skinless, boneless chicken breast (about 1 pound)
1 cup water
1 tablespoon pulverized oatmeal

BABY CHOPPED CHICKEN LIVER

Combine the livers and water in a small saucepan and bring to a boil. Reduce the heat and simmer for 10 minutes. Put the livers, eggs, and ¼ cup of the cooking liquid in the container of a blender or food processor and purée. Alternately, livers and eggs can be ground in a grinder or food mill and then blended with the liquid.
Yield: One and one-third cups.

½ pound fresh chicken livers
½ cup water
2 hard-cooked eggs (yolks only for babies under six months)

POACHED FISH FILLETS

Put the fillets in a skillet and cover with boiling water. Add the lemon juice and simmer for 7 to 10 minutes, or until the fish is opaque. Purée the fish with about 6 tablespoons of the cooking liquid.
Yield: About one and one-half cups.
Note: Try serving poached fish purée blended with half the quantity of potato, carrot, or pea purée.

1 pound lean fish fillets
Boiling water
1 tablespoon lemon juice

One-Dish Dinners

Make your own meat and vegetable dinners by combining ¼ cup meat purée, ½ cup vegetable purée, and ¼ cup medium white sauce made with enriched or whole wheat flour. Once your baby really gets into solids, you can add ¼ cup cooked pasta or rice to the combinations that do not include other starchy vegetables.

Good blends

chicken and potato
turkey and spinach
veal and broccoli
chicken, tomato, pasta
veal and winter squash
fish, potato, spinach

fish and broccoli
chicken liver and potato
chicken and carrots
turkey and green peas
veal and sweet potatoes
chicken, eggplant, rice

Eggs

Egg yolk can be introduced at five months, whole egg at six. After soft-cooked, cereal-camouflaged yolks, mashed hard-cooked whole eggs, and simple scrambles, your baby may enjoy some of these simple custards or no-cook puddings.

CUSTARD FRUIT

1 cup milk
2 eggs
½ cup fruit purée
2 tablespoons honey (for babies over one year only), brown sugar, or maple syrup

Combine all ingredients in the container of a blender and blend on low speed just until blended. Pour into four custard cups and put the cups in a shallow baking pan. Fill the pan with hot water to a depth of 1½ inches and bake in a 350-degree oven for 40 minutes, or until a knife inserted 1 inch from edge comes out clean. Remove the cups from the pan and chill before serving.

Vegetable variation: Substitute ½ cup vegetable purée for the fruit. Omit the sweetener and add ¼ cup grated cheese.

BANANA SMOOTHIE PUDDING

Combine all the ingredients in the container of a food processor or blender and process until smooth. You can also push the ingredients through a food mill. Refrigerate the unused portion for up to two days.
Yield: Two servings.

1 hard-cooked egg
1 very ripe banana
½ cup creamed cottage cheese
1 tablespoon lemon juice
1 teaspoon honey (omit for babies under one year)

PEANUT BUTTER CUSTARD

Put the peanut butter, honey or sugar, and eggs in the container of a blender. Add the milk and blend on low speed just until well mixed. Preheat the oven to 350 degrees. Pour the custard into four to six custard cups and arrange the cups in a shallow baking pan. Fill the pan with warm water to a depth of 1½ inches and bake for 40 minutes, or until custard is set and a knife inserted 1 inch from the edge comes out clean. Remove the cups from the pan and chill before serving.
Yield: Four or six servings.
Note: To satisfy the taste of the more sophisticated toddler palate, increase honey or brown sugar to 3 or 4 tablespoons.

¼ cup smooth peanut butter
2 tablespoons honey (for babies over one year) or brown sugar
3 eggs
1½ cups scalded milk

ALL-IN-ONE-CUSTARD

Milk, egg, cereal, and fruit in one dish . . . for the beginning eater.

2 tablespoons wheat germ
½ cup milk
2 egg yolks
½ cup fruit purée

Soak the wheat germ in milk for 10 minutes. Beat in the yolks and fruit. Pour into 2 to 4 custard cups or recycled baby food jars. Put the cups in a saucepan and add water to a depth of 1½ inches. Cover the pan and simmer for 15 minutes, or until the custard is set. Remove the custard cups from the water, cool, and chill before serving. The custard will keep chilled for up to three days.
Yield: Two meals or four desserts.

Treats and Teethers

JUICY GELATIN

½ cup water
1 envelope unflavored gelatin
2 tablespoons sugar (optional)
1½ cups fruit juice
¾ cup finely diced fruit, puréed for babies under 1 year

Put the water, gelatin, and sugar in a small saucepan and stir over low heat until the gelatin and sugar are thoroughly dissolved. Stir in the juice. Pour into a 2½-cup mold or bowl and refrigerate for about 30 minutes, or until the gelatin thickens to the consistency of unbeaten egg white. Stir in the fruit and chill until set.
Yield: Two and one-half cups.

FRUITSICLES

Great for teething gums or over-heated toddlers.

2 cups unsweetened fruit juice
2 tablespoons superfine sugar, optional

Combine the juice with sugar and blend well. Pour the juice into eight 2-ounce popsicle molds, 3-ounce paper cups, or ice cube trays (this is a good size for babies). Freeze until the ice is fairly firm. Insert popsicle sticks in cups or ice cubes and freeze solid.

YOGIES

Combine the yogurt and concentrate and blend well. Pour into popsicle molds, small paper cups, or ice cube trays and freeze as above. Thaw slightly before serving.

1 pint plain yogurt (see page 324)
1 6-ounce can frozen orange juice concentrate, partially thawed

AVOCADO AND BANANA YOGURT

In a small bowl mash equal amounts of ripe banana and avocado until fairly smooth. Stir in enough plain yogurt to make the mixture creamy. Serve immediately or freeze.

EASY TEETHERS

The main criterion for successful teething biscuits is that they taste okay to babies and are easily clenched in tiny fists and that they hold together long enough to serve the purpose for which they are intended. These work on all counts.

In a bowl, beat the eggs until foamy. Beat in the sugar and, when the sugar dissolves, add the flours. Beat until the dough is thick and only slightly sticky. You may have to add up to ½ cup more flour. Flour your hands and shape tablespoons of the dough into chubby logs slightly narrower than the width of your baby's mouth. Arrange the logs on lightly oiled baking sheets. Bake in a 300-degree oven for 30 minutes. Reduce the oven temperature to 200 degrees and bake for 15 minutes. Turn each biscuit over and bake for 10 minutes longer, or until very hard and brown, but not burned. Cool thoroughly before using. These crumble-free cookies will keep almost indefinitely in an airtight container.
Yield: About twenty-four biscuits.

2 eggs
1 cup brown sugar
1 cup unbleached flour
1 cup whole wheat flour

CRACKERS FOR KIDS

These are good munchibles for babies over nine months and they are a good thing to bake for toddlers instead of cookies.

1½ cups oatmeal
½ cup toasted wheat germ
1 cup whole wheat flour
1½ tablespoons sugar
½ teaspoon salt
2 tablespoons chilled butter, cut up
¼ cup vegetable oil
6 tablespoons cold water
Sesame seeds, optional

Put the oatmeal in the container of a food processor and process until the oats form a fine powder. Add the wheat germ, flour, salt, and sugar and process to mix. Add the butter and process just until the butter disappears into the dry ingredients. With the machine running, slowly add the oil, then water and process just until the dough forms a ball. Divide the dough in half and refrigerate half of the dough. On a lightly floured board, roll the dough out to ⅛-inch thickness. Cut into 1- by 2-inch rectangles or with cookie cutters into shapes. Place on ungreased baking sheets. Prick each cracker in several places with a fork. Sprinkle with sesame seeds and bake in a 300-degree oven for 30 to 35 minutes, or until the crackers are rich brown and firm. They will crisp further on cooling. Remove the crackers to a wire rack to cool completely. Roll out and bake the remaining dough.

Yield: About fifty crackers.

Note: Crackers can be made "by hand" without a food processor. A blender or grinder is necessary, however, to grind the oatmeal.

RECYCLED ZWEIBACK

You can turn any whole grain bread or plain cake into healthy teethers by slicing it into finger-length sticks and baking in a 250-degree oven for 30 to 60 minutes, or until very hard. Cool thoroughly before using and store in airtight containers.

HOMEMADE WHOLE WHEAT PRETZELS

Another great play-group or rainy day activity, or, for when you just want some delicious, warm, chewy pretzels with a conscience.

Put the yeast in a bowl. Add both flours, wheat germ, sugar, and salt. Add the water and mix until the dough forms a ball. On a lightly floured board, knead the dough for 5 minutes, or until it is smooth and elastic. Break off walnut-sized pieces of dough. Roll each piece between the palms to form a rope and shape into pretzels. Young children may be happy inventing their own pretzel shapes. Preheat the oven to 425 degrees. Brush some of the beaten egg over each pretzel. Sprinkle with sesame seeds and with a spatula, transfer each pretzel to a lightly greased baking sheet. Bake for 10 to 12 minutes, or until browned. Cool the pretzels to warm before serving.

Yield: About two dozen medium-sized pretzels.

1 package dry yeast
3 cups whole wheat flour
1 cup unbleached all-purpose flour
¼ cup wheat germ
4 teaspoons brown sugar
Salt to taste, optional
¾ cup hot water
1 egg, lightly beaten
Sesame seeds

BABY GRANOLA

Once your baby has been introduced to several different grains individually, you may want to put together this mixed fruit, nut, and grain cereal.

Grind the oatmeal and rice in the container of an electric blender until they are fine and powdery. Add the remaining ingredients and process again until the mixture is fairly uniform in texture. To prepare 1 serving, combine 2 tablespoons of the cereal mixture with ⅓ cup milk in a saucepan and bring to a boil. Reduce the heat and simmer for 10 minutes, stirring often. Thin with milk before serving. Store the granola at room temperature in an airtight container.

Note: Depending on absorbency of grains, it may be necessary to add a small amount of extra milk as the cereal cooks.

1 cup uncooked oatmeal
1 cup uncooked brown rice
½ cup wheat germ
½ cup toasted walnuts or almonds, optional
1 cup banana chips

BIBLIOGRAPHY

1. COOKBOOKS

General

Albright, Nancy, *The Rodale Cookbook*. Emmaus, Pa.: Rodale Press, 1973
———, *Rodale's Naturally Great Foods Cookbook*. Emmaus, Pa.: Rodale Press, 1977
Hall, Nancy and Walter, *The Wild Palate*. Emmaus, Pa.: Rodale Press, 1980
Hunter, Beatrice Trum, *The Natural Foods Cookbook*. New York: Simon & Schuster, 1969 (Paperback)
LaCore, Kathleen, *The Return to Natural Foods Cookery*. New Jersey: Spectrum Books, Prentice-Hall, Inc., 1978 (Paperback)
Levitt, Eleanor, *The Wonderful World of Natural Foods*. New York: Hearthside Press, 1971 (Paperback: Natural Food Cookery, Dover)
Rombauer, Irma S., and Becker, Marion R., *Joy of Cooking*. Indianapolis: Bobbs-Merrill, 1975 (Paperback: New American Library)
Shepard, Sigrid M., *Natural Food Feasts from the Eastern World*. New York: Arco Publishing, Inc. 1979
Toms, Agnes, *Eat, Drink and Be Healthy*. New York: BJ Publishing Group, 1968 (Paperback)
Worstman, Gail L. *The Natural Fast Food Cookbook*. Seattle: Pacific Search Press, 1980

Breads & Grains

Baylis, Maggie, and Castle, Coralie, *Real Bread*. San Francisco: 101 Productions, 1980 (Paperback)
Beard, James, *Beard on Bread*. New York: Alfred A. Knopf, 1973
Brave, John Rahn, *Uncle John's Original Bread Book*. New York: BJ Publishing Group, 1976
Brown, Edward Espe, *The Tassajara Bread Book*. Boulder, Co.: Shambhala Publications, 1980 (Paperback: Shambhala)
Cole, John N., *The Amaranth Book: From the Past for the Future*. Emmaus, Pa.: Rodale Press, 1979
Ford, Marjorie W., Hillyard, Susan, and Koock, Mary F., *The Deaf Smith Country Cookbook*. New York: Macmillan and Collier Books, 1973
Hunter, Beatrice Trum, *Beatrice Trum Hunter's Whole-Grain Baking Sampler*. New Canaan, Conn.: Keats Publishing, 1972 (Paperback)
London, Mel, *Bread Winners*. Emmaus, Pa.: Rodale Press, 1979
Orton, Mildred Ellen, *Cooking with Wholegrains*. New York: Farrar, Straus & Giroux, 1971 (Paperback)
Rosenvall, Vernice G., et al., *The Classic Wheat for Man Cookbook: 300 Ways with Stone Ground Wheat*. Santa Barbara, Calif.: Woodbridge Press, 1975 (Paperback)
Sandler, Sandra and Bruce, *Home Bakebook of Natural Breads and Goodies*. New York: Galahad Books, 1972
Standard, Stella, *Our Daily Bread*. New York: Berkeley Publishing, 1976 (Paperback)

Dairy

Hazelton, Nika, *The Art of Cheese Cookery.* Berkeley, Calif.: Ross Books, 1978 (Paperback)
Hunter, Beatrice Trum, *Beatrice Trum Hunter's Fact/Book on Yogurt, Kefir and Other Milk Cultures.* New Canaan, Conn.: Keats Publishing, 1973 (Paperback)
Marshall, Mel E. *The Delectable Egg.* New York: Pocket Books, 1970 (Paperback)
Pappas, Lou Seibert, *Egg Cookery.* San Francisco: 101 Productions, 1976 (Paperback)
Smetinoff, Olga, *The Yogurt Cookbook.* New York: Frederick Fell, 1966 (Paperback)
Townsend, Doris McFerran, *Cheese Cookery.* Tucson, Az.: HP Books, 1980 (Paperback)
Uvezian, Sonia, *The Book of Yogurt.* San Francisco: 101 Productions, 1978 (Paperback)

Desserts

Collier, Carole, *The Natural Sugarless Dessert Cookbook.* New York: Walker and Company, 1980
Dworkin, Stan and Floss, *Good Goodies—Recipes for Natural Snacks 'n' Sweets.* Emmaus, Pa.: Rodale Press, 1974 (Paperback: Fawcett)
Martin, Faye, *Rodale's Naturally Delicious Desserts & Snacks.* Emmaus, Pa.: Rodale Press, 1978

Salads

Lerman, Ann, *The Big Green Salad Book.* Philadelphia, Pa.: Running Press, 1977 (Paperback)
Nelson, Kay Shaw, *The Complete International Salad Book.* New York: Stein & Day, 1978
Time-Life Books, *Salads.* The Good Cook Series. Boston: Little Brown & Co., 1980
Uvezian, Sonia, *The Book of Salads.* San Francisco: 101 Productions, 1977 (Paperback)

Vegetables/Vegetarian Cooking

Bauer, Cathy, and Andersen, Juel, *The Tofu Cookbook.* Emmaus, Pa.: Rodale Press, 1979 (Paperback)
Brooks, Karen, *The Forget-About-Meat Cookbook.* Emmaus, Pa.: Rodale Press, 1974 (Paperback)
Brown, Edward Espe, *Tassajara Cooking: A Vegetarian Cooking Book.* Boulder, Co.: Shambhala Publications, 1973
Dalsass, Diana, *Cashews and Lentils, Apples and Oats.* Chicago: Contemporary Books, Inc., 1981
Deeming, Sue and Bill, *Bean Cookery.* Tucson, Az.: HP Books, 1980 (Paperback)
Editors of *Organic Gardening and Farming, The Green Thumb Cookbook.* Emmaus, Pa.: Rodale Press, 1977
Goulart, Frances Sheridan, *Bum Steers.* Old Greenwich, Conn.: The Chatham Press, 1975
Hewitt, Jean, *International Meatless Cookbook.* New York: Times Books, 1980; New American Library (NAL) 1981 (Paperback)
Hooker, Alan, *Vegetarian Gourmet Cookery.* San Francisco: 101 Productions, 1970 (Paperback)
Kasin, Miriam, *The Age of Enlightenment Cook Book.* New York: Arco Publishing, 1980 (Paperback)
Katzen, Mollie, *The Moosewood Cookbook.* Ithaca, N.Y.: Ten Speed Press, 1977 (Paperback)
Kendig, Joan and Keith, *Modern Vegetable Protein Cookery.* New York: Arco, 1980
Lager, Mildred, and Van Grundy Jones, Dorothea, *The Soybean Cookbook.* New York: Arc Books, 1968 (Paperback)
Lin, Florence, *Florence Lin's Chinese Vegetarian Cookbook.* New York: Dutton, 1977 (Paperback)
Lo, Kenneth H.C., *Chinese Vegetarian Cooking.* New York: Pantheon, 1974 (Paperback)
Manners, Ann and William, *The Quick and Easy Vegetarian Cookbook.* New York: M. Evans & Co., 1980 (Paperback)
Null, Gary, *The New Vegetarian Cookbook.* New York: Macmillan, 1980
Richmond, Sonya, *International Vegetarian Cookery.* New York: Arco Publishing, 1980 (Paperback)
Robertson, Laurel, et al., *Laurel's Kitchen: A Handbook for Vegetarian Cookery and Nutrition.* Petaluma, Calif.: Nilgiri Press, 1976 (Paperback: Bantam)
Sacharoff, Shanta Nimbark, *Flavors of India.* San Francisco: 101 Productions, 1972 (Paperback)
Shurtleff, William, and Aoyagi, Akiko, *The Book of Tempeh.* New York: Harper & Row, Colophon Books, 1979 (Paperback)
Southey, Paul, *The Vegetarian Gourmet Cookbook.* New York: Van Nostrand Reinhold Co., 1980
Thomas, Anna, *The Vegetarian Epicure.* New York: Alfred A. Knopf, 1972 (Paperback)

——, *The Vegetarian Epicure Book Two*. New York: Alfred A. Knopf, 1978 (Paperback)
Turvey, Valerie, *Bean Feast*. San Francisco: 101 Productions, 1979 (Paperback)
Walker, Janet, *Vegetarian Cookery*. Hollywood, Calif.: Wilshire Book Co., 1970 (Paperback)

Other Specialties

Berglund, Berndt, and Bolsby, Clare E., *The Edible Wild*. New York: Scribners, 1971 (Paperback)
Burum, Linda, *The Junk Food Alternative*. San Francisco: 101 Productions, 1980 (Paperback)
Castle, Coralie, and Gin, Margaret, *Country Cookery—Recipes of Many Lands*. San Francisco: 101 Productions, 1972 (Paperback)
Chen, Joyce, *Joyce Chen Cook Book*. Philadelphia: Lippincott, 1962 (Paperback)
Chu, Grace, *Madame Chu's Chinese Cooking School*. New York: Simon & Schuster, 1975
——, *Pleasures of Chinese Cooking*. New York: Simon & Schuster, 1976 (Paperback)
Ellis, Eleanor, *Northern Cookbook*. Ottawa: Indian Affairs & Northern Development, Canadian Government, Queen's Printer, 1967
Gerras, Charles, *Feasting on Raw Foods*. Emmaus, Pa.: Rodale Press, 1980
Hunter, Kathleen, *Health Foods and Herbs*. New York: Arc Books, 1968 (Paperback)
Kimball, Yeffe, and Anderson, Jean, *The Art of American Indian Cooking*. New York: Doubleday, 1965
Miller, Amy Bess, and Fuller, Persis, *The Best of Shaker Cooking*. New York: Macmillan, 1970
Zane, Eva, *Middle Eastern Cookery*. San Francisco: 101 Productions, 1974 (Paperback)

2. COOKBOOKS WITH HISTORY, FOLKLORE, OR OTHER INFORMATION

Berquist, Edna Smith, *High Maple Farm Cookbook*. New York: Macmillan, 1974 (Paperback)
Freitus, Joe, *The Natural World Cookbook*. Washington, D.C.: Stone Wall Press, 1980
Garland, Sarah, *The Complete Book of Herbs and Spices*. New York: Viking Press, 1979
Gewanter, Vera, *A Passion for Vegetables*. New York: Viking Press, 1980
Gibbons, Euell, *Stalking the Blue-Eyed Scallop*. New York: David McKay, 1964 (Paperback)
——, Euell, *Stalking the Healthful Herbs*. New York: David McKay, 1970
——, Euell, *Stalking the Wild Asparagus*. New York: David McKay, 1970 (Paperback)
Hawkes, Alex D., *A World of Vegetable Cookery*. New York: Simon & Schuster, 1968
Jones, Muskie, *Muskie Jones's Northwoods Cookbook*. Toronto: Algonquin Publishing, 1965 (Paperback)
Keys, Margaret and Ancel, *The Benevolent Bean*. New York: Doubleday, 1967
Wason, Betty, *Cooks, Gluttons and Gourmets*. Garden City, New York: Doubleday, 1962

3. COOKBOOKS WITH HEALTH THEORIES OR CLAIMS AND/OR PHILOSOPHIES

Abehsera, Michel, *Zen Macrobiotic Cooking*. Secaucus, N.J.: Citadel Press, 1971 (Paperback)
Bircher, Ruth, *Eating Your Way to Health*. London: Faber & Faber, 1961
Bragg, Paul C., *Bragg New Generation Health Food Cookbook*. Burbank, Calif.: Health Science (Paperback)
Davis, Adelle, *Let's Cook It Right*. New York: Harcourt, Brace, Jovanovich, 1962 (Paperback: New American Library)
Doyle, Rodger, *The Vegetarian Handbook*. New York: Crown Publishers, 1979 (Paperback)
Elwood Catharyn, *Feel Like a Million*. New York: Pocket Books, 1971 (Paperback)
Hauser, Gayelord, *The Gayelord Hauser Cookbook*. New York: Putnam, 1980 (Paperback)
Helferich, William, and Westhoff, Dennis, *All About Yogurt*. Englewood Cliffs, N.J.: Prentice-Hall, 1980 (Paperback)
Herdt, Sheryll Patterson, *Nitty Gritty Foodbook*. New York: Praeger Publications, 1975
Kinderlehrer, Jane, *Confessions of a Sneaky Organic Cook . . . or How to Make Your Family Healthy When They're Not Looking*. Emmaus, Pa.: Rodale Press, 1971 (Paperback: New American Library)

Lappé, Frances M., *Diet for a Small Planet*. New York: Ballantine, 1975 (Paperback)
Tobe, John, *"No-Cook" Book*. St. Catherine's, Ontario: Provoker Press, 1969
Walker, N.W., *Raw Vegetable Juices*. New York: BJ Publishing, 1971 (Paperback)
Warmbrand, Max, *Eat Well to Keep Well*. New York: BJ Publishing, 1970 (Paperback)

4. NUTRITION BOOKS

Brody, Jane, *Jane Brody's Nutrition Book*. New York: W. W. Norton & Co., 1981
Clark, Linda, *Know Your Nutrition*. New Canaan, Conn.: Keats Publishing, 1973 (Paperback)
Composition of Foods—Baby Foods, Raw, Processed, Prepared, Agricultural Handbook No. 8-3. Washington, D.C.: Government Printing Office (Paperback)
Composition of Foods—Dairy and Egg Products, Raw, Processed, Prepared, Agricultural Handbook No. 8-1. Washington, D.C.: Government Printing Office, 1976 (Paperback)
Composition of Foods, Spices and Herbs, Raw, Processed, Prepared, Agricultural Handbook No. 8-2. Washington, D.C.: Government Printing Office, 1977 (Paperback)
Dietary Allowances Committee & Food and Nutrition Board, *Recommended Dietary Allowances*. Washington, D.C.: National Academy of Sciences, 1980 (Paperback)
Deutsch, Ronald M., *The Family Guide to Better Food and Better Health*. New York: Bantam Books, 1977 (Paperback)
Echols, Barbara E., and Arena, Jay M., *The Commonsense Guide to Good Eating*. Woodbury, New York: Barron's, 1978
Fleck, Henrietta, *Introduction to Nutrition*. New York: Macmillan, 1976
Fredericks, Carlton, Ph.D., and Bailey, Herbert, *Foods Facts & Fallacies*. New York: Arco Publishing, 1978 (Paperback)
Leverton, Ruth, *Food Becomes You*. Ames, Iowa: Iowa State University Press, 1965
Margie, Joyce D., Levy, Robert I., and Hunt, James C., *Living Better Recipes for a Healthy Heart*. Radnor, Pa.: Chilton Books, 1980
Nutritive Value of American Foods, in Common Units, Agricultural Handbook No. 456. Washington, D.C.: Government Printing Office, 1975 (Paperback)
Pennington, Jean, and Church, Helen N., *Food Values of Portions Commonly Used*. New York: Harper & Row, 1980 (Paperback)
Tarr, Yvonne Young, *The New York Times Natural Foods Dieting Book*. New York: Ballantine Books, 1972 (Paperback)
White, Alice, *Family Health Cookbook*. New York: David McKay, Inc., 1980

5. CONSUMERISM AND ENVIRONMENTAL BOOKS

Bernarde, M. A., *Chemicals We Eat*. New York: McGraw-Hill, 1971 (Paperback)
Carson, Rachel, *Silent Spring*. Boston: Houghton Mifflin, 1962
Goldbeck, Nikki and David, *The Supermarket Handbook*. New York: New American Library, 1976 (Paperback)
Harmer, Ruth Mulvey, *Unfit for Human Consumption*. Englewood Cliffs, N.J.: Prentice-Hall, 1971
Hunter, Beatrice Trum, *Beatrice Trum Hunter's Additives Book*. New Canaan, Conn.: Keats Publishing, 1980 (Paperback)
——, *Consumer Beware!* New York: Simon & Schuster, 1972 (Paperback)
——, *Food and Your Health*. New Canaan, Conn.: Keats Publishing, 1974 (Paperback)
Kramer, Amihud, *Food and the Consumer*. Westport, Conn.: AVI Publishing, 1973 (Paperback)
Marine, Gene and Van Allen, *Food Pollution*. New York: Holt, Rinehart and Winston, 1972
Reinow, Robert, and Reinow, Leona Train, *Moment in the Sun*. New York: Dial, 1967
Turner, James S. (Ralph Nader Study Group), *The Chemical Feast, the Report on The Food and Drug Administration*. New York: Viking Press, 1970
Whelan, Elizabeth, and Stare, Fredrick, *Panic in the Pantry*. New York: Atheneum, 1975
Whorton, James, *Before Silent Spring*. Princeton, N.J.: Princeton University Press, 1974
Wiley, Farida A., ed., *John Burrough's America*. Old Greenwich, Conn.: Devin-Adair, 1951 (Paperback)
Winter, Ruth, *A Consumer's Dictionary of Food Additives*. New York: Crown Publishers, 1978 (Paperback)

6. HEALTH THEORY BOOKS

Airola, Paavo O., *Health Secrets from Europe*. New York: Arc Books, 1971 (Paperback)

Bieler, Henry, M.D., *Food is Your Best Medicine*. New York: Random House, 1973 (Paperback)

Bragg, Paul C. and Patricia, *Healthful Eating Without Confusion*. Burbank, Calif.: Health Science, 1971 (Paperback)

Burkitt, Denis, M.D., *Eat Right to Keep Healthy and Enjoy Life More*. New York: Arco Publishing, 1979 (Paperback)

Clark, Linda, *Get Well Naturally*. Old Greenwich, Conn.: Devin-Adair, 1975 (Paperback: Arc Books)

————, *Secrets of Health and Beauty*. New York: BJ Publishing, 1979 (Paperback)

Davis, Adelle, *Let's Eat Right to Keep Fit*. New York: Harcourt, Brace, Jovanovich, 1970 (Paperback: New American Library)

————, *Let's Get Well*. New York: Harcourt, Brace, Jovanovich, 1965 (Paperback: New American Library)

Hauser, Gayelord, *Look Younger, Live Longer*. New York: Fawcett Crest Books, 1977 (Paperback)

Kloss, Jethro, *Back to Eden*. New York: Beneficial Books, 1971 (Paperback)

Lust, John, *The Herb Book*. New York: Benedict Lust Publications, 1974 (Paperback)

Marsh, Edward E., *How to be Healthy with Natural Foods*. New York: Arc Books, 1978 (Paperback)

Newman, Laura, *Make Your Juicer Your Drug Store*. New York: Benedict Lust Publications, 1970

Pelstring, Linda, and Hauck, JoAnn, *Food to Improve Your Health*. New York: Walker and Company, 1974

Pritikin, Nathan, *The Pritikin Program*. New York: Bantam Books, 1980 (Paperback)

Sheinkin, David, Schachter, Michael, and Hutton, Richard, *The Food Connection*. New York: Bobbs-Merrill, 1979

Sussman, Vic, *The Vegetarian Alternative*. Emmaus, Pa.: Rodale Press, 1978

Waerland, Ebba, *Rebuilding Health*. New York: Arc Books, 1968 (Paperback)

7. DICTIONARIES AND DIRECTORIES

Daystar Publishing Co., *The Annual Directory of Vegetarian Restaurants*. Angwin, Calif., 1980

Editors of *Vegetarian Times*, *The Vegetarian Times Guide to Dining in the U.S.A.* New York: Atheneum, 1980 (Paperback)

Hauser, Benjamin Gayelord, and Berg, Ragnar, *Dictionary of Foods*. New York: Benedict Lust Publications, 1970 (Paperback)

Peterson, Vicki, *The Natural Food Catalog*. New York: Arco Publishing, 1978 (Paperback)

Riker, Tom, and Roberts, Richard, *The Directory of Natural and Health Foods*. New York: Paragon Books published by G. P. Putnam's Sons, 1979

Rodale, J. I., and Staff, *The Organic Directory*. Emmaus, Pa.: Rodale Press, 1959

Staff of *Organic Gardening* Magazine, *The Encyclopedia of Organic Gardening*. Emmaus, Pa.: Rodale Press, 1978

Whole Foods Magazine Staff, *Whole Foods Natural Foods Guide*. Berkeley, Calif.: And/Or Press, 1979 (Paperback)

8. MISCELLANEOUS BOOKS

Burros, Marian, *Pure and Simple*. New York: William Morrow & Co., Inc., 1978

DeLong, Deanna, *How to Dry Foods*. Tucson, Az.: HP Books, 1979 (Paperback)

Gerras, Charles, *Feasting on Raw Foods*. Emmaus, Pa.: Rodale Press, 1980

Harris, Ben Charles, *Eat the Weeds*. New Canaan, Conn.: Keats Publishing, 1973 (Paperback)

Kluger, Marilyn, *Preserving Summer's Bounty*. New York: M. Evans and Company, 1979

Medsger, Oliver Perry, *Edible Wild Plants*. New York: Macmillan, 1972

Ogden, Samuel, *Step by Step to Organic Vegetable Growing*. Emmaus, Pa.: Rodale Press, 1971 (Paperback)

Pond, Barbara, *A Sampler of Wayside Herbs*. Riverside, Conn.: The Chatham Press, 1974

The Rodale Herb Book: An Organic Gardening and Farming Book. Emmaus, Pa.: Rodale Press, 1974

Rodale, J. I., and Staff, *How to Grow Vegetables and Fruits by the Organic Method*. Emmaus, Pa.: Rodale Press, 1961

Rollins, R. L., Fernald, M. L., and Kinsy, A. C., *Edible Wild Plants of Eastern North America*. New York: Harper & Row, 1958

Stout, Ruth, *Gardening Without Work*. New York: Cornerstone Library, 1974

Tarr, Yvonne Young, *The Up-With-Wholesome, Down-With-Store-Bought Book of Recipes and Household Formulas*. New York: Random House, 1975 (Paperback)

Witty, Helen, and Colchie, Elizabeth S., *Better Than Store-Bought*. New York: Harper & Row, 1979

9. PERIODICALS

Country Journal, Blair & Ketchum's, Box 870, Manchester Center, VT 05235
East West Journal, 17 Station Street, Brookline, MA 02146
Let's Live Magazine, 444 No. Larchmont Blvd., Los Angeles, CA 90004
Mother Earth News, 105 Stoney Mt. Road, Hendersonville, NC 28791
Mother Jones, 1886 Haymarket Square, Marion OH 43302
New Roots, Box 548, Greenfield, MA 01302
Organic Gardening and Farming, Rodale Press, 33 East Minor St., Emmaus, PA 18049
Prevention, Rodale Press, 33 East Minor St., Emmaus, PA 18049
Vegetarian Times, 41 East 42 St., Suite 921, New York, N.Y. 10017
Well-Being, 41 East 42 St., New York, NY 10017

MAIL ORDER SOURCES FOR NATURAL AND ORGANICALLY GROWN FOODS

General Suppliers

Arrowhead Mills, Box 866, Hereford, TX 79045
El Molino Mills, 345 North Baldwin Park Blvd., City of Industry, CA 91746
Erewhon Trading Corp., 3 East St., Cambridge, MA 02146
Jaffee Bros., P. O. Box 636, Valley Center, CA 92082
Natural Sales Corp., P. O. Box 25, Pittsburgh, PA 15230
Shiloh Farms, P. O. Box 97, Sulphur Springs, AR 72768
Walnut Acres, Penns Creek, PA 17862

Specialties

Elam Mills, 2625 Gardner Rd., Broadview, IL 60513 (grains, peanut butter, soy flour, mixes)
Golden Acres Orchard, Box 770, Route 2, Fort Royal, VA 22630 (apples and apple products)
Grain Process Enterprises, Ltd., 1570 Brimley Rd., Scarborough, Ontario, Canada
Great Valley Mills, Box 260, Quakertown, Bucks County, PA 18451
Herbal Market, Piermont, NY 10968
Lang Apiaries, 8448 N.Y. Route 77, Gasport, NY 14067 (honey)
Lee Anderson's Covalda Date Co., P. O. Box 908, Coachella, CA 92236
Lee's Fruit Co., Box 450, Leesburg, FL 32748 (citrus and honey)
Thousand Island Apiaries, Clayton, NY 13624 (honey)
Wolf's Neck Farms, Freeport, ME 04082 (meats)

Seeds for Sprouting

Johnny's Selected Seeds, Albion, ME 04910
Natural Development Co., Box 215, Bainbridge, PA 17502
Nichols Garden Nursery, 1190 No. Pacific Highway, Albany, OR 97321
George W. Park Seed Co., Greenwood, SC 29647
Thompson and Morgan, Box 24, 401 Kennedy Blvd., Sommerdale, NJ 08083
Walnut Acres, Penns Creek, PA 17862

INDEX